Work Songs

TED GIOIA

Work Songs

Duke University Press   Durham and London   2006

© 2006 Duke University Press

All rights reserved

Printed in the United States

of America on acid-free paper ∞

Designed by C. H. Westmoreland

Typeset in Minion

by Keystone Typesetting, Inc.

Library of Congress Cataloging-in-

Publication Data appear on the last

printed page of this book.

To my mother

DOROTHY GIOIA

✳ CONTENTS

Can songs born of hard labor and the workaday life hold relevance for us today? In 1996 Anna Chairetakis and Mary Taylor conducted a fascinating experiment, assembling a group of tough, young former inmates in the inner city, and asking them to listen to the old work song recordings made half a century earlier by convicts at Parchman Farm. What would be their reaction? Would they see this music as an embarrassment, or perhaps a degrading spectacle of a bygone era that, like bare-fisted boxing or bearbaiting, had persisted too long and was best forgotten? Or would the music speak to them in terms they could understand?

Let's hear some of their responses:

"I think these songs have a great value, a great lesson: the will of the human spirit—the will to survive and go on, no matter what, and in spite of everything."

"Oh man, it really makes me grateful for this moment. A lot of times in the day I sit down and complain about my problems and my troubles. And just listening to them [the convicts], they went through so much more than I can ever dream of going through, and they were still able to sing."

"It's almost like they suffered so that we don't have to, you know, suffer as much as they did."

"They sing with a lot of hope and strength. They sing for inspiration, survival."

"The songs were a way to vocalize that they can get to a better life."

I began this project a decade ago convinced (much like these listeners) that this music possessed multilayered meanings and rich implications—aesthetic, social, and perhaps even moral; qualities that were lost in the typical one-dimensional presentation of work songs found in textbooks and other writings or, even worse, in films and various forms of popular culture. Even more, I believed that the work song could teach us lessons about music making in general, lessons that might enhance our appreciation and understanding of other styles of performance. But, above all, I was drawn to these songs because the music moved me deeply. And I was convinced that others might have a similar response if they were brought into closer contact with it. For me, this was not a dispassionate matter of scholarship, but a very personal exploration.

Midway through my project, an unexpected event crystallized these perceptions in a very telling manner. I had been invited to give a talk on my current research to a group of faculty and graduate students at Stanford's Department of Music. In the course of preparing my lecture I deliberated at length over the first musical selection to play for my audience. Eventually I chose a song I admired greatly: an obscure performance of a prison work song titled "Po' Lazarus," which was recorded by Alan Lomax at the Mississippi State Penitentiary in 1959 and performed in a gripping rendition led by inmate James Carter. Imagine my disappointment (and tinge of self-doubt) when my listeners showed few signs of enthusiasm for this song.

Yet if I was looking for external validation, it came to me to a stunning degree during the coming months. A few weeks after the lecture at Stanford, a friend cornered me and insisted that I listen to what he felt was an exceptional soundtrack recording of a new Hollywood movie. He then played for me the compact disc of the soundtrack to *O Brother, Where Art Thou?*, and my mild interest turned to startled surprise as I heard the opening track, "Po' Lazarus," the same prison work song I had played to the Stanford group. But my amazement grew apace during the passing months as *O Brother, Where Art Thou?* skyrocketed to the top of the charts—bypassing the cutest boy bands and trendiest hip hoppers—soon going gold, then platinum, then double platinum, and eventually selling more than seven million copies. And, as if this were not remarkable enough, at the music industry's annual Grammy awards the soundtrack was given a bevy of honors including album of the year—an award rarely given to any soundtrack, and unheard of for a compilation of traditional music. If I had had any lingering concerns that my interest in work songs might be a mere personal obsession unlikely to be shared by others, here was compelling evidence to the contrary.

I could offer other examples of the music born of hard labor achieving unexpected commercial success, and in the course of this book I will cite many such cases. But these instances, however gratifying, raise many unanswered questions. Why does this music move us? Why do such raw performances, made without commercial intent, not intended for "audiences" in any conventional meaning of the term, lacking the polish and perfection imparted by the entertainment industry—why do these songs affect us so profoundly? Is our interest a proper one, or a reprehensible, voyeuristic intrusion on the workers who made them? Is our response a reaction to the music itself or merely to the social conditions that made it necessary? Or is it (as I suspect) due to something even more profound: that is, to our fascination and reverence for the transformational power of music, for its hidden dynamism as a change agent in everyday lives? And what does it mean for music to serve as a "change agent" in work and in other situations? In the simplest possible terms: Why do workers (and others) sing? Can we learn something about the power of music, about its capacity to enchant and transform everyday situations, by exploring the intersection of song and human labor? Above all, can we bring this transformational power to bear, in some degree, on situations in our own day-to-day lives?

To probe the inner meaning of this music, I have taken an approach that is discursive and synthetic, seeking broader connections and meanings, trying to construct the big picture rather than isolate a few small strands. As a result, my definition of a "work song" may strike some readers as overly inclusive. I did not restrict myself to the African American tradition—the most bountiful source of this style of singing, deserving though it is of special attention—since I believed that coming to grips with this music required looking at the songs of a wide range of laborers operating in diverse settings, assessing the similarities and the differences that came to light. Nor did I focus solely on vocal efforts, since increasingly as my research progressed I found that instrumental music has also played a critical, but often neglected, role in the daily tasks of laborers. Finally, I found that it was sometimes important to address songs *about* work, as well as the songs actually sung while working, since the interactions between these two approaches are a vital part of the story, critical to understanding the evolution of the music under discussion. In essence, I hoped that by casting my net wide I would uncover truths that might elude me in a narrower search.

I have aimed to be equally wide-ranging in my sources of information. This study and others like it are increasingly seen as part of the academic discipline known as ethnomusicology. Certainly I have benefited enormously from the research of ethnomusicologists, but I have also felt free to draw on travel literature, anthropological writings, slave narratives, personal journals and correspondence, historical accounts, WPA documents and archival material of other sorts, the work of psychologists and scientists, myths and legends, folklore, biographies and memoirs, labor union writings, archeological evidence, business tracts, the speculations of philosophers and sociologists, and, obviously, songbooks and recordings in my attempt to construct a holistic view of the interrelationship between labor and its music. Wherever a lead would take me, I followed it, often plunging into disciplines and debates in fields far outside the usual sources for books on music. Often I drew on the most recent research in various fields, seeking new insights to illuminate the subject at hand; but just as often I probed into the oldest source documents I could find, trusting that they too had wisdom to offer.

I undertook this endeavor based on my conviction that only a broad, multidisciplinary approach would shed the requisite light on the ways in which music and social institutions interact. Although this discursive approach may introduce as many questions as it resolves, I hope my readers will be forgiving of this indiscretion. Perhaps some will find these connections, as I do, revealing and sometimes even exhilarating. And maybe a few later researchers will derive inspiration from these open questions for efforts of their own, efforts which likely will go beyond the hints and speculations sketched out in these pages.

Although the literature on music and work is abundant, virtually all of it focuses on a specific occupation, period of time, nationality, or geographic region. Certainly no synthesis of the scope presented here has yet been attempted. In light of this I have included detailed footnotes and a comprehensive bibliography to aid the efforts of future scholars working in this area. I have felt it wisest, however, to place all notes at the close of the book so as to avoid weighing down the text with the excesses of my academic zeal. In contrast, my list of recommended recordings, which also appears at the end of the text, makes no claims for completeness (a true discography of the subject would require a book-length manuscript in its own right), but will point the interested reader in the direction of some of the best music described within these pages.

It would have been impossible for me to address the subject of work songs without the input and assistance of other people. I would like to thank in particular Evelyn Alloy, Peter Berryman, Gill Burns, Eric Charry, Marianne Fisher-Giorlando, John Flower, Paul Garon, Dana Gioia, Michael Golston, Chris Heppa, Robin Johnson, Fern Zalin Jones, Andy

Karp, Robert Kraut, Joseph Mailander, Alan V. Miller, Chuck Perdue, Michael L. Richmond, Antoinet Schimmelpenninck, Carla Sciaky, Eleanor Selfridge-Field, John Sloboda, Yuval Taylor, Ranko Vujosevic, and Steve Waller. I would also like to acknowledge the support and advice of Ken Wissoker and his colleagues at Duke University Press. Any limitations of the present work are, however, solely my responsibility. Finally, I owe the greatest debt to my wife, Tara, whose support and advice throughout this project were invaluable, and without which this book would have never seen its way to completion.

Before concluding, I would like to stress here that for me my research is not so much about exploring a facet of the history of music as it is about understanding its potentialities in the present and future. This may sound odd given that the subject of this book, the work song, is no longer a vital form of musical expression. And a quick perusal of the book and its notes and bibliography may convey the impression that my concern is with distant events described in dusty tomes and manuscripts; an antiquarian's fascination with times and places whose charm derives from their contrast with (not their relevance to) the modern day. But the exact opposite is the case. From the very beginning, my interest in the work song was driven by the firm conviction that the music of traditional societies and situations can teach us something critical about art making and about its role in our own hectic, postmodern lives. In particular, I believe that coming to grips with these old songs of labor can serve, in some measure, to revitalize our relationships both to music and to our day-to-day work. Certainly it is my hope that this timeless music, so radically different from contemporary commercial entertainment, may very well still be able to show us ways of connecting to song that as a society we have all but forgotten.

For if the study of work songs teaches us anything, it is that music should not be relegated to the concert hall or recording studio, where it is the domain of a small group of professionals. Music exists for all of us, as part of our shared heritage. The songs of laborers who put their music to practical use every day, yet could still extract great beauty from it, should remind us of this every time we hear it.

 **INTRODUCTION**

Why Work Songs?

Music was created not only for pleasing the ear: it must have

a meaning, express an activity, a natural or supernatural force,

a feeling. Without meaning, it loses its reason for being.

—*Yaya Diallo, Malian drummer*

A prevailing characteristic of art has long been its growing distance from
the daily concerns of human beings. Most artists and critics have seen this
as a positive development. "I think what an audience wants from a concert or a recording is to get something larger than life, something more
than going to work at nine and coming home at five," explains one
performer. "I think that's the function of art in our society. It's relief from
the gray and the noise and the din."

Probing this same sensibility, Lydia Goehr has given it a name, the
"separability principle," which represents the now-dominant attitude toward art that separates it "completely from the world of the ordinary,
mundane and everyday." Ralph Vaughan Williams makes a similar point
in his essay "Why Do We Make Music?" when he confidently answers the
question phrased in his title by proclaiming, "One thing we can be certain
of: we do not compose, sing or play music for any useful purpose." For
Vaughan Williams, this represents a tremendous achievement—waxing
enthusiastically, he continues: "Music is just music, and that is, to my
mind, its great glory."

Lowbrow art forms embrace this same "separability" mandate. Yes, we
can dismiss these offerings as simple "escapism"—which is another name

for Goehr's principle, I would suggest—but a panoply of so-called entertainment industries expend billions of dollars each year trying to create, package, and sell it. Popular art eschews "relevance," almost luxuriates in its absence. Yet even highbrow critics express the same attitude, although they do so frequently in jargon-laden pronouncements that few pay any attention to, praising the "autonomy of the text" or the "incommensurability" of the work of art—hard, cold phrases that are outside the vocabulary of the average person, yet act as significant code words for creative endeavors drained of their connections to everyday life. This is truly an odd alliance. Yet both movie moguls and deconstructionist academics share the same determination to relieve art from the burden of its relevance, its linkages to a boring quotidian existence. They want to set free the surface images of art to play and dance, unfettered by the need to serve a higher purpose or function. The student writing a term paper has always fretted over the "deep inner meaning" of the work of art—in my day they even gave it an acronym, the "DIM." Ah, but this bugbear has finally been put on the run. The work of art now merely *is,* it no longer *means* anything and it is expected to *do* even less . . . except perhaps generate a good return on investment.

At first glance, this is an approach that seems to elevate art so as to distinguish it from the merely human. On closer inspection, it consigns art to the dustbin. In lacking a connection to our day-to-day experience as human beings, art can achieve nothing more than to distract us for a few idle moments. In the disheartening words of another respected scholar, Steven Pinker, music is nothing more than "auditory chessecake" for the brain, merely one more pleasurable stimulus little different from junk food or "recreational drugs"; it "could vanish from our species," he adds, "and the rest of our lifestyle would be virtually unchanged."

Compare the "separability" or "auditory chessecake" view of the role of music to the part it plays in less leisure-driven cultures. In describing the music of Native American tribes, for example, John Bierhorst writes: "There were very few songs that did not have some definite purpose, and it is this purposefulness, more than anything else, that distinguishes Indian music from the music of modern Europe or America." Native American songs would assist in healing, courtship, propitiating spirits, greeting visitors, giving thanks, or preparing for war. Sometimes a single song might have multiple purposes, such as the one sung by Native American women of the Southwest while grinding corn, which both made their physical labor less draining and also served as a prayer for rain to ensure the continuance of the corn supply. Probing these many purposes of music, we are tempted to concur with the Motu tribesman of New Guinea who told James Chalmers, "No drums are beaten uselessly. There are no dances that are merely useless." We are now far afield from Vaughan Williams's one certainty, that music has no purpose, as far away from such a view as can be imagined.

We are faced here with two incompatible attitudes. One celebrates music for its very uselessness; the other demands that music enter into the many varied spheres of day-to-day life. Is Vaughan Williams right? Must music merely *be*, and never *do?* Are our songs like those grand kings of olden times whose very glory demanded that they sit aloof on the throne, languorous and inactive, forbidden from entering into the streets and fields, inns and taverns, schools and playing fields where real life flourished? Or should we expect something more of music? It is one of the premises of this book that we should; that music has many roles to play in our lives; that it becomes richer, not poorer, by taking on these added dimensions.

Some years ago, the philosopher Arthur Danto made a striking prediction about the future of art. The current era represents, he suggested, the end of the history of art as a series of progressive movements: "The time for next things is past. The end of art coincides with the end of a history of art that has that kind of structure. After that there is nothing to do but live happily ever after. It was like coming to the end of the world with no more continents to discover. One must now begin to make habitable the only continents that there are. One must learn to live within the limits of the world. As I see it, this means returning art to the serving of largely human ends."

Danto is vague about what these "human ends" might be. And, at first, it must seem puzzling to view art in this manner. Everywhere we hear the mantra of "art for art's sake," yet almost never do we hear about art for *our* sake. It is almost as if the "separability principle" has become so ingrained in our cultural thinking that we have lost sight of the many other ways of relating to art. As a society, we have put art on a stage . . . and kept it there, safely out of the way. Above all, any suggestion that people might be able to *put art to use* in their lives will strike many as an archaic, perhaps even dangerous, notion. But once we adjust our vision to art as an essentially human endeavor, and comprehend that all such endeavors are purposive to some degree—indeed, people stop putting things to use only when they no longer see value in them—then the fear and befuddlement may perhaps disappear. Instead, lifting itself above the horizon a broad landscape of art integrated into the day-to-day lives of people can suddenly become visible.

Music and the other arts have no greater role to play than to enchant and transform our everyday existence. The average person knows this on a deep, almost intuitive, level, even if many critics and reviewers, and indeed some artists themselves, appear to have lost the thread. And in recent years, a growing cadre of scholars, immersed in a wide range of disciplines, have undertaken the task of reassessing this rich if little understood process, each working from the distinctive vantage point of a specific area of expertise, often in ignorance of each other's efforts but nonetheless striving toward a common end. Their efforts have helped in paving the way for my own work and also, I believe, have the potential to influence and enhance the ways in which art and art making are situated in contemporary society. The academic field of ethnomusicology has an especially important part to play in this process, given its focus on that critical nexus point at which music and social forces intersect. One wonders how widely the works of John Blacking, Charles Keil, Bruno Nettl, Steven Feld, and others are read outside of this field, but their focus on how music shapes and enhances individual and social activities would be worthwhile for anyone dealing with creative pursuits to consider. Christopher Small, a secondary school teacher in New Zealand who later became a lecturer in education, might seem to be an unlikely ally, and even less a potent force to revolutionize our thinking on music. But he has probed deeply into these issues, in thoughtful works such as *Music, Society, Education, Music of the Common Tongue* and *Musicking,* forcing us to re-assess our most basic notions of what an artist is and does. During this same period, cognitive psychologist John Sloboda has approached these issues from a completely different perspective, but has perhaps done more than anyone else to reveal the richness in how people use music in their daily lives. Sloboda's work also deserves to be far better known outside his field, for his research establishes in many ways the psychological basis for a completely different aesthetic approach to music and other arts. I must also call attention here to the insightful studies of the anthropologist Ellen Dissanyake, the bioevolutionary theories of Frederick Turner, the writings of the sociologist Tia DeNora, the historical inquiries of William H. McNeill, the research into soundscapes and acoustic ecology conducted by the composer and scholar R. Murray Schafer, and other efforts by experts operating in a range of diverse fields. Given the fragmentation of contemporary scholarship, few researchers pay attention to the linkages between these different currents of contemporary thought. And even fewer people involved in creative fields—performers, painters, dancers, poets, and the like—comprehend the tremendous implications of what they mean. A completely different attitude to artistic creation and consumption is presently being outlined and developed—one that, I believe, may emerge as the dominant approach in the coming decades and may serve as a potent alternative to the "separability" model described above. If (as I believe) art making is enriched, not lessened, by entering into the fabric of our day-to-day lives, then the outlines of a roadmap for appreciating its riches and untapped potential can be traced in the works of the authors cited above.

The present work and its companion *Healing Songs,* as well as a planned third volume *Love Songs,* will attempt to provide the historical underpinnings for these lines of inquiry, connect them to the other emerging areas of research, show their roots in timeless patterns of behavior, and above all, reveal their implications for artistic creation today. My goal is to comprehend a history of music not as an account of great composers, of artistic movements, or of evolving styles, but rather by focusing on the points of impact, on those decisive moments in which artistic creation and consumption meet and in which the lives—of individuals, of communities, of tribes and nations—are transformed. For me, this is not a small matter, but rather the critical component in the whole equation, the key to understanding what music has been and can be.

But as much as I want to write good history, my motivation is even more rooted in a desire to create good practice. I believe that the current paradigms of assessing art and fostering art making are at a point of exhaustion. In essence, we have come to a crossroads. The most powerful model for the last five hundred years has postulated that arts must progress, much like sciences, with each generation going beyond the boundaries set by its predecessors. This view is so deeply ingrained in our approach to artistic creation that many people merely assume that we have *always* thought about art in these terms. In fact, this approach was initially little more than an organizing principle employed by a few critics and commentators (most notably Giorgio Vasari in the early sixteenth century), who found it a useful perspective for assessing the rapid progress of artistic innovations after the end of the Middle Ages. And it did prove useful, and continued to prove useful until quite recently. But gradually over the last several decades, this positivistic model of artist movements has lost its power to explain and enlighten. In the area of music, for example, the progressive view cannot explain the rise of minimalism, the abandonment of serialism, the vitality of jazz and popular forms of music, the pervasiveness and influence of "ambient" music, the resurgence of many traditional and regional forms of music, the emergence of music linked to New Age philosophies, and many other unmistakable trends and developments. For any critic who accepts this ingrained progressive view of the arts, these movements must be ignored, explained away (often under the convenient rubric of "postmodernism," which still betrays the chronological, progressive bias of our time, as illustrated even more tellingly by the more recent and lamentable term "post-postmodernism"), or denounced as reactionary tendencies of the worst sort. In short, much of what is interesting or appealing or provocative in contemporary music cannot be addressed by the models of progressivism and separability that permeate our critical perspectives. A new paradigm is demanded: one that gives due attention to the living reality of creating and experiencing music as part of our personal and social soundscapes.

Mapping this terrain has been the key focus of my thinking about music for most of the last decade. But even earlier I sensed that contemporary theories of artistic production and consumption were missing a rich and vital part of how people actually respond to music. In trying to come to grips with the nature of jazz while writing my first book, *The Imperfect Art,* I vaguely understood even then that the human and personal element was what made it special. By grappling with the imperfections of jazz as an *improvised* art I instinctively comprehended that these human flaws could not be eradicated from the music, and in fact were the elements that gave jazz its allure and special magic. At the same time, I had learned—perhaps most clearly from Ortega y Gasset in his brilliant essay, "The Dehumanization of Art"—that this same intimate, personal element was being purged from virtually every other sphere of creative endeavor. An exploration of the underlying causes and dramatic scope of this shift are beyond the scope of this volume—indeed, these elements are more driven by tendencies in the social sciences and philosophical currents than by the needs of artistic pursuits—but composers, musicians, and lovers of music are left to cope with the end result, namely a cultural environment in which artistic pursuits have been cut off from the purposes, meanings, and values that gave them vitality for thousands of years.

Back then I still subscribed half-heartedly to the separability principle. Or, perhaps it is more accurate to say, I did not comprehend at the time how art could focus on meeting human needs without diminishing its scope, without limiting it to the narrowest, most utilitarian purposes. But, as I see it now, the exact opposite is true. When allowed to serve the needs of people, music actually broadens its scope. It becomes more than just the isolated pursuit of performers on a stage or in a recording studio, and enters into a myriad of intimate relationships with individuals and the surrounding world. How does music meet human needs? Let us count some of the ways. There are work songs, the topic of this study; but also songs of courtship and love; of spirituality and worship; healing music; game songs; storytelling ballads which relate an important event, or capture the history or mythology of a people; military music; lullabies; school or team songs which create cohesion among a community; patriotic anthems which do the same for an entire nation; mnemonic melodies which assist in learning everything from the alphabet to the periodic table of elements; music for social dancing; or for exercise, or stimulation or meditation; songs of greeting or thanks, or for boasting or praise; or ritual music for all passages of life from births to funerals . . . the list goes on and on. In essence, the music of human needs is as broad as music itself, tapping every source of inspiration and addressing all situations. Even the escapism of popular music, when seen from this perspective, is yet another example of a human need being met. In truth, the moguls of pop music would be standing in unemployment lines if it were not for the public's persistence in integrating music into all the steps of love and courtship, from the quasi-licentious slow number at the high school prom to the sobering first dance at the wedding reception. Even when artists think they are making art for art's sake . . . the cussed public insists on using it for other, more functional, purposes.

Seeing this broad array of purposeful songs, deeply integrated into the fabric of social and individual life, I am tempted to propose a "connectedness principle"—the mirror image of Lydia Goehr's mandate of separability. The "connectedness principle" would suggest that all music creates linkages with our daily lived experiences, and that this is its greatest blessing for us. A music totally divorced from human concerns is as impossible as a cuisine made without food or a dance without movement. How can music, a social institution, exist in isolation from human needs? John Blacking makes this point persuasively when he writes, "A person may create music for financial gain, for private pleasure, for entertainment, or to accompany a variety of social events, and he need not express open concern for the human condition. But his music cannot escape the stamp of the society that made its creator human, and the kind of music he composes will be related to his consciousness of, and concern for, his fellow human beings." Even when the uses of music are frivolous or contrived—perhaps to secure tenure in a music department or to please an insistent piano instructor—they are still part of the connectedness principle.

I am reminded here of the British philosopher J. L. Austin, who turned linguistic philosophy on its head with his book *How to Do Things with Words*. Most philosophers, focusing on the meaning of words, viewed them as mere symbols. In contrast, Austin described a class of speech acts that he called "performatives" because they could actually perform tasks, could literally "do" things. How so? When someone says "I promise to pay you ten dollars tomorrow," or "I take thee Susan to be my wife," or "I christen this boat the HMS *Bounty*" they are not just describing the world but are actually changing it in some small measure, altering it through the words they are speaking. Music can do this too, although we are often oblivious to the fact. For many years now, I have felt increasingly drawn to these musical performatives, sensing that they may hold the key to revitalizing our sense of the enchantment of song; that in them may reside the power that music still has to change our lives and not just provide an unobtrusive background soundtrack.

Applying Austin's view to music, for all its apparent novelty, literally returns us to the earliest stirrings of song in human societies. The Latin word for singing—*cantare*—contained as part of its original meaning the working of magic, a sense still held for us by the word "incantation." Perhaps all songs actually did something in their early days, revealing their magical powers in the process. In his study of music among the Flathead Indians of Montana, Alan Merriam reports a concept strikingly similar to Austin's idea of performatives. "For the Flathead, the most important single fact about music and its relationship to the total world is its origin in the supernatural sphere. . . . A sharp distinction is drawn by the Flathead between what they call 'make-up' and all other songs. 'Make-up' songs are those which are composed by individuals in a conscious process of creation and those which are known to be borrowed from other peoples. These songs have no inherent power and, according to the Flathead, are 'used for enjoyment.'" The other songs convey specific powers in a range of social situations. From a Flathead perspective, the music of the West is comprised almost exclusively of those songs that have "no inherent power," while the efficacious music is marginalized, dismissed, neglected, or even destroyed.

In traditional African cultures, music is similarly integrated into day-to-day life to a degree hardly imaginable in Western societies. In a host of African languages—Igbo, Tiv, Yoruba, Efik, Birom, Hausa, and others—it is difficult to find a word corresponding to the Western concept of music as a stand-alone practice abstracted from particular activities. As Charles Keil reminds us, in these languages "it is easy to talk about song and dance, singers and drummers, blowing a flute, beating a bell . . . but the general terms 'music' and 'musician' require long and awkward circumlocutions that still fall short . . . So what seems to us a very basic, useful and rather concrete term is apparently a useless abstraction from a Tiv, Yoruba, perhaps even a pan-African or non-Western point of view." In his explorations of the Tiv language, Keil shows how the verb *dugh*, which is used to describe the act of composing music, can also refer to catching fish, gathering yams, collecting honey, or digging a well. The terminology is revealing: the study of music in such a setting seems to lead inevitably back to the workaday activities of daily existence.

The degree to which we have lost this "connectedness" is made clear by a review of the early travel literature written by Western visitors to Africa. In 1795, twenty-four-year-old Mungo Park embarked on a risky journey into the interior of Africa—an eighteen-month trip that found him, at various points, robbed, imprisoned, enslaved, left for dead, stricken with malaria, fending off lions, nearly overcome by thirst or famine, and finally reduced to beggary. When he eventually returned to the coastal settlements at the end of his ordeals, Park was almost unrecognizable: unkempt, unshaven, and dressed in rags. The scraps of notes he took during his travels were his only surviving possessions, and formed the basis for his celebrated 1799 book *Travels in the Interior Districts of Africa*. Although Park was ostensibly writing about geography and describing travel routes, his work also bears witness to the wide range of music and its social importance in the many towns and villages he visited. He describes war drums used to raise four thousand fighting men; women singing to while away the hours spent spinning cotton; villagers called to evening prayers by sounds blown through hollowed elephants' teeth ("the sound is melodious," Park wrote, "and, in my opinion, comes nearer to the human voice than any other artificial sound"); songs employed to conciliate and praise a political leader ("they are so loaded with gross adulation, that no man but a Moorish despot could hear them without blushing"); drums used to announce a wedding and accompany singers at the celebration; initiation into adulthood marked by the formation of groups of youngsters who spend two months traveling throughout a neighborhood singing and dancing; numerous encounters with *jilli kea,* or singing men ("one or more of these may be found in every town"), who sing of historical events, accompany soldiers into war, and compose various extemporaneous songs; songs used to request hospitality, to uplift the crestfallen, to describe a trip, or to greet a returned villager after a long absence. Presented with vivid descriptions of this rich mosaic of music—music that was truly lived and experienced, not watched dispassionately as a mere performance—I am forced to wonder at how much we have lost.

But much can also be regained. I mentioned above that the "separability principle" is now the dominant view in the world of art. Yet I should clarify that statement. Yes, it is the dominant view of theorists and critics, and perhaps some artists. But, as I have already suggested, when one looks at how most individuals approach art, we find something quite different. Cognitive psychologist John Sloboda has undertaken a number of fascinating studies of how music plays a role in people's lives. Sloboda's findings are invigorating and surprising. Most might assume that the modern listener treats music as an inobtrusive background soundtrack, diverting or entertaining perhaps, but counting for little else. But through a growing and impressive body of research, Sloboda has shown that the exact opposite is true. Music is not only deeply embedded in day-to-day lives, but in fact serves as an invaluable tool in meeting demands and necessities, and in navigating through challenges and crises. In a survey of sixty-seven respondents, he found that forty-one called particular attention to this role of music in their lives. "The most commonly mentioned concept," he writes, "was that of music as *change agent.*" In another study, Sloboda and Susan O'Neill asked subjects to carry a pager that was rung once during each two-hour time period between the hours of 8:00 AM and 10:00 PM, although the specific moment within these 120-minute slots was determined at random. At each paging, the subjects would note in a logbook their most recent musical experience. The study results conveyed both the pervasiveness of music in our lives—44 percent of the entries indicated a musical experience since the last paging—and its integration into day-to-day activities. Active listening to music accounted for only 2 percent of the instances; the rest of the time, people were doing other things while the music was being heard. But the music did not merely provide a sonic background. As Sloboda and O'Neill note, "We found, on average, the experience of music resulted in participants becoming more positive, more alert and more focused in the present." Other research by Sloboda has highlighted the particular importance of music in various work situations—desk work, housework, traveling to and from places of employment, unwinding after work—which in totality account for close to half of all listening experiences. Who can deny that the need for song to accompany labor is just as important in our postindustrial age as it was for earlier generations who wielded hammers and axes, or spears and clubs? Sloboda's research can leave little doubt about this matter. Songs still make things happen, can change us, and even in some degree alter the world around us. This capacity of music is not restricted to Native American tribes and traditional societies but continues everywhere, everyday.

And even our highbrow cultural legacy is not without precedents for bringing music and other creative pursuits into the center of our activities, where they are no longer restricted to the periphery of our experiences. As M. I. Finley points out with regard to ancient Greece, it was a culture that reached the pinnacle of artistic achievement, yet totally lacked museums: "Art was meshed in with daily living, not set apart for occasional leisure time or for the enjoyment of rich collectors and aesthetes." In contrast, musical performance for the purpose of mere entertainment was seen by the ancients not simply as a lesser art but in fact as a low art. Tacitus, for example, describes as a "national disgrace" the emperor Nero's desire to perform music on a public stage. In fact, the "connectedness principle" is not very far from Aristotle's ancient view of the complicated, various roles of music, which included alleviating toils and pains, providing refreshment, strengthening the soul, firming the character, and—yes, but almost as an afterthought—also offering entertainment. If we have forgotten all but the last of these roles in our media-dominated commercial culture, we need do nothing more than listen with open ears to the pathos and intrinsic dignity of the work song to be called back to this richer view of the role of music.

For this reason, paying attention to the work songs and healing songs, the love songs and ritual music, the "embedded music" of different times and places, can be much more than a mere antiquarian pursuit; more than just another revival of some forgotten craft. Such a study represents, rather, a return to first principles and a much-needed corrective. Above all, it serves as a telling reminder of the most essential element in all music, namely its ability to enter into intimate communion with our everyday lives in multifaceted ways, addressing our deepest concerns and most heartfelt needs, both as consumers and as creators. Traditional work songs, so deeply woven into the meanings and manners of everday life, may never come back, but the spirit that gave them impetus can and should be nurtured. Certainly we need what they had to offer more than ever today, in our sad and dehumanized musical culture, with its machine-made songs that are bought and sold like one more commodity, no different than barrels of oil or crates of produce.

The future of music cannot simply be an extension of these stultifying trends—that way madness lay. Instead we must reclaim our heritage, and this starts by comprehending what a music might be if it were truly our own, meeting the exigencies of our human condition. There is no better place to begin this process than by coming to terms with the music that enlivened our labors, gave continuity and substance to our life's vocation, and empowered our efforts.

CHAPTER ONE

The Hunter

Without a song, the bush knife grows dull.

—*West African proverb*

In 1988, two researchers probing caves in the south of France made a remarkable discovery, one that deserves far greater recognition by those concerned with the origins and evolution of music. Here at the foot of the French Pyrenees, Iegor Reznikoff and Michel Dauvois were testing a new technique for exploring the caves of Lascaux, famous for their vivid prehistoric paintings. These celebrated images—of wild beasts, of hunters, and of strange hybrid creatures that seem part human and part animal—have captivated the imagination of experts and laity alike since their discovery in 1940 and have altered our notions about the evolution of the visual arts in early societies. The sheer scope of the images, and the difficulties in lighting and scaffolding that must have been overcome by their creators, are fascinating issues in their own right. But the role that these paintings may have played in the lives of the hunting societies that made them is an even stronger stimulant for speculation. Indeed, one is hard pressed to categorize these works as "aesthetic" in any conventional sense. So vital and intense are the figures on the walls of the caves that the hunters who made them seem to have used the pictures to capture the very energy and life force of the creatures depicted.

Yet, unlike previous visitors, Reznikoff and Dauvois were not interested in looking at these famous walls. Instead, they focused their attention on the rather unconventional question of how they *sounded*. Carefully mapping the acoustical properties of different parts of the caves, they reached the significant conclusion that the very places where the paintings were located were those that demonstrated the *greatest acoustical resonance*. It was hard to escape the inevitable corollary: the people who made these paintings must have gathered around them for singing, chanting or other forms of music making. And the music making was so important to them that the location of the images—some of them in places almost impossible to reach—was apparently dictated by the need to create the loudest sounds possible.

What purpose motivated this singing or chanting? As I describe later, we have enough evidence from other hunting societies to hazard an educated guess. To start, these songs were probably not made for entertainment or diversion, to while away the long hours of darkness or inclement weather, or other such idle pursuits—although these purposes may have been served in some supplementary way by the music making. More to the point, the songs of the tribe were almost certainly cultivated for their efficacy and potency. As such, this music was performed, taught, and preserved for enhancing success in hunting, for exercising magical control over the wild creatures that surrounded them, to increase the sometimes precarious supply of food, and to reduce the ever present risks to the hunters who secured it. If this theory is true—as the cumulative evidence of the following pages will, I hope, substantiate—it has telling implications for the present study. Here, at the first stirrings of music as a social enterprise, it appears already linked to the economic basis of the community. But even more striking, the "work song" of the hunter—if such we can call it—was already much more than a rhythmic accompaniment to labor. It also carried a power of enchantment, served as a spur to courage, and acted as a force of social solidarity. True, it enhanced the success of the work at hand, but not in the cut-and-dried, functionalistic way that we normally associate with such music.

For the groups who joined together in singing and chanting at these places of high resonance, the sounds themselves must have been awe-inspiring. The natural world is mostly quiet. Except for rare events, a fierce storm or avalanche, or a visit to unusual locations—such as the foot of a waterfall—an individual of this period might go through an entire lifetime without hearing a single very loud sound. In such circumstances, the invention of social music making on a large scale must have been a dramatic moment of self-discovery, inspiring the entire community with its intensity. And bringing this practice into enclosed locations with resonant acoustics may very well have made the very animals tremble with apprehension, perhaps literally or at least in the imagination of the hunters. If one of my goals in this volume is to show that music can be life changing and world changing, we may have already found a striking example here at the very start of our story.

It is, of course, a long start. Measured on a timeline, this beginning of our account takes us almost to the end. Since homo sapiens first appeared, they have lived during 99 percent of this period as hunter-gatherers. Ten thousand years ago, most of the habitable parts of the globe served as hunting grounds for human societies. Even now, after our emergence as a post-industrial economy, experts estimate that over half of the people who ever lived depended on hunting and gathering for their subsistence.

Yet our understanding of these cultures—and of the role they played in shaping our biological, psychological, and communal lives today—is flimsy at best. Like culprits leaving the scene of a crime, we have done our best to destroy the evidence. In a tragic and ironic reversal, played out over the last two hundred years, the great hunting societies of the globe— the San of South Africa, the Sioux of North America, the Birhor of India, the Aboriginal natives of Tasmania, the Khanty of Siberia, and so many others—themselves became the victims of more powerful poachers who coveted their ancestral lands. No communities have been more decimated, more marginalized than these last reminders of the socioeconomic lives we all once led. Today hunting societies have all but vanished, some overcome by the hostile forces surrounding them, others converted to different means of procuring the necessities of life, and only a hearty few pursuing traditional ways in areas too remote or inhospitable for most other purposes. A whole way of life, with its songs and other trappings, has become extinct. Hunter and hunted came to share the same fate, both superseded by more robust economic models of supply and demand.

Given this long and murky lineage, any inquiry into the origin of hunting songs is tantamount to a search for the birth of music itself. To ask why hunters first sang forces us to confront profound questions about why the earliest individuals and societies required *any* musical forms of expression. One theorist has suggested that "if Homo erectus bands learned to consolidate sentiments of social solidarity by dancing together, their hunting would have become more efficient." In short, singing led to teamwork, and teamwork led to successful hunting. Who dares argue with such pat logic? But, as we shall see, the matter is much richer and deeper than indicated by such neat models of pure functionality. One of my chief goals in this work is to show that songs associated with various tasks and professions cannot be reduced to their purely utilitarian aspects, but rather fulfilled varied and complicated roles within their societies. In our study of hunting music, we will not be disappointed in this regard. Many layers of meaning, of purpose, emotion, and beauty in this music will demand our attention and earn our respect.

Members of agricultural communities are well known for singing while at work in the fields, as are herders in their pastoral lands. In contrast, the music of the last remaining hunting societies is little known or appreciated. This obscurity is partly due, no doubt, to the remote and often inaccessible locations in which traditional hunting still takes place. The hunters themselves also contribute to this neglect: they rarely seek out opportunities to share their music beyond the confines of their community, often reluctant to perform it when outsiders, even sympathetic ones, are present. But our own biases also play a role here. Above all, the prevalent image of primitive hunting as marked by silence and caution may lead many to suspect that songs play a comparatively modest role in the day-to-day life of these societies. But nothing could be further from the truth. Hunting cultures typically enjoy a rich musical life, and much of their song and dance influences or is influenced by their mode of economic sustenance, although the linkages between music and the act of hunting itself, as I have already suggested, can often be allusive and indirect.

The more we probe into the songs of the hunt, the more we uncover these ethereal and magical—one is sometimes even tempted to use the word "spiritual"—elements lurking below the surface. We have already caught a glimpse of these elements in the findings from Lascaux. We can easily imagine that the hunt was first enacted in a representational manner before these images (also representational in nature), probably with the accompaniment of music and dance. This fictive hunt takes place before the real pursuit begins, the ceremony prefiguring the success of the ensuing expedition. Sympathetic magic is the formal term given to such activities: the belief that depicting or enacting an event—usually in a transformed, ritualized manner—will assist in bringing it about in real life. This simple concept that "like produces like" stands out as one of the most potent and persistent ideas in the history of human societies. To the true believer, it offers everything: it is religion, science, medicine, philosophy, psychological support, and moral guide all rolled into one. Its influence on early music and on the incorporation of song into ritual and social settings is still insufficiently understood and appreciated.

Vestiges of this belief system survived until modern times in the music and dance of hunting societies, as illustrated in particular by the ceremonies that preceded or followed the chase. While visiting the Mandan tribe of the upper Missouri during the 1830s, George Catlin observed the tribe's buffalo dance, held during a period in which game was scarce and the people faced starvation. "My ears have been almost continually ringing since I came here, with the din of yelping and beating of drums . . . In any emergency of this kind, every man musters and brings out of his lodge his mask (the skin of a buffalo's head with the horns on), which he is obliged to keep in readiness for this occasion; and then commences the buffalo dance, of which I have above spoken, which is held for the purpose of making 'buffalo come' (as they term it), of inducing the buffalo herds to change the direction of their wanderings, and bend their course towards the Mandan village." Numerous other examples of this use of sympathetic magic in hunting music could be cited. Among the Wahehe of Tanganyika, for example, the imitation of elephant cries form part of a hunting song. The turtle-hunting song of the Andaman Islanders is accompanied by a dance in which the motion of the turtle swimming through the water is emulated. In describing a hunting dance he witnessed in Yamoussoukro in the Ivory Coast, Geoffrey Gorer explains how performers armed with bows and arrows enacted in pantomime the killing of an antelope, which was played by a fifteen-year-old-boy wearing a realistic animal mask and dangling a straw tail. As this example makes clear, the hunter often imitated not only the sound or appearance of the animal to be stalked, but might even act out the entire process of pursuit and capture. Describing an "opossum dance" among the Aboriginal people of southeastern Australia, A.W. Howitt wrote in 1904: "Every action of finding the animal—the ineffectual attempt to poke it out of its retreat, the smoking it out with fire, and the killing of it by the hunters as it runs out—is rendered, not only by the words of the song, but also by the concerted actions and movements of the performers in their pantomimic dancing."

In fact, this magical linkage between preparatory music and the success of the hunt is found in all regions of the world. The Danish explorer

Knud Rassmussen offers a translation of a song used by the tribal elders of the Igloolik Inuit when there is a dearth of meat. The song assists the wizard who will invoke the Mistress of the Sea to come to their aid and "release some of the creatures she is holding back."

> We stretch forth our hands
> To lift thee up.
> We are without food,
> Without fruits of our hunting.
> Come up then from below,
> From the hollow place
> Force a way through.
> We are without food,
> And here we lie down.
> We stretch forth our hands
> To lift thee up.

Frances Densmore found a similar practice in use among the Seminoles, who begin their songs the night before important expeditions in the belief that the music will bring the animals to "feed close in" and thus be more easily discovered by the hunting party. T. G. H. Strehlow wrote a detailed account of the "kangaroo increase" ceremonies of central Australia, which he witnessed at Alice Springs in 1933 and at Jay Creek in 1950, the latter instance documented on film. This sacred ritual involves the laying down of a ground painting depicting the kangaroo ancestors, as well as singing, acting, and a concluding symbolic fertilization rite—the latter activity surrounded by such a strong veil of secrecy that Strehlow believed that he was the first white man allowed to observe it. Of course, European traditions of this sort also existed at one time, but vanished so long ago that little documentation remains. Writing of the Laplanders in 1673, John Scheffer noted that "they believe they can effect very strange things by the drum. . . . These are three, belonging to their hunting, their sacred affairs, or lastly the enquiring into things far distant. . . . In order to the knowing this, they place the bunch of rings on the picture of the Sun in the drum; then they beat, singing at the same time." Scheffer adds that the direction in which the keys move indicates the location in which game will be found.

Even if the magical efficacy of such ceremonies seems doubtful, their role in enhancing the confidence of the hunters can hardly be denied. The

Israeli ethnomusicologist Simha Arom documented a striking example of this ritual music among the Aka Pygmies, which is presented in part on his 1987 recording *Centrafique: Anthologie de la musique des Pygmees Aka.* Before embarking on their great collective hunts—large-scale undertakings that can last weeks or months—the Aka conduct their Zoboko, a rite that enables a seer, selected from among members of the tribe, to predict the dangers ahead and the prey to be caught. At nightfall on the evening before the start of the hunt, the diviner dances by a large fire in the center of the camp, while others surround him singing and clapping. A few men, crouched in front of a tree trunk lying flat on the ground, strike it with sticks to provide a ground beat. As the music progresses, the seer begins to call out the names of the animals that will be taken in the hunt; at times he falls to the ground in front of one or another of the men, indicating that this hunter will have success in stalking game. At the end of the ceremony the men return in silence to their dwellings, emboldened by the predictions of their valor and ultimate triumph.

But for the Aka and other hunting societies of central Africa, their hunting music has at this point only just begun. In the following weeks, numerous specialized songs, dances, and melodic calls will be used at various stages of the hunt and its aftermath, filling many roles, both functional and ritualistic. True, hunting may be the quietest of professions. But, paradoxically, the hunting efforts of these traditional communities are also rich in musical accompaniment, almost as if the stalkers need to compensate at all other times for their enforced moments of silence. Here we might be reminded of that odd passage in Vico's *New Science,* where the author postulates that the first human languages were sung melodies: the founders of nations, "having wandered about in the wild state of dumb beasts and being therefore sluggish, were inexpressive save under the impulse of violent passions, and formed their first languages by singing." Vico offers us vague conjecture in the guise of science, and his theories may well make a modern linguist blush, but the student of early hunting societies recognizes a certain poetic truth to the notion. Song permeates day-to-day life in these cultures, and in terms of value to the community it rivals spoken language.

Colin Turnbull, in his moving account of his life among the Mbuti Pygmies of the Congo, confirms that virtually the "only time they are silent is when actually hunting." Concentration and quiet are essential here, not just to ensure success in the hunt, but also to avoid serious injury, since unwittingly surprising a dangerous animal is one of the great risks of life in the African rainforest. But at other times song is pervasive. Hunters will invariably sing and banter when not actually on the prowl. But the importance of song is perhaps even more obvious in the gathering activities that supplement the hunter's production; and here again ritual, aesthetic and functional concerns merge. When the Mbuti gather mushrooms, roots and other food, singing keeps them aware of each other's location, adds a quality of playfulness to their activities, and may keep potentially dangerous animals away.

This brief description conveys something of the key uses of this music. But it cannot do justice to its grandeur. To my mind, the songs of the Pygmies—the term is a bad one, given its general derogatory use in English, but no widely accepted alternative has arisen to replace it—are the most awe-inspiring music to emerge from traditional African societies. Listening to it is like hearing an aural equivalent to the carnival house of mirrors: every sound reverberates and is re-echoed from another angle; it is impossible to tell where phrases end or begin; all is perpetual momentum. There is nothing to grab hold to, only shifting textures, tantalizing but evanescent. You perhaps associate African music with vital rhythms, and this too is found in the songs of the Aka, the Mbuti, and the other remaining Pygmy tribes. But the swirling, pulsating vocal textures provide a delicate membrane structure over the powerful rhythms below. The music conveys, in some paradoxical way, both strength and gentleness at the same time.

Sound takes on an importance in hunting cultures that we post-industrialists can only vaguely appreciate. With vision impaired by the closed-in surroundings, the hunter invariably first learns of both predators and prey through auditory signals. Even the absence of sound—the sudden silence of the crickets, the termination of the bird's song—is a warning that must be heeded immediately. Hunters adapt to these demands, paying obsessive attention both to the sounds they hear as well as to the ones they themselves make. Pastoral people, with their wide-open spaces, can rely on visual cues; trusting in what they can see, they have less need to pay attention to what they hear. As a result, they can afford to let their sonic and musical cultures become more stylized—more an accompaniment to the activities of their life and less an essential part of the meaning of things. But for the hunter, only hearing is believing. There is no higher arbiter, no truer means of insight, than sound itself. Steven Feld, an ethnomusicologist studying the Kaluli in Papua New Guinea, learned this when trying to classify local bird lore according to Western ornithological methods. "Listen," his informant insisted, "to you they are birds. To me they are voices in the forest." These voices had a life of their own, distinct from the classifications of wing, beak, color, and other determinants of ornithological taxonomy. Here the sound of the animal is its ultimate reality, its essence, more vivid and less elusive than its often fleeting appearance.

And even the visual cues used by the hunter evoke a sonic landscape. The hunter "learnt to know animals by the rhythm of their movement," explains Elias Canetti in his *Crowds and Power*. "The earliest writing he learnt to read was that of their tracks; it was a kind of rhythmic notation imprinted on the soft ground and, as he read it, he connected it with the sound of its formation." The intricacy of the criss-crossing tracks, of many animals and their human pursuers, provided a veritable orchestral score of rhythmic counterpoint, strikingly similar to the actual music of these societies. And only the smallest gap existed between the silent and realized sound of these imprints in the earth: for the hunter was always listening, always straining his ears for the clip-clop, clip-clop of real footsteps. Few concepts can be more alien to the modern Western mind than this linkage between music and topography, but for traditional hunting cultures, the connection is almost self-evident. We find it demonstrated in stunning fashion, for example, in the "Songlines" of Australia, where songs were not only used by the Ancestors to call into existence the trees, hills, and waterways, but continued to serve as infallible guides for later journeys of considerable distances. Here Bruce Chatwin concluded that "the whole of Australia could be read as a musical score. There was hardly a rock or creek in the country that could not or had not been sung."

Such philosophical speculations should not blind us to the many overtly functional uses of the hunter's music—which, even in the case of the Songlines, were far from negligible, the songs serving, as Chatwin points out, as "map and direction-finder . . . passport and meal-ticket." True, in other instances the utilitarian nature of the hunting music is more readily apparent. We find many examples of songs, for instance, serving to frighten animals in an attempt to bring them out of their hiding spots. An Egyptian relief sculpture from the fourteenth century BC, found at el-Amarna and now housed in the Brooklyn Museum, shows women beating tambourines to scare birds into flight. Although no hunters are depicted, it may well be that they were represented on an adjacent block that has not survived. A comparable depiction from the Old Kingdom shows a boy in a boat holding two decoy birds and blowing into a tube—essential parts of the image are damaged, nonetheless some have speculated that the instrument depicted is a trumpet—in an apparent attempt to stir waterfowl into motion. The Aka Pygmies have a similar music: their *mongombi* calls serve to scare the game out of hiding and into the nets of the waiting captors. But these calls serve another equally utilitarian role—that of allowing the hunters to contact each other when out of visual sight and thus coordinate their efforts. Other hunting cultures employ similar musical signals, sometimes elaborating them into complicated communication systems. The Bariba of Benin, for example, rely on a variety of these melodies, each with a precise meaning. They serve as a code language enabling hunters to communicate without alerting the animals of the wild. Here, the role of music in the hunt is overt and easily subsumed under our logical concepts of cause and effect: the song directly facilitates capturing the prey.

But the relationship between the hunter and the hunted is not always purely adversarial, and the music itself often reflects this ambiguity. Many of the songs used to bring success in hunting were believed by the hunting communities to be transmitted by powerful animal spirits, whose support could be enlisted by the proper propitiatory actions. In essence, the prey is to some extent also the guide. These two roles are not contradictory, but rather reinforce each other in a cosmology in which interdependency, not dominance, is the primary ecological attitude. Among Native American tribes, the songs and dances associated with important animals—the buffalo, the deer—are often among the most precious parts of their cultural legacy. As such, they continue to hold meaning and are cherished even after hunting has ceased to become a critical source of food supply. The Teton Sioux medicine men, for example, employed a special song that could secure buffalo during times of famine. In the song, which is performed in the dark, the buffalo itself speaks:

> a pipe
> they mentioned
> as they walked
> many times
> I have offered this

as I walked
a red earth
they mentioned
as they walked
many times
it has been place upon me
as I walked
a blue earth
     they mentioned
as they walked
many times
it has been place upon me
as I walked

Siyaka, the source of this song, vouched for its great power. The pipe mentioned in the song refers to the one given to the Sioux by the White Buffalo Woman. This sacred object, still in existence, symbolizes many things for the Sioux, especially the tribe's intimate relationship with the buffalo, whose fate they share not only in a ritualistic sense—the identification of hunter and prey, as we have seen, playing a role in such instances—but also from a strictly historical perspective. "The buffalo was part of us," writes Lame Deer, the Sioux medicine man, "his flesh and blood being absorbed by us until it became our own flesh and blood. . . . It was hard to say where the animal ended and the man began. . . . If brother buffalo could talk he would say, 'They put me on a reservation like the Indians.' In life and death we and the buffalo have always shared the same fate." Such songs might have originated as a means of interceding with the prey, asking it—odd though it seems to Western hunters with their adversarial relationship to the creatures of the wild—for assistance in the very process that would lead to the animal's demise. Writing of the Yaqui deer songs, Larry Evers and Felipe Molina note this theme of propitiation in the traditions associated with the music, explaining that they "were first used to placate *malichi* [little fawn] and to ask his permission for hunting and killing him." This ideal of permission and forgiveness, which the traditional hunter often seeks to inculcate in the animals killed, creates a heightened sense of interdependency and balance that contrasts markedly with the lop-sided winner-and-loser view of such relationships now prevalent in modern societies.

I have discussed here the role of music before and during the hunt, but songs continue to play a role even after the hunt's conclusion, often occurring with redoubled energy, especially when an expedition has been successful. Virtually all hunting societies cherish these songs of celebration and boasting. We encounter them in ancient texts, such as the *Shijing* from China and the *Kinkafu* from Japan, and they are preserved in oral traditions among nonliterate cultures. "I have shot a bull elephant and a wild boar," sings a young hunter of the Lakher in India. "I am beside myself with joy. I have actually shot what till now I had only seen in dreams." Among the Inuit, we find a similar song:

> When hunting we found hares and deers.
> The little brother was frightened
> And knew not what to do.
> As for myself I chased them
> And caught them.
> Ah, ja, ja!

For the Netsilik Inuit "the most common time for song composition is the return journey after a hunting trip when the adventures of the hunt are still vividly recalled by the hunter," writes Beverly Cavanagh. "The song composed in this manner then serves as a kind of narrative account of the hunter's experiences to be shared with the community at the drum dance which would be held on his return." Among the Mande of West Africa, hunters do not need to boast of their prowess—instead they rely on musicians who compose songs of praise specifically in their honor. The Aka also possess a wide range of celebratory hunting songs and dances, which are often reserved for festive occasions. One such ritual is the Monzoli, which is performed for several evenings in a row after the killing of an elephant (a major event given that the carcass of this animal can feed an entire community for weeks). (The gradual extinction of forest elephants in this region has made the Monzoli every bit as endangered as the animal that inspires it.) Among the Akan of Ghana, the killing of an elephant is a moment of such great excitement that, writes J. H. Nketia, the hunter "climbs on to the beast and bursts into song with mixed feelings of triumph and lament for the dead elephant." Other songs are used on the return from a successful expedition as a signal to those left behind at camp, while still others are sung after the arrival of the hunters. An additional hunting ritual of the Aka, the Mbenzele dance, has multiple uses: it can serve as celebration after the successful capture of prey, as a lament following a burial, or as entertainment on evenings marked by the full moon. The combination of praise and lamentation can also be found in the funeral dirges for Yoruba hunters, which, as Bade Ajuwon tells us, "can only be chanted at night and in front of the house of a deceased hunter." Enumerating the successes of their departed colleague offers the gathered hunters an opportunity to vent emotions as well as to inspire themselves with accounts of prowess in the chase.

As these varied examples amply demonstrate, music informs and enriches virtually all aspects of a hunter's life. Indeed, my researches have convinced me that no communities value music more highly or embrace its social and symbolic uses with greater fervor and vitality than these now neglected, if not overtly oppressed, hunters-gatherers living outside the currents of modern life. Perhaps the critical factor contributing to this apparent abundance of music is simply the large amount of leisure time enjoyed by the members of hunting societies. This may seem surprising, given the view that technology has made our modern lives easier, and that traditional societies face days marked by relentless hardships. But, in many ways, the hunting life is far more leisurely than our own. One scholar has gone so far as to call these communities the "first affluent societies." A time/motion study of a hunting group of Aboriginal Australians living in Arnhem Land calculated that they work for around four hours per day. Napoleon Chagnon, in his study of the Yanomamo, estimates that this tribe "earns its living"—which involves both hunting and cultivating—with about three hours of work per day. By comparison, France's recently legislated thirty-five-hour work week would seem like a recipe for exhaustion to traditional hunters, given their relaxed and comparatively unstructured pace of life. Author and music preservationist Louis Sarno, who began accompanying the Ba-Benjellé Pygmies on their hunting trips in an attempt to become integrated into their community, at first found the work unpleasant and tiring—especially because he was lugging heavy recording equipment with him through cramped and potentially dangerous rain forest terrain. Yet his attitude changed imperceptibly with the passing days until he came to realize the exhilaration and enjoyment that was forever lost to the modern world. "As I developed the stamina for hunting, I began to enjoy our expeditions more and more," he writes. "Hunting was fun! I thought of the contrasts between hunting and agriculture. Who in his right mind would want to trade such an invigorating day's work for the drudgery of life in the fields? And for what? Manioc? Bananas? Hunting gave you meat. And as for gathering—it was sheer delight. The women strolled through the forest as though they were in a vast grocery store—only here everything was for free. And each day's hunt was full of little adventures, excitement, moments of idyllic contemplation or laughter. No two days were the same."

No listener can hear the music of these traditional hunting cultures without sensing this joy and exultation, this expression of intense connection with the surrounding environment. The songs of herders and farmers are, by comparison, pensive and sober, only rarely achieving the vivacity that is a constitutive element of the hunter's daily music. Such differences defy precise analysis using the conventional tools of musicology, but they can be heard nonetheless, as much a part of the songs' essence as anything that can be reduced to staff paper.

But, above all, the prevalence of music in hunting societies must be due, at least in part, to the unpredictability of the hunting economy. The success or failure of the hunt may vary dramatically from day to day or week to week. Hence, many of the musical rituals associated with the hunt are designed to ensure good fortune or reverse a spell of bad luck. I have already described a number of the music-infused rituals of the hunters themselves. At other times, however, the hunting music may be sung by those left behind, and here the emphasis on securing good luck is especially prominent. Chagnon explains that although Yanomamo hunters perform these songs at appropriate times, the young women and girls are not exempted from musical responsibilities but must sing and dance every evening while the men are away on their *heniomou,* the week-long hunt. Throughout the course of this book I examine many modes of economic sustenance for communities, but none is more volatile than hunting and gathering, none less easy to systematize and build into a successful routine, and none more dependent on a range of complex external factors—weather, terrain, ecology, and the like. Is it any wonder that these societies sought magical power through their music? Or, convinced of the potency of their songs, that music figures so prominently in their communal life?

Many of these hunting-oriented cultures embrace practices that are associated, either now or in the past, with shamanism—for example, the Tungus of Siberia (from whom the term "shaman" comes to us), the

Aboriginal Australians, the Native Americans, the Bushmen (or San) of Africa, and the Lapps of northern Europe, among others. In all of these settings the shaman relies on music—typically drumming and singing—to achieve ecstatic states in which communication with spirits is made possible. The linkages between shamanism and hunting are striking. Many of the shaman's helping spirits or intermediaries take the form of animals. In some instances, the shaman himself is said to be capable of taking on an animal form. "Each time a shaman succeeds in sharing in the animal mode of being," writes Mircea Eliade in his classic study of the subject, "he in a manner re-establishes the situation that existed *in illo tempore*, in mythical times, when the divorce between man and the animal world had not yet occurred." This skill in mediating between man and beast makes a shaman or priest especially useful in ensuring the success of the hunt. Among the Tungus, for instance, the shaman often finds that hostile spirits are impeding the hunters or fishermen, and thus ecstatic intervention is required to counter their malevolent influence. The Ndembu of Zambia consult their "doctors" for a host of "afflictions," a category in which both physical illness and the inability to find game while hunting are included. Eric Charry notes that the "hunter's musician" among the Mande in Senegal "functions more like a priest" than a performer and is especially important in intervening with the supernatural forces at work in the midst of the bush. Rose Brandel, in *The Music of Central Africa,* states that the same music and dance employed in connection with healing rituals may often form part of the hunting ceremonies—among the Kuyu of equatorial Africa, for example, the shaman's song *Kabe* is used to attract alligators. Among the Crow Indians, the shaman plays a prominent role in the preparation for the hunt, and magical music useful in this regard may be taught to him during the course of vision or dreams. Luther Standing Bear, describing the "last great Sun Dance of the Sioux," which he saw in 1879, notes that the two main objectives of participants in this grueling ritual (which eventually was banned because of the self-mutilation it entailed) were to cure illness and to secure a supply of game for the hunters. Many other examples might be cited of the linkages between shamanic healing ceremonies and preparations for the hunt.

As such, the shaman or priest in these rituals appears to rely on techniques that had their origin, or at least their counterparts, in prehistoric times. The research of Reznikoff and Dauvois mentioned at the start of this chapter has furthered our understanding of the possible linkage between shamanic rituals and the famous cave paintings of southern France. But even without their studies of resonance, we might have reached similar conclusions simply by examining the subject matter of many of the paintings. Within the caves at Les Trois Freres in the Pyrenees there is an engraving of a man with a bison head playing a musical bow. A hunting scene painted at Alpere depicts nearly one hundred animals— antelopes, wolves, birds, stags—and an almost comparable number of humans, many with bows drawn and some engaged in movements that can only be described as dancelike. Here music is never depicted as an idle pursuit to amuse or to while away the time, but rather always appears to have a larger purpose, a greater efficacy, a deeper meaning.

A study of the musical instruments associated with hunting music often reveals this rich universe of meanings and associations. For example, the bow, frequently shown in early paintings of music making, is both a hunting implement as well as a musical instrument. The Scythians, according to Plutarch, played music on their hunter bows, but the history of the musical hunting bow goes back long before recorded history, with evidence of its archaic use found in various areas around the globe. Scholars have debated the origins of this tradition: Which came first, they ponder, the musical instrument or the weapon? Or did both develop simultaneously? But the widespread use of this double tool links traditions as disparate as those of southern India, classical Greece, Africa, Brazil, and the Native American southwest. Sometimes one end of the bow is placed in the hunter's mouth, which serves as a resonator. In other instances, a half-gourd piece or other object is permanently attached to the bow to fill this purpose, amplifying the sound, increasing the bow's power as a sounding device, but lessening its value as a hunting tool— thus showing that even pre-historic societies faced the trade-off between functionality and musical considerations.

When Sir Laurens van der Post discovered a hidden Bushman community in the heart of the Kalahari Desert during his 1955 expedition, he was struck by the prominence of the bow in so many aspects of the tribe's day-to-day life. The leading hunter of the community, Nxou, was also its chief musician, and the bow served as his unfailing instrument in both fields of endeavor. Nxou's name translated literally to "bowl of life," and van der Post commented on the appropriateness of the name—for "that is what he was as hunter to the bodies and as musician to the spirit of his people."

Because much of their music related to hunting, the intersection of these two disciplines came naturally to the Bushman community: women would sing paeans to returning hunters; elaborate and intense song and dance celebrations would follow especially successful hunting expeditions; and game songs would revolve around imitations of different animals and their response to the hunter.

In such societies, the uses of the song and the bow are more than practical or aesthetic matters, but also are rich in symbolic meanings that permeate even apparently unrelated areas. As such, few artifacts from these cultures are richer in implication or more intriguing to the outside observer. Van der Post was surprised to learn that a Bushman who wished to court a young woman would carve a miniature bow and arrow from a sliver of animal bone. He would then dip the arrowhead into a special love potion and shoot it into the rump of the desired woman. If the arrow struck its target, and the woman did not immediately pull it out and destroy it, this was a sign that his suit had succeeded. The similarity of this act to the Western myth of Cupid is striking, and it suggests that perhaps carryovers from prehistoric hunting cultures also color our own traditions of courtship and romance. Indeed, the idea that the bow might be used to stalk a lover as well as an animal has occurred to more than a few suitors in traditional societies. Michael Harner found a similar custom among the Jivaro of South America where, he writes, "young men frequently play love songs softly on bows at sunset and hope, thereby, magically to cause their sweethearts to think of them, no matter how distant they may be." The efficacy of the bow is also vouched for among the Ndembu where, according to Victor Turner, young girls are given a *mankunkundimba,* or a musical bow, as part of their ritual transition into adulthood. They play this bow during a period of seclusion—at dawn, or when hungry or frightened—but are forbidden to show it to men, otherwise they will be barren. The linkage between the bow and procreation is so strong in the mind of the Ndembu that they construct miniature bows, called *kasenzi,* around which are entwined white beads. These are then placed in the apex of the seclusion hut, where they represent fertility and the children to come. On the day after a wedding the beads are given to the bride's mother, who keeps them until the first pregnancy, when they are placed first around the wife's neck and then around her stomach, "to help her grow big."

As these examples show, the musical bow takes on a magical potency for hunting cultures, and it represents powers that go far beyond the production of sounds or the securing of food. As noted above, Plutarch tells how the ancient Scythians used the twanging of their bows to awaken their courage from the languor of idle leisure, often listening to the sound during an intense bout of drinking to counter the dissipation caused by alcohol. This same paradoxical mixture of relaxation and intensity figures in the Afro-Brazilian tradition of capoeira, where a playful dance is combined with violent fighting movements—all accompanied by a musical bow: the berimbau, made from a branch of a biriba tree. The dance is now treated as an important cultural tradition but was once banned in Brazil, its very intensity and potency no doubt contributing to the efforts made to marginalize it.

Other instruments also play a significant role in hunting music. The hunter musicians of western Africa, for example, sometimes play harp-type instruments. But even here linkages to weapons used in stalking prey can be seen. As Eric Charry writes: "The fundamental unity of West African harp culture may have its ancient roots in the bolon, which has the uncanny look of a calabash drum slipped on to a warrior's or hunter's bow. Hunter's harps (donso ngoni, kori, kon, simbi) look as if someone had straightened out the bow of the bolon and added a few more strings." Plucking the strings with their fingers, musicians will perform before hunts or at the funerals of hunters. Those familiar with jazz percussion may note similarities between the rhythms of this music and the patterns played by a jazz drummer on the ride cymbal. Perhaps hunting music formed a critical part of the heritage of the African slave immigrants whose traditions later influenced the jazz idiom and other forms of American performance arts. Such speculations, although beyond the scope of this study, are worthy of further research.

Most of the music we will explore in later chapters will be vocal in nature, but here at the start of our study we cannot afford to neglect the varied sound-making implements used by hunting communities. Their very appearance signals to us their importance. Musical instruments that have survived from prehistoric days often reveal a remarkable craftsmanship. Much more care and labor had been put into their creation than was done for many far more functional items, causing us to wonder why the necessities of life took a back seat to these purely "aesthetic" considerations. But this line of thought shows a misunderstanding of the role of music in these early societies—a role that had little or nothing to do with mere appearances. Among other purposes, musical instruments, fashioned from animal bones or horns, may have been thought to strengthen this sympathetic pull on the living beast. In discussing their discovery and analysis of what may be the oldest surviving musical instrument—a fifty-thousand-year-old flute constructed from the left thigh bone of a young cave bear—Drago Kunej and Ivan Turk speculate that such artifacts may be linked to the very birth of instrumental music. They write: "The following is possible. Paleolithic hunters were predators just like carnivores with whom they came in contact daily. They therefore identified with them. They saw that carnivores left traces on bones that long remained visible. Holes punctured by teeth made a great impression and they started to copy them by adding their own chipped holes, which meant simply, I, too, was here. Later, by adding holes and experimenting on other materials, a flute was created."

"In the spiritual horizon of hunters and herdsmen," as Mircea Eliade reminds us, "bone represents the very source of life, both human and animal." Thus, for the primitive hunter, its choice as the material for his musical instruments is not merely functional, but quasi-magical in purpose. Just as the voodoo practitioner wants a piece of clothing or item associated with an individual before making a doll or fetish, primitive man may have felt that an instrument made from an animal would have greater potency in assuring success in the hunt. Some have seen the later legend of the "singing bone"—in which a murdered man's bone, fashioned into pipe, sings out an accusation revealing the identity of the murderer—as echoing this primitive belief. In other traditional narratives, the bone is transformed into a more conventional instrument, yet its power to attract animals, both wild and tame, is retained in the story. The tale of the Pied Piper, immortalized by Browning, is the best known of these accounts, but folklore is full of other stories of the magical power of musical instruments to attract animals.

One more musical instrument must be addressed before we close this chapter. In Western culture, the horn stands out as the most well-known source of music associated with the chase—almost as prominent in the popular imagination as gun or bow, net or arrow. Hunting horns are mentioned as early as Oppian's *De Venatione,* circa 180 AD. An anonymous French poem from the twelfth century, "La chace dou cerf," describes several special calls on the horns. Around this same time, hunting music began to fuse in surprising ways with other styles of performance.

Although fanfares are described in literary documents dating back to antiquity, the first clear musical examples come to us by means of French hunting treatises from the fourteenth century. The jaunty rhythms of Italian hunting songs from the Trecento, known as *caccie,* may have found their way into liturgical music, as seen for instance in the lilting mass settings from the Old Hall manuscript, a major source of early English polyphonic compositions. Hunting songs were incorporated into plays early in the seventeenth century—indeed the only place where they were heard more often than on stage was perhaps at the tavern. In essence, the music of the hunt found itself magnetically drawn to that most unexpected place of all: indoors. Here it discovers a new home, surrounded by walls and far from the activities that gave it birth. Yet in an odd way the move indoors is also a return to the original setting of hunting music: enclosed in caves, among large groups safe from the dangers of the wild.

During the late sixteenth century, hunting horns became prevalent in France. Around this time, instruments made from animal horn were being replaced by metal ones—although the former would continue to be used in France occasionally until the eighteenth century, and even later in other parts of the world. Great lords would now take pride in possessing elaborate hunting horns made from gold and silver and embellished with precious stones. But the sound of the horns was far from neglected. Louis XIV took great care in the composition and selection of hunting fanfares, relying on the assistance of his master of the hunt, Monsieur de Dampierre. But around 1650 the hunting horns also began finding their way into opera houses, where they appeared in works by Pietro Cavalli and Jean-Baptiste Lully. They were later used by Handel for his *Water Music* and by Bach for his *Mass in B Minor.* The instrument then went through a period of refinement and modification, spurred by changes such as the addition of crooks (coiled tubing added to the main pipe of the horn to lower the pitch) and the use of valves—innovations that gave the performer greater flexibility in addressing chromatic tones. *La Juive,* an opera by Fromental Halevy, featured the new valved horns, and Wagner also embraced the innovation in his early operas (although he used valveless horns as well). By the time Fritz Kruspe introduced his modern French horn around 1900, the transition from hunting implement to concert hall instrument was all but complete.

A similar process took place in Russia, where hunting expeditions often involved large numbers of peasants who blew primitive hunting horns made from mostly straight, conical tubes of brass, bent slightly at their smaller ends. Johann Maresch, a native of Bohemia who came to St. Petersburg in 1744, established his reputation by making improvements to the horn and forming a peasant ensemble for performances. The latter proved quite challenging, and Maresch was forced to construct twenty-five different horns, each tuned to a different note, and invent a crude system of notation to show untrained performers when to blow and when to keep silent. But the results were stunning: Maresch's 1757 concert at a grand hunt in honor of the empress set off a craze for hunting-horn ensembles in Russia. Before the close of the century, St. Petersburg could boast nine separate hunting music ensembles, and their skill was such that it was not uncommon to hear one perform a four-part fugue flawlessly. Once again, the practical music of the hunt had been transformed into concert hall fare.

In modern times, hunting has largely ceased to be a pursuit of the working class and has emerged as a leisure activity for a small subgroup of society. As a result, hunting figures little in the vernacular music of the industrial and postindustrial working class. There are a few examples in American popular music—from "Fox Chase" by DeFord Bailey, the first African American musician to perform at the Grand Ole Opry, who imitated the sounds of the hunt on his harmonica, to Tom Lehrer's tongue-in-cheek "The Hunting Song"—but this subject has never exercised the fascination that made trains and desperados into perennial topics for folk singers. In Britain, one might expect more, since fox hunting is often romanticized as exemplifying the traditions of rural life, yet it rarely figures in the folk music of the countryside. Reg Hall, who spent four decades studying the traditional music of Ireland and the United Kingdom, has remarked on the "relatively few references to fox-hunting in the traditional song repertory." Alexander Mackay-Smith, the historian of fox hunting, has had more success in collecting examples of this music, but even he notes that before the beginning of the sixteenth century, the pursuit was restricted to persons of high rank, while the oldest song in his collection was first published in 1685. Hunting with hounds was perhaps too far from the concerns of ordinary working folk, except perhaps in sheep farming communities where it served to protect and preserve the flock. In these parts, songs such as "The Kielder Hunt" and "The Irthing Water Hounds" would often be sung in the pubs to celebrate the successful hunt and, even more important, the much-prized local dogs.

Here we encounter a transition that we will see again in our study of work songs. Instead of serving as part of an occupation, music takes on a subsidiary role, merely commemorating or commenting on the activity it once enriched directly. This remains true even when substantial effort has been put into the preservation of traditional hunting songs. For example, commenting on the deer song tradition of the Yaqui, Larry Evers and Felipe S. Molina boast that their "deer songs and the traditions which surround them are very much alive and that more than sixty years of recording and printing versions of them has complemented and rein-forced more traditional oral modes of continuance." Yet they must add that "Yaqui traditions tell of the deer dance and deer singing as a part of a ritual performance before the hunting of deer. That connection seems only a memory now. Some Yaquis, especially in the Sonoran commu-nities, continue to hunt deer regularly. And deer songs and the deer dance are still performed regularly on a variety of occasions in every Yaqui community we know. There seems now, however, to be no direct connec-tion made between the two activities."

In such instances the songs of the hunters become less important, while songs about hunters or those borrowed from them continue in some form. The former may survive in books or recordings, or perhaps, although less frequently, even in performance. But they are transformed by the very steps—laudable, no doubt—that allowed them to survive long after the conditions that gave them their purpose have disappeared. We will see many more instances of this tendency, in which occupational songs take on new meanings and are forced into unfamiliar settings, as we pursue our inquiry into the music associated with other economic ac-tivities and livelihoods.

CHAPTER TWO

The Cultivator

Ain't no more cane on this Brazos.

They done ground it all down to molasses.

—African American song, Brazos

River Valley, Texas

As far back as we can trace, the pursuit of farming is linked with music. Singing accompanied the tasks of cultivation; music contained powerful magic to secure the fertility of the crops; song and dance adorned the festivals and rites of agricultural communities. Music was sustenance, guiding communities, solidifying the social bonds, bringing order and organization into the art of cultivation, intervening with the gods, and placating the creatures of the earth. As we shall see, the sound itself may even have helped the crops grow. But even if the impact on celestial powers and terrestrial flowers were purely imaginary, we can hardly doubt that song aided the farmers in rich and varied ways, providing a rhythmic support for work, and creating a crystalline network of meanings and practices that informed virtually all aspects of day-to-day life. The farther back we peer, the more limited our sources, the sketchier our conception of day-to-day life. But music is always there.

Even bare scratchings on ancient walls in the scattered remains of archeological sites testify to the importance of music. The Egyptian hieroglyph that represents grain also signifies a drum or a period of time, pointing to the ancient linkage between musical rhythms and the cycles of agricultural life. The Babylonian epic *Gilgamesh* refers to the farmer's work song. Various passages in the Hebrew scriptures, especially *Isaiah* and *Jeremiah,* describe singing in the vineyards. Japanese work songs, known as *rosaku minyo* (literally, "songs of laborious work") are among that culture's oldest folk music. Evidence suggests that music and agricultural labor were intimately linked in prehistoric China as well. The eight songs of the Pa Ch'üeh, which may date back to the third millennium BC, deal with the importance of good weather and abundant crops, and were accompanied by a dance in which three men stamped their feet and waved an ox tail, hinting at a symbolic or totemic link to plowing.

In the Western classical tradition, we discover a similar connection of song and cultivation. Indeed, it is worth recalling the explicit linkage of the Greek word *melos,* meaning limb, to *melody*—the birth of music equated to the working of arms and legs. This connection may well be personified in the figure of Orpheus, who is heralded as the greatest musician of antiquity, as well as, in some accounts, the first to teach the arts of agriculture to the Greeks. We find other tantalizing hints of the work song traditions, mostly lost, of the ancient Greek farmers. A number of sources refer to the *Lityerses,* a well-known reaping and threshing song. In the *Iliad,* grape gatherers working to music are depicted on the famous shield of Achilles. While they toil, a youth plays the lyre and sings, and the laborers move in time to the music.

We can imagine the benefits that song brought to these laborers engaged in sowing, reaping, and various other tasks associated with the agricultural life. The work movements themselves were almost dancelike, with a rhythmic symmetry that invited musical accompaniment. "The simplest form of activity is two-phasic, one phase is the exertion and the second phase is the recuperation," writes Irmgard Bartenieff, a pioneering researcher (and collaborator in the 1960s with Alan Lomax on his cantometric and choreometric projects) who undertook detailed studies of body movement in numerous fields, including physical therapy, dance, sports, and work. "As activities become more complex, canoeing for example, or threshing or hoeing, simple two-phasic forms are still central, but there are more of them—repetitions of the same two-phasic forms or several different two-phasic forms in series." Here is the simplest rhythmic pattern of work. Given the back-and-forth motions required by many of the constituent activities involved in cultivation, we should not be surprised to see a preponderance of songs in duple meters accompanying these labors.

Yet the ability of the worker to impose more complicated rhythmic patterns on a "two-phasic" foundation, to use Bartenieff's term, or sometimes even to leave the duple orientation entirely behind, is also remarkable. The ingenuity and variety of this music deserves our appreciation. Rose Brandel notes that the pounding songs of the Bongili women of equatorial Africa are in a strict 4/4 meter. She believes that this is virtually required by the activity, explaining that the "evenly spaced sounds of the pestle seem to shape and sustain the vocal rhythm." Patrick Kersale, however, recorded in the mid-1990s a millstone grinding song in Burkina Faso (formerly Upper Volta) that is in a pronounced waltz meter. Hahn Man-young transcribed a pounding song from Korean rice farming communities that is notated in 12/8 with a marked triple feel to the rhythm, which is fairly typical for this type of Korean music. The corn grinding songs notated by Natalie Curtis among the Zuni at the dawn of the twentieth century—which she transcribed from the performances of women "whose white hair and quavering voices told of well-nigh fourscore years"—are all in a strict duple meter. A similar rhythm can be heard in a *hie*-pounding song from a Japanese collection. But a cassava root grating song performed by women among the Garifuna of Belize is in 6/8, as is an acorn grinding song transcribed from a recording of the Tachi Yokuts of California. Among the Navajo music recorded on 78 rpm disks by Laura Bolton before World War II, one finds a corn grinding song that stays comfortably in 5/4 time for most of its duration. And Gerhard Kubik has transcribed a maize grinding song, performed by a Tikar woman from central Cameroon, which follows a pattern of thirty-six pulse units. These examples are drawn solely from pounding and grinding songs, which one might suppose, would involve the simplest types of rhythms. As more complicated tasks are accompanied by song, the opportunity for rhythmic variety only increases.

Today the music of the working class—passively consumed on the job, in the car, or at leisure—is mostly in 4/4 time, which has all but replaced the metrical variety of the earlier work songs, a diversity that must often have been linked to the variegated rhythmic requirements of work itself. Can it be pure coincidence that, nowadays, when an increasing percentage of people work with their brains and fingers rather than their limbs, back and shoulders, that 4/4—the music of counting, even more than of movement—reigns supreme, while duple meters are less common? Yet even for the highly repetitive tasks of the farm life, the rhythmic variety and subtlety of the accompanying songs demand the respect of careful listeners.

In our historical development as a species we may very well have emulated the maturing process that is still followed by each newborn infant: until the age of four or five, a child finds it difficult to sing without moving and is incapable of separating the rhythms of a piece of music from the accompanying physical actions. In essence, the *melos* of the Greeks surfaces again in each youngster's development: the music resides first in the limbs as much as in the mind, and only gradually does it become our modern *melody*, savored now as an aesthetic, not kinaesthetic, experience. Only the sober adult can approach music as a phenomenon completely disassociated from body movement. Is it possible that, on a social level, the same process is played out? Over time, as a society becomes increasingly differentiated in its occupations and ambitions, do its songs grow more distant from the needs—muscular, respiratory, rhythmic—of the tasks they accompany? Certainly, much is lost in this maturing process: just as adults add more spice to their meals, attempting to recapture the intensity of flavor that all foods possess in their simplest form for children, so do advanced industrial societies—or what I like to call the "indoor societies"—seem to demand in their music increasingly exotic harmonies and compositional structures, the auditory equivalents of paprika and cumin, hoping thereby to compensate for the loss of *melos* in their collective arms and legs. The traditional work song stands out as a telling reminder of this almost forgotten facet of our musical heritage, this neglected legacy of song as an extension of our bodies doing things in the world around us.

We still do not understand the causes of the initial shift from hunting to agriculture in many parts of the world. Three types of causes are often mentioned: environmental changes in the climate or other conditions of life; the pressure of rising population density; and changes in forms of social organization. All of the offered theories raise as many questions as they answer. Yet the sheer breadth and impact of the transition cannot be doubted. Around ten thousand years ago, communities in very different parts of the world—South America, the eastern regions of North America, Southwest Asia, and China—all began to embrace cultivation in various degrees, gradually leaving behind their economic dependence on hunting and gathering.

The music of this shift dimly echoes through various sources. The oldest surviving secular songs from ancient Egypt are agricultural work songs. Indeed, some work song texts from the Egyptian New Kingdom have survived in identical form at sites considerable distances apart, implying that these were well known to agricultural laborers throughout the region. The text of a sowing song has been encountered in many Old Kingdom tombs; it follows a question and answer form, indicating that two individuals or groups—or perhaps a leader and a team—were likely involved in the singing, much as in the call-and-response work songs of more recent times. Instrumental music also figured prominently in this tradition. A flute might be played at harvest time, often in tandem with singing.

Although manual labor may have formed the backbone of Egyptian civilization, the workers themselves were little prized. Egyptian scribes never ceased extolling the superiority of their own profession as compared with that of the despised laborers in the fields. Nonetheless, some hints of the workers' day-to-day life can be heard in the surviving texts. The following lament, for example, suggests that almost from their first recorded historical use, work songs could be used not only to accompany and alleviate labor, but also to complain against its harsh conditions:

> Must we spend all day carrying barley and white emmer?
> The granaries are full, heaps are pouring over the opening.
> The barges are heavily laden, the grain is spilling out.
> But one hurries us to go. Is our heart of copper?

Here, at the dawn of our story, we find the first work songs and the first protest songs, almost side by side.

Yet not all of the songs of cultivation are designed to accompany the physical movements of work. Of course, plowing, harvesting, threshing, grinding, and other strenuous activities have rich musical traditions, but the agricultural life also possesses a spiritual component related to the fertility of the land, reflected in ritualistic practices that also typically require music. Among Native American tribes that practiced cultivation as a major source of food, the communities often possessed traditional songs and dances that they believed contributed in some metaphysical manner to the growth of the crops. The green corn dance was widespread among many tribes—including the Cherokee, Iroquois, Seminole, and Creek, among others—although the timing and specifics of their respective ceremonies show marked variations. A similar ritual was noted as early as the mid-sixteenth century by the artist Jacques Le Moyne, but the wide geographical spread of the green corn dance suggests a much earlier date of origin. Writing in 1851, Lewis Henry Morgan described part of this ceremony, as witnessed among the Iroquois: "Each song lasted about two minutes, during which the band danced around the room, in column, with great animation. When the song ceased, the dancers walked around the council-house, about the same length of time, to the beat of the rattles. The thanksgiving speeches were made during these intervals between the songs." A dim recollection of this tradition is retained in the American celebration of Thanksgiving—a holiday that most people associate with pilgrims and European settlers, but that more properly relates to the Native Americans—and even in its modern form betrays linkages with this indigenous ceremony.

In the twentieth century, the songs and dances associated with the cultivation and preparation of corn could still be found in tribal settings, although often only the oldest members of the community retained a deep knowledge of their meaning. In 1922, Frances Densmore interviewed an old Yuman tribal member named Katcora, who claimed that "his power was such that his singing of these [corn dance] songs caused the corn to grow faster." With his assistance, Densmore assembled a group who could perform the songs for her ponderous recording device. Both the antiquity of the music and its dying links to contemporary practices were all too evident. "The words of these songs," Densmore later wrote, "are in what is known as the 'old language.' The singers repeat the songs by rote and have a general knowledge of their meaning, but the language is obsolete." Only a few years before Densmore wrote these words, Sir James Frazer had laboriously documented, in over a dozen densely footnoted volumes of *The Golden Bough*, a similarly half-forgotten tradition of fertility songs and dances, related both to the land and its residents, as part of the cultural heritage of western Europe.

In my discussion of the music of hunting societies presented in chapter 1, I described how the rhythms of the shamans played an important role in the securing of food and in furthering the general cohesiveness of the tribe or community. In agricultural societies, a similar—if subtly different—importance is assigned to fertility songs and rites. Both types of music combine spirituality with practical efficacy by intertwining a decisive intercession with higher powers with a purely human thirst for music as a force for social bonding. Above all, both remind us how song mixed with ritual can be a potent force both in the everyday sphere, as well as in offering access to the divine currents that are often missing from our quotidian existence.

Yet the differences between these two spheres of musical activity are also noteworthy. The shamanic music of hunting societies is often intensely personal, accompanying a visionary quest made by a single chosen individual. Others may participate in the music and the ritual, but rarely in the transcendent manner of the shaman, who alone has the power to intercede with animal spirits and ensure the abundance of game for the hunters. In agricultural societies, this unstable emphasis on the visions of a chosen individual are replaced with a more symbolic and impersonal approach. The shaman is replaced by the high priest. The hypnotic rhythmic intensity of the music is replaced by a sing-song lyricism—indeed, "real" melodies that can be easily remembered (and sometimes even notated by musicologists) take on a far greater prominence than ever before. At the same time, a personal experience of the divine force is now seen as unnecessary, or perhaps even as a dangerous pursuit to be discouraged or forbidden. True, ecstatic elements sometimes persist for greater or lesser periods in the cults and rites of agricultural societies, but the inevitable tendency is to sublimate these into more formalized practices. Institutions arise that preserve the gods and traditions of the community, often through rote performances where the original meaning of the fertility rites (and other practices) are forgotten or only vaguely recalled. This historical shift from shaman to priest, from individual vision to group ritual, may have happened gradually in some societies, while in others it was perhaps precipitated by some sudden, disruptive event. In any event, the spiritual guideposts of agricultural societies invariably mutated from those that propelled the early hunting cultures. And, with this change, the songs of these societies are equally transformed. Conditions demand new music to match the new needs, both secular and religious, of the people and their institutions.

Women singers often played the predominant role in these songs of fertility and cultivation. Although we tend to view agricultural labor as a masculine activity, in many cultures women have played a decisive role in performing and preserving the songs associated with toil in the fields. The anthropologist Judith Brown has suggested that a gender-based division of labor derives not from any difference in strength or stamina between the sexes, but rather from a woman's preference to pursue tasks close to home, and hence compatible with child rearing. The role of women as gatherers of vegetable products must have imperceptibly developed over time into active cultivation. In any event, field work songs performed by women are known in most parts of the world. "In Europe well into this century," writes Elizabeth Wayland Barber, "the women often sang or chanted ritual songs to set the rhythm of the endless repetitive motions of handwork in the fields." Hem Barua, in his *Folk Songs of India,* provides a number of examples of such songs, including the following two examples sung by the Uraons during the rains of June and July when women are engaged in the transplantation of paddy in the fields:

> The lightning dazzles in Jashpur,
> The rain is streaming, mother,
> The fields are filling . . .

> Raining, raining water,
> Raining faster,
> Where is a sheltering rock my sister?
> Raining, raining water,
> Raining faster.

In the Balkans also, such pieces are usually sung by women in unison or in a stylized form of two-part singing that is not used by men. "The upper voice sings the melody," explains Patricia K. Shehan, "while the accompanying voice sounds a syllabic drone on the tonic or the subtonic." This approach to singing field work songs is especially common in Bulgaria, Macedonia, and Serbia. Shehan provides a translation of an example from Skopje, Macedonia, which, with its "shrill ringing timbre," is performed both for the amusement of the singers, as well as "for the benefit of workers in neighboring fields":

> Why didn't you come last night for supper, young man?
> We had white bread and roasted lamb, dear young man.
> We had roasted lamb and red wine, young man.

In traditional Japanese rice cultivation, men tilled the soil but women took responsibility for transplanting the seedlings. Known as *sa-otome,* these female laborers would don new clothes, tie red cords around their waists, and wear white towels on their heads. Many would play flutes and beat gongs or drums. This activity had the look and feel of a religious or magical ritual—as indeed it essentially was, since this initiating step in the process of cultivation was nothing less than the quasi-divine act of creating new life where previously there was only barren soil. Sometimes the magic was made explicit, as among the Kammu people of Laos, where women also play a critical role in sowing: in preparing the rice seed, in establishing the order in which the various kinds of rice will be sown, and in leading the work. Every day during sowing season, an incantation is uttered at the start of work in the morning and when resuming after the midday break:

> Oh, sowing this field,
> Let sowing be fast,
> Let sowing be easy,
> Moving up the mountain,
> Crossing the slope,
> Finishing early,
> Eating by daylight.

In this instance, the magical intention of the chant is obvious. But in other instances—for example, in the butter churning and the milking songs discussed in the next chapter—it can be difficult to determine whether a song is used primarily to provide a rhythmic underpinning to the labor or to enlist mystical powers in the successful fulfillment of the task at hand.

The disappearance of this traditional music of sowing and reaping represents a great loss. There is a primal beauty to the work songs of agrarian societies. In a striking passage in his book *What Is Art?*, Leo Tolstoy favorably compared the singing of peasant women "with shouts and banging on scythes," to Beethoven's late sonatas. The peasant women's song conveyed a "definite, strong feeling" while the Beethoven work contained "no definite feeling." Almost at the same moment that Tolstoy was writing these words—no doubt shocking many readers, both then and today—but half a world away in Jamaica, English expatriate Walter Jekyll, was observing a similar grandeur in the neglected "digging-sings" of the island's agriculture workers. While others dismissed these Jamaican works as vulgar and worthless, Jekyll spent long hours with the men and boys who worked for him, listening to their songs and stories and writing them down for posterity. "Nothing more joyous," he wrote, "can be imagined than a good 'digging sing' from twenty throats, with the pickers —so they call their pick-axes—falling in regular beat." Jekyll preserved dozens of these songs—once so prevalent, now all but vanished.

As this last example demonstrates, along with so many other comparable ones, the African diaspora served as the greatest source and repository of songs of agricultural labor. Virtually every aspect of cultivation— cutting sugarcane, shucking corn, picking cotton, turning water through the rice fields, threshing—had its associated songs. The earliest collectors of these songs found an almost inexhaustible supply; and if they ever feared that they were running out of new material to catalog, a short trip to a nearby community or county was bound to produce a wealth of additional examples. "Upon a rough calculation, made with no statistics to refer to, I have concluded that there are, at least, thirty thousand slave plantations in the United States," noted a journalist writing in *Putnam's Monthly Magazine* in 1855. "Is it unreasonable to suppose that on each of these plantations, one song may be found of undisputed genuineness and excellence? It will be a proud day for America when these thirty thousand songs are collected into several volumes, handsomely bound in Turkey morocco and superbly embellished." Yet this same author was quick to add, in words that were all too true: "But long ere that time the hand that writes these lines will have mouldered and become dust." Some seventy years later, when the documentation of African American work songs was finally beginning to gain momentum, Dorothy Scarborough consulted Dr. Boyd, an elderly resident of Nashville knowledgeable about work songs, who, like the *Putnam's* journalist, stressed the abundance and mutability of these ephemeral melodies. Boyd explained that "the music and the words changed in every state." In Virginia, the "singing was like that of a choir." In South Carolina, "the leader would start off with a song, and the other laborers would follow as they came up to him." In Mississippi, the workers would sometimes sing alone, scattered throughout the cotton fields, other times joining together. In Louisiana, the cane cutters and haulers each practiced their own distinctive style of singing. In Texas, "the singing was made up of almost all types." As odd as these distinctions may seem, they perhaps had a functional basis in the different rhythms required by various crops and activities. On one extreme, the sugarcane demanded an aggressive, slashing attack to clear the fields, in sharp contrast to tobacco, which needed to be handled with greater delicacy. Cotton was somewhere in the middle, but though collecting it demanded considerable handwork, it was still picked in rows and required an organized, paced flow of work. As the nature of labor varied, the music inevitably must have adapted, to a greater or lesser extent, to its specific movements.

Whatever truth there might be to these generalizations, the growing mobility of the African American workforce in the final decades of the nineteenth century ensured that a tremendous cross-fertilization of songs and singing styles would take place. Black farm laborers would follow the ripening crops, migrating from place to place to find communities where pickers were in demand. Delta bluesman Muddy Waters recalled moving from the cotton fields to the berry harvest and the sugar beet harvest, then to the pea and bean harvest. His song "Rolling Stone" was written to describe these travels, which were often made by hopping onto passing trains (and the song's title even took a second life, I am told, when picked up by some British fans of Waters as the name of their successful blues-based ensemble). And where workers traveled, music came as well, thereby providing a constant exchange of work songs throughout the South and even beyond, as the shipping industries of Mobile Bay, New Orleans, and other locales hired African American sailors, who brought these songs on board and to other ports.

Corn shucking may well have provided the pre-eminent setting in which African American music and culture invigorated the demands of agricultural labor. In an environment in which work was typically brutal and dehumanizing, corn shucking offered a marked contrast, with its quasi-festive atmosphere. "With the exception of the Christmas holiday —and not always that—former slaves recalled having looked forward to corn shucking most of all," writes historian Eugene Genovese. Some remembered this work, indeed, "as their only good time." In an interview with Bernice Lewis of the Virginia Writers' Project, which compiled interviews with exslaves in the late 1930s, Uncle John Spencer provided the following details of these all-night affairs:

> They always selected a bright moonlight [night] for the shucking. A week or so more from the time, the news began to spread around when it was going to be; and as soon as it was dark, the neighbors began to drop in. The one with the most powerful voice was selected to stand on top of the corn pile and lead the singing. They would all get in a working mood to the tune of the shucking song:

> Come to shuck that corn to-night
> Come to shuck with all your might,
> Come for to shuck all in sight,
> Come to shuck that corn to-night . . .

The shucking would last until late in the night, but after all the corn was shucked, they had a feast of roasted pigs, mutton, beef, pies and cakes.

Other narratives describe how as many as several hundred people would be in attendance, and the corn pile might be as large as a house, or even a city block—one account mentions a massive accumulation of corn that spread out for one hundred and eighty yards. "Even after allowing for the fact that these were reminiscences and therefore potentially subject to exaggeration, the event clearly was extraordinarily outsized in relation to everyday life," writes Roger Abrahams, who has documented numerous accounts of corn shuckings on plantations. Given the ample food, alcohol, and music that usually attended the gathering, the nineteenth-century corn shucking may well have been the closest the black underclass would get to recapturing the gaiety of the harvest festivals of Africa.

In contrast, documents from the era rarely mention the use of songs while picking cotton—despite the stereotyped image that often primarily associates work songs with this particular task. A rare example was collected by Cora Folsom, of Hampton Institute in Virginia, from a Florida student who had in turn learned it from the older residents of a plantation where he had worked. The refrain goes:

> Dis cotton want a-pickin,'
> So bad!
> Dis cotton want a-pickin,'
> So bad!
> Dis cotton want a-pickin,'
> So bad!
> Gwine clean all ober dis farm.

At one point in the song, however, part of the Emancipation Proclamation is quoted, which raises the question of how much of this music actually dates back to antebellum days. Lydia Parrish, in her study *Slave Songs of the Georgia Sea Islands,* provides another example of a cotton picking song, "Five Fingers in the Boll":

Way down in the bottom—whah the cotton boll's a rotten
Won' get my hundud all day.
Way down in the bottom—whah the cotton boll's a rotten
Won' get my hundud all day.
Befo'e I'll be beated—befo'e I'll be cheated
I'll leave five finguhs in the boll.

The reference in the song to "fingers" indicates the compartments in the boll that contain the white fiber, and the "hundud" relates to the view that ninety pounds was the minimum amount a hand should pick in a day. But only one firsthand account of Southern slaves singing while picking cotton can be found in a verified antebellum source. The author of an article from 1859, published in *Great Republic Monthly,* describes the following scene:

> The negroes were at work in the fields, picking cotton and stowing it in long baskets. They worked in gangs, or companies, men, women and children, selected and classified according to age and physical ability—each slave being required to pick as many pounds of cotton in a day as his master, or overseer, had prescribed. . . . While at work in the cotton fields, the slaves often sing some wild, simple melody, by way of mutual cheer, which usually ends in a chorus, in which all join with a right hearty good will, in a key so loud as to be heard from one plantation to another, and the welkin is made to ring for miles with musical echoes.

The account concludes with the admission that the author "could not comprehend the words of the songs or chorus."

One of the truisms of American music is that songs move between social and racial strata with greater ease than do people, power, or money. Indeed, if one measures the success of a currency by how far it circulates and how eagerly it is accepted on its journey, song would rival the greenback as the true American exchange medium. Hence, by the dawn of the twentieth century, the agricultural work song in the United States may have been largely a reflection of the black cultural experience. Yet the white European tradition of folk singing sometimes returned the favor, enriching the musical practices of the South while sometimes making its presence felt in surprising ways. Katherine Pettit, who founded the Hindman Settlement School in 1902 in Kentucky, was struck one day by the singing of a student, Josiah Combs, who came from the southern Appalachians. While working in the fields or hauling coal and wood, Combs sang long ballads he had learned at home about nobles and fine ladies and life in old London town—experiences that went far beyond those of a child from the Bluegrass State. Pettit contacted George Kittredge, a professor at Harvard, and the two of them transcribed and edited the youth's ballads for publication. Later, Combs himself went on to become a noteworthy scholar in the field of folk music.

Combs's extensive knowledge of Old World songs was not, however, an isolated case, as subsequent research proved. Olive Dame Campbell, on her travels with her husband John Campbell during his work on a project to upgrade the Appalachian school system, had collected over two hundred ballads, many of them revealing foreign antecedents. In 1915 she shared some of her research with Cecil Sharp, the Cambridge-educated scholar who was then visiting America as dance advisor for a production of *A Midsummer Night's Dream*. Sharp immediately recognized the great importance of Campbell's work, noting the English, Irish, and Scottish roots of the music, and the linkages with the pioneering work of Francis James Child, Kittredge's predecessor at Harvard, whose cataloguing of 305 classic English and Scottish popular ballads had been a major achievement in furthering and legitimizing this field of study. Sharp's enthusiasm was heightened by his realization that much of the music collected by Campbell had disappeared from the popular culture of Britain, even as it miraculously seemed to continue to flourish in the American South.

Determined to follow up on this lead, Sharp began soliciting funds to support research into the Appalachian ballads. A request to the Carnegie Foundation was turned down, but an individual patron—Mrs. J. J. Storrow of Boston—provided $1,000 to initiate the project. In July 1916, Sharp arrived at the Asheville, North Carolina, home of the Campbells to begin his fieldwork, accompanied by his assistant Maud Karpeles. He soon came to the realization that the New World offered a far more fruitful source of English folk songs than even he had suspected. Again and again, he heard the melodies of songs that in England he had been able to study only as written texts. Sharp surmised that one would have to go back fifty years to find such a rich tradition of ballad singing in Great Britain. A single informant, a woman in Hot Springs, North Carolina, provided him with no fewer than 30 songs, and by mid-September he had collected a total of more than 250. A little over a year later, the number surpassed 1,000. By the close of 1917, Sharp published the first results of his research, combined with the earlier work of Campbell. In December 1918, he returned to Britain, having revolutionized research in the English folk song tradition thousands of miles from its land of origin.

Later researchers in the South continued to find these ballads in the most surprising locales. John Lomax boasted that to his knowledge the single best source for Child's English and Scottish ballads was Emma Dusenberry, a blind woman living in a log cabin on two acres of land in the southern Ozarks. To get to her home, Lomax needed to bring his car over a wagon trail through the woods. "Ours was perhaps the first automobile the startled squirrels had ever seen," he later wrote. Dusenberry was seventy-nine years old at the time, and had been blind for most of her life. Her cabin consisted of two rooms with no glass windows, just slabs of rough pine board hung up at night on rawhide hinges. Yet the woman's musical knowledge was extraordinarily rich and bespoke a familiarity with a far-off world. "You see I am blind, and never could read, so I think about lords and ladies, the fair lady and the gallant knight, dressed in gold and purple," she explained to Lomax. (Did anyone ever defend the universality of art, and its ability to transcend geographic and cultural boundaries, quite so succinctly?) During the course of two days, Lomax recorded for the Library of Congress Dusenberry's version of some eighty-two songs.

Yet the efforts of John Lomax, and those of his son Alan, coincided with the end of this era of vernacular music. The farming communities were the last to abandon time-honored ways: long after manual labor of other sorts was transformed by mechanization and automation, the farm worker retained many traditional practices. In England, too, well into the modern era a worker continued to trod some eleven miles to plow a single acre of land—considered a typical honest day's work. Even as modern methods of agriculture permeated the farms, many workers continued to work and live as in bygone days, insulated from the trends, both liberating and pernicious, of urban society. In its inward focus, this resilience and self-reliance of the farm economy not only preserved but also kept vital and relevant the songs of the agricultural laborer long after work songs had mostly disappeared from other occupations. But these factors could only delay, not deflect, the inevitable assimilation of modern ways. Song largely disappeared as a constitutive element of rural life, or to the extent that it remained it came to the farm by means of radios, phonographs, and other innovations offered by the purveyors of what is now charmingly called "consumer electronics."

As noted earlier, most of the research on agricultural work songs examines them as social or aesthetic phenomena. But perhaps a third perspective, a purely *botanical* aspect, is also worth considering: put simply, the crops may respond to the music. Although speculation on this topic has a long history—even Charles Darwin played the bassoon to a plant, hoping to gauge its reaction—the belief that crops are influenced by music has achieved a modicum of scientific respectability only in the last several decades. In the 1950s the botanist T. C. Singh, head of the Department of Botany at Annamalai University in Madras, determined that vegetation exposed to music showed acceleration in the streaming of its protoplasm. Singh began testing the influence of raga music on groups of balsam plants, during which, relative to a control group, he measured a 72 percent increase in leaf count and a 20 percent improvement in height. In 1960, the botanist George E. Smith, following up on Singh's work, began playing George Gershwin's *Rhapsody in Blue* throughout the day and night in a greenhouse where he grew corn and soybean plants. In doing so he noted that the plants exposed to Gershwin achieved faster growth with thicker and tougher stems; were heavier in weight and greener in appearance; and enjoyed higher survival rates compared to a comparable group deprived of music. But before Gershwin fans had much time to rejoice, a follow-up experiment showed even better results when the plants were serenaded with excruciatingly loud tones held at a constant pitch. In another experiment George Milstein, of Long Island City in New York, showed that a persistent humming tone accelerated the growth of his plants; he later supervised the release of a commercial recording in which the sound was incorporated into musical selections.

Other researchers have delved into the subject with more overtly aesthetic considerations guiding their efforts. Work undertaken by Dorothy Retallack in the late 1960s at Temple Buell College in Colorado aimed at understanding the specific musical preferences of plants. Retallack carefully measured water consumption and the degree and direction of the lean of the leaves both away from and toward the music source. An interesting finding showed that the plants noticeably leaned away from the rock music of Led Zepplin, Jimi Hendrix, and Vanilla Fudge. Even after Retallack rotated the plants 180 degrees, the plants changed their position, now leaning in the opposite direction, again trying to get away from the source of the music. In contrast, plants would markedly lean toward classical music—both Bach and the atonal music of Weber, Berg, and

Schoenberg did the trick—as well as toward the jazz of Duke Ellington and Louis Armstrong. The vegetative audience especially favored the sitar music of Ravi Shankar, bending more than sixty degrees, well over half way to horizontal, toward the music, with the nearest plant almost embracing the speaker. Other findings showed a vegetative dislike to percussion music, a preference for strings, and plain indifference to folk and country and western music. Television producers, who contacted Retallack to report on her work, enlisted her help in setting up a sitar versus rock battle of the leaves, which was eventually featured on Walter Cronkite's CBS Evening News in October 1970. Mulling over this odd and intriguing body of research, we are led to conclude that not only do plants respond to the songs that are performed for them, but that they are also apparently discerning, clearly favoring some sounds and disliking others. Unlocking the mysteries of this phenomenon might eventually lead to commercial innovations. Some have gone so far as to suggest that farm equipment in the future will come equipped with oscillators and speakers, to spread the nurturing vibrations to the crops. Perhaps the claims of Densmore's Yuman informant—that his songs could make the corn grow faster—had more scientific grounding than she may have realized!

We tend to dismiss these purely vegetative consequences of work songs, in favor of more sociological or ethnomusicological considerations. Some readers may even brand those of us who sing to our plants as crackpots or worse. However, the history of vernacular song is full of examples in which the influence of music on the crops was a paramount concern. Examine, for instance, the art of rain-making, where music and magic are often intertwined in strange and wondrous ways. Among the most prized bits of knowledge of the "clever men" of the Australian Aborigines, rank the rain-making songs and rituals. The rainmaker invokes the assistance of the rainbow serpent, a huge snake who resides in waterholes, swamps or lakes—paintings of this powerful mythic figure in the Australian imagination date back to before the time of the earliest Egyptian dynasties. In the belief systems of some tribes, the rainbow serpent is the sole source of life-giving water, and without his intercession the rains would cease and the land would become parched and dry. Writing a century ago, the pioneering anthropologist A. W. Howitt described the various methods of the Bunjil-willung, or rain men: "[They] would fill the mouth with water and then squirt in the direction appropriate to the particular clan, and each one sang his especial rain-song. . . . These rain-makers could also bring thunder, and it was said of them, as of the other medicine-men, that they obtained their songs in dreams." Other songs helped end storms, or summoned the winds. So pervasive is the linkage in the aboriginal mind between music and rainfall that, among the Kurnai, the croaking of the frogs is sometimes described as their "singing for rain."

Natalie Curtis found rainmaking songs in East Africa; Bela Bartok transcribed them in Turkish Asia Minor; and Verrier Elwin documented them in India. Indeed, wherever cultivation sustains human life, and the skies are sometimes parsimonious with their supply of waters, they have had a role to play in social life. These songs play an especially prominent role in the indigenous societies of the Americas. Curtis tells of a group of Navajos who traveled to California in 1903, where they saw the ocean for the first time. Amazed by the sight, they chanted and sprinkled pollen on the waves, while engaged in prayer. "So much of water is here," their prayer exclaimed, "here where there seems no need. With us the need is great. As we give of our offering, so may there be given to us of these Great Waters." These songs can be found in the traditions of a wide range of Native American cultures, from the indigenous tribes of South America to the Inuit of the Arctic regions. Even today, some villages retain rainmaking ceremonies and customs; for example, in Peru in the small village of Tinta to the south of Cuzco, the Queros—whose heritage may even date back to the Inca civilization—celebrate a ritual on the third Sunday in June. Called the Raq'chi festival, the event offers an annual opportunity to thank the rain god for favorable weather. The *paras* dance performed at this time derives its name from a Quechua word meaning "rain."

Rainmaking songs also figure prominently in European traditions. James Frazer, in *The Golden Bough,* cites a fascinating ritual of southeastern Europe, in which a girl is clothed in a makeshift apparel constructed from flowers, grass, and herbs. This girl, called the Dodola, goes through the village and dances in front of various houses, accompanied by other young women, who form a ring around her and sing:

> We go through the village;
> The clouds go in the sky;
> We go faster,
> Faster go the clouds;
> They have overtaken us,
> And wetted the corn and the vine.

Frazer cites numerous other instances, from a range of cultures, in which singing plays a significant role in rites and ceremonies related to fertility, both of the crops and of people. In most of these instances, the singers are not important officials, priests, or magicians but members of the agricultural working class, or their children. Their involvement is driven by the most practical of motives—they were the members of the community who stood to gain or lose the most from the fertility of the crops. Many examples of sympathetic magic can be found in these songs, in which activities or sounds emulate the desired results. For instance, rainmaking songs often find the musicians imitating the splashing sound of rain or the noise of thunder in an attempt to create a similar effect in the skies, or spitting out water as a token of the showers to come.

Rainmaking is only one example of how song plays a practical role in cultivation. In many instances, music is employed to prevent animals or birds from destroying the cultivated fields. The ancient Indian collection of some four hundred songs, the *Ahananuru*, includes the tale of a young girl stopping an elephant from eating the crops by her song, which so fascinated the animal that it forgot its hunger. An Egyptian relief sculpture from 1365 BC shows women beating tambourines in order to scare birds into flight, perhaps away from crops or in the direction of hunters. Two thousand years later, a similar usage could be found in the following songs, from nineteenth-century England, employed to frighten the birds:

> O, you nasty black-a-tops [blackbirds],
> Get off my master's radish tops,
> For he's a-comin' with his long gun,
> And you must fly and I must run.

And

> Gee, hallo, hallo, blackie cap,
> Let us lie down and take a nap.
> Suppose our master chance to come?
> You must fly and I must run.

In such instances the songs appear to be purely functional, yet not without a certain playfulness that survives even when sung away from the fields and the pestering blackbirds. To serve the same purpose the Kammu of Laos construct "musical scarecrows"—idiophones that produce sound by means of wind, water, ropes, or other comparable methods. But this is a much more serious endeavor than the bird-shooing songs of England; and here we even encounter the almost unique case of a musical performance that the performer does not care a whit to hear. When operated by a rope, the musical scarecrow "player" may be situated several hundred meters away from the "instrument." But the success of the tune is keenly followed nonetheless, measured in this instance by the observable movement of wings above the rice field as the intruders take flight.

Ah, what tremendous diversity and vitality we have already noted among the songs of cultivation, ranging from impassioned rain-making dances to the rattles and jangles of musical scarecrows, from ballads of knights errant to magical fertility rituals, encompassing vocal outpourings of thanksgiving or protest, songs for amusement or propitiation, performed solo, or in unison, or in the timeless patterns of call-and-response. The typical stereotyped view of the songs of manual labor depicts them as repetitive, one-dimensional affairs, a mere rhythmic spur to get the work done. One of the purposes of this book is to show how much is missed by this blasé attitude. Yes, the songs often served a utilitarian purpose, but we find a similar "purposefulness" in many other things—a modern skyscraper, a Minoan vase, a batik cloth, Cellini's salt cellar, Brunelleschi's dome, Ghiberti's door—without that purpose exhausting their meanings, or preventing them from demonstrating an aesthetic component, sometimes one of surprising intensity.

The field call, one of the most common and least elaborate forms of agricultural work song, epitomizes this richness and complexity. No musical performance could be simpler than a field call. Yet, at the same time, its emotional content and social significations can be as rich as what one finds in the sweetest aria or the proudest anthem. In its most basic form, the field call was a specialized type of work song used to convey information. "Field calls grew up alongside work songs," Frederic Ramsey writes. "They probably began as high, wordless chants, sung in falsetto." Unlike the work song, which usually involved a group of laborers, the field holler was often sung by a solitary individual. "The call was a variation of *la hoo hoo*," Ramsey continues, "a gentle, whooping sound, that nevertheless carried far. The response came back; *yehee, lahee*. During slavery they were used for communication between squads in neighboring fields.

Sometimes the call-and-response was followed by a brief exchange of information not meant for the master's ears." But even when forced to serve functional ends such as these, the agricultural songs still retained an aesthetic element—one not entirely separated from the utility of the music but rather intertwined with it. Frederick Law Olmsted has left us an evocative account of a field holler he heard late one evening in January 1853 somewhere in South Carolina.

> Suddenly one [worker] raised such a sound as I never heard before: a long, loud musical shout, rising and falling and breaking into falsetto, his voice ringing through the woods in the clear frosty night air, like a bugle-call. As he finished, the melody was caught up by another, and then, another, and then, by several in chorus.

The Harvard archeologist Charles Peabody was so moved by the hollers he heard during his 1901–1902 excavations in Mississippi, that he wrote an article for the *American Journal of Folk-Lore* in which he marveled over these "strains of apparently genuine African music, sometimes with words, sometimes without. Long phrases there were without apparent measured rhythm, singularly hard to copy in notes." Peabody makes particular mention of the extraordinary music he heard at John Stovall's plantation—the same location where Alan Lomax would discover Muddy Waters almost exactly forty years later. Very few recordings of field hollers have been made commercially available. It is perhaps interesting to note that one of the best surviving examples was performed by Waters's brother-in-law, Charley Berry. Anyone listening to Berry's "Cornfield Holler," recorded by Alan Lomax in 1942 at Clarksdale, Mississippi, or to Thomas J. Marshall's "Cornfield Holler" (also known as the "arwhoolie" or "hoolie"), recorded by Herbert Halpert in 1939, cannot fail to be moved by the sheer beauty of this music. There is no conflict between the two roles fulfilled by such songs: the purposefulness of the music makes it all the more compelling; its beauty enhances its utility.

This multifaceted psychological dimension of the work song—its inner meaning—is far richer than its mere musicological trappings. The "Cornfield Holler" mentioned above is only a few seconds in duration, a snippet of melody that is almost impossible to notate, let alone analyze in accordance with the tools of academic musicology. But its psychological and emotional depth compensates for this paucity of formal contents. How else do we explain the discomfort or near embarrassment that many people feel when listening to work songs such as this one—almost as if one were intruding on an intimate, private moment? No music was more ostensibly "public" than these songs of labor; they literally took place in the open, in the midst of commercial activity. Yet, paradoxically, no music was so personal and private.

Any discussion of agricultural work songs and field hollers brings us inevitably to the redoubtable subject of slavery. Much has been written and debated about the music of the black slave workers, but unfortunately the terms of the discussion have too often simplified the matter into the heated question of whether slaves sang because "they were sad" or because "they were happy." "I have often been utterly astonished, since I came to the north, to find persons who could speak of the singing, among slaves, as evidence of their contentment and happiness," wrote Frederick Douglass in a famous passage in his autobiography. "It is impossible to conceive of a greater mistake. Slaves sing most when they are most unhappy. The songs of the slave represent the sorrows of his heart; and he is relieved by them, only as an aching heart is relieved by its tears." The use of the African American's songs as circumstantial evidence in support of their own oppression and enslavement was a reprehensible deception. But we should no longer let this lie set the terms on which we assess this body of music a century and a half later. The work song was part of the heritage of the Africans, brought by them to the New World, predating the plantations of the South, and surviving after the demise of slavery. The work songs became part of a shameful history, but the songs themselves are not shameful. The ethnomusicologist Rose Brandel has stressed that African tribes do "not deliberately project the 'work music' upon the scene in the manner of modern factory psychologists. Rather, the music seems to be an expressive outgrowth of the labor itself." Brandel does not deny that "the music also alleviates the burden of muscular monotony and spurs on to more energetic endeavors," but these benefits are not causal forces, nor can any functionalist interpretation drawing on them as motivating factors exhaust the meaning of this music. In short, these songs refuse to be reduced to tools or symbols, whether in the name of economics or of political ideology.

Robert Nathaniel Dett, reviewing the book *Negro Workaday Songs,* focused on this complexity—and the contrary feelings it generates—from the perspective of black Americans. He mulls over "a shame akin to that which led Burns to labor so hard over the folk songs of his beloved Scotland," and he offers a gripping metaphor: "An artist recently employed to make drawings of deep sea life related how when the dredges were drawn up they contained only what appeared to be vast quantities of mud and slime, but that sometimes in this apparently noisome mass were found choice specimens, often so rare and beautiful as to be almost beyond human imagination . . . What professors Odum and Johnson have done [in their study of work songs] . . . may be a parallel case."

In the final analysis, the work song of the slave, the prisoner, and other oppressed laborers, is never purely or even primarily about "feelings," however defined, whether happy or sad. It is as much about "being" and "doing" as about feeling. Sometimes this doing is little more than coping, surviving, or maintaining a human dignity in the face of the inhuman; at other times the doing itself takes on the substance of grandeur, of an artistry that persists even when separated from the song. Yet these other meanings do not detract from the emotional content of the song; rather they heighten it. Here is a poetry amplified by its purpose, a beauty that is conveyed not only in melody and rhythm but also in actions and effects. In his book *Tiv Song*, Charles Keil talks about "shifting our conceptual frame from 'emotion' to 'motion,' from 'beauty' to 'energy,' from 'esthetics' to 'ontology' "—and it is precisely this change in perspective that is required here. The work song, for African Americans, "got things done," got many things done.

Yet despite this immediacy, the songs were also capable of a level of artistic distance between singer and subject, one that at times almost defied belief. Sometimes the most horrible aspects of slavery served as subjects for songs. The listener who knows the story behind the music shudders to recall the personal travails that were transmuted into art, so bitter is the root from which the song grows. Matthew Lewis, the novelist who also owned a sugarcane plantation in Jamaica during the early years of the nineteenth century, describes one such refrain:

"Take him to the Gulley! Take him to the Gulley!
But bringee back the frock and board."—
"Oh! Massa, massa! me no deadee yet!"
"Take him to the Gulley! Take him to the Gulley!"
"Carry him along!"

The story of the song relates to a slave-owner named Bedward who, some thirty years before, had gained notoriety for his extreme cruelty. Lewis explains:

> It was his constant practice, whenever a sick negro was pronounced incurable, to order the poor wretch to be carried to a solitary vale upon his estate, called the Gulley, where he was thrown down, and abandoned to his fate; which fate was generally to be half-devoured by the john-crows, before death had put an end to his sufferings. By this proceeding, the avaricious owner avoided the expense of maintaining the slave during his last illness; and in order that he might be as little a loser as possible, he always enjoined the negro bearers of the dying man to strip him naked before leaving the Gulley, and not to forget to bring back his frock and the board on which he had been carried down.

The slaveowner was unmoved by the cries and protestations of the victim, but sometimes the fellow slaves would take matters into their own hands. In at least one instance, they brought the man back to the slave quarters at night, and tended him back to good health in the following days—all unbeknownst to the owner—at which point the slave left the plantation undetected and escaped to Kingston. Lewis continues:

> Unluckily, one day the master was passing through Kingston, when, on turning the corner of a street suddenly, he found himself face to face with the negro, whom he had supposed long ago to have been picked to the bones. . . . He immediately seized him, claimed him as his slave, and ordered his attendants to convey him to his house; but the fellow's cries attracted a crowd round them, before he could be dragged away. He related his melancholy story, and the singular manner in which he had recovered his life and liberty; and the public indignation was so forcibly excited by the shocking tale, that Mr. Bedward was glad to save himself from being torn to pieces by a precipitate retreat from Kingston, and never ventured to advance his claim to the negro a second time.

As was often the case, the resulting song served as a musical protest, a testimony and denunciation by those whose evidence was never allowed in a court of law, whose personal advocacy was reduced to these almost unbearably poignant refrains.

How do we come to grips with the inner experience of the field work song? What did it mean to sing these songs, day after day, month after month, year after year? A number of researchers, most notably Mihaly

Csikszentmihalyi, have written about the "flow state"—namely, the attitude of mind most conducive to high levels of performance in sports, the arts, and other areas of endeavor. In the flow state, the work becomes effortless and almost seems to happen of its own accord. Csikszentmihalyi explains this sense of flow as follows:

> We have all experienced times when, instead of being buffeted by anonymous forces, we do feel in control of our actions, masters of our own fate. On the rare occasions that it happens, we feel a sense of exhilaration. . . . Such events occur not only when the external conditions are favorable, however: people who have survived concentration camps or who have lived through near-fatal physical dangers often recall that in the midst of their ordeal they experienced extraordinarily rich epiphanies in response to such simple events as hearing the song of a bird in the forest, completing a hard task, or sharing a crust of bread with a friend.

In this passage, Csikszentmihalyi does not mention slavery or field work, or the music that it produced, but his comments are quite applicable to these matters. It is worth keeping this in mind as we interpret firsthand accounts of the music of Africans and the African diaspora. Reading passages such as the one from Brandel noted above, or the one following from 1666 in Charles de Rochefort's *The History of the Caribby-Islands*, we are inescapably reminded of these flow experiences: "They do also by singing alleviate the hard labour they are addicted unto, and yet what they do, seems to be done rather out of divertisement, and to avoid idleness, than out of any considerations of advantage that they make thereof."

The workers themselves recognized this intrinsic benefit of the music, as illustrated by the laborer who when asked by Alan Lomax why he sang, replied simply: "It go so better when you singing, you might nigh forget and the time just pass away." It is worth noting that much of the research on flow experiences has focused independently on the subjects of work and music. Csikszentmihalyi has stated that one of the primary goals of his research has been to "transform jobs into flow-producing activities." Music making is often cited by researchers in this area as an endeavor in which achieving the flow state is relatively easy for a skilled practitioner. So it is no great exaggeration to say that the ideal work experience would be much like singing a song. Given this intersection of work, music, and flow, one might even be justified in saying that the work song is the quintessential facilitator of the flow experience.

The ability of music to create this altered state of consciousness is well known from anecdotal accounts and, even more forcefully, from our own firsthand experiences. (At least for the vast majority of us: drawing on surveys, Csikszentmihalyi estimates that 15 to 20 percent never experience the flow state, while a comparable percentage achieve it virtually everyday.) In attempting to explain the prevalence and obvious value of songs used in hoeing, reaping, weeding, and related activities observed during two years of research in southeastern Africa, Thomas F. Johnston speculated on the neurological bases for these experiences, and he drew conclusions compatible with those of Csikszentmihalyi. In his study titled "The Function of Tsonga Work Songs," Johnston writes that "communal 'immersion' in polyrhythmic kinesthesia has a reinforcing, feedback effect upon individual susceptibility to auditory driving . . . polyrhythms tap the basic brain wave frequency of the whole group rather than solely that of the individual . . . These various components and aspects of Tsonga work-group music are functional in alleviating the unabatedness and monotony of women's horticultural labor, and in ensuring attainment of at least a minimal subsistence level for the population by coordinating the physical manipulations of individuals in task forces and spurring on their efforts." A few researchers have explored the neurological conditions for these experiences—for example, V. J. Walter and W. G. Walter, Andrew Neher, Gilbert Rouget, Melinda Maxfield, and others. Despite the collective work of these various experts, both those out in the field and others inside the laboratory, our understanding of the neurological implications of singing at work is still relatively modest, yet what we do know makes it clear that real physiological changes are involved. If the work song, as we have suggested, "got things done," it did so in a very holistic way, with its effects taking place inside the singer as well as in the external environment.

Because of this inherent complexity, the multiple purposes it enbodies, the work song follows musical rules of its own, far distant from the cultural and formal considerations that hold sway in virtually all other types of performance art. Indeed, in almost every regard the work song defies our conception of an "artistic performance." Its pace can be repetitive and predictable; often it strives to achieve effects that, in other settings, would be dismissed as merely monotonous. The time and setting of the performance, the number of singers—these factors and others are usually determined by external forces. No artists have less control over their "medium" than do the singers of these songs. The rhythms are typically slower than most other types of traditional songs, sometimes positively sluggish—they need to be, if the laborer is to last until the end of the workday. Even when the work song is brought into the arena of high art it retains this stubborn lethargy: recall that Verdi, when introducing his "Anvil Chorus," is forced to cut the tempo in half to accommodate the rhythm of the real work taking place on stage. By the same token, the length of the performance can be stretched far beyond conventional bounds. An amusing anecdote is told of Doc Reese, a former prisoner, who was asked to sing a work song at a dinner given by Alan Lomax in New York. Reese started singing, and then went on and on for some twenty-five minutes before stopping with the half-apology: "It just goes along just about like that." Needless to say, such music was not designed for performance at social events, and it was even less suited for airplay in neat three-minute installments. But if we define "performance" more broadly—as more than just an activity that takes place on a stage in front of a paying audience; or, above all, if we embrace the aspects of ritual, propitiation, world creating, and world changing that are hidden within the term (reminiscent of Austin's performatives as discussed in the introduction), we reach a far different conclusion. From such a perspective, the work songs that developed within the world of the cultivator, during that long-forgotten shift from hunting and gathering to agriculture as a basis of society and economic life, stand out as quintessential performances, as pre-eminent demonstrations that artistic expression can make things happen.

With the concept of flow serving as a key, we can better appreciate the significance of anecdotes such as the one related about Doc Reese; more to the point, we can uncover the intimate links between song and agricultural work and their overlapping role in the formation of cultures. A. L. Lloyd has suggested that all European folk songs share a common origin in the "lyrical song of the *coloni*—tenant farmers of the Roman Empire— and the communal and hardly differentiated work songs and cult songs of barbarian tribesmen." It is worth recalling that the lands that sprouted the oldest historical societies of note—Mesopotamia of the Sumerians and Babylonians; the Nile and adjacent deserts of the Egyptian dynasties; Attic Greece; the Central American lands of the Mayans, where agriculture could only be pursued by burning and clearing jungle—were largely inhospitable areas requiring back-breaking labor to tame and develop.

Thucydides argues at the outset of his *History of the Peloponnesian War* that Athens enjoyed stability in its early history, because the poverty of its soil attracted only a few hostile parties, who then were happy to let the Athenians toil away in relative peace. More recently, the scholar Victor Hanson has gone so far as to see the flowering of Greek civilization as rooted in family farming and agricultural labor, and not, as so commonly assumed, in the leisure activities of the Greek city dwellers. Farmers not philosophers, agrarian workers not tragic poets, laid the foundation for Western Culture—an achievement which built on "small-scale, intensive working of the soil, a complete rethinking of the way Greeks produced food and owned land, and the emergence of a new sort of person for whom work was not merely a means of subsistence or profit but an ennobling way of life, a crucible of moral excellence in which pragmatism, moderation, and a search for proportion were the fundamental values." Can we avoid surmising that the natural challenges of topology, and the requisite ingenuity and labor they necessitated, were what inspired early societies to great achievement, both in economic and artistic endeavors? Is it possible that work—indeed, hard and relentless work—is the greatest spur to our creative energies, growing not only the crops but also our creative capacity for song and other cultural productions in the process?

If so, perhaps we can easily believe that the farmer's perspiration and his musical inspiration might very well have developed hand in hand. Instead of an urban setting for artistry, we should not be surprised to find it flourishing alongside sickles and plows. And the field work song, rather than being treated as a peripheral activity on the fringes of the economy, on the outskirts of the city, and neglected in the annals of artistic achievement, may have played a more constitutive role than can now be measured.

CHAPTER THREE

The Herder

Makes no difference

How you shear um

Just so you shear um clean.

—*Shearing song*

The shepherd's vocation is fraught with paradox. No domesticated animal is as defenseless or as vulnerable as the sheep. Yet, as the herder can attest, the sheep proudly refuse to acknowledge their helplessness. Instead, they are stubborn and foolish, fickle in their choice of pasture and water, and often blissfully unaware of their reputation for docility and—is there a better word?—sheepishness.

But the shepherd's position is even more contradictory than that of the flock. On the one hand, this vocation offers ample leisure, hours of idleness, and uneventful waiting while the flocks roam over the pasture land. But it is also a position of unceasing vigilance, of constant worry and supervision. Recall that the biblical story of the Good Shepherd literally holds the herder up as a model of the ultimate worrywart, as the individual who frets about everything and everyone. Here we have two incompatible views of the herder: on one hand a restful pastoralist enjoying idyllic leisure; on the other, a nervous Nellie anxiously guarding over the flock.

For both these types of herders, however, music was a useful tool. Music helped avoid the extremes of each role, allowing the herder to relax when pressing concerns dominated and, perhaps even more important, to maintain alertness when indolence might otherwise jeopardize the flock. Above all, song helped to combat the shepherd's two implacable enemies—no, not the wolf and the thief, but boredom and sleepiness. Counting sheep? Is it not, even in our postindustrial society, the proverbial precursor to falling asleep?

The Roman author Columella advised shepherds to neither recline nor sit, "for if he is not walking he ought to stand, since the task of the herdsman calls for a lofty and commanding elevation from which his eyes may observe as from a watchtower. . . . lest a thief or predator cheat the shepherd while he is daydreaming." But the ancients realized that music was not incompatible with the vigilance required by shepherding. Macrobius notes, in his *Commentary on the Dream of Scipio,* that the "shepherd's pipes bring rest to the flocks in pasture." Conveying both calmness and alertness—again, the paradox—the shepherd's song could serve as a musical accompaniment to virtually every situation and activity of the pastoral life.

The efficacy of these songs, which some might be tempted to dismiss, must not be underestimated. Even a small movement—a stray rabbit coming unexpectedly into view, a wind-blown object making a noise—can create confusion and danger. The sheep have no defense except their instinct to flee. The song calms the uneasy flock and keeps it at pasture. The sound of the shepherd's voice prevents panic and the dangers of an unwarranted stampede. Here lies the origin of pastoral music: with its soothing strains acting as a sonic cushion of comfort, it was originally conceived not to please human ears but rather the more acute sensibilities of the animal, for whom listening is often a matter of survival.

But the practicality of the shepherd's song is sometimes hard to perceive after centuries of idealized views of singing shepherds. The image of the poet and singer as shepherd has become trite and conventional. Even the earliest examples of the pastoral genre in literature—such as Theocritus's *Idylls* or Virgil's *Eclogues,* with their lavish praise of the herder's life—are clothed in an aura of unreality. "It is generally assumed that literary pastoral developed from singing competitions," Raymond Williams tells us in his provocative study *The Country and the City.* Yet by the time this tradition made its way into written texts, the linkage with rustic activities was only a dim memory from the past, liable more to confuse than to illuminate the reader. Virgil's masterpiece is a jumble of contradictions—sometimes it seems to take place in his native Mantua, at other times in ancient Arcadia or Sicily. As one expert on pastoral literature remarks: "To insist on a realistic (or even recognizably 'natural') presentation of actual shepherd life would exclude the greater part of the compositions that are called pastoral." As pastoral songs evolved and spread, this element of fantasy and unreality remained constant, even as other aspects of the music changed dramatically. It is unclear, for example, whether the *pastorela* songs of the medieval period can be traced back to classical antecedents, but these pieces are every bit as utopian as the musings of Theocritus and his followers. In the *pastorela,* a high-born man of status courts a lowly shepherdess, creating an Arcadian story that blissfully ignored barriers of birth, the demands of arranged marriages, feudal laws and customs, and religious mandates.

Yet the faint echoes between these idealized poems and the real songs of shepherds cannot be totally ignored. We may detect them perhaps when assessing the traditional *yoik* or *joik* of the Sami people of northern Europe, for whom reindeer herding has long served as an important way of life. Even today a few thousand herders continue in this traditional livelihood, and preserve some of its evocative music. When the young Finnish composer Armas Launis collected yoiks during 1904 and 1905, the vast majority were songs about other people. One fisherman's wife, Biret Peltovuoma, sang some seventy-nine different yoiks for her curious visitor, of which all but seven were about specific individuals, including friends, relatives, neighbors, the postmaster, the shopkeeper and his son, various reindeer owners and the local schoolmaster. One sees the same emphasis on singing the merits, or flaws, of the "other" in formal pastoral poetry. In fact, each of the three main types of pastoral poetry finds its counterpart in the music of the modern European herder: the "eclogue," which is properly described as a singing contest between shepherds; the "complaint," which is a shepherd's song praising his beloved and bewailing her indifference or cruelty; and the pastoral "elegy" which is a herder's lament for another shepherd who has died. Two other common themes for yoiks—animals and nature—are also important concerns for the pastoral poet. The following yoik, documented by Johan Turi—a herder who was also the first published author to write in the Sami language—deals specifically with the endearing qualities of reindeer.

> Silke-njávvi,
> the one with the soft silk hair
> voya voya nana nana

they dashed away like the beams of the sun
voya voya nana nana
the little calves grunted
voya voya nana nana
the herd moves like the swiftest streams
voya voya nana nana.

In many yoiks, as with pastoral music in general, we can sense a plaintive, melancholy tone—perhaps inculcated by the long lonely hours spent by the herder with only the company of animals. And this pervasive tone may also help explain why, for us, listening to pastoral music often seems to summon up feelings of bittersweet nostalgia for simpler bygone eras and lifestyles. True, this is part of our inherited cultural associations with the music of herders, but it also comes from the sounds themselves, which only rarely attempt to express gaiety, and more often settle for a pensive moodiness. A. Hyatt King has gone so far as to trace the characteristic elements of eighteenth- and nineteenth-century Romanticism in music—with its idealization of nature and its preoccupation with emotional immediacy—back to the Alpine melodies of herding communities. Although Beethoven apparently never visited Switzerland, either before or after composing his Pastoral Symphony, this does not prevent King from speculating that the great composer may have been inspired by a chance encounter with Austrian Alphorn players, or that he may have gained access to the music through his Swiss friend Dr. Ignaz Troxler. Yet the association of pastoral music with nostalgic sentiments may be as old as the herding songs themselves. As we have already noted, the ancients saw "complaints" and "laments" as two of the three most common themes for pastoral poetic expression. Long before Beethoven's day, no visit to an isolated and lonely Alpine pasture land was required in order to understand the emotional associations of the herder's life.

But classical poetry is far from the only ancient source of idealized views of the shepherd's life. Clearly the most influential use of the herder's vocation as a metaphor for other concerns took root shortly after the death of Virgil, when the early Christians drew on the image of shepherd and flock to symbolize the watchfulness of their Messiah. They took seriously the proclamation by Jesus, in chapter 10 of the book of John, "I am the Good Shepherd. The Good Shepherd giveth His life for the sheep." Some tried to link these two ancient views of the good shepherd, the pastoral idealization of the poets and the Christian metaphor, seeing in Virgil's *Eclogues* (in particular the fourth one), semicryptic predictions of the coming of Christ. Yet the Judaic tradition of shepherd-musician predates all of these examples—whether Roman or Greek, Christian or Pagan—and especially the example of the quintessential shepherd-musician: King David of Israel. No herder's songs are more venerable than the Psalms of David, none more influential or better known, none more beautiful:

> The Lord is my Shepherd; I shall not want.
> He maketh me to lie down in green pastures:
> He leadeth me beside the still waters.
> He restoreth my soul.
> Yea, though I walk through the valley of the shadow of death, I will fear
> no evil: for thou art with me; thy rod and thy staff they comfort me.

Experts place the time of King David at almost 1000 years before Christ. But the shepherd's vocation probably predates King David by at least five thousand years. Wherever shepherding is found, a musical tradition is invariably discovered coexisting with it. Indeed, the origin of music and the development of cattle ranching are oddly linked in the fourth book of Genesis, where the two pursuits are described as arising almost simultaneously. Decorations from the tomb of Wensu at Thebes, from around 1500 BC, show a herdsman playing a primitive reed instrument, pleasantly passing the long hours watching his sheep and goats. When Vasco de Gama rounded the Cape of Good Horn during his 1497–1498 voyage to India, among the first things he discovered were shepherd-musicians on the east coast of Africa. After firing his guns to attract attention, a small band of herders came to greet him, accompanied by their sheep and cattle, and entertained his sailors with an elaborate performance on four flutes. The Spanish explorer was so charmed that he ordered the trumpets to be played in response, and a spontaneous dance was held at this meeting of musical cultures.

Although not as old a vocation as that of the hunter, the shepherd's livelihood was an inevitable extension of the former. The keeping of animals served as the most secure way of accumulating the surplus wealth of a community, family, or individual. At first, the herds were probably kept to supply meat for periods when hunting was unsuccessful or impractical, but in time the wool-bearing capability of the sheep must have become important in its own right. Around 4000 BC, we can observe a growing realization in Mesopotamia that herd animals are potentially more valuable alive than dead—that their wool, milk, and sheer muscle power could confer benefits as substantial as meat and hides. Initially the herders may have simply waited for the wool to shed on its own—which happened naturally with these prehistoric breeds—but later they would develop the shearer's art.

Even today, surviving traditions of singing herders bespeak great antiquity. Often living in remote areas, far from the influence of other cultures and classes, the herders are sometimes the last practitioners of venerable songs and instruments that have been forgotten elsewhere. When Alan Lomax conducted research among the shepherds of Spain, he was often overwhelmed by the evident antiquity of their songs, which were much older than anything he had encountered in the New World. "I remember the night I spent in the straw hut of a shepherd on the moonlit plains of Extremadura," Lomax later wrote. "He played the one-string *vihuela,* the instrument of the medieval minstrels, and sang ballads of the wars of Charlemagne, while his two ancient cronies sighed over the woes of courtly lovers now five hundred years in the dust." Lomax had expected to find the most vibrant musical traditions in the south of Spain, with its gypsies and its long ties to North Africa, but instead he learned that the lonely shepherds of the northern highlands had been the most loyal custodians of the ancient songs.

The ability of herders to preserve complicated historical narratives over a period of many generations may surprise some readers. Yet researchers have long noted that their best sources of traditional material are usually the individuals who are the most remote from other influences, and the least well educated, at least in the formal sense. Indeed, the illiterate singer is typically the one who knows the most songs, who displays the best memory, and who offers the most reliable information. In her study *Roadside Songs of Tuscany,* published with the assistance of John Ruskin, Francesca Alexander describes one such herder, Beatrice Bernardi:

> She had no education in the common sense of the word, never learning even the alphabet, but she had a wonderful memory, and could sing or recite long pieces of poetry. As a girl, she used in summer to follow the sheep, with her distaff at her waist; and would fill up her hours of solitude by singing such

ballads as "The war of St. Michael and the dragon! The creation of the world!! and the Fall of man!!!" or "The history of San Pellegrino, the son of Romano, King of Scotland"; and now, in her old age, she knows nearly all the New Testament history, and much of the Old, in poetical form.

Some fifty years later, Albert Lord and Milman Parry found similar prodigies among herders in Yugoslavia. "When I was a shepherd boy, they used to come for an evening to my house, or sometimes we would go to someone else's for the evening, somewhere in the village" recounted Seco Kolic, one of Lord and Parry's informants. "Then a singer would pick up the gusle [a one-string bowed instrument], and I would listen to the song. The next day when I was with the flock, I would put the song together, word for word, without the gusle, but I would sing it from memory, word for word, just as the singer had sung it." Scholars were so dazzled by what Lord and Parry had encountered—illiterate bards who could perform epics of more than twelve thousand lines—that it is scarcely an exaggeration to say that this fieldwork changed forever our conceptions of epic verse and the origins of Western literature. Here, on the pasturelands of Tuscany and central Europe, we gained a glimpse into the frame of mind that preserved and polished the *Iliad* and the *Odyssey*.

Some researchers have thought that herders rarely use songs in their work. "As the Corsicans are by tradition a people of shepherds," writes one ethnomusicologist, "one cannot expect many types of work songs there." Even the briefest survey of herding communities around the world disproves this wrong-headed generalization. Pastoral work songs are used to herd camels in sub-Saharan Africa and to calm sheep in the Basque country. With the emigration of many Basque shepherds to the United States—their services were so much in demand that the Western Range Association established a special program in 1950 to assist in their entry into the country—their remarkable *bertsolari* tradition of singing, in which new words are improvised to traditional melodies, came along with them. In Albania, A. L. Lloyd has documented a rich variety of pastoral music, including the melodic calls employed by shepherds to transmit news across the valleys, whether of weddings and local events or about the location of the flocks. The Kuria of East Africa know that their flute music is not just a diversion but an important part of their liveli-hood: "Playing flutes makes them [the cattle] feel better," one informant told researcher John Varnum. Varnum adds: "Whereas every male child takes part in the caring of cattle, so must every male child become a performer of the flute." Throughout Europe, herders have long relied on a wide range of musical and rhythmic devices—yodels, calls, the sounding of horns, even the cracking of whips—as methods of signaling and communication, both with their animals and among themselves. The nomadic Armenian shepherds play their pastoral music on the *shvi,* a wind instrument whose high-pitched tones are reminiscent of the songs of birds. Their ancient equivalents may have done much the same: double flutes made from bones, probably used by shepherds, have been uncovered at excavations in Garni and Dvin. In the Andes, herding songs are also of great antiquity, and include both vocal pieces as well as music played on the *kena,* a flute with a venerable tradition and perhaps the oldest such instrument in the Americas. "The music both comforts and directs the animals," writes John Cohen. "It also serves to locate the shepherd in space."

In the nearby Mantaro Valley of Peru, Raúl R. Romero has recorded a wide range of songs used by herders in marking cows, sheep, and goats. The chants of camel drivers rank among the oldest vernacular songs of the Middle East and northeastern Africa—they are among the few styles of singing from this region that we are certain predate the rise of Islam. In some communities, camel songs have persisted until modern times. In *Somali Pastoral Work Songs,* Axmed Cali Abokor differentiates between a half-dozen separate types of work songs related to camels: some are used to drive the animals to grazing lands, different melodies are employed when loading them, still others for bringing them back into the corral. This specialization is so extreme, that the first and second watering each have their own songs. "The pitch of the re-watering songs is lower," Abokor writes, "and the voice seems to be emotionally more appealing." Other herding cultures show an equally discriminating sensibility to subtle gradations of song and sound. A. L. Lloyd describes Bulgarian herders devoting hours to selecting and combining bells for their sheep or cattle: they hear fine distinctions where outsiders are merely aware of a brief metallic clash and jangle. As these examples make clear, music is as indispensable to the shepherd as the shanty to the sailor, the march to the soldier.

There is a further misconception that herders undertake little rhythmic manual labor—that their lives, so it seems, are spent idly watching while animals graze and hence they have no need for music to help organize and propel their movements. Their songs, to the extent that they employ them, are more about mood than movement. Nothing could be further from the truth. Many of the day-to-day tasks of herding communities are, in fact, highly rhythmic and often accompanied by music. Milking songs are found virtually wherever cattle are raised, and have been documented by researchers in locations ranging from the shores of the Black Sea to sub-Saharan Africa; from the Hebrides to various parts of the Americas, and throughout Asia. Jean Jenkins has recorded a number of milking songs in Mongolia, noting their great profusion: "These differ not only from place to place, but more important differences occur with each type of animal. Each man or woman sings to his own animal, to soothe her; the combined voices give a polyphonic (or possible heterophonic!) effect." Milking songs represent an important part of the folk music traditions of Scotland. Margaret Fay Shaw provides the following example from the Hebrides:

> Darling of the cattle, love of the cattle,
> Darling of the cattle, you are mine . . .
> My heifer will wait, my heifer will stay,
> My heifer will wait for me.

Sula Benet has noted the use, in certain parts of Poland, of a repeated incantation that is said to spur the cows to yield abundant quantities of milk. The idea that the song possesses a magical linkage to the amount of milk produced may well be at the root of many of these singing or chanting traditions. Songs and rituals associated with the dairy are so common among the Toda of South India that W. H. R. Rivers devoted over a third of his classic 1906 study to the subject, and the topic recurs frequently in linguist M. B. Emeneau's thousand-page opus *Toda Songs*.

Shearing songs are also widely known around the world, such as the following one, collected by Alton C. Morris in Florida:

> Makes no difference
> How you shear um;
> Makes no difference
> How or when;
> Makes no difference
> How you shear um
> Just so you shear um clean.

Jim Copper's *Song Book,* a fascinating collection of traditional music compiled by a Sussex farmer in 1936, includes another example, which begins:

> Come all my jolly boys and we'll together go,
> Together with our masters to shear the lambs and "yowes."
> All in the month of June of all times in the year
> It always comes in season the lambs and "yowes" to shear.
> And then we will work hard, my boys, until our backs do break,
> Our master he will bring us beer whenever we do lack.

Most activities in a shearer's life would seem hardly worthy of commemoration in a ballad, let alone a patriotic anthem, yet the best-known Australian song, "Waltzing Matilda," was inspired by the events of an 1894 shearers' strike. Little more than a hundred years have transpired since the composition of this song, yet few ancient inscriptions require as much esoteric knowledge to interpret as do these now famous words:

> Along came a jumbuck to drink at the billabong,
> Up jumped the swagman and grabbed him with glee,
> And he sang as he stowed that jumbuck in his tucker bag,
> "You'll come a-waltzing, Matilda, with me."

Those curious about these lyrics can find an exegesis—which amounts to a miniprimer in Australian shearer lingo—among the notes in the back of this book.

Butter churning songs are equally widespread. The best-known example, "Come, butter, come" was documented in England as early as 1656, and, according to Chuck Perdue, undoubtedly the song has "ushered in countless tons of butter" in the intervening years.

> Come, butter, come
> Come, butter, come
> Peter's standing at the gate
> Waiting for a butter cake,
> Come butter come.

Such songs filled a double purpose: to provide momentum for the labor, as well as to serve as a charm against evil magic that might prevent the butter from forming. In Arkansas, housewives were known to drop a silver coin into the churn for a similar purpose. Not just the magic of butter churning but also its music came to the New World along with other traditions of immigrants. Frank C. Brown, a professor of English at Duke University during the early decades of the twentieth century, gathered more than a dozen butter churning chants in North Carolina, and Chuck Perdue documented thirty-four examples from Georgia alone.

The list of examples could continue almost indefinitely, but my point should now be quite clear: the vocation of animal husbandry is full of rhythmic work often accompanied by song, contrary to the widespread view that it is a slow-paced life of idyllic leisure. But one of the great mysteries of the musical life of herders is the relatively modest role played by drums. After all, drums are frequently made out of the skins of the very animals these pastoralists raise. Yet panpipes and flutes, string instruments, and singing are more commonly found accompanying these pastoral pursuits. Is this perhaps due to the deference of the herder, who is unwilling to make the much-prized animal into a musical instrument? Probably not. Certainly herding communities have shown no reluctance to use their animals, dead or alive, for virtually every other purpose. Among the Nuer, E. E. Evans-Pritchard found that the herders extracted nearly every necessity, and more than a few luxuries, from these four-legged bank accounts. The cattle supplied milk, a daily staple of the Nuer diet. Meat and blood were also provided, both used as foodstuffs. Skins were made into bedding, tethering cords, carrying pouches, and collars for cattle. Tail hairs were used to make decorative tassels. Scrota were transformed into small bags for tobacco, snuff, and other various and sundry items. Bones could serve both functional and decorative roles, being made, for instance, into armlets as well as tools and other implements. The horn would be cut into spoons or used as part of a harpoon for hunting. Cattle dung served as plaster for housing or covering for wounds, or was burnt as fuel. The ashes of burnt dung served as tooth powder and mouthwash, and as a hair treatment and body decoration. Cattle urine assisted in the tanning of leather, and it was used in cheese making or washing. In short, the Nuer derived a whole general store supply of goods and services from this unique source of wealth and sustenance. So important is herding to the Nuer, that Evans-Pritchard was compelled to say they were "always talking about their beasts. I used sometimes to despair that I never discussed anything with the young men but live stock and girls, and even the subject of girls led inevitably to that of cattle. Start on whatever subject I would, and approach it from whatever angle, we would soon be speaking of cows and oxen, heifers and steers, rams and sheep, he-goats and she-goats, calves and lambs and kids." The center of this universe exerts such a strong gravitational pull, the men and women even come to take on the names of their cattle.

Yes, for the Nuer herders, the animals did play an important role in their herding music—but less as a source of skins for drums, and more, as with the Sami, as a subject for their songs. Although the Nuer are not unaware of drumming, for the most part they would prefer to sing to their animals rather than make drums from them. Evans-Pritchard noted that most of the Nuer compose songs about cattle, which can be sung in the pasture to pass the long hours, or at dances and festivities. During the rite of initiation, a man is assigned a name according to the coloring of a ritual bull given to him at that time (the Nuer have numerous words to indicate subtleties in the spot patterns on cattle). In return he is expected to compose songs of praise for the bull. Few cultures boast a love song tradition as rich as that lavished on the cattle of the Nuer by their affectionate owners.

The comparatively modest role of drumming in herding activities may be simply a matter of the animal's (no, *not* the herder's) preference for other sounds. The drum may alarm or upset the herd or flock, while the sound of the flute or human voice exerts a calming influence. As Nils L. Wallin, in his study *Biomusicology,* writes: "The tonal patterns in the high pitch range present acoustic features which have the strongest recognition effect on cattle." Wallin's assertion is made in the context of his study of yodeling, which he believed arose in conjunction with a shift from hunting to herding activities at an early state in human history—a theory I will discuss in greater detail below. But, if true, his view would also help us understand the cultural importance of panpipes and flutes, small stringed instruments, and vocal music (especially falsetto styles such as the yodel) in herding communities in far distant parts of the world.

The tradition of pastoral musicians, thousands of years old, is now disappearing. In 1996, only one surviving member of the Gan people of Burkina Faso in Africa could be found to play the shepherd's side-blown bamboo flute for a recording. This last remaining pastoral flautist died the following year, leaving no one to continue the tradition. In tracking down the herding songs of China, Antoinet Schimmelpenninck found that they were recalled only by the oldest members of the community. During the late nineteenth century and the first half of the twentieth century, Bela Bartók and other collectors found an almost inexhaustible supply of folk music in Hungarian herding communities. But later researchers faced a far different situation. When Balint Sarosi sought a surviving practitioner of the traditional Hungarian "long flute" among the herders of Somogy County, he could find only two old men, both born in the late nineteenth century. His best source, an old swineherd named Vince Nemet, took out of hiding a dozen flutes kept under his straw mattress. But this venerable gentleman, with his old lungs and stiff, tired fingers, refused to play more than a few notes.

But at least one musical tradition of ancient herders has survived in modern times and still finds willing practitioners: the yodel. This sinus-clearing call moves from low tones produced in the chest to higher head tones, often sung in a falsetto voice. Although casual listeners associate this tradition with the cow and goat herders of Switzerland, its history is much older and its geographic spread far wider than most suspect. Violet Alford has traced its presence "from the Alps through Dauphiné and Auvergne, down to the Pyrenees. Along this range it goes, rising and falling in piercing falsetto, reaching its maximum of intensity in Basque country, dropping to something less horrifying across the Spanish frontier, nevertheless shrill enough to make one apprehensive along the Cantabrian coast, to finish mildly among the mild Portuguese." Well, not quite finish: Alford neglects to add that yodel-type calls have been noted among traditional music makers in a range of places outside of Europe, from central Africa to the Solomon Islands. A century and a half ago, Frederick Law Olmstead described the field holler of the Southern slaves as "jodeling," and his observation, far from inviting ridicule, should lead us to ponder the linkages between the African American field holler and the yodel-like musical calls of Africa itself. But in this style of work song, unlike most others, Africa must take a back seat to Europe, where herding communities have been the most prolific and influential yodelers.

Over five hundred years ago, cattle thieves in the Scottish Highlands may have yodeled as a method of communicating with one another. A thousand years before this, Emperor Julian complained about the wild shrieking songs made by the mountain people of the north, and a chronicle from the fourth century AD describes the execution of a missionary, accompanied by the ringing of cowbells, the sounding of the Alpine horn, and yodeling—suggesting that the linkage between herding and the distinctive singing style predates by many centuries the formation of the country now known as Switzerland. In time, the style became best known for calling and soothing cattle—rather than for stealing them or accompanying executions—as well as for signaling across long distances. In Britain, too, yodeling has been widely known for centuries, although there it is often referred to by the less romantic name of "throat-warbling." During the late eighteenth century and the early nineteenth, yodeling became associated with Swiss national culture, and in 1805 a festival featuring yodels, alphorns, and traditional songs was held at Unspunnen near Interlaken. In the ensuing decades, a veritable yodeling renaissance could be witnessed: various singing families from the Alpine region entertained audiences in Europe and abroad with their yodels; wordless yodels were incorporated by innovative composers into instrumental music; yodel clubs were established as an outgrowth of gymnastic clubs, whose members were delighted to sing the praises of the cowherd and the life of the dairy farmer; and even popular song writers overseas, cowboy composers on the range, or city slickers such as John Hill Hewitt, one of the first professional American tunesmiths, were inspired to pen new songs drawing on the venerable yodeling tradition. This style of singing is far from extinct in its native land, although Hugo Zemp—who made field recordings of yodels in the Muota River valley of central Switzerland in 1979—has remarked that "everyone agrees that there is far less yodelling now than in the old days."

James Leary has documented the U.S. yodeling tradition in his authoritative work *Yodeling in Dairyland,* one of the lesser-known classics of fringe ethnomusicology. Leary highlights the evocative yodeling activities of Swiss immigrants in Wisconsin, but other parts of the country were not immune to the attractions of chest-to-head singing. The early cowboy music tradition, in particular, demonstrated a surprising affinity for the yodel. This might seem odd, given the macho image of the American cowboy and the effeminate associations of falsetto singing. Yet the strong linkages between cowboys and herding communities no doubt explains this natural carryover of singing styles from the dairies of the Midwest to the great outdoors of the Wild West.

Despite the grumbles of a few about the "good old days" of yodeling, this singing tradition has no shortage of new adherents. Even today, yodeling competitions are routinely held, and awards are given out to the heartiest contestants. Students of the art can learn from older practitioners, but if no senior throat-warbler is nearby, they can purchase instructional books, cassette tapes, and even videos by mail order. Those impatient to start can immediately access www.yodelcourse.com, where an online tutorial in ten lessons is available around the clock. And, yes, a German-language version was recently established at www.jodelkurs.de so that even the Swiss can learn yodeling without having to step out into the cold Alpine air.

But this quaint singing style may be much more than a stylized national or local cultural tradition, or a pastime for the aficionado of old-time ways; rather, it may hold a key for our enhanced understanding of the development of music in human societies. Nils Wallin has suggested that this vocal technique "developed in biocultural symbiosis with a transition from hunting to breeding of domesticated flock animals, a process of enormous impact on human evolution." He stops just short of claiming that the yodel was "*the* way music became music," but he does argue that a study of its history is of great value in illustrating the "ultimate biological and cultural qualifications for such an evolution." Wallin recognizes that acoustical signals may have existed in some form in hunting cultures during the Lower and Middle Pleistocene age—and we have already seen in the course of this study that hunting societies employ melodic calls that are reminiscent of the yodel. But as the basis of economic life shifted, these sounds took on a new role in keeping together animals that were not yet completely domesticated. Song served as an important tool in creating a "new relationship between man and animal." As Wallin writes: "The distance-field calls in particular, normally developed harmonious, steady-state structures of relatively long duration combined into repetitive patterns, thereby appealing to the animal's mechanisms for long term memory . . . In contrast, the near-field exclamations were probably always accompanied by commanding gestures and other sudden changes in locomotion to be visually perceived by the animals; this conglomerate of near-field stimuli with rapidly varying and bifurcating acoustical and visual features appealed to the short term memory of the animal." Thus the role of sound increased in importance the farther the animal roamed, while visual and tactile means of control became less effective. The emphasis on song also increased as the herd grew more numerous and thus larger areas of land were devoted to pasture.

In time, these calls would also serve other purposes: for example, to train the herd; or to alert and ward away threatening animals as well as competing human societies; in essence serving as territorial markers. Here we are inevitably reminded not only of the territorial songs of birds, but even more of the singing competitions so common in traditional myths and legends, as well as of anthropological accounts, such as those of the famous "songlines" of Australia, in which roads and geographical landmarks are literally sung into being. In such instances, music becomes not only an auditory map demarcating the "lay of the land" but also a way of asserting and staking claims—literally a source of power. In our later study of more developed work songs in modern societies, we shall repeatedly encounter music's almost preternatural ability to organize, to create a locus of power, to forge order out of the social mishmash of conflicting personal rhythms and inclinations. But even here, in the depths of prehistoric time, we see this same force.

We are often inclined to view music as intoxicating, liberating, breaking through the restraining bonds of habit and culture. But its value as a source of control and cohesion is much more ancient and probably far more important in the rise of civilizations. In the herding communities, music exerts its quasi-magical pull on the animal world, but in other settings it imposes a similar order on people, their tasks, and even their surroundings. Long before it became a source of entertainment, song was embraced because, preeminently among all types of sound, it could change and enhance the world, imparting structure where previously confusion reigned. Its ability to exert this force on four-legged creatures was simply the mirror image of its even greater power, one that would gradually be felt within a wider and wider range of human economic and social institutions.

CHAPTER FOUR

Thread and Cloth

Sweet mother, I cannot weave—

Slender Aphrodite has overwhelmed me

With longing for a boy.

—Sappho

The oldest preserved spun fiber, found accidentally in a Lascaux cave, dates from around 15,000 BC. But this fossilized specimen, made from an unidentifiable vegetable source, comes to us from a relatively late period in the long history of twisting fibers into thread. Some ten thousand years earlier, needles became fairly abundant in many communities. Clay shards dating from this period, found in the Czech Republic, also show the clear impression of woven fabric. Around this same time, beads made from bones, shells, and teeth began to feature increasingly tiny holes, through which thread must have passed. These have been found arranged in burial sites in patterns that suggest they were once sewn together. In the words of one scholar, the "String Revolution" had begun.

We can only speculate about the nature of this so-called string. Could the sinews of animals have held these beads in place? Or was it something more akin to modern thread? A surviving bone statue, found at Lespugue in France and dating from around 20,000 BC, plainly represents a woman wearing a skirt of twisted strings—the sculptor took care to engrave the tell-tale windings in the fibers and their fraying at the ends. A new industry had obviously, by this time, emerged—one which, like the control of fire, was marked by its ability to transform and improve other materials.

The growing abundance of woven artifacts from later years—cord, netting, and baskets—testifies to its spread and development.

Were women the main protagonists in this technological leap forward? We cannot ascertain this with any certainty, but a number of factors point in that direction. Certainly women could and did hunt, as well as perform many other tasks traditionally assigned to men. But, as the anthropologist Judith Brown has argued in an influential article, women inevitably gravitated toward work that was compatible with child rearing. Tasks that could be undertaken at or near home were preferred over those requiring lengthy absences. The latter activities—stalking prey or engaging in battle—were relegated mostly to men. A gender-based division of labor was born. At some point, perhaps even at the start of the "String Revolution," women took on the primary responsibility for the production of woven items in most communities. The earliest artistic depictions and historical records support this thesis.

Not only are women shown as the makers of the garments, but they also may have been the chief beneficiaries of this work. Elizabeth Wayland Barber has noted that the earliest string skirts were only worn by females, and suggests that, given the garment's dubious utility in providing warmth or assisting the claims of modesty, they may have served primarily to signal that a woman had reached her child-bearing years. Putting on clothes as a symbolic act? Little has changed today, as readers of *Vogue* and *GQ* can attest. Perhaps, as Remy de Gourmont suggested over a half-century ago, the invention of apparel gave birth to modesty, and not the other way around. But the weaver's craft ultimately brought innumerable practical benefits as well, transforming virtually every aspect of daily life with its end products.

At some early point, perhaps from the very beginning, songs accompanied the work of producing cloth. Among the Ewe, the word *lo* means both "to weave" and "to sing," which indicates a long-associated history between the two activities in Africa. Even today, an attractive metaphor is provided in the concept of weaving a song or spinning a tale, and possibly suggests an intrinsic similarity between making cloth and making music. In any event, the antiquity of these songs is well documented. As we shall see, the first African work song to be widely circulated in the West was a cotton spinning melody improvised by women while they labored, and jotted down by an explorer. Almost three thousand years ago, Homer described Circe singing at the loom, no doubt summoning up an image that even then would have been familiar to his audience. At the very birth of Greek lyric song, among the surviving fragments of Sappho, we find

Sweet mother, I cannot weave—
Slender Aphrodite has overwhelmed me
With longing for a boy.

We can easily imagine these words sung over the loom. A lament from ancient Egypt also makes clear that women sang as they made flax into linen.

Ladies suffer like maidservants,
Singers are at the looms in the weaving rooms,
What they sing to the goddess are dirges.

We have little detailed information on these songs in Europe during antiquity or the early Middle Ages, although St. John Chrysostom (who died in 407 AD) assures us that "women who are weaving, or disentangling the threads on their spindle, often sing: sometimes each of them sings for herself, at other times they all harmonize a melody together." We have a far better basis for knowledge of the songs from the late Middle Ages, when the *chansons de toile* of France—sometimes translated as "spinning songs"—were sung by women while weaving or doing needlework. The topics of these songs usually had only the most remote connection to the task at hand. They would usually begin by introducing a young heroine, noted for her beauty, who might indeed be sitting by a window sewing or pursuing some other domestic task; yet before long the thread and cloth would be forgotten in some amorous adventure. A line from a romance of the early thirteenth century proclaims that "ladies and queens of days gone by were always singing spinning songs as they embroidered," suggesting that even at that early date, this way of whiling away the hours of toil with music was already seen as a venerable practice. These songs have been performed and recorded by modern singers, but since the melodies of the *chansons* have typically not survived, a fair amount of interpretive license has been exercised in such efforts. But the spirit of these songs, their promise of romance and escape, are immediately recognizable to a modern audience.

Some years back, Charles Bertram Lewis attempted to explain the origin of these songs by linking them to traditions associated with the Annunciation. From the fifth century to the thirteenth century, visual representations of the Virgin Mary often showed her weaving when visited by the angel Gabriel. Widely circulated early Christian writings excluded from the Bible—known as the apocryphal Gospels; for example, the *Protevangelium of James* and the *Pseudo-Matthew*—added to the credibility of this tradition. And certainly a number of characteristics of the *chansons de toile*—the feminine viewpoint of the stories, the humble attitude of the unmarried female protagonist, the physical separation of the woman from her beloved—remind us of some aspects of the Christian story. But the theory collapses when we consider the ancient and widespread traditions of weaving songs from various non-Christian cultures and settings that also have thematic content similar to the *chansons de toile.*

Indeed, the religious sensibility of the singer seems to have little influence on these songs, which invariably deal with courtship, romance, and marriage, and more often reflect a profane rather than religious perspective. In discussing the work songs of the Assam region of India, Hem Barua notes that "proficiency in weaving was considered an asset for marriage. This has given rise to a number of songs. These songs are not concerned with the actual process of weaving. Their motif is mostly love." As an example, Barua offers the following:

> I sit at my loom,
> But my eyes are there in the street;
> And the shuttle drops,
> And drops.

Ruth Rubin, in her study of Yiddish folk songs, *Voices of a People,* notes that "many love songs and ballads were created by women as they sewed the garments for the rich. . . . Following the 1880s, when women entered industry in increasing numbers, these working girls poured out their heart in plaintive songs which described their hard, colorless, often celibate lives. No rosy future awaited them, and they saw for themselves only a long life of sewing and stitching, stitching and sewing, unloved alone until the 'grey hair sprouted.' Only a prince charming in a dream could take them out of their misery." Rubin provides an example of one of these sewing songs, which she translates as follows:

Day and night and night and day,
And stitching, stitching, stitching!
Help me, dear God, may my handsome one come along.
And take me away from this toil.

In Galicia in 1952, Alan Lomax found women who still made linen by hand while singing. A woman named Evangelina Carballo prepared her flax by beating it to pulp against a stone block with a piece of firewood. All the while, she sang

The root of the green yew
Is very hard to pull up,
And first loves
Are very hard to forget.

In Balkan culture, as Patricia Shehan writes, domestic work parties called *sedankas* have continued to play an important role in community life. As the women and young girls engage in spinning, weaving, and other tasks, they sing "unaccompanied songs referring to the village boys and men, with mention of some as potential husbands who will later determine a young woman's future economic and social situation."

Many of the love lyrics in *The Book of Songs* from ancient China incorporate images of textiles and fiber plants, and it is not hard to imagine them sung during the process of weaving and doing needlework. At the birth of Western lyrics, we see the same images in the surviving fragments of Sappho and Erinna. The antiquity of much of this music is not surprising. Indeed, long before a robust and evocative *male* perspective on love emerges in song form—from the mouths of troubadours in the twelfth and thirteenth centuries—women had already long refined this form of self-expression, a process no doubt assisted by the sedentary domestic pursuits that provided an inviting context—away from the inquisitive ears of husbands and fathers, brothers and kinsmen—for these narrative and lyrical pieces.

The themes of love and romance also play a prominent role in the waulking songs of Scotland, which comprise a special category of songs employed in cloth making. After being removed from the loom, tartan cloth needs to be shrunk before it can be used. This process, known as waulking, is traditionally accompanied by song. Margaret Fay Shaw, who documented numerous waulking songs in the Hebrides, describes the process: "The ends of a length of newly woven cloth are sewn together to make it a circle, and the cloth is then placed on a long trestle table and soaked with hot urine. An even number of women sit at the table, say twelve with six a side, and the cloth is passed around sunwise, to the left, with a kneading motion. They reach to the right and clutch the cloth, draw in, pass to the left, push out and free the hands to grasp again to the right. One, two, three, four, slowly the rhythm emerges." One woman will lead the singing, which usually relates a tale, with the others joining in during the chorus, called the *fonn* or ground. "The choruses of waulking songs are usually meaningless, consisting of syllables that carry the air; but they have a mnemonic significance, and must always be sung correctly." Shaw's collection includes thirty-two waulking songs gathered from the region of South Uist. At the time of her volume's publication in 1955, however, she estimated that as many as two hundred songs were still extant in the region, although in other parts of Scotland the tradition was all but extinct. Many of the waulking songs appear to be quite old, and from linguistic clues can be dated back some four hundred years.

Occasionally the waulking songs address directly the task at hand, as in the following example collected and translated from Gaelic by Shaw. Each line of the verse, sung by the soloist, is followed by the chorus "Waulk, o hó, the cloth of the lads" repeated three times, the first line of which is usually sung alone by the soloist, with others joining in on the repetitions.

> From hand to hand, the cloth of the lads.
> Let me waulk quickly, the cloth of the lads,
> Let me waulk with joy, the cloth of the lads,
> Sing with love, the cloth of the lads,
> Put into a roll, the cloth of the lads.

More often, however, the waulking songs waste little time talking of tartan cloth, and concentrate again on issues of love, with a primary focus on heartbreak and the absence of the beloved. "Wet is the night and cold," runs another song: "It is not the care of the cattlefield, nor care of herding cows with calves that weighs upon me, but anxiety about you, Roderick, my love." Or another example: "Heavy is my step, I am not joyful. Heavy is the burden which I bear. The burden I bear is a broken heart."

Here, as with other work songs, we need to avoid the temptation to dismiss this music as merely functional or as deprived of value once separated from the accompanying task. True, these songs served a purpose, sometimes even a banal purpose, but this did not prevent them from achieving a level of emotional depth, even artistry. From time to time, a measure of this beauty has survived, even when the music itself has not. Jean-Jacques Rousseau has left us one such moving testimony. Toward the end of his life, he recalled with intense feelings the songs his Aunt Susan sang while embroidering so many decades before. This scholar of cultivated taste and deep understanding of the performing arts (recall that Rousseau achieved some renown as a composer and worked for many years as a music teacher and copyist) was not ashamed to attribute his love of song to these early experiences, paying homage to them for a "charm that I cannot express." He adds: "It may seem incredible but, old dotard that I am, eaten up with cares and infirmities, I still find myself weeping like a child as I hum her airs in my broken, tremulous voice." Such is the power of this music, excluded from performance halls and rarely preserved for posterity. Indeed, even during his own day, Rousseau despaired of tracking down the words of these ephemeral melodies; yet although only half remembered, the music's emotional force remained strong and undiluted for him.

During the several decades following Rousseau's heartfelt recollection many others apparently came to share his sentiments, realizing that the songs of work could serve as inspiration for high art. Goethe's composition of Gretchen's monologue at the spinning wheel from *Faust,* later set to music by Schubert and others, is perhaps the most celebrated example. Around this same time Baron van Swieten, charged with the task of creating the text for Haydn's *The Seasons* found a measure of inspiration in Gottfried August Bürger's poem "The Spinning Song." In time, Wagner, Mendelssohn, and others would follow suit. But the most interesting musical example from this period comes from the unlikely source of Mungo Park, an adventurer who traveled extensively in Africa toward the close of the eighteenth century. Park had taken note how African women spinning cotton "lightened their labor by songs," and was so moved by one such piece that he brought it back with him to England. This melody, the oldest African work song to gain notoriety in the West, was deemed so captivating by its hearers that it inspired several other artistic efforts, including poems by James Montgomery and Georgiana, Duchess of Devonshire (the daughter of the Earl of Spencer), as well as a musical arrangement by G. G. Ferrari. Was this the birth of "world music" as a cultural phenomenon? Other scholars will need to decide such matters, but it was clear that a recognition of the value of work songs was beginning to be felt by those far distant from their sources of inspiration. We studied a similar phenomenon in the first chapter, exploring the growing fascination with hunting horn ensembles and their incorporation into highbrow cultural and elite social circles during this same period. We can only surmise that as the arts became more rarefied, the vitality of these vernacular forms must have been all the more prized.

As the example from Mungo Park suggests, the traditions of Africa and the African diaspora were especially prominent in spinning and weaving songs, as in so many other types of work songs. Numerous examples have been documented in the Americas, such as this one collected by Dorothy Scarborough, which was sung by women while hand spinning at home.

Spin, ladies, spin all day,
Spin, ladies, spin all day.
Sheep shell corn,
Rain rattles up a horn,
Spin, ladies, spin all day,
Spin, ladies, spin all day,
Spin, ladies, spin all day.

Mildred Carter, born in Virginia in 1856, described the weaving songs of her mother's generation in an interview with a researcher in the late 1930s. "Mother said dey would always spin in pairs—one would treadle whilst de other would wind the ball. You got to wind it fast, too, an' take de thread right off the spindle, else it git tangled up. An' mamma told me dey would all pat dey feet an' sing

Wind de ball, wind de ball,
Wind de ball, lady, wind de ball,
Don't care how you wind de ball,
Wind de ball, lady, wind de ball,
Ding, ding, ding,—wind de ball,
Wind de ball, lady, wind de ball.

Although these songs were typically sung by female workers, examples performed by men have also been documented. Michael Harner found a parallel tradition among the Jívaro of South America, where spinning, dyeing, and weaving are handled exclusively by men. Like their female counterparts in other cultures, these manual laborers maintained a rich singing tradition, and used their music to boast of their superiority over the women at these tasks. Harner provides the following translation of one of their songs:

> For me it is very easy
> To spin yarn,
> For I am a man-spider.
> Therefore I am adept.
> My hand is like the hand
> Of a spider.
> Because of this
> I make the spindle hum.

But such examples are rare exceptions. And even after the industrialization of the textile industry, women continued to serve as the major source of labor in making both the cloth and the songs that accompanied its creation.

Until the middle of the eighteenth century, this work often took place entirely at home. After the sheep were sheared, the fleece was cleaned and then carded. The latter step involved untangling and straightening short fibers from the mass with the use of a hand-card, a simple process that could often be done by children. If vegetable fibers were used, such as flax, they would be removed from the stalk and made ready for spinning. The spinning wheel, operated by a single person, twisted the fibers into yarn. The hand loom, an ancient device which served its purpose admirably for thousand of years, interlaced sets of threads at right angles to one another—the warp and the weft—making them into cloth. The process was cumbersome, but well within the capability of a typical family to undertake at home.

All of this would change dramatically during the closing decades of the eighteenth century. In 1764, James Hargreaves constructed the first "spinning jenny," which allowed a single operator to spin eight threads at once, and represented a major improvement in productivity. Hargreaves, who was illiterate, failed to file a patent, and soon others were imitating and improving on his design. By the time of his death fourteen years later, over twenty thousand spinning jenny machines were in use throughout

Britain. Richard Arkwright's spinning frame was an even more powerful tool, allowing sturdier yarn to be spun, but the machine was too large to be operated by hand. An attempt was made to use horses to propel the mechanism, but finally a water wheel proved even more practical. The first factory using this new technology, which became known as the water frame, was established in Cromford, Derbyshire, in 1771. Arkwright rapidly expanded his business, building new factories and hiring a large number of workers, many of them children, who labored from six in the morning until seven at night. He continued to experiment and improve his process, and in 1775 he took out a patent for a new carding engine. Eight years later, Arkwright became one of the first businessmen to adopt the newly invented steam engine for industrial use, incorporating it into his factories.

This rapid improvement in the manufacture of yarn inevitably required other inventions to support it, as pressure for increased output moved up and down the supply chain. British imports of cotton grew from a modest 1,000 tons in 1760 to 220,000 tons in 1850. Pressures were also felt overseas in America, as the need to supply the British factories with cotton led to a rapid increase in exports, and thus put the onus on cultivators to increase their efficiency and output. The need of plantation owners for slave labor grew proportionately. It is not going too far to suggest that industrialization, which often reduces the demand for labor, had the paradoxical effect in this instance of heightening its importance in many sectors of the economy. But this, in turn, furthered the demand for even more automation, as industrialists attempted to wring additional efficiencies from their growing operations. Eli Whitney's invention of the cotton gin in 1793 marked a further response to the push for industrialization overseas. This machine, which separates the seed and hulls from the cotton fibers, could do work that previously required fifty manual laborers. And, as thread output increased, the old hand looms no longer had sufficient capacity to process it into cloth. Many aspiring entrepreneurs tackled the challenging task of automating the process of weaving. By the early years of the nineteenth century, fairly reliable power looms had been developed and were being established throughout England.

Soon William Blake would denounce the "dark Satanic mills" of England—lines first published as part of his 1804 epic "Milton." Yet by then the zeal for automation had taken a life of its own and it would be impossible to get the genie of the spinning jenny back in the bottle. The literally homespun method of making cloth was irreversibly changing itself into an almost fully automated, large-scale industry, with each step in the production process now relentlessly echoing the rhythm of machines. It had taken less than forty years for this major economic transformation to happen.

Yet, the cultural influences spurred by these changes would be felt only gradually. The first impact of the spinning jenny and water frame was to increase the need for home-based hand loom operators. Small farmers turned to the weaving trade in hopes of raising their standard of living, and tumbledown barns, attics, and homes were converted into work areas. By 1800, Britain contained a staggering 250,000 hand looms, which employed a significant portion of the country's labor force—but still this work took place primarily at home, on the farm, or in other traditional environments. In *Silas Marner*, set during this period, George Eliot castigates the "questionable sound" and "half-fearful fascination" of the old loom, as compared with the "natural cheerful trotting of the winnowing machine, or the simpler rhythm of the flail." Yet the rhythm of the household hand loom, as operated by Silas Marner and so many others, would now itself be superseded as more automated technologies made it redundant. The following song, drawn from a broadside of the period, crystallizes the tensions of this transition in a love story between a traditional hand loom operator and a woman working at the newer power loom factories.

> I am a hand-weaver to my trade.
> I fell in love with a factory maid.
> And if I could but her favor win,
> I'd stand beside her and weave by steam.

The song closes:

> Where are the girls? I'll tell you plain.
> The girls have gone to weave by steam,
> And if you'd find 'em, you must rise at dawn,
> And trudge to the factory in the early morn.

Here the love story angle so typical of the genre remains, but everything else has changed, radically modified by the tremendous changes in the economic and social conditions underlying the production of cloth.

Hand loom operators saw the impact of this shift in lower prices for their output, and as power looms proliferated, the value of manual weaving continued to decline. Soon, operating a hand loom was no longer a pathway to prosperity but rather associated with dire poverty. This shift was reflected in songs such as "The Poor Cotton Weaver" (sometimes called "The Hand-loom Weaver"), which begins

> I'm a poor cotton weaver as many one knows.
> I've nowt to eat i' th' house an' I've wore out my cloas.
> You'd hardly give sixpence for all I have on.
> My clugs they are brossen an' stockins I've none.

This song was not published until around 1860, but by that time it had probably circulated for a half century. Sometime after 1820, "The Hand-Loom Weaver's Lament" also became well-known among English workers, clearly demarcating in its lyrics the sharp conflict between the masters, addressed as the "tyrants of England," and laborers.

> When we look on our poor children
> It grieves our hearts full sore,
> The clothing it is worn to rags
> And we can get no more.
> With little in their bellies
> As they to work must go,
> While yours do dress as monkeys,
> Monkeys in the show.

Songs had always played an important role in the work day of British spinners and weavers, but previously the music had rarely shown such levels of despair and anger. When Henry VIII visited a spinning operation run by a clothier, he had been delighted to hear the young women singing like nightingales at their work. Even with the arrival of the power loom, songs continued in the noisy factories, with workers, especially the women laborers, diverting themselves with hymns and ballads during their long hours of toil. Yet songs of protest and complaint increasingly found their way into these industrial settings, such as the following refrain, which could be sung out of the earshot of the masters:

> Poverty, poverty knock!
> Me loom is a-sayin' all day.

Poverty, poverty knock!
Gaffer's too skinny to pay.
Poverty, poverty knock!
Keepin' one eye on the clock.
Ah know I can guttle [eat]
When ah hear me shuttle
Go: poverty, poverty knock!

A similar process of industrialization transformed the production of cloth from vegetable fibers such as flax and hemp, altering both the type of labor and the music involved in its creation. In traditional communities, these practices were almost always accompanied by song, as seen above in the example found by Alan Lomax in Galicia. The Croatian song "Pukala Sam Lenek" is another striking example, describing the manual production of linen from flax—the title is translated "I cut the flax," and the refrain means "Oh linen, beautiful linen." Unlike so many other spinning songs that are preoccupied with romance and courtship, "Pukala Sam Lenek" describes the process at hand: "I spin the flax, I sew the flax, I don the linen." The traditional textile workers of Okinawa also found work songs invaluable in the production of cloth from hemp. These melodies mitigated in some measure the toil involved in the labor-intensive process of producing *yaeyama jofu*, a fine woven cloth that requires lengthy drying in the sun and bleaching in the sea. In the 1970s, efforts by preservationists on the island focused on reviving traditional crafts, and more than twenty songs used in the production of *yaeyama jofu* have come down to us. But this emphasis on the protection and celebration of time-honored practices—both the manufacturing processes and the songs that accompanied them—is a rare exception. For the most part, industrialization swept away all vestiges of the culture of craftsmanship and hand labor.

A study of the Irish linen industry also makes clear the disruptive changes brought about by the introduction of new production methods, and how these methods transformed the role played by music in the daily life of the workers. Until the eighteenth century, the production of Irish linen took place primarily in domestic settings, especially on farms where flax was grown. Here wives and daughters, with some assistance perhaps from servants, would spin the flax into yarn. The yarn would then be transformed into cloth using hand looms, often operated by men when they were not busy with cultivation. The cloth was then bleached at home.

Much of the output was also used at home, but excess amounts could be sold. This process would change dramatically after the introduction into Ireland, starting in the 1780s, of modern methods of cotton production. Efficiently produced cotton now began displacing linen in the market-place, and only with the adoption of automation and modern work practices could linen cloth recover its lost market share. At the close of the 1820s, the introduction of wet spinning technology and the adoption of steam power in the production of linen yarn proved to be major catalysts in signaling the inevitable decline of hand labor in the industry. Around 1850, the introduction of power looms hastened this irreversible shift.

But for a time, singing continued to play a major role in the production of linen, especially among the female workforce, despite the noise of machinery and the dehumanized setting of the factory. In fact, songs may have grown even more important in the face of these social and economic changes, as women who had been raised on farms and had migrated to cities sought to hold onto reminders of more traditional ways of life. "You stood all day at your work and sung them songs," explained a female mill worker to folklorist Betty Messenger. "You'd a heard you with the frames on, singin' then. We had no pay hardly, but we were happy." Here, as in many other industrial settings, men were less inclined to join in the music making. "You never got the boys singin'" remarked a male mill worker. "They used to play more pranks than anything else." Yet even this unwilling vocalist provided a song to Messenger, an interesting lyric that testifies to the strict manner in which workers were managed:

Tilly is our doffing mistress,
She is very cross,
And if you break a spindle,
She will tell the boss.
And when you get your wages
You'll find they will be short,
For they fine you on a shilling,
For the spindle you have lost.

Despite the efforts of British industrialists to prevent textile equipment and expertise from spreading to other countries, comparable operations inevitably sprang up overseas. In 1790, Samuel Slater, an English immigrant, established the first modern cotton spinning mill in the United

States in Pawtucket, Rhode Island. However, this approach to manufacture, which became known as the Rhode Island system, still relied on independent loom operators, who converted the yarn into cloth, often at their home. By 1815, a fully integrated textile factory had been established in Waltham, Massachusetts, by Francis Cabot Lowell, who had observed power looms in Britain and was determined to bring the technology to the United States. Now a single facility could handle the entire process of converting raw cotton into cloth. Yet this advance in the means of production brought few tangible gains to workers. When Lowell's employees went on strike in 1836, fifteen hundred women workers paraded through the streets singing:

> Oh! Isn't it a pity that such a pretty girl as I
> Should be sent to the factory to pine away and die?
> Oh, I cannot be a slave; I will not be a slave.
> For I'm so fond of liberty
> That I cannot be a slave.

Another song from Lowell's workers includes the following verses:

> Come all ye weary factory girls,
> I'll have you understand,
> I'm going to leave the factory
> And return to my native land . . .
> No more I'll get my overseer
> To come and fix my loom,
> No more I'll say to my overseer
> Can't I stay out 'til noon?
> Then since they've cut my wages down
> To nine shillings per week,
> If I cannot better wages make,
> Some other place I'll seek.

By 1890, garment manufacturing employed close to four hundred thousand women in the United States—a considerable number given that fewer than five million American women held paying jobs at the time. But the prominence of female workers had little to do with progressive notions held by mill owners. The bottom line was a far more powerful motivator. At the time, a typical woman's wage was 54 percent below the average earned by men. In the mills, spinning jobs were held almost exclusively by women, with men and women sharing the weaving operations. In contrast, lifting and loading and other heavy labor were the undisputed domain of the male workforce.

As this production process became increasingly organized and specialized, song continued to play an important role in the lives of laborers, but less often as an accompaniment for work. Mill workers would often play the guitar or banjo during breaks from their labor—which could be frequent in rural mills that relied on the water power of streams and rivers to keep the machines in motion. "We run by water then," worker Ethel Faucette recalled to an interviewer, "and when the water'd get low they'd stop off for an hour or two." During the break, according to Faucette, a "gang of boys would get their instruments and get out there in front of the mill, and they would sing and pick the guitar and the banjo, and different kinds of string music. Get out in front of the mill under two big trees, get out there in the shade and sing. And maybe they'd stand an hour or two and the water'd gain up, and they'd start back up." Although an interesting note to the history of mill work, these moments of musical recreation were so rare that it would be difficult to call them a tradition. They are perhaps best understood as signs of the declining role of musical performance in industrial settings—singing first pushed outside the factory doors, and later lost completely.

Indeed, the textile industry would become best known not for recreational music but as a breeding ground for songs of protest and complaint. In the United States, the textile trade served as a significant source of material for John Greenway's *American Folksongs of Protest,* in which the author notes that only miners have produced more songs of social and economic unrest. In the Gastonia, North Carolina, strike of 1929, for example, the songs of striker Ella May Wiggins played a critical role in organizing worker resistance; and, in the aftermath of the Marion strike of the same year, ballads commemorated the deaths of six men who were shot by deputies during a walkout. Wiggins was also a victim of violence —in September 1929 she was killed by a stray bullet during a confrontation with anti-union demonstrators in Gastonia. Her most famous song is "Mill Mother's Lament," which begins

> We leave our homes in the morning,
> We kiss our children goodbye

While we slave for the bosses
Our children scream and cry.
And when we draw our money
Our grocery bills to pay,
Not a cent to spend for clothing,
Not a cent to lay away. . . .
How it grieves the heart of a mother
You everyone must know,
But we cannot buy for our children
Our wages are too low.

In some instances, this music found its way into recording studios and then onto the airwaves. The year following the Gastonia and Marion strikes a recording of "Cotton Mill Colic," written by Gaston County native Dave McCarn in 1926, was released, and the song was soon taken up by striking Piedmont mill workers as part of their protest against working conditions. McCarn had worked from an early age in the textile industry, but he also chose to pursue a part time career in a string band. In 1926 these two areas came together in his composition of "Cotton Mill Colic":

When you go to work you work like the devil,
At the end of the week you're not on the level.
Payday comes, you pay your rent,
When you get through you've not got a cent
To buy fat-back meat, pinto beans,
Now and then you get turnip greens.

At one point the song caught the attention of Alan Lomax, and it subsequently appeared in a number of compilations of folk music. "Cotton Mill Colic" eventually entered the repertoires of countless folk singers, and was recorded by Pete Seeger and Mike Seeger, as well as Lester Pete Bivins and the Blue Sky Boys, among others. But these later successes did little for the career of the song's composer. McCarn eventually returned to the very millwork he had complained about with such bitter words.

This example serves as a telling indicator of things to come. The final stage in the evolution of the songs of the textile industry found these "dark Satanic mills" playing a meaningful, if often unappreciated, role as a source of supply and demand for the nascent recording business, as the latter attempted to package and market country and western along with other traditional music styles for regional markets in the South. Like McCarn, a number of mill workers attempted to join the ranks of southern musicians who were signed by record companies such as Columbia, Okeh, Paramount, and Victor during the 1920s and 1930s. Others found opportunities in radio, as southern broadcasters looked to feature local guitarists, fiddlers, singers, and other musicians. In the early 1930s, for example, more than one hundred musicians from the Carolinas performed on Charlotte's WBT station. Yet the same recording and radio industries that provided opportunities for a few textile workers to reach broader audiences as musicians also contributed to the decline of singing traditions in mill towns. For example, workers in Gastonia petitioned management in 1930 for permission to begin work a quarter hour earlier, so that they could get home in time to listen to the radio program *Amos and Andy*, which started at 6 PM. From now on, music and entertainment would increasingly be driven by the decisions of network executives rather than by members of the local community.

As we will see again and again in the course of this study, the spread of new technologies involved in the dissemination of music—by radio, phonograph, Muzak, and so on—during the years between World War I and World War II happened almost simultaneously with the decline in singing by workers. It was almost as if workers were unwilling to give up their musical traditions until some adequate substitutes were provided. Even today, we can almost imagine that if all of these technologies were to disappear tomorrow, a brief silence would pass. But then one especially brave or bored worker would begin a song. Then another worker would pick up the melody, and still another, until the sounds of music again reverberated in the halls of industry.

The rise of a vibrant country-and-western recording industry in the South provided the most alluring of these substitutes. It came, in time, to serve as nothing less than an alternative voice for the southern workers who kept the textile mills and other factories running. It was a voice, however, that sapped the workers' own voices of vitality and relevance, both in music making and in social protest. In 1925, live Saturday-night broadcasts from the stage of the Grand Ole Opry in Nashville began introducing the rising stars of southern music to a wider audience. Two years later, Victor Records signed Jimmy Rodgers and the Carter Family to contracts on the same day, a signal event in the process of "star formation" that would sharply delineate the population into two groups: those (few) who sang, and the many who merely listened. In the years leading up to World War II, the market would be finely segmented into subgenres —Western swing, cowboy songs, bluegrass, and so on—each with its target audience and economic base. Work songs, so significant in traditional societies, were not a marketing category recognized by the recording industry, and as such were marginalized along with the other indigenous music-making activities of the laboring class. In effect, the new genres promoted by the record companies became the new work songs, and gained acceptance as symbolic musical expressions of the sentiments of the modern industrial worker. Spinning songs were no longer necessary, since spinning records now filled the void.

These alternatives to individual and community singing would do more to eradicate musical performance from the life of textile workers in the South than any purely mechanical innovation or adversarial response from the owners of capital assets. And similar shifts were taking place in other industrial settings throughout the United States and overseas. The musical life of workers would be, from now on, a passive one driven by the consumption of products created and disseminated for the purposes of realizing profits.

Only in communities—invariably in the Third World—where the entertainment industry had not yet become a dominant social force would the active practice of song be retained in the lives of textile workers. And even in these traditional societies, the forces of modernization in music were at work. For example, a song for twisting the thread and threading the needle from Vietnam, "Xe chi luon kim," has been arranged and modernized, and made suitable for airplay as popular music. Here we see a syndrome that I will examine in more detail later in this volume— namely that work-related songs, in order to survive in the modern age, need to find a path of rapprochement with the forces of popular music. Only in the rarest situation do we see this process handled with dignity and care—as, for example, in Carla Sciaky's recording *Spin the Weaver's Song*, where traditional songs associated with spinning and weaving have been meticulously researched and lovingly performed. Far more typical is Dolly Parton belting out *Nine to Five* as a workers' anthem; while anyone looking for the modern equivalent of a waulking song or *chansons de toile* may encounter groups named the Spinners or the Weavers, and songs called "Spinning Wheels" or "Silver Threads and Golden

Needles" or "Dream Weaver," but their link to cloth making goes no further than the name. As we shall see, the modern pop songwriter can deal with such workaday concerns only to deride them or, at times, to use them as a metaphor from some other, more overtly commercial, subject. Although the music industry and the world of day-to-day work have a dialogue of sorts even today, it is a negotiation in which the more monolithic force predominates.

CHAPTER FIVE

The New Rhythms of Work

I ring at 6 to let men know when to and from

theair worke to go. —Inscription on a bell

from Coventry (1675)

The pulse of labor originally mimicked the rhythms of nature. The largest increments of time, for the worker, were annual or seasonal; the smallest and most basic unit of human labor was the day, bracketed by the diurnal course of the sun. This framework is reflected even today in business and organizational terminology such as journeyman, journal, diary, per diem, adjourn—all of which have etymologies linked to words for "day."

Even without clocks and chimes, societies needed to measure their work against the passage of time, but methods of doing this were imprecise by modern standards. This function was often filled by music— or, at a minimum, musical tones. Sulaiman al-Tajir, an Arab traveler to China in the ninth century, described the highly organized use of music to tell time: "Each city has four gates, at each of which there are five trumpets, which are sounded by the Chinese at certain hours of the day and night. There are also in each city ten drums, which they beat at the same time . . . to give knowledge of the hours of the day and night." In other instances, a single singer might fill this function. Many examples of the "Alba" or dawn song can be found in European traditional music, and equivalents are seen in other regions, for example in the Confucian classic *The Book of Songs*. In rare situations, these traditions survived well into modern times. As late as 1940, researchers from the Federal Writers' Project found recollections of the Alba, brought to the American Southwest by early missionaries. "The Alba hymn was the song of dawn. In each little settlement the *resador* arose at dawn, and walked around the placita singing the Alba. That was a call for everyone to arise, day was coming. Anyone—unless sick—that was found in bed after the Alba had been sung was considered lazy and a disgrace to the village."

In other cases, natural surrogates for the clock were sought. The passage of time might be measured by changes in the appearance of plants and flowers, in the level of water, in the sound of animals, or in the movement of shadows and sunlight. The ingenuity of tribal timekeepers was sometimes remarkable. The San of South Africa could even use a banana as a clock—the hunters would bring an unripe banana with them on their trip, and the time to return home would be signaled when the fruit became ripe. Other tribes could reportedly tell by the fragrance of the surrounding vegetation that the time to begin or conclude an activity had come.

But the rough measurements of solar and lunar time, whether marked by songs or smells or even ripening bananas, would eventually be seen as insufficiently accurate for the needs of more organized types of labor. As such, the pace of work would evolve in tandem with changes in technology. "Time and the calendar were just about the only aspect of medieval science that moved ahead in this period," writes David Landes in *Revolution in Time*, his study of clocks and timekeeping during the Middle Ages. "In every other domain, these centuries saw a drastic regression from the knowledge of the ancients." Time itself would now be put under the yoke and made to serve the needs of economic progress. Yet Landes ascribes this to changes in religious organization, rather than to the evolution of the means of production. The Rule of St. Benedict was especially influential, guiding the monk through a rigorous schedule of daily devotion, which needed to be followed with hitherto unknown precision. Landes explains: "For hundreds of years there were no rules, only practices," but now regulation became inextricably linked to religious life. Timekeeping was so integral to this approach that monks now even spoke of "reciting the hours," the measurement of time becoming almost synonymous with the ritual itself.

In this environment, the relationship between song and work was often debated. Was it proper for a monk to sing, for instance, while engaged in manual work, or should their chants be reserved for specific times of worship? For St. Basil, prayer and psalmody were suitable at every hour so "that while one's hands are busy with their tasks we may praise God sometimes with our tongue, or if not, with the heart." But Pope Gregory disagreed, seeing that "rest from exterior motion" was an essential part of the monk's pursuit of the contemplative life. But though the views of local abbots and bishops may have differed on the degree of control required, the new regimentation of religious life would eventually be accepted by all to some degree. Previously aspiring saints merely needed to do things "by the book"; now they were expected to do them "by the clock" as well.

Or by the bells, to be more specific. The importance of following the dictates of their tones is commemorated by youngsters even today when they sing of "Frere Jacques," who scandalously continued to sleep while morning bells were ringing. But over and above their spiritual importance, the bells were also temporal, in the most basic sense of the word. Inevitably this sensibility of measuring the hours infiltrated the broader currents of economic life, transforming the pulse of labor outside the monastery walls. For centuries, both religious institutions and secular labor would be guided by the same musical source, no one needing to ask for whom the bells tolled, for they now rang for saints and sinners alike. As such, bells and belfries began showing up in locations where few monks ventured to go. In 1324, for example, the abbot of Saint-Pierre authorizes the fullers of Ghent to install a bell in a newly established workhouse. In 1335 the aldermen of Amiens decide that a new bell should be set up to regulate the cloth trade. In Artois in 1355, the royal governor approves the construction of a belfry to assist the textile trade, by signaling working hours and the times for commercial transactions. "This was the beginning of the organization of work," writes the historian Jacques Le Goff, "a distant precursor of Taylorism." Sometimes the overarching economic purpose was even etched into the bell's surface. The inscription, dated 1675, on a bell at Coventry reads: "I ring at 6 to let men know when to and from theair worke to go."

The bells would never lose their spiritual significance but now this role would pale beside their importance as tools of social control and organization. Then as now, if you wished to understand a society's priorities, you merely need travel into its largest cities and look for the biggest buildings and the loudest sounds. Today, perhaps the Mall of America and football stadiums define our preferences and lifestyle choices, but for a thousand years European culture, lacking such boons, stretched out in concentric circles around its bells and the immense structures that housed them. These titans of sound came to figure so prominently in civic life that they were given names—historian Johan Huizinga tells us of "Big Jacqueline" or the "Bell Roland." Sometimes they were even assigned personalities: "Whoever cares to peer into the records of that era of naïve credulity which we call the Middle Ages," writes John Frederick Rowbotham, "shall find the superstitions which were connected with the drum re-appearing in connection with the bell. He shall read of bells being thought to speak, of bells thought to be alive, of bells dressed, and arrayed with ornaments." For centuries, the ringing of the bells—sometimes "hideous to hear" in the words of one chronicler—surpassed all other sounds, much as the church itself towered over all other structures. Bells were rung not only at set hours, but also to signal special events. When a peace was concluded or a new pope elected, the bells of churches and monasteries might ring all day long and even into the night. These traditions persisted well into the modern era, at least in some communities. Writing in 1772, Charles Burney remonstrates that the people of Bavaria were "three hundred years behind the rest of Europe," offering as evidence the fact that "nothing can cure them of the folly of ringing the bells whenever it thunders." Given this prominence, the bell could not help but become a symbol of the society and worldview whose sonic life it dominated. "Wherever the missionaries took Christianity," writes R. Murray Schafer, "the church bell was soon to follow, acoustically demarking the civilization of the parish from the wilderness beyond its earshot."

Time may seem to be value neutral, favoring neither one class nor another. But in practice the precise measurement of its rhythms, the tabulation of its ebbs and flows, inevitably becomes a support of the individuals in power. How else to explain that on the first day of fighting in Paris during the French Revolution various groups in different sectors of the city each decided to destroy the church clocks, without any prior plan or communication on that account? The revolutionaries realized, either explicitly or intuitively, that the chiming bells were complicit in their oppression. Alain Corbin, in his study of French village life during the nineteenth century, offers the surprising conclusion that "the majority" of local conflicts, tensions, and rivalries "seem, at least during certain periods, to have hinged on conflicts over access to bell towers and the use of bells." This hostility toward timekeeping devices has lasted until recent times, again sometimes taking the form of a spontaneous outburst of social protest. When the nation of Brazil prepared to celebrate the five hundredth anniversary of the arrival of the first Portuguese explorers, the leading broadcasting network, TV Globo, set up numerous "countdown clocks" in various parts of the country—only to find them subjected to assaults and sometimes even destroyed, by a loosely organized group of homeless workers. Many denounced the attacks as senseless, but to laborers whose every movement at work is regulated by the hour and the minute, the choice of these particular targets seemed all too obvious.

Such assaults can only be symbolic gestures. Long before the storming of the Bastille, the clock had become an indispensable tool to the ruling class. "God confound the man who first found out how to distinguish hours," writes an ancient Roman author. "Confound him, too, who set up a sundial, to cut and hack my days so wretchedly into small pieces!" And though time-keeping technologies might change, the nature of work might change, even the ruling class might change, still this mechanism of control and coercion would be far too valuable for any new master to renounce.

By the time of the French Revolution, of course, the sundial and the ticking of the clock had been supplemented by many other new rhythms of labor—a panoply of distinctive pulsations that imparted their character to the work environment. The fundamental tempo of work, once demarcated and paced by song, would now be established by the much different sound of machines in motion. The invention of the weaving loom in 1733 and the spinning jenny in 1767 paved the way for the establishment of the first advanced textile factory in the world, built at Cromford Mill in England in 1771. Both capitalists and consumers benefited from the change—the price of textiles in Britain fell 90 percent and the volume produced increased 150-fold, all in a fifty-year span. But as we have seen, the textile worker's lot changed mostly for the worse. The laborer would become one more raw material consumed, used up, and discarded when no longer of use. Not only were working conditions far more dehumanized, far more separated from the organic rhythms that had previously dominated the common life of the laborer, but some commentators have gone so far as to link the growing mechanization of labor with a concomitant strengthening of the institution of slavery. As

Peter Drucker writes: "Considered to be practically dead by the founders of the American Republic, slavery roared back to life as the cotton gin—soon steam-driven—created a huge demand for low-cost labor and made breeding slaves America's most profitable industry for several decades."

The introduction of steam power to textile production was a landmark achievement of the Industrial Revolution, but other less visible changes were also taking place, altering the pace and flow of working lives. "Singing and steam are irreconcilable," wrote William Alden in 1882—and as industry after industry fell under the sway of cheap energy, using it to replace workers and increase efficiency and profits, the music of work was forced to mutate into new forms, or sometimes to disappear altogether. Steam was soon everywhere—by the middle of the nineteenth century, the boom in railroad building was underway and steamships were replacing sailing vessels. Further, as human labor was replaced by steam power, coal grew in importance, leading to an expansion in mining industries. Shortly after the mid-nineteenth century, Britain was producing two-thirds of the world's coal. Henry Bessemer's innovations in steel making around this time led to a similar expansion in the production and use of metal. Josiah Wedgwood brought mass production techniques to bear on the manufacture of pottery—he organized his workers into production lines and invented the modern system of having the laborer "clock in" and "clock out" at the beginning and end of shifts. And just as the advent of the steamship would mark the decisive moment signaling the decline of the sea shanty, the embrace of modern manufacturing technologies and their associated management practices would lead to a similar decline in singing as a constituent part of the production of the necessities of life.

Even agricultural life was being transformed by the trend toward industrialization. Open-field cultivation gave way to the improvement of closed farms and fields, a process that gained momentum in the West during the eighteenth and nineteenth centuries. Techniques of scientific agriculture and stock breeding were disseminated. Old patterns of organizing farm labor, some dating back to medieval times, were replaced by modern systems of hire for labor similar to those practiced by industrialists. Steel plows allowed an expansion in the cultivation of land—for example, in 1833 virtually no farms existed in Iowa because the thick prairie grass was too great an obstacle for wooden plows, but less than thirty years later Iowa farmers were producing more than forty million bushels of corn. But for farms the most striking impact of industrialization was what it took away—namely, masses of people. Migration to the cities became an irreversible trend in the U.S. West. By 1850, more than half of the British population lived in cities and worked in industrial or commercial establishments. And even though agricultural communities would continue to maintain vibrant musical traditions—at least until the rise of radio and sound recordings—these songs would no longer exert the cultural influence they had once possessed. From now on, city sounds would dominate the aural imagination of the working class.

The historical relationships between song and commerce are complex and sometimes contradictory. In the previous chapter, I began to explore the importance of music in *industrial* practices—a topic that will recur later in this chapter as well as elsewhere in this volume. Yet not only the manufacture of goods but also their trading and retailing activities have been known to possess distinct songs and musical culture. Indeed, this held true long before the rise of modern capitalism—among the Inuit, for example, who could not imagine trading goods without also exchanging music; or among the Australian Aborigines, who commemorate their trade routes in songs of exceptional detail and vividness. Petroglyphs in the American Southwest depict the flute-playing Kokopelli, a quasi-divine figure who may also represent traders who used music to signal their arrival with goods ready for commerce. A source in Arabic from the twelfth century tells of African merchants who "beat great drums which they have brought with them, and which may be heard from the horizon where these people of the Sudan live." Even earlier, in the *Book of Songs* of Abu al-Faraj al-Isfahani, an important tenth-century source document, we learn of the musician Adarmi, who composed a song, "The Good Red Wine," to help a proprietor sell his wine—and did so quite successfully, with buyers flocking to purchase the vintage in response to the alluring music.

The Chinese also have a long tradition of street music, which has survived into modern times: Antoinet Schimmelpenninck recorded examples in the late 1980s. A half a century earlier, Alexander Tcherepnin had been overwhelmed by the music of the Shanghai streets—what would now be described as their "soundscape." Writing in the *Musical Quarterly* in 1935, Tcherepnin marvels at the sheer abundance of street music:

Then you will notice that, whatever work is going on, it is done in a distinct rhythm: the shoemaker will hammer nails into a shoe-sole at a regular beat; the carpenter will work according to a certain "pulse"; likewise the mason, the dish-washer, and everyone else. When a job offers no opportunity to produce rhythmic sound, the worker will mutter a sort of song, or rather of rhythmic recitation . . . In attracting your attention by sound, the ingenuity of the Chinese knows no limit: each motor-man of the street cars proudly clings to his own rhythm for the sounding of his gong, to warn you of coming danger; there are hardly two Chinese chauffeurs who would use the same rhythmic phrase for the blowing of their horns; the street vendors tax your imagination by the variety of their rhythms and by the percussion instruments they use in order to produce those rhythms. You soon discover that rhythm is fundamentally related to the life and work of the Chinese people.

The West has also been familiar with this cacophonous music of supply and demand. As trading in merchandise became the major activity of cities in the West, the melodic street cries of sellers grew apace, attracting onlookers as well as paying customers. Musical calls promoting goods and services coexisted alongside begging songs, the calls of the watch-men, and the shouts of the town crier. The calls are documented in English at the beginning of the fifteenth century in "London Lackpenny," a poem attributed to John Lydgate. These melodies often served as in-spiration for formal composition. English composers in Shakespeare's day—Orlando Gibbons, Thomas Weelkes, and Richard Dering—incor-porated these songs into their music; while the French composer Clém-ent Janequin drew on more than three dozen street cries in his a cappella part-song "Voulez ouyr les cris de Paris." Handel is known to have been so intrigued by a match-seller's cry that he transcribed it on a loose sheet of paper. In 1687, Marcellus Laroon published his best-selling *Cryes of the City of London Drawne after the Life,* and its huge and lasting success testified to the inherent appeal of the subject. Edmé Bouchardon drew on this same source of inspiration in a series of well-known drawings of French street merchants, the *Cris de Paris,* some seventy years after Laroon. These images were widely distributed as engravings, testifying to the public's persistent fascination with singing peddlers and vendors. Even earlier, Annibale Carracci documented the street life of Bolgona in his drawings. In an age in which the visual arts were still mostly focused on the concerns of ruling classes and religious institutions, the recurring image of the singing merchant in such efforts was indicative of a growing populist strain, spurred by a demand for greater social realism as well as by the transformation of creative pursuits into economic enterprises in their own right. From one perspective, the depiction of street vendors by professional artists was merely one commercial trade taking interest in another, just as the composers who borrowed their cries revealed that both were, despite all differences, purveyors of music.

Street cries and the songs of peddlers survived until very recently as an important component of American urban culture. In 1908, Commissioner Theodore Bingham of the New York Police issued an order for the suppression of unnecessary noise in the city, as part of which musical street cries were forbidden. Yet the practice continued despite the prohibition. Thirty years later a report titled the "Street Cries and Criers of New York," completed for the Federal Writers' Project, documented numerous examples of a still vital tradition. Terry Roth, who wrote the report, noted that around three thousand licensed pushcart peddlers graced the city streets, many of them boasting their own distinctive songs, chants, and jingles. Sometimes a simple call was employed—"Ahps!" (for apples), "Peeeeeches!" "Flowwwwhers!"—but frequently entire songs were performed. The streets of Harlem were especially rich in this music of commerce, and the report includes a number of song titles, such as "The Street Chef," "Ice Cream Man," "Vegetable Song," "Hot Dawg Dan," and "Yallah Yams." The report also gave the full texts of some of the songs, such as the following transcribed from a man "wheeling a white cart, laden with foodstuffs":

> Sund'y folk eats chicken'
> Mond'y ham an' greens,
> Tuesd'y's de day fo' po'k chops;
> Wednesd'y rice an' beans.
> Thuhsd'y de day fo' 'tatoes,
> Candied sweets or French fried leans,
> Fish on Frid'y some foks says,
> But Sat'd'y gimme kidney beans,
> Yassah! Plain kidney beans!

Another example goes as follows:

> Ah got string beans!
> Ah got cabbage!

Ah got collard greens!
Ah got um! Ah got um! . . .
Ah got anythin' you need,
Ah'm de Ah-got-um man!

Around this same time, Gershwin was drawing on the cries of street vendors as a source of inspiration for his opera *Porgy and Bess*, emulating the same path Handel and others had pursued two centuries earlier. This simplest form of vernacular music was, again, earning begrudging respect and proving once more that it could serve as inspiration for high art.

But the influence of capitalism was not always quite so favorable to the creation of song, especially within the factory walls. A new medical term entered the doctor's lexicon around this time: "boilermakers' deafness." This affliction, characterized by high-frequency hearing loss associated with the din of industrial processes, was first diagnosed in 1886, but was no doubt felt by factory workers long before being assigned a formal name. As Luigi Russolo pointed out in his 1913 futurist manifesto, *The Art of Noises,* the modern concept of noise could hardly be said to have existed before the advent of machinery. "Ancient life was all silence. In the 19th century, with the invention of machines, Noise was born." He continues: "Today, Noise is triumphant and reigns sovereign over the sensibilities of men. Through many centuries, life unfolded silently, or at least quietly. The loudest of noises that interrupted this silence was neither intense nor prolonged, nor varied. After all, if we overlook the exceptional movements of the earth's crust, hurricanes, storms, avalanches, and waterfalls, nature is silent." The rise of industrialization had brought with it this new paean to profit—noise, which now resounded constantly in the heart of the economy, booming and bellowing with a relentless energy far beyond the scope of any merely human work song.

As production processes became increasingly mechanized—and inevitably noisier—many laborers tried nonetheless to hold onto the singing traditions that had played an important role in less industrialized settings. The ways they did this were many, and the immediate results not always the same, but the inevitable long-term solution in almost every instance was that the workers were forced either to sing outside the factory walls or to change the music inside from active singing to passive listening. The only remaining option was, of course, for music to halt altogether. And this, too, frequently happened. Other compromises were sometimes tried—in some instances the machines would even be shut down for brief periods to allow the workers to sing—but these efforts did not prove to be practical.

A survey of the tobacco industry over a seventy-five-year period provides insight into the complexity and sometimes the surprising twists that took place in this uneasy rapprochement between music and machines. Frederika Bremer, who published a series of letters in 1854 about her travels in the Americas, was very much struck by the extraordinary singing she heard during a visit to a Virginia tobacco factory, where production processes continued to emphasize manual labor, and even the screw machinery used in packing was still turned by hand. "Here I heard the slaves," she wrote, "about a hundred in number, singing at their work in large rooms; they sung quartettes, choruses and anthems, and that so purely, and in such perfect harmony, and with such exquisite feeling, that it was difficult to believe them self-taught. But so they were." Bremer noted, however, that the environment was unhealthy; and she calls attention to "the smell and the dirt" and the frequency of lung disease, but the sound of heavy automation did not yet drown out the singing. By the time Dorothy Scarborough wrote about the same industry, seventy years later, the nature of the worker's environment had apparently changed enough to make music and machinery almost incompatible. Noting the slow demise of singing traditions in southern tobacco factories, Scarborough adds that the machinery's tendency to "drive out song" was not always successful: "In some factories, the machinery is stopped for brief periods during the day and the toilers rest themselves by singing." Around this same time, African American workers at the Lorillard Tobacco Company of Richmond, Virginia, took another approach to preserving their traditional songs: they formed a chorus to sing during leisure hours the music formerly performed while on the job. Scarborough reports that 175 workers participated in the ensemble. The tobacco industry of Cuba witnessed another type of conflict between music and modern ways, but with precisely the opposite result. In 1923—at virtually the same time that Scarborough was researching her book in the United States—the Cabanas Cigar Factory installed a radio to allow the workers to listen to recorded music, a practice that was sometimes supplemented by live performances. Cuban songwriter Benny Moré started his performing career at the factories, and later he commemorated the cigar in his classic song "Se te cayò el tabaco." The Arturo Fuente cigar factory in the Dominican Republic reportedly instituted a similar policy of employing musicians. In one setting, the advent of new manufacturing technology tended to eliminate music at the tobacco factory, while in another, related, environment, the progress of technology—in this instance, the radio—served to bring music to the laborers. But the consistent, over-riding trend—which we will assess in detail when we come to the impact of Muzak—was for active singing to be replaced by passive listening in those work environments where music remained.

In other instances, workers would change careers and attempt to bring the traditional songs into their new place of employment. Creola Johnson, who was recorded by Glenn Hinson in 1979 as part of a project to preserve Virginia work songs, explained that the melodies she sang in a Danville tobacco factory were the same she had heard her grandmother singing in the fields. Later when she began working as an oyster shucker, she brought her grandmother's music with her, and her spirited singing soon established her as the songleader in a tradition that was on the brink of disappearing. Only a few shuckers sang along with Johnson, although the small crew of vocalists made up for their lack of numbers by the undiminished enthusiasm of their efforts. Hinson states that by the time of his encounter with Johnson it had become increasingly difficult to find any traces of the local work song heritage, adding that "greater mechanization, the radio and an attitude among younger African-Americans associating work songs with 'slavery days' have all contributed to the tradition's demise."

Within the factory walls, a new type of all-encompassing rhythm now dominated both the sound and appearance of work activities. Populist rhetoric might well assert that the worker became one more cog in the machinery that kept the plant running. As such, the worker needed increasingly to adapt to—and sometimes even to imitate—the rhythms and flow of the equipment. Although Henry Ford is often credited with the invention of continuous flow manufacturing, many previous examples can be found. In the fifteenth century, Venetian war galleys were built in an assembly line process—one in which the work flow was literally that: flow. Ships were constructed as they moved down a channel lined with warehouses and fitting stations. In 1771 Josiah Wedgwood—heralded above as the inventor of the now venerable practice of having workers "clock in" and "clock out"—established a new factory called Etruria, where he applied production line techniques to the manufacture of pottery. The establishment near Philadelphia in 1785 of a continuous process gristmill, powered by water, signaled another major advance, which was widely imitated around the world. The development in 1799 of the Fourdrinier machine in France, which produced paper in a continuous roll, was another milestone. Henry Ford's introduction of assembly line processes in 1913 may have had the greatest social impact of any of these moves by bringing down the cost of the car to a level that many could afford—yet it was not an innovation in the rhythms of work but rather merely the recognition of best practices that were already half a millennium old.

The rise of industrial processes was accompanied by a growing literature on music, rhythm, and work. For example, Karl Bucher's 1896 book *Arbeit und Rhythmus* explored in great detail the relationship between these two forces, seeing a rhythmic impetus at the root of economic development. Although Bucher had mixed feelings about industrialization, he looked forward to a time when men and machines would achieve a higher rhythmical unity. Bruno Nettl has criticized Bucher's theories, countering that many traditional cultures lack work songs, and even in those cultures that have them, there is often no recognition that rhythms enhance the efficiency of work. "Indeed, it is only in quite sophisticated cultures that the advantages of rhythmic work, and specifically singing to accompany work, have been discovered. On examination, Bucher's theory appears unsubstantiated; apparently its opposite is closer to the truth."

But does a society need to recognize the functional reasons for a practice in order for it to thrive? If this were so, Darwinian processes would never take place in the natural (or social) world. Functionalist explanations of cultural phenomenon have bedeviled sociologists for decades and are often problematic, but especially so in this case. The ability of sound to impart order may have more to do with the inherent properties of music, rather than with the intentions of the singers or those who lead them. Certainly there are instances, as in the military, when music is intentionally encouraged by commanders in order to instill order and discipline. And the potency of music in assisting physical activities has been well known since ancient times; in addition to the many work songs outlined in these pages, we might also note that athletes in ancient Greece often brought a musician to their practices, and sometimes to their competitions, to provide additional stimulus to their efforts. We know, for instance, that music was used in ancient times to accompany boxing, wrestling, the long jump, and the discus and javelin competitions. But these examples are exceptions to the far more widespread, spontaneous, and almost unconscious ways in which song has served as an aid to activity in social settings. In fact, the societies that make most use of music at work are usually those that are the least hierarchical, and where bosses and overseers spend little time worrying about regimentation and the optimal organization of human resources.

This same spontaneous tendency is also reflected in natural processes. Perhaps you recall the scientific experiment, used by many schoolteachers, in which small sand grains and particles are scattered on a glass plate, but take on patterns of great order and symmetry when a violin bow is passed over the edge of the plate. Other experiments reflect this same tendency of sound to create its own patterns of organization: for instance, the Dutch scientist Christian Huygens noted in 1665 that two pendulum clocks, when mounted side by side, soon come to swing in precisely the same rhythm with greater exactitude than human intervention could, on its own, create. Hans Jenny devoted years to studying and photographing these processes, with much of his research published in the fascinating book *Cymatics*. It appears that even inanimate matter wants to come together in musical union. Yes, the tendency of the universe to harmonize apparently has little or nothing to do with the intentions of individual agents. It is, rather, an inherent property of the order of things. Some scientists have even given this process a name—"negenthropy"—a term that demarcates the constant natural transformation of random flows of energy (sunlight, vibration, matter) into trees, vegetation, human and animal life, and other highly organized entities. Music has its own negenthropy, as amply demonstrated in examples provided throughout this book.

American researchers were already reaching conclusions similar to Bucher's. Two years before *Arbeit und Rhythmus* appeared, Thaddeus Bolton published a lengthy study of rhythm in the *American Journal of Psychology*, which included a detailed historical survey as well as the results of his experimental work on the topic. "Most subjects felt themselves impelled by an irresistible force to make muscular movements of some sort accompanying the rhythms," he announced. "A corresponding rhythmical series of motions associates itself in dancing, marching and beating time, with almost irresistible force to the changes of strength in the clang." Yet Bolton stops short of specifying the use of rhythmic accompaniment for modern work, since the "tendency for sensation to find expression in visible muscular movements is stronger with children and primitive peoples than it is with highly civilized and especially well-trained persons." But other American thinkers would soon push ahead into the economic implications of rhythmical movement, some merely seeking to understand these issues better, others determined to make money by finding more efficient ways of managing workers. Bolton had lamented that few researchers took seriously the issues he was addressing. Yet less than twenty years later, another psychologist writing in the same publication could pronounce that the "experimental investigation of rhythm has grown so extensive and, at the same time, so indefinite in scope that the writing of an introduction which shall be adequate to the general problem is now altogether out of the question. The subject of rhythm has been carried over into many fields both inside and outside of the science of psychology: within it has been related to attention, work, fatigue, temporal estimation, affection, and melody; without, it is frequently mentioned in connection with music, literature, biology, geology, gymnastics, physiology, and pedagogy."

The author of this study, Christian Ruckmich, cited dozens of learned authorities during the course of his exploration of "The Role of Kinaesthesis in the Perception of Rhythm." But he missed the most important one. Frederick Winslow Taylor, whose *Principles of Scientific Management*, published only a few months before Ruckmich's article, would take these theoretical speculations and transform them into a practical regimen that would influence the lives of tens of millions of workers. Under the influence of Taylor, the benefits of harmony and rhythm in the work environment, forces initially arising spontaneously, would now be studied, systematized, and propagated. Like mighty water currents redirected to provide hydroelectric power, the natural rhythms of work would be channeled in new directions in the pursuit of efficiency and profit. Indeed, the worker would now mimic the processes of machinery, adopting the repetitive motions and unwavering pace of a piece of equipment. The rhythm of manual work would thus be forced to match the tempo and instrumentation of automation.

Describing the "general steps" required to implement this regimen at a factory, Taylor wrote:

First. Find, say 10 or 15 different men (preferably in as many separate establishments and different parts of the country) who are especially skillful in doing the particular work to be analyzed.

Second. Study the exact series of elementary operations or motions which each of these men uses in doing the work which is being investigated, as well as the implements each man uses.

Third. Study with a stop-watch the time required to make each of these elementary movements and then select the quickest way of doing each element of the work.

Fourth. Eliminate all false movements, slow movements and useless movements.

Fifth. After doing away with all unnecessary movements, collect into one series the quickest and best movements as well as the best implements.

After forming this list, Taylor concludes: "In this simple way one element after another of the science is developed."

Even while Taylor was writing these words, the concept of a "scientific study" of the relationship between workers and capitalists would be taking on a much different meaning in the writings and organizing efforts of Marxist thinkers. And only six years later, a revolution based on this new Marxist science of economic progress would alter the political landscape of Russia and, eventually, of much of the world. Yet Taylor's writings would, from the point of view of the average laborer, have far more influence on the realities of the work environment than the inflammatory exhortations of Marx or the armed conflicts of Lenin and Mao. Even governments supposedly committed to the rights of the worker would find it necessary to embrace Taylorism, emulating his practices even if his name were never mentioned. Work may have always had its music, but now it would be a type of music itself. And the worker now would become the equivalent of a musical instrument, one whose tempo and modulations were to be carefully monitored, controlled, and modified. After Taylor there could be no turning back. The rhythms of work had been fundamentally, and perhaps permanently, changed.

CHAPTER SIX

Sea and Shore

A song is as good as ten men.

—*Sailor's proverb*

"Nothing is more common than to hear people say—'Are not sailors very idle at sea?—what can they find to do?'" complains Richard Henry Dana in his 1841 memoir *Two Years before the Mast*. "This is a very natural mistake, and being very frequently made, it is one which every sailor feels interested in having corrected." Dana proceeds to do precisely this:

> It is the officers' duty to keep every one at work, even if there is nothing to be done but to scrape the rust from the chain cables. In no state prison are the convicts more regularly set to work, and more closely watched. . . . When I first left port, and found that we were kept regularly employed for a week or two, I supposed that we were getting the vessel into sea trim, and that it would soon be over, and we should have nothing to do but to sail the ship; but I found that it continued so for two years, and at the end of the two years there was as much to be done as ever.

Yet, as Dana came to discover, the songs onboard the ship proved to be as abundant as the work at hand. "A song is as necessary to sailors as a drum and fife to a soldier," he writes. "They can't pull in time, or pull with a will, without it." These songs of sea labor—the sea shanties, or chanteys—mimicked their counterparts on shore, with their group interplay, their unflagging energy, and their reliance on call-and-response forms. "The burden is usually sung by one alone, and, at the chorus, all hands join in,—and the louder the noise, the better. With us, the chorus seemed almost to raise the decks of the ship."

The use of song and music to ease the labor and tedium of life at sea is as old as the art of navigation itself. An ancient work song of Egyptian fishermen, circa 2500 BC, has survived: "It comes and brings us a fine catch!" bellowed the men with optimism as they pulled the rope that lifted the net on board. A model of an ancient Egyptian boat, now in the Metropolitan Museum in New York, shows a harpist and singer facing the rowers, no doubt encouraging their labors with the sound of music. The model, found in the eleventh-dynasty tomb of nobleman Meket-Re, dates from circa 2000 BC. Bronze Age rock carvings discovered in the south of Sweden and the border area with Norway also show unmistakable images of musicians playing onboard boats. Greek legend tells of Jason enlisting the services of the great Orpheus on the journey of the Argonauts, where, among his other responsibilities, he served as *keleustes,* the man who marked time for the rowers. This was usually done by banging on a copper drum or a wooden block, but Orpheus's music held magical power, and his singing was prized not only for coordinating labor but also for soothing the tempers of his colleagues and, at one critical juncture in the journey, causing a turbulent storm to subside.

On board these ships, music served as much more than a primitive "engine room," pushing the rowers to work harder. The Swedish rock carvings mentioned above also show dancers, and indicate that the music-making was festive as well as functional. The first recorded observation of Native American dance in the New World, made in 1534 by Jacques Cartier from the deck of his ship near the mouth of the St. Lawrence River, describes warriors in their canoes "dancing and making many signes of joy and mirth" while some of the women stood "up to their knees in water, singing and dancing." Herodotus also tells of singers and musicians playing while aboard a boat traveling to a festival in honor of the goddess Bastet. Thucydides notes the Peloponnesian sailors singing a paean of victory after their first major naval victory over Athenian ships at Naupactus. Viking ships often relied on *skalds,* or officers who led the rowers with rhythmic chants; these might also include laudatory passages praising the captains and the achievements of the ship and its crew. Like music on shore, the songs of the sea filled many roles, from the merely utilitarian to the overtly aesthetic.

During the Middle Ages, the trumpet and drums were the most frequently mentioned instruments in descriptions of seafaring musical activities. The statutes of the city of Venice went so far as to specify the presence of trumpeters and drummers onboard ships, with their number varying based on the tonnage. The Venetian ships that brought the Crusaders to the Holy Land also carried hundreds of trumpets, employed in signaling, celebrating, and even in battle where their sound was thought to strike fear in the enemy. Yet the Crusaders no doubt brought back an even richer military and seafaring musical tradition from their encounters: some warriors came home with *naggara* drums—small conical percussion instruments approximately ten inches in diameter and somewhat similar to our modern bongos. In Europe, the naggara became known as the *naccaire* or *naker*, just as the Persian-style *taburak*, also brought back from the Crusades, evolved into the *tabor* or *tabour*. This tabour is described as part of the spectacle of King Edward I's Great Feast of 1306, held in Westminster Hall. His son, Edward II, hired a foreigner from the East, Janino le Nakerer, to serve as minstrel and drummer. A few decades later, Chaucer mentions the naker in *The Canterbury Tales*.

Henry Farmer has speculated (although not with the agreement of all) that the Saracens relied on the sound of their military bands, the *tabl khana,* to give them courage in battle. This sound only ceased in retreat, so as long as the martial music continued, the soldiers knew that their forces were still battling the enemy. The extent to which these borrowings influenced the music made onboard ship is unclear. Yet it is likely that the impact of Middle Eastern and Asian practices on the music of Western sailors has always been richer and deeper than we are able to measure. The assimilation of techniques and compositions from other cultures and settings is, of course, evident in virtually every genre of music; but sea songs are especially prone to such syncrenistic admixtures, given the constant travel of the sailors and their repeated exposure to new and different cultures. Both military and trading contacts between East and West must have inevitably created strange musical hybrids: for example, Vasco de Gama, the explorer who opened up the trade route to India around the Cape of Good Hope in 1497–1498, called his trumpeters to perform in response to the music of the African shepherds, who had regaled his crew with their indigenous flute music. The records of the trip tell us that the men danced in celebration. One would give much to have been an eavesdropper at this early meeting of European and African musical traditions.

Most of the examples cited above refer to instrumentalists, but vocal music also figured prominently onboard ship, increasingly so after the close of the Middle Ages, as various historical references make clear. Henry V of England was typically accompanied on his journeys by a large choir, whose repertoire included both religious and secular songs. Christopher Columbus may not have brought trumpeters or drummers on his expedition to the New World—at least the records make no mention of them—but he was accompanied by choirboys who sang chants at dawn and sunset and other important junctures of the journey. Many other voyages of exploration also relied on singers and performers of various sorts for, in the words of one journal, the "solace of our people and allurement of the savages." In other instances, especially when royal personages were onboard, the singers primarily served for pomp and splendor. In 1520, when Henry VIII sailed to meet Francis I of France at the Field of Cloth of Gold near Guisnes, he brought with him composer and pageant-master William Cornyshe and ten children singers. When Philip II of Spain journeyed to England in 1554 for his marriage to Queen Mary Tudor, his retinue included a choir and a full complement of musicians.

Around this time, however, the role of song onboard ships increasingly took on a functional, work-a-day aspect. *The Complaynt of Scotland* from 1549 may well have been, as Stan Hugill notes, the "earliest work giving the words of shanties" (although the shanty tradition, as commonly defined by Hugill and others, encompasses the work songs of large sailing ships, and thus excludes many other types of songs associated with sea labor, including many used in rowing and fishing). The following anchor song comes to us from this source:

> Vayra, veyra, vayra, veyra,
> Gentil gallantis veynde;
> I see hym, veynde, I see hym,
> Porbossa, porbossa,
> Hail all and ane, hail all and ane;
> Hail hym up til us,
> Hail hym up til us.

The mixture of cultures, so common in the songs of sailors, is evident even at this early stage of shantying: "vayra" or "veyra" probably comes from the Spanish command "Vira!"—a call to heave or hoist. Certainly the influence over the seas of both the Spanish and the English was on the rise during this period, and a commensurate increase in seafaring music from these sources would have been likely. In particular, a number of popular British shanties, such "Haul the Bowline," "A-rovin,'" and "Whiskey Johnny," may have originated during the Elizabethan era if not earlier.

Yet for the two centuries following this early outburst of shantying, little documentation exists. William Doerflinger believes that the "custom had fallen into comparative disuse during the wars of the seventeenth and eighteenth centuries." Nonetheless, this silence is puzzling, given the extraordinary vigor of singing on ship before and after this period. How could such a vibrant and much-loved practice take a hiatus? Doerflinger elaborates on his hypothesis: "Imperiled by hostile men-of-war and privateers and, during both the seventeenth and eighteenth centuries, by piracy, larger merchantmen had to carry ample crews and armament with which to defend themselves. Conditions aboard many merchant vessels were to some extent comparable to those existing on war ships." True, merchant ships and whalers have always been more conducive settings for sailor songs than warships, yet it is hard to imagine that extra armaments on board these trading vessels during outbursts of naval tensions would be sufficient to put a halt to such an important part of the sailor's daily life. Also, the survival of Elizabethan shanties into the nineteenth century suggests that a singing tradition onboard ship continued even during the years in which little was documented in writing.

I suspect that the apparent revival of the shanty in the nineteenth century may be less a matter of a peaceful political climate than a question of the increased racial and cultural diversity of most crews. This development both spurred the interaction of musical traditions onboard ship and made singing a more important pursuit—music being, after all, the universal language which brings groups together when language barriers prevent other means of communication from creating social and work bonds. The growing number of African American sailors serving in the merchant fleets must have been an especially important factor in the increasing prominence of shanties during the nineteenth century. In the eighteenth century, in contrast, opportunities for black sailors had been extremely limited. In 1780, a group of black Americans from Massachusetts petitioned the state legislature, arguing that "we have not an equal chance with white people neither by Sea nur Land." Even when offers to sail were presented, many free African Americans feared to take them, given the genuine risk they faced of being kidnapped and sold into slavery while onboard ship or in an unfamiliar port. The autobiography of the African sailor Olaudah Equiano, published in London in 1789, tells of numerous situations in which the author was threatened, robbed, or confronted with the risk of seizure and enforced servitude. "I had suffered so many impositions in my commercial transactions," he notes in the concluding chapter of his memoir, "that I became heartily disgusted with the seafaring life, and was determined not to return to it." Yet Equiano was one of the more fortunate black sailors of his day, earning his freedom, and serving in important expeditions, including a scientific voyage toward the North Pole to find a northeast passage to India, as well as a missionary visit to Sierra Leone. The opportunities for black sailors did, however, improve somewhat as the nineteenth century progressed. Between 1815 and 1860, American shipping emerged as a booming industry, with its tonnage quadrupling during this period. The extent to which African Americans benefited from this growth can be read in the pages of the *Providence City Directory* of 1832, where fully one-quarter of the household heads of black families are listed as mariners. Directories from other cities ranging from Maine to Maryland tell a similar story. Who can doubt that this tremendous influx of African Americans into the ranks of sailors played a major role in the flourishing of sea songs during this same period?

Shanties, as they evolved, became almost as specialized as the types of labor they accompanied. Halyard or long-drag songs were sung while raising or lowering sails, which were hung from cross-bars called yards— a demanding task given that these sails could weigh more than a half-dozen men. During halyard shanties, such as "Reuben Ranzo," the crew would haul during the chorus and pause during the verse:

LEADER: Oh, poor old Reuben Ranzo
CHORUS: Ranzo, boys, Ranzo!
LEADER: Oh, poor old Reuben Ranzo
CHORUS: Ranzo, boys, Ranzo!
LEADER: Oh Ranzo wuz no sailor.
CHORUS: Ranzo, boys, Ranzo!
LEADER: He wuz a Boston tailor.
CHORUS: Ranzo, boys, Ranzo!

LEADER: Shanghaied aboard of a whaler.
CHORUS: Ranzo, boys, Ranzo!
LEADER: They tried to make him a sailor.
CHORUS: Ranzo, boys, Ranzo!

Hugill testifies to the efficacy of this shanty: "A man just had to pull when he roared out 'Rrranzo!'" Yet even more popular was the following halyard shanty, the most famous of all—even young children today know its chorus:

LEADER: "As I was a' rollin' down Paradise Street."
CHORUS: "To me, way, hey, blow the man down!"
LEADER: "A sassy flash clipper I chanced for to meet."
CHORUS: "Ooh! Give me some time to blow the man down!"

Less-arduous hauling—such as unfurling sails—would employ short-drag (or short-haul) shanties. Other hauling songs would be used for storing sails or boarding tacks and sheets. Pumping—frequently required to rid the bilge of water—demanded its own set of songs, and even different types of pumps might necessitate specific rhythms and refrains. The most exhausting task, however, was usually heaving the anchor, and this required special capstan or windlass songs, with measured tempos and many verses since this job could take hours to complete. Long, drawn-out versions of shanties such as "Shenandoah" and "Santa Anna" kept the sailors primed and focused during this draining work. Finally, forebitters were sung by the sailors during moments of leisure, and include many of the best-known songs of the sea, such as "Spanish Ladies" and "Maggie May." These songs were often accompanied by the squeezebox, fiddle, or whatever other instruments might be available onboard ship.

Sometime the song failed to fit the task at hand, a matter that could cause serious problems. Dana tells of the difficulty in finding the right shanty for heavy "raise-the-dead" pulls. "Two or three songs would be tried, one after the other, with no effect;—not an inch could be got on the tackles—when a new song, struck up, seemed to hit the humor of the moment, and drove the tackles 'two blocks' at once." New songs, passed along by another crew or a recently arrived sailor, were greeted with enthusiasm—sometimes the old ones had simply worn out their staying power and needed replacing, no different than a sail or piece of rigging.

Of course, for simpler tasks, the crew might be forgiving of a less-than-ideal shanty: "Tom's Gone to Hilo" (or "John's Gone to Hilo") was simply too slow to serve as a proper tops'l halyard song—it invariably took ages to hoist a yard given its languorous tempo; but nonetheless it was popular with sailors, who liked its melody and often put it to use despite this functional limitation. Other songs only found their true calling over time, such as "Santa Anna," examined in more detail below, which started life as a pumping shanty and gradually made its way to the capstan, where it served yeoman's duty.

The word "shanty" (and, as mentioned above, sometimes "shantey," "chanty," or "chantey") did not make its appearance until the middle of the nineteenth century, an era that might properly be described as the golden age of sea songs. Hugill tends to believe that the word owed its derivation to the shanties that housed the Africans transported to the West Indies—the songs may well have been sung in the process of moving these houses, as well as for tasks on ship and shore. Others feel that the word's derivation lies in its similarity to the English word "chant" or the French "chantez" or "chanson." Whatever the origin of the term, there can be little doubt that the influence of the African diaspora on the art of shanty singing was pervasive, as even the white shanty singers were quick to admit. W. F. Arnold, in the introduction to his 1914 collection *Songs of Sea Labor*, states unequivocally that "the majority of Chanties are negroid in origin." Joanna Colcord, in her *Songs of American Sailormen*, supports this view, stating that "even on American ships, Irishmen, of whom there were always a few in every crew, were admitted to rank ahead of the white Americans as shantymen; though they in turn were outstripped by the American Negroes—the best singers that ever lifted a shanty aboard ship." Hugill speculates that the West Indies served as a major breeding ground for the songs, adding that he learned much of his extensive repertoire from West Indian shantymen. Roger Abrahams supports Hugill's views and argues that the influence of the West Indies has been underestimated by many writers on shantying—the singing tradition there was so rich and vital, in fact, that Abrahams found it still flourishing when he undertook field work on St. Vincent, Tobago, and Nevis during the 1960s, a time when few ports elsewhere resounded with these time-honored melodies. Despite these differences of opinion, few scholars would dispute W. Jeffrey Bolster's contention that "the shantey's late-eighteenth-century origins corresponded with rising numbers of black sailors." Nor can one dismiss as mere coincidence the fact that, as Bolster notes, "the period of the shantey's greatest development after 1820 was one of black prominence at sea."

Although the words of the shanties rarely referred back to Africa, the singing style itself reflected an unmistakably African aesthetic. The call-and-response form, so typical of African and African American music, figured prominently in these songs, providing a back-and-forth interplay that established a hierarchy among the workers, gave encouragement to their efforts, and imparted a structure to both music and labor. Improvisation also played an important role, and was encouraged by the sailors, looking to relieve the monotony of their tasks. "Many a Chanty-man was prized in spite of his poor voice because of his improvisations," wrote Frank Bullen in 1913; "Poor doggerel they were mostly and often very lewd and filthy, but they gave the knowing and appreciative ship-mates, who roared the refrain, much opportunity for laughter." As such, the shanty texts that have been handed down to us are often only a faint representation, cleaned up for public consumption, of their more vulgar and perhaps vigorous originals. (Before his death, Stan Hugill talked about publishing a book featuring the unbowdlerized versions of the songs; and though he never fulfilled this ambition, some of the coarser lyrics have found their way into print—although no doubt only a small sampling of what once circulated onboard ship.) Indeed, it is probably misleading to even use the term "original" to describe a shanty, since these songs, like other African-influenced forms of music, do not hark back to some initial manuscript or moment of creation but rather were developed organically over time, picking up much of their essence in the process. Even if we could trace the genealogy of any given shanty back to its source, the results would be unlikely to shed much light on the music: like a newborn infant, the shanty at its birth is merely a bundle of possibilities, with all that is most magical and mysterious still lying ahead of it. In this regard, the shanty is no different than the African American work songs found on land, which continued to evolve and change in meaning for as long as this style of singing remained vital. When the songs stopped mutating, it was merely a sign that they no longer served an important role in the culture.

As a result of these various influences, states Bolster, "by the nineteenth century, white sailors spent a significant amount of time singing in what had once been a characteristically black style." But African influences mixed with many other musical traditions in creating a strikingly varied repertoire for the singing sailors. As we have seen, some hauling songs of Elizabethan seamen continued to be used hundreds of years after their first appearance. British folk songs and ballads were also popular with sailors, as were operatic airs, marches, dance and fiddler music, hymns, and military airs of various sorts. Sailors also borrowed from other occupations, and their repetoire included work songs that originated on the plantations or in logging camps or other settings. Also, as suggested above, the influence of foreign sea songs was quite substantial: Hugill surmises that "new shanties would be made up from scraps of tunes heard in Oriental and Latin ports." Virtually every major harbor or waterway in the world had its associated musical traditions, although few were documented as thoroughly as those found in the Anglo-American world. But British sailors probably gave back as much as they took. Sometimes a song in English would be translated into a new language: Konrad Tegtmeier, for example, discovered a Platt-Deutsch version of "The Banks of the Sacramento" as well as a Swedish translation of "Rolling Home." Few original shanties seemed to have been sung in German, yet at least one, which begins "Glori—Glori—Glori—Gloria, / Schön schmeckt der Wein in Batavia," may have served as the source for the British shanty "Gloria Victoria." In other instances, shanties from outside the Anglo-American tradition not only survived in their native tongue but even found a global audience, such as that most famous of Russian work songs, the "Ey ukhnem" of the Volga boatmen. Nautical memoirs include many examples of these local singing traditions, including the Indonesian shanty below, picked up by sailor Frederick Pease Harlow during a voyage to Surabaya:

> *Ah,* hoo-e *la*-e.
> *Ah,* hoo-e *la*-e.
> *Ah*-e, *hoo*-e, *ah,* hoo-e *la*-e,
> *Ung!*

Or the following example, which was a great favorite with the Yankee sailors, who would often join in singing:

> Sum go cool-ie ah-o ah ang, sor Sou-ra-ba-ya.
> Hoo-e la-e la-e la, hoo-e la-e la-e la,
> Sum go Sou-ra-ba-ya, sor, Pa-su-ru-an.

The meaning of the words was of little importance to the American crew—Harlow merely comments that "as nearly as I could tell the chantey was a tale about going from Sourabaya to Pasuruan." But the tune was contagious, even if the words remained obscure to the singers.

The various cultures of Asia and the Pacific Islands were especially rich in fishing and rowing songs; and though these traditions were rarely disseminated as widely as the shanties of the sailing ships, their local importance should not be minimized. These songs can be found in the pages of *The Tale of Genji,* the classic eleventh-century Japanese novel by Murasaki Shikibu, just as half a millennium later the poet Bashô would describe the pleasing "voices of the fishermen as they divided up the catch." Sir James George Scott, writing in his 1882 book *The Burman: His Life and Notions,* waxes with enthusiasm over the rowing songs he heard during his lengthy residence in present-day Myanmar, with their "mysterious, gusty air that has suggestions of the swirl of the river eddies and the rustle of the wind." In his essay on the "Music and Folklore of East Pakistan," Abbasuddin Ahmad stresses that "the rivers play a prominent role in the life and culture of the people," and he supports this claim with an account of the Bhatiali or "boatman's songs"—the call-and-response performances that express "sometimes the hissing sounds of water, sometimes the sound of beckoning." Describing the songs of the fishers of Lamalera of Indonesia, R. H. Barnes writes that "the crew must sing as long as the animal is under the surface of the sea, although the songs appropriate to each species are quite different."

In Polynesia, special work songs known as *tangi* or *fakalangilangi* have been used to attract fish, while canoe hauling and paddling songs were quite common and sometimes were made use of in odd ways. Mervyn McLean notes that the canoe hauling songs served double duty in New Zealand and the Tuamotu Islands, where they were also sung to welcome visitors. Richard Moyle, in his study *Tongan Music,* has provided many examples of *tau'a'alo,* or songs used to accompany paddling and rowing. These songs, first documented almost two hundred years ago, have undergone many changes during the intervening period, including adaptation for land-based uses. Dana describes with great interest the work songs used by the Kanaka (Hawaiian) sailors employed in the Pacific trade during the early nineteenth century, and it is likely that one of these song inspired the shanty "John Kanaka" with its call and response:

LEADER: "I heard, I heard, the old man say,"
CHORUS: "John Kanaka-naka too-lye-ay."
LEADER: "We'll work tomorrer, but no work terday."
CHORUS: "John Kanaka-naka too-lye-ay."

Perhaps this constant borrowing across linguistic barriers explains the frequent use of what are apparently nonsense syllables, such as "yo-ho," "way-ay-ay," "do-a-day," and the like. Just as scat singing in jazz began—or at least legend tells us—when Louis Armstrong knocked over his music during a recording session and had to make up syllables to replace the original lyrics, so perhaps many shanties came to include their puzzling and apparently meaningless syllables as a similar replacement for the forgotten original words in a foreign tongue. Others have seen these cryptic shanty phrases as carryovers from wild yells and cries that evolved later into proper songs. In either case, the relative indifference of sailors to the meaning of the words, as long as the melody and rhythm were right, is one of the notable characteristics of the shanty tradition.

Certainly these songs, once brought onboard sailing ships, traveled far and wide, often taking on new meanings in the process. Tracing the history of the classic shanty "Santa Anna" provides us with an insight into this colorful and convoluted process. This song probably first came into existence on land, not sea, as an account of General Antonio López de Santa Anna, well known for leading his Mexican soldiers to victory at the Alamo in 1836. The song later became popular among the cowboys of the Wild West, who surprisingly celebrated the defeat of the Texas forces.

Santiana gained the day,
Hooray Santiana!
Santiana gained the day,
Upon the plains of Mexico.

It is not clear whether this counts as "remembering the Alamo"; but in any event, the original impetus of the song became even more forgotten with each passing generation. How a song about the "plains of Mexico" became so well known on ship is a mystery in its own right, but it is likely that British seamen, many of whom favored the cause of Santa Anna and had deserted their ships to join his troops, brought it back with them from their land campaigns. From here the song spread widely and was especially popular with the crews of whalers. While toiling at the pump or capstan, the sailors sang many different versions of "Santa Anna," which varied considerably from ship to ship, but most often the shanty now seemed to refer to a sea voyage to Mexico. A Norwegian captain of a whaling ship, singing it for Stan Hugill, declared:

> Heave an' weigh, we're bound for Mexico.
> All across the plains of Mexico.
> All along the shores of Mexico.

On some ships, the song was known as "Round the Bay of Mexico," and General Santa Anna was not mentioned in it at all. In contrast Captain David Bone, writing in the early 1930s, knew about the reference to Santa Anna but interpreted it as a sailor's prayer to Saint Anne, the patron of Breton seamen. When the *Charles Morgan*, the last active American whaling ship, was hauled into port for the final time, her crew chose "Santa Anna" as their curtain call—and accounts tell that the old tars on the quayside had tears in their eyes. But the song proved more durable than the whaling industry, and it took on new life on shore. The song that had started on land returned there once again, but the words and meanings had changed so drastically in the intervening years that its historical roots were now totally obscured. The song shows up, for example, on field recordings made in the Bahamas in 1935, and though the setting is still "the Bay of Mexico," the protagonist has become a woman Suziana. Finally, writing in 1942, Lydia Parrish refers to a musical chant, commonly heard in Brunswick, known as "Sandy Anna."

> Seaman, what's the madda?
> Hooray, Sandy Anna.
> Seaman stole my dolla's
> Hooray 'o-ray
> He stole it in Savannah
> Hooray, Sandy Anna.
> He spend it in Havana
> Hooray 'oray
> I caught 'im in his colla'
> Hooray, Sandy Anna.

Over the course of a hundred years, the famous general had been transformed into a damsel by the seashore and the setting shifted from

Mexico to Georgia and Cuba. Such arcane genealogies are daunting for researchers faced with the difficulty of interpreting the meaning of any given sea song. Clearly, the sailors employing these songs were far more interested in their spirit than in their literal meaning, and were apt to take such great liberties that the initial spark that brought any given song into being could easily be hidden within a few years.

Although the British and American shanty traditions contributed the most widely known songs of sea labor, this had more to do with the dominance of these countries on the sea than to any monopoly of singing talent. Merchant ships tended to be the best source of songs, and virtually every country that provided crew members for the world's commercial fleets also made some contribution to the music sung and performed onboard. Even nationalistic Yankee and British tars took notice of these different, and by no means inferior, traditions. "The most beautiful chanty I have ever heard was sung by a Norwegian crew," writes John Masefield. "I have heard two Greek chanties of great beauty, and I am told that the Russians have at least one as beautiful as any of our own." Dana describes with admiration the songs of the Italian and Hawaiian sailors he encountered during his travels. Hugill praises lavishly the shanty tradition of the West Indies. In the international commerce of music, as opposed to more tangible types of trade, no tariffs or duties hindered the import and export of new material, and the natural resources of one nation were readily taken up by sailors in their travels and exploited for their own use.

But songs moved around the world in written form as well as by word of mouth. Printed ballads on seafaring subjects circulated widely, in quarto sheets covered with old black-letter or gothic type. Sometimes these items were mere literary affectations, produced by land-lubbers, but the sailors themselves often got involved in their creation and dissemination. Herman Melville's 1849 novel *Redburn,* based on his first-hand experiences serving on a packet ship, describes a telling detail of the Liverpool docks, noting the "number of sailor ballad-singers, who, after singing their verses, hand you a printed copy, and beg you to buy." Virtually every major event of seafaring life, from the defeat of the Spanish Armada to the sinking of the *Titanic,* served as inspiration for popular ballads, but also modest affairs of merely local interest—tales of smuggling or press-gangs—found their way into these songs, testifying to their authentic linkages with real sailors and their doings.

The American South may well have rivaled or surpassed the West Indies and Liverpool as a fertile source of songs to accompany labor on ship or shore. The great river ways of the South not only served as a magnet for the music of the region, but also reached deep into the American heartland, bringing back songs along with the more pedestrian commerce of crops, animals, raw materials, and manufactured goods. "Black watermen carried their special worksongs, along with other kinds of Negro folksongs, up and down the rivers," writes Eileen Southern, "from Wheeling, West Virginia, and Cincinnati on the Ohio River, from Omaha, Nebraska, Kansas City and St. Louis on the Missouri River, to the towns on the Mississippi itself, Cairo, Illinois, Memphis, Tennessee, and finally, to New Orleans. The same songs or similar ones could be heard on the Gulf Coast in Mobile Bay, and on the Atlantic Coast in Savannah, Georgia; Charleston, South Carolina; Norfolk, Virginia; and in Northern ports." By the middle of the nineteenth century, half of the free African Americans in Alabama lived in Mobile, which was second only to New Orleans as a center of cotton shipments, and perhaps second to none as a source of sea songs. The diverse workforce of blacks, European immigrants, and visiting sailors created a rich musical environment, which Hugill has described as the "shanty mart or work-song exchange." Yet no port or waterway could match the great Mississippi in its abundance of music during the nineteenth century. Frederika Bremer, in a letter describing her American travels published in 1854, describes a memorable and unexpected musical interlude during her travels down the river:

[My companion] asked me whether I should like to hear the negroes of the ship sing, and led me for this purpose to the lowest deck, where I beheld a strange scene. The immense engine-fires are all on this deck, eight or nine apertures all in a row; they are like yawning fiery throats, and beside each throat stood a negro naked to his middle, who flung in fire-wood. . . . The negro up aloft on the pile of fire-wood began immediately an improvised song in stanzas, and at the close of each the negroes down below joined in vigorous chorus. It was a fantastic and grand sight to see these energetic black athletes lit up by the wildly flashing flames from the fiery throats, while they, amid their equally fantastic song, keeping time most exquisitely, hurled one piece of fire-wood after another into the yawning fiery gulf. Every thing went on with so much life, and so methodically, and the whole scene was so accordant and well arranged, that it would have produced a fine effect upon any theater whatever.

In 1882, as part of a fascinating article discussed below, William Alden declared the death of the shanty tradition, yet a half century later Mary Wheeler was still able to find numerous work songs linked to the Mississippi and its tributaries. Her 1944 book *Steamboatin' Days* contains dozens of these songs, many of which were gathered from black residents living in cabins along the river banks. At virtually the same time that Alden was writing his lament, Samuel Clemens was preparing his *Life on the Mississippi*, in which he describes the workers on the steamboats roaring out songs "inspired to unimaginable exaltation by the chaos of turmoil and racket." He also recounts the musical sounding calls used to determine the depth of the river, from which he derived his literary name: "M-a-r-k three! .... M-a-r-k three! .... Quarter-less three! .... Half twain! .... Quarter twain! .... Quarter twain! ... Mark twain!" The term "mark twain' signals a depth of two fathoms, or twelve feet, the clearance needed to allow the passage of the boat. "In order to make themselves understood, often through wind and rain, the measurements are sung in a sustained chant," notes Wheeler, "and each leadsman evolves his own tune and rhythm that he associates with the various depths." The African American workers, who often filled this role, would refer to this as "passin' the word." Clemens liked the pleasant sound of the call, and the symbolic meaning it conveyed of safe depths for navigating. He was not, however, the first to adopt this pseudonym: Captain Isaiah Sellers, who had written news stories about the river for the *New Orleans Picayune* had also called himself Mark Twain some time before. In 1939 Herbert Halpert, seeking to document what might remain of these sounding calls, made a memorable recording of eighty-six-year-old Sam Hazel, who obliged his interlocutor by calling out:

> Quarter less twain,
> Quarter less twain,
> Lawd, Lawd, no send me quarter less twain.
> Throw the lead line a little higher out.
> I've gone low down, so mark twain,
> Mark twain.
> Come ahead, Mr. Pilot, a little bit strong.
> I've done got over, and I believe we're gonna
> Throw the lead line over—
> No bottom here.

The levees and levee camps of the Mississippi region were another fertile source of work songs. The construction of the levee system of the Mississippi, a structure longer and taller than the Great Wall of China, stands out as one of the largest public works projects in the history of the United States. This ambitious undertaking created a mini-industry in the region, involving countless workers both in its construction and in ongoing maintenance. The levee camps were rough, violent places, known as hideouts for escaped prisoners and other desperate characters. As a New England engineer who worked in one of the camps wrote in a letter home: "Everybody carries a gun . . . and is always in a state of preparedness . . . One got shot in a crap game in a camp above here. It didn't even stop the game." Yet songs could flourish even in this harsh environment, where they would serve as a constitutive part of the work experience. The levee camp "hollers"—melismatic, slow solo work songs, free in rhythm—were perhaps the best-known music of the camps, and some examples have been preserved in field recordings made during the 1930s and 1940s. But more-structured songs and ballads were also part of the repertoire of the levee workers. R. Emmet Kennedy, who began collecting songs in Louisiana during the 1880s, recalled his intense surprise at first hearing the song "Casey Jones": Kennedy had transcribed an identical melody several years earlier from a levee worker named Willie. In the original version, the lyrics told of Aunt Dinah and her old mule:

> Ole Aunt Dinah had a rawbone mule,
> Got up one mawnin' wen de air was cool—
> Hitched him to de wagon an' wat she do.
> Stahted down de road fo' de bah-be-cue.

Other now-familiar songs can also be traced back to the work songs of southern waterways. The well-known children's melody "Michael, Row the Boat Ashore" was first documented as a rowing song (although it may have an even earlier history as a spiritual, with reference to Michael the Archangel). William Francis Allen published a transcription of this piece shortly after the Civil War in his seminal collection *Slave Songs of the United States,* a work he compiled with assistance from Charles Pickard Ware and Lucy McKim Garrison. Here he notes that "Michael, Row the Boat Ashore" was described by workers as especially popular when "the load was heavy or the tide was against us." But the melody languished in obscurity for close to a century. In 1954, Tony Saletan ran across a dusty copy of Allen's book in the Widener Library at Harvard University; he took notice of the song and added it to his repertoire, later teaching it to Pete Seeger, who performed it with the Weavers. The song was then picked up by a pop group called the Highwaymen, who transformed it into a hit single in 1961.

> Michael, row the boat ashore, al-le-lu-yah
> Michael, row the boat ashore, al-le-lu-oo-yah.
> The river is deep and the river is wide, al-le-lu-yah
> Milk and honey on the other side, al-le-lu-oo-yah.
> Michael, row the boat ashore, al-le-lu-yah
> Michael, row the boat ashore, al-le-lu-oo-yah.

The evolution of a sea song into a pop hit is not as rare as one might first assume. The "Sloop John B"—popularized by the Weavers, the Kingston Trio, and the Beach Boys—also started life among sailors, was featured in Carl Sandburg's *The American Songbag,* and recorded as early as 1935 by Alan Lomax and Mary Elizabeth Barnicle in the Bahamas. "Kumbaya" was first heard as a spiritual in the Georgia Sea Islands (and it was only later brought to Africa, when missionaries introduced it into Angola), and may very well have been used as a rowing song in its early days, given its tempo and relaxed momentum. It is even possible that America's most popular hymn, "Amazing Grace," had a similar start, originating as a plantation song or perhaps even as an African melody, then traveling onboard ship, where it was picked up by its credited composer, Reverend John Newton. Before becoming a preacher and abolitionist, Newton had worked as a slave trader, during which time he frequented ports where such songs circulated. Although some accounts suggest that Newton borrowed the melody from an earlier folk song, the plaintive tone, measured pace, and swaying rhythm of the music all point to an origin accompanying physical labor. The song's later history also seems to support this view: "Amazing Grace" is frequently presented alongside pieces from the African American tradition, where it seems comfortably at home, much more so than when it is sung as a conventional folk song. And we can well imagine that composer Newton, who commemorated his change of heart from slave trader to abolitionist in this powerful piece, would have happily drawn on African American sources of inspiration in articulating this heartfelt call for spiritual and temporal deliverance.

The ability of traditional sailing and rowing songs—such as "Michael, Row the Boat Ashore," "The Sloop John B," and, possibly, "Amazing Grace" or "Kumbaya"—to enter the pantheon of popular music is testimony to the intrinsic appeal that many of these songs possess. Their melodies and rhythms, in essence, had already stood the toughest test long before they appeared on a hit record: they had energized a crew to greater heights of achievement, and as such had earned the hard-won loyalty and respect of the sailors themselves. Few workers possessed catchier or more uplifting work songs than did sailors, and we can easily imagine other pieces from this tradition becoming well known if given the right degree of exposure to a mass audience.

For the most part, however, the history of these songs over the past century and a half has been one of neglect and obscurity, if not total loss. The advent of new technologies accelerated the disappearance of the sea songs. In particular, the gradual replacement of sailing ships with steamships during the second half of the nineteenth century put an end to many of the most demanding tasks of sea labor, and thus made redundant the songs that had accompanied these efforts. In some small pockets of the American maritime industry, a few tasks remained that required song well into the middle of the twentieth century. For example, in the Chesapeake Bay and along the Atlantic seaboard the singing of the menhaden fisherman, which was a routine part of hauling in the nets, continued with vigor until the 1950s. Captain Hudnall Haynie recalled the occasions when the catch was so large that he would need to signal to another steamer to help him, otherwise the risk of capsizing was too great: "Then there'd be about sixty men in there, all doing the chanty. That was something you could hear all over the Chesapeake Bay!" But the inevitable adoption of hydraulic power blocks on the pursing boats dramatically reduced the need for coordinated physical labor among large numbers of men. As a result, by the early 1960s the work song tradition disappeared there as well.

In the parts of the world where labor is cheap—and thus less likely to be replaced by automating technologies—work songs, on ship and shore, have proven to be more resilient than in most developed economies. But even in labor-intensive places the decline of the tradition has been merely delayed, not halted. Such is the case in China, for example, where rowing and fishing songs flourished for many centuries. Johann Hüttner, who traveled in China toward the close of the eighteenth century, described this music with delight, noting that "in the northern provinces of China, especially along the coasts, boatmen have the habit of synchronizing the strokes of their oars with a song, which is a very agreeable one and has a surprising effect when heard from a distance." As Hüttner continues:

> The captain begins and his crewmen respond. This prevents fatigue, keeps up attention and promotes a regular rowing-motion among the oarsmen. I remember with the liveliest pleasure the evening when . . . [we] met hundreds of large and small boats, each one passing by us with the song *Highodee highau* as they put out from the harbor with the falling tide. The crowd on the boats, the measured movement of the many oarsmen and the repetition of this song by many hundreds of voices striking up on all sides—how full of liveliness, what a tumult! London, Liverpool, Venice and other ports seemed to me to have nothing like it. . . . The oriental custom of singing by oarsmen is observable around all Asiatic coasts and islands. I myself heard a similar song of the Malayans in Batavia and also in Cochin China, but neither of these came near the tune of the Chinese oarsmen.

The collection *Min River Boat Songs,* published by Stella Marie Graves in 1946, drew on over one hundred examples collected by Malcolm F. Farley in the years between the two World Wars. Huang Bai, who grew up in China's Jiangsu province in the early 1940s, recalls how fascinated she was, during these years, with the work songs (*laodong haozi*) of the fishermen, dock workers, and boatmen. Yet within two decades, the Jiangsu waterfront also suffered a marked decline in its music. Shortly after entering the Shanghai Conservatory in 1958, Bai attempted to track down these songs among harbor workers. To her dismay, the songs were no longer sung on the boats or on the docks, and it was only when she found some aged workers and convinced them to perform the old music, that she was able to hear this tradition brought back to life, albeit briefly. Antoinet Schimmelpenninck, who conducted field research in southern Jiangsu in the late 1980s and early 1990s, attempted to document the singing traditions among the fishermen in the region. She had little luck, however, and concluded that "except for working cries (*hazoi*), no folk songs can be heard during fishing today." An older folk song collector, Ren Mei, who had spent time in the early 1950s in a village near Lake Tai, related that even at that time "fishermen's songs were already a thing of the past."

During the 1990s, Elsa Guggino, a professor at the University of Palermo specializing in the history of Sicilian folklore, encountered a similar situation when she attempted to document the songs known as the *mattanza*, which are associated with the Mediterranean tuna harvest. During the process of pulling in the nets and hauling in the tuna, one man typically was exempted from physical work in order to sing, the rhythm of his song enabling the others to maintain the proper pace in their efforts. In the mid-1950s, Alan Lomax found this singing tradition still very much alive, and he encountered no shortage of performers willing to show him exactly how the music should sound. Two topics of interest—no more—inspired their songs: "the pleasures of the bed which awaited them on shore, and the villainy of the tuna fishery owner." But this limited range of subjects inspired a surprisingly large number of songs. Lomax even hauled his equipment onboard a tuna fishing barge sailing in the Mediterranean, for what he believed was the first in situ recording of such music. It must also have been one of the last. When seeking out these songs among the fishermen of Favignana four decades later, Guggino found Gioacchino Ernandes—the retired *rais,* or leader, of the local fishing crew—to be one of the few residents who could respond to her requests for renditions of the old material. "I am the last one who really knows the songs," he told the researcher.

Other traditions have persisted as younger singers have consciously made an effort to preserve the past, as with, for example, the pearl diving songs of the Persian Gulf. This difficult job required divers to make repeated plunges into the waters without the benefit of oxygen tanks, an exhausting process that left even the most vigorous worn out by the end of the day's labors. Singers, or *nahams*, played an important role in the work, both encouraging and entertaining the divers, as well as offering prayers to Allah for their protection. This diving industry declined in the face of increasing sales of cultured pearls, and the overshadowing importance of oil to the local economy. When composer David Fanshawe traveled to Bahrain in the late 1960s with hopes of hearing the diving songs, he eventually had to settle for performers who tied an old rope to the wheel of a bus and, while they sang, pretended that it represented the anchor on the end of a chain. But here an apparently dying custom came back to life in the 1970s, when the pearl diving songs returned to prominence as part of a conscious effort to preserve traditional practices. Still, they are no longer a functional part of day-to-day work, but are more often performed at weddings and official functions than in the environment that gave them their original meaning and purpose.

The same fate has beset the once vibrant Anglo-American sea shanty tradition. Interest in shanties is on the rise, with performances and sing-a-longs held, recordings released and preservation societies formed. But the music is no longer part of the working lives of sailors, and has not been for well over a century. Most sea shanties today are doubtless sung on terra firma, and those seeking them would have better luck in a library than on a dock.

In an important essay, "Sailor Songs," published in *Harper's* in 1882, William Alden could already lament that the spread of steam engines had killed the shanty: "In the place of a rousing 'pulling-song' we now hear the rattle of the steam-winch; and the modern windlass worked by steam, or the modern steam-pump, gives us the clatter of cog wheels and the hiss of steam in place of the wilder choruses of other days. Singing and steam are irreconcilable." Yet even at this terminal stage, Alden noted that one pulling song could still be heard occasionally on steam ships. But soon even it would be forgotten. Cut off from the activities that gave it meaning, the shanty has become just another song. This transition can only be lamented, for the work-a-day circumstances that gave birth to the shanties also imparted the rough-and-ready beauty that made them so inspirational, and this charm all but disappears when the music is brought inside the concert hall or recording studio. As poet John Masefield wrote: "They are songs to be sung under certain conditions, and where those conditions do not exist they appear out of place. At sea, when they are sung in the quiet dog-watch, or over the rope, they are the most beautiful of all songs. It is difficult to write them down without emotion; for they are a part of life."

Did these songs actually help the sailors in their work, or were they a mere diversion, a way of making the hours of toil pass more quickly? Let's close this chapter by allowing the sailors themselves to settle this matter. Richard Henry Dana reminds his readers, in true Yankee fashion, that "music may be 'turned to account,' " and recalls the proverb, commonly told onboard, that "a song is as good as ten men." "I have often thought how easy it would be for a crew of deep-water sailors to enter a tug-of-war contest," adds Frederick Pease Harlow, who sailed American merchant ships in the second half of the nineteenth century, "with every man's son, flat on his back and with feet braced with the stretch of the rope, pulling his utmost, then a nice little chantey like 'Haul away, Joe' would completely up-end the men on the opposite side and bring home the bacon."

CHAPTER SEVEN

The Lumberjack

LEADER *(singing): I'm a lumberjack, and I'm okay.*

I sleep all night and I work all day.

RESPONSE: *He's a lumberjack, and he's okay.*

He sleeps all night and he works all day.

—*A late example of the call-and-response work song*

An ancient record of sea commerce, dating from circa 2600 BC, describes the delivery of forty shiploads of cedar from Lebanon to Egypt. No wood was more prized in its day than the timber from these legendary trees. Many other inscriptions and documents refer to the famous cedars of Lebanon—perhaps most notably the Biblical description of their use in the construction of the First Temple and Solomon's Palace. Yet we also find references to other types of lumber from our ancient sources: to acacia from Lower Nubia, to tribute gifts of timber paid to Sumerian rulers, and to various other transfers of valuable wood into major cities from distant lands. Despite these records, we know all too little about the circumstances in which these trees were harvested and transported, and possess only a rudimentary idea of the end products made from wood. An ancient relief from Karnak shows the princes of Lebanon cutting trees for the Egyptians, and a column erected by Trajan depicts a similar scene, but with their representations of a handful of dignified laborers these images barely hint at the massive workforces that must have been mobilized in such undertakings. Archeological sites offer few clues, since wooden structures and objects rarely survive long enough to form a major source of information.

Documents about ship building and other types of construction fill in some gaps, but also leave much to our imagination.

Yet we can have little doubt about the value of the timber. Many of the early civilizations of the Middle East emerged in areas where few native trees existed, and the types that were plentiful served poorly for construction. The quest for timber also figures repeatedly in the Icelandic sagas, motivating many protagonists to undertake long and arduous journeys. Whatever the nature of the early timber industry, it is safe to assume that the processes of harvesting and moving wood consumed large amounts of human capital. And where workers tackled such enormous projects, songs almost certainly played a major role in coordinating and motivating their efforts. The cutting of trees and wood figure, for example, in several of the songs of the Confucian classic, the *Shijing*, and perhaps were even used in the process of harvesting timber.

> Chop, chop they cut the hardwood
> And lay it on the river bank
> By the waters so clear and rippling.

A Chinese document from around 100 BC includes a possible description of a call-and-response song performed by timber workers. This passage from Liu An reads: "Now the men carry big wood, in front they cry 'xie xu,' at the back they reply. This is a song to carry heavy loads."

The *Shijing* tells how "the oak forests were laid low" as a result of incessant building. By the same token, only a few cedars remain in modern-day Lebanon. Such accounts remind us that deforestation and the expansion of societies have gone hand in hand throughout recorded history. At the dawn of the second millennium, almost 80 percent of Europe was forested; today, most of this woodland has been cleared. Like the cedars of Lebanon, Sherwood Forest of Robin Hood fame is a paltry reminder of the grandeur that once was, and the majority of the remaining trees in the Black Forest are sick or dying. Indeed, so grievous was this task of deforestation that the workmen themselves often felt compelled to offer apologies in song as they cut down the trees. An old travel journal recounts the following rhyme, sung as the laborers cleared an oak forest in order to construct the city of Berne in the twelfth century: "Wood let us willingly cut thee: this Citie must Bern named be." Yet, apologies or not, the trees came down. The same process repeated itself in the New World.

When European settlers first came to land now called the United States, almost half of it was covered by trees, representing over one billion acres of pristine woodlands. Yet, as was done in Lebanon and Europe, the building of the nation also signaled the clearing of the country's forests. Timberland was converted to agricultural and pastoral use—for a period of fifty years, American farmers chopped down an average of over eight thousand trees per day—or made way for a variety of other commercial and private uses.

Yet wood was more than just an obstacle to expanding economies. It increasingly became a valuable commodity in its own right, serving as fuel, construction material, paper or in some other capacity. Tree cutting on a large scale had always taken place—at least, ever since Columbus constructed the first colonial village on the east bank of the Bajabonico River, where builders and craftsmen were numbered among the fifteen hundred settlers—but logging would now become a major industry in its own right. At first, the exploitation of this resource was handled haphazardly. Communities drew on the woodlands near at hand. As commerce developed, areas near waterways and major commercial centers were the first locations to be cleared. In the United States, portions of New England, the mid-Atlantic, and the coastal southeast were the earliest to relinquish their tree cover in the name of progress. The initial logging camps might have included only three or four men, but eventually grew to encompass one hundred or more workers. Logging gradually expanded into the Ohio Valley, the Great Lake states, the south central region, and, eventually, the Pacific Northwest, feeding the growing nation's insatiable appetite for wood and its by-products. Today this process continues, although more often in poorer regions of the world, with virgin timberland from Siberia or plantation forests in countries such as Uruguay, Indonesia, South Africa and Thailand serving as increasingly important suppliers to global markets.

Ethnomusicologists have provided us with some understanding of tree-cutting songs from traditional societies—for example, Dale Olsen has documented their use among the Warao of Venezuela, and Steven Feld has recorded them in Papua New Guinea. Other scattered examples, from Africa to Russia, can be found in various collections, but these are mere glimpses compared to the panoramic views provided by the folklorists who have studied the culture of North American logging camps. For an earlier generation of scholars in Canada and the United States, these camps with their rough characters, and their stories and songs, proved to be an alluring subject, and many researchers rose to the challenge of documenting and interpreting the folklore and musical life of these isolated workplaces in the wilderness. As the late Canadian folklorist Edith Fowke wrote in 1970: "Some years ago I proposed that the lumber camp setting had played a key role in maintaining and transmitting a significant body of traditional song. I suggested that this role went beyond the confines of song text topics of occupational reference." Stan Hugill has also called attention to the frequent interaction between lumber workers and sailors on the waterways where timber was transported, and suggests that a "close alliance" between the two led to the frequent exchange of songs. The loggers, researchers discovered, were tremendous songsters, as exhibited both in their composition of new songs and lyrics, as well as in their ability to remember and share the older music they had heard. "One clear sign of this is the number of parallels to Canadian and United States lumber camp tunes that have turned up in recently available collections from Australia," Fowke writes. "It would be difficult to argue any extensive cross-influence in accounting for the parallels; rather a pattern of growth from a common origin would be indicated." In essence, the immigrant laborers who came to these logging camps appear to have taken greater care in preserving their traditional music, and in teaching it to others, than did their counterparts in cities and agricultural communities.

As is invariably the case in isolated settings, the logging camps gradually developed their own mannerisms and customs—in essence, their own local culture. Most of the workers were single men quick to develop new ties and habits amid the camaraderie of their round-the-clock companions. After months together, the loggers came to act alike, think alike, and even talk alike. A curious observer once counted some four thousand words indigenous to the lumber trade—a veritable private language for lumberjacks. Even today we frequently employ colloquial expression drawn from the camps, almost always when discussing unpleasant matters. When we speak of a "logjam" or even of a traffic "jam" on the road we are merely adopting the term used for the jamming of logs during a river drive. "Going haywire" refers to the baling wire used by loggers for mending sleds and tools. "Skid row" hails back to the skid roads on which logs were hauled by oxen into mill towns.

But not all was unpleasant in a logger's life. The conviviality of the camp served as the theme for what may be the most widely disseminated of the lumbering songs—so central to the logger's repertoire, that it is often simply called "The Lumbercamp Song." Doerflinger assigned its origins to the northeast, where he believed it dated back at least to the 1840s. Fowke writes that "it probably originated in Maine or New Brunswick, but it turns up in much the same form in nearly every collection from the northeastern states and eastern Canda." The song often took on the name of the specific camp where it was learned, where it might be called "Jim Murphy's Camp," "Jim Lockwood's Camp," "Jim Porter's Shanty Song," or some other such name. But no matter what the title or where the locale, the words invariably celebrated the joie de vivre of the logging life.

> Come all you jolly boys, I will sing to you a song.
> 'Tis all about the shanty lads and how they get along.
> They're a bunch of jolly fellows so merrily and so fine,
> And they spend a pleasant winter in cutting down the pine.

The song continues, in its various versions, to describe the daily schedule and the different tasks involved in logging, all conveyed in the most boisterous spirit.

The song's opening words as quoted above (along with its close variants, such as "come all ye") reappear in countless logging camp songs. These words reflect the Old World antecedents of this music, much of it created by immigrants and their children, and they convey as well the collegial nature of the camp environment. Like students with their school-team fight songs, the shantyboys, as they were called (the term shares no clear link with the shanties of sailors), liked to sing of the superiority of their group. Numerous songs have survived that tout a specific camp and its crew. Edward Ives recalls searching through the old issues of the *Carleton Sentinel*, a New Brunswick newspaper, and finding a dozen such lyrics published there during the course of a single winter. "In spirit they are akin to the old photographs one often sees of the whole crowd standing outside the camp, posing with the tools of their particular tasks," he writes. Both the songs and photos serve as "souvenirs, something to call back, in years to come, the camaraderie of one's winter work."

This general tone of gaiety puts the lumber camp songs almost in a class by themselves in the area of work-related music. Here is another representative example, drawn from E. C. Beck's collection *Songs of the*

Michigan Lumberjacks, where even the logger's old patched clothes becomes a source of merriment.

> I am a jolly shanty boy
> Who loves to sing and dance.
> I wonder what my girls would say
> If they could see my pants!
> With fourteen patches on the knee
> And six upon the stern,
> I'll wear them while I'm in the woods
> And home when I return.
> For I am on my jolly way,
> I spend my money free.
> I have plenty—come and drink
> Lager beer with me.

Elsewhere in this book I describe occupational songs that relate the shabby clothing of laborers, a common image in working-class lyrics, but outside of the logging camps these descriptions are never delivered with such glee, and certainly not in the context of bragging about riches. For example, from Maine comes "The Logger's Boast," as documented by Roland P. Gray in his *Songs and Ballads of the Maine Lumberjacks,* with its tone of cheerful bragging:

> When you pass through the dense city,
> and pity all you meet,
> To hear their teeth chattering
> as they hurry down the street;
> In the red frost-proof flannel
> we're incased from top to toe,
> While we range the wild woods over,
> and a lumbering we go;
> And a lumbering we'll go,
> so a lumbering will go,
> O! we'll range the wild woods over
> while a lumbering we go.
> You may boast of your gay parties,
> your pleasures, and your plays,
> And pity us poor lumbermen
> while dashing in your sleighs;

We want no better pastime
than to chase the buck and doe;
O! we'll range the wild woods over.
and a lumbering we will go;
And a lumbering we'll go,
so a lumbering will go,
O! we'll range the wild woods over
while a lumbering we go.

During the early years of the twentieth century, when such songs were actively circulated in the camps, few other professions could boast such a plethora of proud and cheery songs. During this era, the songs of most occupations were frequently sober in tone, and sometimes could take on a mien of outright bitterness or anger. The coal mine, the factory, the prison: these places of labor served as sources of many of the most poignant songs in the traditional repertoire. In the songs of the field and the pasture, as well, one often finds a melancholy strain, even when the lyrics contain no overt words of lamentation or protest—in the songs of shepherds, for instance, where the loneliness of the vocation is almost always betrayed by the plaintive music. In contrast, the shantyboys of the timberlands had little patience for self-pity, and although they might be fond of a sad song, such as "The Plain Golden Band" or other ballads of disappointed love, these rarely dealt directly with work matters.

Attempts were made at various times to organize workers in the timber industry and, as in other vocations, songs were used to raise awareness of labor issues and to mount protests. But it is revealing to note that in the numerous examples of poems and hymns cited by Jeff Ferrell in his study of the songs of the Brotherhood of Timber Workers, he is unable to provide even one example of a timber worker actually singing these pieces. Instead, they were drawn from trade journals, socialist newspapers, and other periodicals. When complaints about working conditions found their way into the camp music, they were invariably softened by a bit of humor or irony. A death in camp would often be commemorated in music, but unlike the songs recounting mining disasters, for example, the aim of these compositions was to recall or praise the departed rather than to call for reform of working conditions. "Jimmy Judge," the account of an Ontario tragedy that was sung in many camps, is typical in this regard:

Jimmy Judge was this young man's name, I'm going to let you know,
And I mean to sing his praises wherever I do go,
For he was as fine a young man as ever the sun shone on,
And 'twas on that Bonneshai River that he was drownded on. . . .
It would melt your heart with pity when they brought him on the shore
For to see his handsome features with the rocks all cut and tore,
To see so fine a young man all in his youthful bloom.
Down on these foaming waters he found a dismal doom.

Here no blame is cast; no threats of retribution are made. The song ends with the confident assertion: "But now he is in Paradise and happy he may be."

Despite such tragic ballads, the songs of the camps were mostly lighthearted and apparently carefree. Even the interludes between songs betrayed this sensibility. Edward Ives recounts a verse often sung after a lumberjack had finished with his song so as to encourage someone else to continue the entertainment:

Down in the lonesome pinewoods,
This song is sung with glee.
Now I have sung a song for you
And you may sing one for me.

Perhaps only the sailors could match the lumberjacks in the exuberance of their songs—and, as we have seen, much musical commerce took place between the two occupations; yet, even here, I would give the upper hand to the woodsman. Hence, it comes as little cause for surprise that when the comedy troupe Monty Python wanted to parody the excessive bonhomie of male bonding songs, they focused on the convivial lumberjacks of the logging camps. Thanks to their efforts, the most famous woodsman song is none of the camp ballads cited by the folklorists, but rather

I cut down trees.
I eat my lunch.
I go to the lavatory.
On Wednesdays I go shoppin'
And have buttered scones for tea.

No, logging life was not quite this carefree. In fact, the camp could be a dreary environment to pass long months in virtual isolation. Yet this very dreariness was a spur to the creation of song and the search for amusement: loggers realized that any entertainment at camp must, by necessity, be provided by themselves. "Lumberjack songs are not work songs like those of sailors," explain Paul Glass and Louis Singer in their introduction to *Songs of Forest and River Folk*. "Woodsmen's songs are created for the most part *after* the job is done." Here music co-existed with other diversions. "Story-tellers were almost as welcome as a good cook," Donald MacKay writes in his study *The Lumberjacks*, and notes the prowess of a highly esteemed raconteur who started a story in November to amuse his colleagues each night after dinner, and didn't finish it until after Christmas. Such a knack for narrative invention was greatly appreciated in the old camps, where there were few books, and perhaps even fewer who could read them. But while only the most fortunate camps could boast of a resident Homer or Chaucer, many commanded a decent share of musical talent and musical instruments were common in camp. "Their music was fiddle, accordion, mouth organ, and jew's harps," MacKay explains. Talent in this area was held in high esteem. "Crusty old foremen were known to hire a good singer or fiddler even if he was not much of a logger."

We can rarely identify the composer of a work song with any certainty. These snatches of music come as mysteriously as they go, seemingly born on the wind and seldom arriving on the job site with a pedigree in hand. Yet a surprising amount of documentation on the creators of lumberjack songs is available, partly due to the prolific output of a few singing timbermen whose notoriety spread in tandem with their melodies. Lawrence Gorman, born on Prince Edward Island in 1846, was the foremost of these celebrated composers of the woodlands. The extent of his fame, almost entirely spread by word of mouth, can be measured by recollections that were still strong almost forty years after his death when Edward Ives began conducting research for a biography. After publicizing his project in a few newspapers in the northeast, letters began pouring into his mailbox, full of stories of Gorman's life and times. Before long Ives was corresponding with over 150 people, all of whom had something to say about this long-dead lumberjack. William Doerflinger writes: "If more orally circulated songs—widely circulated ones, too—were composed by any other folk-song maker on this continent than have been traced on good authority to Larry Gorman, the fact hasn't been reported."

Gorman's songs did little to advance his career, however. Despite the popularity and staying power of his music, Gorman died poor in 1917, his energy spent in years of hard work as a woodsman and millhand. Gorman no doubt contributed to his own tribulations: his taste for satire, seldom held in check, was not appreciated by its victims, and on many occasions he was ousted from a camp for a song that raised the ire of a cook or foreman. Gorman even commemorated this fact in an autobiographical song, which asserted:

> And when they see me coming
> Their eyes stick out like prongs,
> Saying, "Beware of Larry Gorman,
> He's the man who makes the songs."

Gorman's compositions show a closer affinity to the popular literary tradition of Robert W. Service, James Whitcomb Riley, and Rudyard Kipling than to the call-and-response efforts of the anonymous work song composers of his day. As with these other poets of the vernacular tongue, Gorman's tales in rhyme were distinguished by their compact narration of a story, their author's unfailing ear for the cadences of spoken language, and their large doses of local color. Hearing the opening of his story about the lovelorn lass who falls in love with "Young Bill Crane," we cannot help but be reminded of other populist verses such as "The Shooting of Dan McGrew" or "Casey at the Bat."

> My name is Nellie Harrison; the truth I'll tell to you.
> I'm in the prime of womanhood, just turning twenty-two.
> I've been admired by earls and squires, and many's the lovesick swain.
> But 'twas beyond their art to gain my heart till I met young Billy Crane.

In this song Nellie Harrison is jilted by her lover, who breaks his promise to marry her and ships aboard the steamer *Andover*. The tale ends with the odd twist so characteristic of these ballads, when Nellie Harrison resolves to disguise herself as a man and take to the sailor's life herself:

> I'll dress myself in man's attire, I'll scorn the raging main;
> I mean to ride the swells and tides till I gain young Billy Crane.

With his lilting momentum and mock-epic language—"scorn the raging main," "lovesick swain," "ride the swells and tides"—Gorman leaves far behind the conventional world of work songs and work-related songs. Yet the shantyboys of the camps loved such tales, with their earthy grandiloquence and accessible subject matter. They may not have been songs about the working man and this travails, but they certainly were songs for the working man.

Joe Scott, a contemporary of Gorman, was almost as well known for his song writing skills. Scott was born in 1867, and sometime before his twentieth birthday he left home to work as a woodsman. In the logging camps of Maine he earned a reputation for his skill with an ax and as a first-rate river driver, as well as for his songs. Moreover, unlike Larry Gorman, whose biting satires made him enemies wherever he went, Scott was well liked. His musical talent and amiability, as well as his undeniable skills as a lumberjack, made him a welcome addition to any logging camp. His friendly disposition may, however, also have hidden a deep streak of melancholy. A failed romance had marked his youth, and it figures as the apparent subject matter for his most famous song.

In October 1893, Scott was engaged to a woman named Lizzie Morse, and he had even reached the point of having the town clerk issue a license for their impending marriage. But no ceremony ever took place, and a few months later she was engaged to a rival. Edward Ives, who wrote an extensive biography of Scott, views this event as "the turning point in his life." The folklorists who researched the songs of the lumberjacks tended to be swept away by the romance of their topic, so we are wise to be wary of their psychological insights. Yet Scott clearly had his moods after this failed early romance, and it didn't take much to turn his laughter into tears—sometimes in the midst of a song or after a few drinks. Like many balladeers, Scott sang of unhappy romance, and for his ballad "The Plain Golden Band" he could draw from firsthand experience. "Uncle Joe" Patterson, interviewed by Doerflinger, noted that the song was "famous" in the Summit Landing, Maine, camp where he worked with Scott in 1905, and he confirmed that it was inspired by a real romance.

> The day that we parted I ne'er can forget;
> I fancy I see those sad tears falling yet,
> My poor heart was sad and with sorrow did sting
> When she took from her finger that plain golden ring,
> Saying, "take back this ring that I fain would retain,
> For wearing it only causes me pain.

I have broken the vows that I made on the strand.
Now take back, I pray you, that plain golden band."

A similar maudlin tone marks "Sacker Shean's Little Girl," another Scott composition:

Now I am only Sacker Shean's
Poor little girl, you know,
Who was cast upon this cruel world,
No home, no place to go.
My father is a drunkard
And my mother, don't you know,
Oh she left me in my infancy,
She died long years ago.

This Dickensian piece, revolving around a poor child in distress, seems a paltry thing today, as does "The Plain Golden Band." But for all their clichés, these songs help us understand the types of simple stories that were popular in the logging camps, where tales and songs with the most time-honored themes—love, family, war, adventure, friendship—found a ready audience. The darker and more realistic approach, evoked by mining or industrial work songs from this era, would have held little appeal for the lumberjacks, who were seeking diversion, not consciousness raising, during their idle hours. And though the songs of Gorman and Scott hardly seem as charming to us as they must have to their logging camp listeners, who among us is not touched in some degree by the images they inspire of sentimental lumberjacks who, for all their roughshod ways, express their emotions by listening to songs about orphans and jilted lovers? The modern music of male bonding, examples of which I will spare you, sounds harsh and crass by comparison.

Scott went to the trouble of having some of his songs professionally printed, and he intended to sell these copies at the camps or lodgings where he stayed. "He used to get twenty-five cents apiece for [his songs]," recalled Thomas Hoy, who first met Scott in New Hampshire around the turn of the century. "They were printed on a little paper, just like a little circular you get, you know. He had them typed somewhere." Scott brought the printed songs along in a briefcase, and would perform the ballads as part of his sales pitch. "He was a good singer. He'd sing any song that he sold there. And then they'd ask him about other songs [and] he'd sing. He knew an awful lot of songs."

Scott died in June 1918, only a few months after Larry Gorman. It was, in many ways, the end of an era. True, the invention of the chain saw was still thirty years in the future, and mechanical tree fellers arrived in the woods even later. Preservation efforts—which would eventually safeguard some 250 million acres of the United States from timber or natural resource exploitation—were only in their infancy. Yet other factors were already at work that would undermine the singing traditions of the lumberjacks. The insulated nature of the lumber camps had already started to give way to modern technologies that allowed greater interaction with the world outside. Spurgeon Allaby told Edward Ives of the surprise in camp, during the winter of 1912 and 1913, when the cook arrived with a cylinder phonograph. "It was the first one I had ever seen," he recalled, "and believe me it was kept busy for a while but he didn't have too many records for it." In succeeding years, crystal sets and radios were, at first, much-cherished luxuries, and eventually necessities. In time, film projectors came to camp, initiating Sunday movies in the cookhouses, where westerns and other Hollywood fare predominated. The flourishing of lumber camp music, which had been inspired by the loggers' need to create their own amusements, now gave way to prepackaged songs and stories from afar. In this way, the camp residents were no different from those countless tribes and communities, studied by ethnomusicologists, who abandon their rich native traditions of music when faced with the oh-so-perfect products of the entertainment industry.

Yet the lumberjacks were well served by the folklorists and ballad collectors who worked to compile and preserve the music and traditions of their profession. Few occupations of the late nineteenth century and early twentieth have been better documented. Songs, stories, photographs, and anecdotes have been collected and published. Individual logging camp composers like Larry Gorman and Joe Scott have served as subjects of full-scale biographies. Above all, this field shows what can be accomplished by meticulous and loving preservation efforts undertaken by caring individuals and, as such, could serve as a model for other researchers who are interested in documenting musical traditions on the brink of disappearance.

 CHAPTER EIGHT

Take This Hammer!

Twenty-one hammers fallin' in a line.

Twenty-one hammers fallin' in a line.

Twenty-one hammers fallin' in a line.

Nobody's hammer, buddy, ring like mine.

—African American work song

In a postindustrial age, when most workers measure their productivity in clicks and bytes, we inevitably forget the erstwhile intimacy between manual laborers and their tools. The carpenter's hammer, the lumberjack's axe, the sailor's knife, even the writer's trusty typewriter (now all but obsolete): these may possess a simple utilitarian function. But for their user, they are something more. The tools may even be said to have their own personality—note how many workers give names to their implement of choice, as well as attribute to them a range of character traits, from fickleness to dependability, that are usually associated with living beings. Under the best circumstances, bonds of affection grow naturally between workers and the tools of their trade. And why not? Measure it however you choose—by the physicality of contact, the successes shared, or the sheer number of hours spent together—the laborer may well have a closer relationship with the much cherished instrument of a lonely craft, than with fellow-workers, or even family and friends. Surviving work songs, captured on recordings or in print, support this hypothesis. Almost as many focus on hammers, shovels, spades and other implements of manual labor, as on spouses and lovers.

Yet just as dealings with a spouse can be complicated and contradictory, so is the worker's relationship to the tools of labor. For the hammer, the axe, and other such instruments are signs of power and assertion, as well as symbols of servitude to hard labor and to the structures of control that workplaces invariably present. Giving up the hammer could often serve as a potent sign of freedom, as in the following song gathered in Alabama and presented in Newman White's 1928 book *American Negro Folk-Songs:*

> Take my hammer,
> Carry it to my captain,
> Tell him I'm gone,
> Tell him I'm gone.
> If he ask you was I running,
> Tell him no,
> Tell him no.
> Tell him I was going across the Blue Ridge Mountains
> Walking slow, yes, walking slow.

At other times, the tool gets the upper hand, as in the lament of the prison worker:

> I say that's all about the hammer,
> 'Bout a-killing me, hammer.

The laborer's hammer, real or symbolic, is thus the center of multiple valences, highly charged and often paradoxical. But all of them link back to one dominant theme: power. Sometimes it is the power of the worker that is foremost, at other times that of the bosses and overseers. But above all, the power of the hammer itself is asserted, again and again. In songs of work this theme is pervasive, and clearly reflects the deeply felt emotions of the men who made the songs. Often this power is merely implied; but occasionally it comes to the fore, as in the following lyric from Andalusia:

> Today, since I'm the anvil.
> I know I must forebear . . .
> If ever I'm the hammer,
> Beware, my friend, beware.

At an extreme, the tool may be thought to possess a quasi-mystical efficacy. From the ancient Minoans to the modern Masons, we find prosaic tools invested with rich symbolic meaning and incorporated into important rituals. Nor should this be surprising. One of the interesting effects of working at peak levels of performance—in what Csikszentmihalyi aptly calls the "flow state"—is the extraordinary effortlessness of the labor. In such moments, the tool can seem to take on a life of its own, do the work by itself, with little guidance from the user. In my experiences playing jazz piano, I have noted this odd phenomenon: the music seems to be at its best when I feel I am doing next to nothing. The black and white keys have taken on a magnetic attraction drawing my fingers to the right places without any deliberation on my part. In contrast, the more conscious I am of being "in command," the less commanding the music turns out to be. To some extent, all manual laborers have experienced this same effect. And the best workers must, almost by definition, do so with greater frequency. Who can blame them, then, for feeling that their tool of choice enjoys a remarkable potency, which the implements of their coworkers fail to possess?

No tool plays a more significant and complex role in the surviving body of work songs than the hammer. As researchers have learned, the word "hammer" took on a world of meanings for the singing laborer. Sometimes it could be used to refer to an axe or other tool—Bruce Jackson found that "Hammer Ring" was the most popular tree cutting song among the convicts he recorded—and was belted out with enthusiasm even when no hammer was present. Half a world away, Vladimir Propp marveled at the prevalence of Russian folk songs that include the refrain "Dubinuška, uxnem" ("oh, sledge hammer"), and he noted that the words were often used in contexts in which hammering plays no part, such as boat hauling. In grasping for an explanation, Propp argued for an etymology linking the songs to the word *dub*, which "once designated any leaf-bearing tree." As such, the scholar was compelled to propose a linkage between the act of hauling and the practice of pulling down a tree with a cable. I am incapable of judging matters of Russian etymology, but the transfer of hammering songs to other tasks is so common elsewhere—due, I believe, to the special intensity of labor they inspire—that it is not surprising to discover such borrowings among boat haulers.

The hammer could also serve as a symbol of the worker's strength or determination, or even virility. A. L. Lloyd, probing the latent meaning of industrial songs, has noted a "fantasy, persistent in folklore since ancient times, in which working techniques are sexualized and the tools and gestures of trade are turned into erotic metaphors." Gershon Legman, in an article in the *Journal of American Folklore*, adopts a similar perspective, calling attention to "the proud phallic ordnance metaphors of hammers and scythes" so characteristic of male work songs. But it is hard to know who is more guilty of concupiscence in this instance, the harried laborer or the erudite folklorist. (Recall that Legman, a great scholar of popular lore and obscure facts, also worked for the Kinsey Institute, coined the term "make love, not war," and gained some renown for calculating all of the possible positions for coition—so what *he* saw in a hammer of scythe may not serve as a good indicator of attitudes down at the Ace Hardware store.)

Of course, students of preindustrial societies are likely to find a different type of symbolic resonance in the hammer, noting the magical efficacy of the tool for many cultures. Writing of the Bambara tribe of West Africa, for example, Harold Courlander describes how blacksmiths were believed to possess "an invisible spiritual force." "Mystic powers" enabled smiths to work metals and were also transmitted by them into the implements they hammered into shape. Echoes of this reverence for the hammering smith can be found in many parts of the world, even in Western European traditions, as evidenced (to cite only the most obvious examples) in the myths associated with Thor and Vulcan. The well-known tradition that associates horseshoes with good luck is also linked to a venerable belief in the supernatural power of the blacksmiths who made them.

Yet we do not need to pursue these erotic and magical themes to grasp why the hammer should take on so much importance in the songs of workers. Indeed, we do not need to seek for symbols or hidden meanings of any sort. Simply as a brute fact (something "ready-to-hand" in Heidegger's usage); as an object that hits, and hits hard, anything in its path, the hammer would inevitably evoke thoughts of unvarnished force. Especially for a prisoner or a manual worker, a nine-pound tool seems highly likely to conjure up images of power and strength, even if only as a reaction against other indignities or as an outlet for pent-up emotions.

Here, a favorite old proverb comes to mind: "To a man with a hammer in his hand, everything looks like a nail." A singer holding such a tool, and swinging it with full force, is unlikely to offer us soothing melodies for whiling away the passing hours. Such music inevitably takes on the power of the hammer—it becomes rough, almost violent. "The most dynamic of Negro work rhythms are to be found in the hammer songs," attest B. A. Botkin and Alan Lomax in their accompanying notes to the recording *Negro Work Songs and Calls.* Frederick Burton, who studied Native American music during the early years of the twentieth century, tended to minimize the role of "industrial songs" (his preferred term for "work songs") in the tribes he observed. Yet even he marveled at the tendency of groups employed in carpentry to become so engrossed in the "roaring chorus" that accompanied their hammering, that sometimes they would even lay aside their tools and become totally absorbed by the music, pushing it ahead to its conclusion with great vigor, forgetful of the task at hand.

Work songs are rarely sung at fast tempos. The demands of physical labor typically require a measured approach—what one might call the "work song law of conservation of energy." Pacing is critical, and the song leader is responsible for seeing that the workers do not exhaust themselves in their efforts but rather can continue on until the end of day. But in the 1934 recording of "Hammer Ring," led by Jesse Bradley at the state penitentiary in Huntsville, Texas, the convicts keep up a jitterbugging tempo that is hardly sustainable and exceptionally rare among documented work songs. The "hammer, ring" literally blurs into "hammering," where the sound of work and the song feed off each other.

> LEADER: This is a very fine hammer.
> RESPONSE: Hammer ring!
> LEADER: This is a very fine hammer.
> RESPONSE: Hammer ring!
> LEADER: Got the same old hammer.
> RESPONSE: Hammer ring!
> LEADER: Got the same old hammer.
> RESPONSE: Hammer ring!
> LEADER: Got to hammerin' in the timber.
> RESPONSE: Hammer ring!
> LEADER: Got to hammerin' in the timber.
> RESPONSE: Hammer ring!

Here the sound of the song emulates the sound of the hammering itself. Half a world away, Verrier Elwin found a similar refrain among the

Agaria, who sing while at work amid the smiths and iron smelters of central India:

> O brother, the ringing of my hammering!
> *Tining tining, tining tining!*
> By my hammering the house is filled with rice!
> *Tining tining tining tining!*

In England, we encounter a comparable attempt to imitate the sound of the smith's hammer and bellows in song.

> Here's a health to the jolly blacksmith, the best of all fellows
> Who works at his anvil while the boy blows the bellows
> Which makes his bright hammer to rise and to fall . . .
> *Twankydillo, Twankydillo, Twankydillo-dillo-dillo-dillo.*

Such songs were probably a staple of the smith's day-to-day life in many communities. For example, in chapter 12 of Dicken's *Great Expectations,* Pip responds to Miss Havisham's demand that he sing, with "a song that imitated the measure of beating upon iron," which the protagonist (and probably Dickens too) had learned at the forge.

Within the context of the work song, as many of these songs make clear, the tools of the trade are more than just a recurring inspiration for music, they *are* the music, or at least a substantial part of it. It may not be going too far to claim that the hammer is the quintessential percussion instrument of the work song. A large portion of field recordings feature the hammer's recurring backbeat, as much a part of the song as the call-and-response between leader and group. Many compelling recordings of work songs would be deprived of their vitality if the sound of the tools were taken away.

William Eleazar Barton, a Lincoln scholar and minister, was among the first to note the importance of hammering songs among the African American workers of the South. He published several articles on plantation hymns in *New England Magazine* in 1898 and 1899, and though he concentrated his research primarily on songs of religious feeling, Barton could not help noticing the men "drowning their low chant to the chink! chink! of the steel." Sometimes the religious music and the hammering songs even coalesced, as Barton noted in his description of "The Christians' Hymn of the Crucifixion," sung at evening service, where the constant refrain was "Ham-mer-ring!" "I do not know that it is used as a song to work with," Barton told his readers, "but suspect that the 'hammer-ring!' which is the constant response, may be used sometimes to time the descent of the pick or sledge." In a collection of African American folk songs collected at Virginia's Hampton Institute and published in 1918 and 1919—and one of the first compilations to devote serious attention to work songs—we find a different, but comparable, example. The accompanying notes indicate that, at the word "huh!" the "hammer falls here, while the men expel their breath with a sharp ejaculation."

Boss is call-in—huh!
Let her drive, boys—huh!
Foller me—huh!
Foller me—huh!
I been hammerin'—huh!
In dis mountain—huh!
Four long year—huh!
Four long year—huh!

For centuries, the hammer was the worker's most versatile tool. It is linked to many trades and is almost ubiquitous in locales where manual labor took place—we find it indoors, outside, underground, behind bars, and on the move. Connoisseurs of hammers can no doubt delineate dozens of different occupational models—meeting the varying requirements of their specific users, from carpenters to surgeons, upholsterers to ship builders. In the early days of railroad construction in the United States, the hammer was used primarily to drive spikes and to drill into rock in preparation for exploding charges of powder. The latter task required a rhythmic coordination between two laborers, one holding and turning the drill and the other handling the hammer. In some instances, a single turner might assist two different drillers, which added to the complexity of the interactions. Drill hammers also played an important role in a range of other occupations, especially those requiring the removal of rock. Working with an inadequate hammer was more than just an inconvenience—it was a positive hazard. The expression "flying off the handle" comes from the unfortunate tendency for an axe or hammer head to come loose during use.

In the African American work song tradition, size and strength were preeminent concerns, for these laborers were typically given the toughest tasks, where sheer force, the more the better, was invariably demanded. That staple of the modern toolkit, the sixteen-ounce curved claw hammer, may be adequate for an unexpected weekend repair, but in an earlier day and age it would only have earned scorn and ridicule. To the extent that work songs or folk songs specify the type of hammer, it is usually expressed by weight and power, with the "nine-pound hammer" owning special pride of place. An especially rich body of song surrounds the topic of this particular tool. Dorothy Scarborough was the first researcher to publish a song under the title "Nine-Pound Hammer," which she includes in her 1925 collection *On the Trail of Negro Folksongs*. She provides this text, sent to her by Evelyn Cary Williams, who had heard it sung by Charles Calloway, a black worker from Bedford County.

> Nine-pound hammer,
> Kill John Henry.
> But 't won't kill me, babe—
> 'T won't kill me.

Scarborough also passes on another, similar work song, which was provided to her by Joseph Turner of Hollins, Virginia:

> Nine-pound hammer,
> Nine-pound hammer,
> Nine-pound hammer,
> Can't kill me,
> Can't kill me,
> Can't kill me.
> Nine pound hammer can't kill me.

Folk songs often present researchers with complicated histories that defy even the best efforts to determine an "authentic" lineage. This particular song offers a striking example of the difficulties involved in tracing the origins of even well-documented material. For example, Joanna Colcord discovered a version of it in an unlikely setting for such hammer songs: namely among sailors who served on U.S. Navy destroyers during World War I.

> This yere hammer kill Jack Johnson,
> Didn't kill me, babe, didn't kill me.

Cecil Sharp linked this same material with the English folk song "Swan-nanoa Town," which his North Carolina source, Julie Borne, sang in 1918 with the following passage:

> I've been a-hammering this old town, O,
> Seven long years, baby, seven long years . . .
> I've got the hammer, killed my partner,
> Can't kill me, baby, can't kill me.

Robert Winslow Gordon uncovered the following version during his visits to prisons to collect songs in the mid-1920s:

> This ole hammer-huh!
> Killed John Henry-huh!
> Can't kill me, baby—huh!
> Can't kill me!
> My old hammer-huh!
> Shine like silver—huh!
> Shina like gol,' baby-huh!
> Shina like gol'!
> Ain't no hammer-huh!
> In this whole mountain-huh!
> Shina like mine, baby-huh!
> Shina like mine!

And as we shall see below, a very similar passage can be found in a Jamaican song that appears to date back to the late-nineteenth century.

The year after Scarborough's book was published, Howard Odum and Guy Johnson, both affiliated with the University of North Carolina, provided further information on hammer songs in their milestone study *Negro Workaday Songs*. In this volume they claim that "no workaday songs are superior to the gang songs, heave-a-horas, steel driving songs, short pick-and-shovel songs, and the scores of other short specimens which accompany special tasks requiring hard work, team unison, or continuous effort. There is, of course, no attempt here to present even an approach to exhaustive lists. We have so far found no intimation of where the number of such songs will stop." Their collection includes the following example:

This ol' hammer, hammer
Mus' be loaded;
This ol hammer, hammer
Mus' be loaded;
This ol hammer, hammer
Mus' be loaded;
Do bear down,
Do bear down.

As well as the following:

If I could hammer like John Henry,
If I could hammer like John Henry,
Lawd, I'd be a man,
Lawd, I'd be a man.

Over the next two decades, hammer songs started showing up in an ever-widening range of musical settings: in Carl Sandburg's popular collection *The American Songbag* (1927), which included "My Old Hammah" and "Drivin' Steel"; in hillbilly songs, such as the Brunswick recording of "Nine-Pound Hammer" by Al Hopkins and his Buckle Busters (1927); and, above all, in the field recordings of work songs conducted by John Lomax and others in the American South. No fewer than nine different recorded versions of "Hammer Ring" are housed in the American folk song archives of the Library of Congress, all but one of them from Texas. Sometimes the refrain "hammer ring!" or "let your hammer ring!" became incorporated into other work song traditions, showing up as a refrain, for instance, in some versions of "Black Betty." The tool traveled even farther west, the nine-pound hammer becoming a ten-pound hammer in Blaine Stubblefield's rendition of "Way Out in Idaho," recorded by Alan Lomax in 1938. Archie Green notes that some thirty hammer songs were issued by record companies—and this does not include the recordings of the ballad "John Henry," of which there were an even greater number. The multiplicity, and variants, of songs about hammering during the years preceding World War II is nothing short of remarkable: in an age of automation and the replacement of manual tools with more complicated machines, the most ancient work implement of all had become a hot topic. Amid this proliferation of hammering songs, moreover, one repeatedly encounters a romanticized and idealized vision of manual labor, which no doubt was accentuated by the gradual disappearance of such work and, with the onset of the Great Depression, by the general scarcity of jobs of all sorts.

The hammer songs persisted to the final days of work songs. These songs, for example, play a significant role in the music preserved by Cortez Reece, who recorded work songs in West Virginia during the period from 1949 to 1953. Almost a third of the songs included in *Prison Worksongs*, the compilation of material collected by Harry Oster in the late 1950s, mention a hammer in some capacity. As late as the mid-1960s, Bruce Jackson recorded no fewer than nineteen versions of "Hammer Ring," sung by thirteen different leaders, as part of his fieldwork in Texas prisons. I have noticed that even today, long after the decline of this tradition, when the topic of work songs is mentioned, the first thought that comes to mind for most people is not the lumberjack and his axe, or the sailor and his shanty, but the chain gang worker with his heavy hammer.

"John Henry," of course, stands in a class by itself; it is the song in which all of these themes come to a head: the inroads of automation, the mythical power of the tool, the idealization of manual work, and the inherent dignity of labor as well as its dangers and degrading circumstances. Indeed, any assessment of work songs in American music and life seems to lead inevitably to the consideration of John Henry—half historical figure and half legend—and his compelling story. He has been commemorated in perhaps the most famous of all American ballads, written about in books, brought to life on stage and in film, and his name or story figures in countless work songs. The work songs may have come first, Guy Johnson asserts, speculating that "the first songs about John Henry were simple, spontaneous hammer songs." These songs provide few details of the story, but "a short time later some person who was familiar with the tradition composed a ballad and had it printed on single sheets for distribution at a low price, say five or ten cents." Later researchers, including Louis Chappell and Archie Green, have taken the opposite view by arguing, in Green's words, that "the narrative form was separately and quickly composed around the particular dramatic conflict of a man and a steam drill."

Certainly the drama of the narrative and its symbolic resonance take center stage in any assessment of John Henry. His story celebrates a classic battle between the worker and the newly introduced steam drill, which threatened to take the place of the "steel-drivin' " laborers constructing the railroads of America.

> John Henry said to his Captain,
> "A man ain't nothin' but a man,
> And before I'll let your steam drill beat me down,
> Gonna die with my hammer in my hand, Lord, Lord,
> Gonna die with my hammer in my hand."

The battle is too much for John Henry, who dies after the exhausting contest—although some versions of the song make sure to specify that the man out-performed the machine. "John Henry made his fourteen feet, while the steam drill made only nine." As early as 1909, folklorists were taking an interest in this story, but long before it became an object of scholarship, the song must have traveled far and wide and entertained many audiences. The fame of the ballad is not surprising, combining as it does a number of powerful themes that would have resonated with turn-of-the-century listeners: the threat of mechanization replacing manual labor jobs; the ability of a black worker to challenge the system; the inherent excitement of a physical competition.

For many earlier researchers in the field of American folklore, seeking the "real" John Henry was their "Holy Grail" quest. Their efforts are much like the amateur detective work practiced by later scholars of African American music, who were determined to discover the true life story behind the legends surrounding Robert Johnson or Buddy Bolden. But as puzzling as Johnson or Bolden were, John Henry presented an even greater enigma. At least with those latter-day legends, some solid evidence—a photograph or a location—was available to the investigator as a starting point. With John Henry, no agreement could be reached on the simplest matters—where he lived, whether John Henry was his real name, or even if he had truly ever existed.

Nonetheless, many witnesses have stepped forward, claiming to possess first hand knowledge. Here are some extracts from correspondence received by Guy Johnson, when he tried to find the real John Henry in the 1920s:

A letter from North Carolina: "With further reference to my letter sometime ago I am herewith giving you more data on John Henry, steel driver. John Henry was born in Caldwell County. His real name was John Henry Dula."

A letter from Utah: "John Henry was a native of Holly Springs, Mississippi, and was shipped to the Cruzee Mountain Tunnel, Alabama, to work on the A.G.S. Railway in the year of 1880 . . . [His] real name was John H. Dabner."

A letter from Ohio: "My father who is 72 years old worked with the original John Henry (Jones) 41 years ago." [Johnson's request for more information from this party only produced the return of his letter, marked "Gone, left no address."]

A letter from West Virginia: "I was also Aquainted with one of his nephews and have talked with one of the men that was turning the steel for him when the Incedent happened that the song was composed from. . . . I live in twenty miles of the Big Ben Tunnel where it all happened."

A letter from Michigan: "My Uncle Gus . . . was working with John Henry and saw him when he beat the steam drill and fell dead. This was in the year 1887. It was at Oak Mountain Alabama."

A letter from Kentucky: "I got most of my information from an old Negro grader. . . . He claimed to have known John Henry personally . . . He said that John Henry died during the Civil War, also that he was a 'free' Negro—but that is hardly possible for no steam drills were used in this country prior to that time."

And on and on, until Johnson found himself awash in a "thousand and one different opinions as to where, when and how John Henry came to his death." As the theories proliferated, they became even more surprising: some suggested that John Henry was the same as the outlaw John Hardy, also celebrated in a ballad, or even that John Henry was a white man. Johnson eventually determined that the preponderance of evidence pointed to either Alabama or the Big Bend Tunnel in West Virginia. His fieldtrip to the latter in June 1927 was a frustrating enterprise. "What a pity that someone did not make an investigation at Big Bend ten or fifteen years ago! Even five years ago would have made a great difference in the richness of the data available." The key informants had mostly died or become too forgetful to answer the relevant questions.

Beginning in 1922, Louis Chappell also undertook research into the historical roots of the John Henry ballad, and his views may have influenced Johnson's conclusions. However, Chappell's book on the subject was not published until four years after Johnson's had appeared. With its detailed documentation—drawing on newspaper articles, research on tunneling, construction reports, correspondence, and interviews—Chappell's *John Henry: A Folk-Lore Study* represented a major step forward in separating fact from fiction. In particular, Chappell could assert with some confidence that John Henry had been a real individual and had been involved in tunneling operations for the railroad. Between 1870 and 1872, around one thousand men, mostly black, had been engaged in tunneling through Big Bend Mountain for the C&O Railroad. The work was arduous and very dangerous. The red shale of the mountain disintegrated easily; slides were a continual threat; and the air was thick with stone dust and noxious fumes from the more than eight hundred pounds of nitroglycerin exploded each day. Chappell believed that here, on the largest tunneling project in American history at the time, the legend and ballad of John Henry may have had its origin.

George Jenkins, who worked in the construction of the tunnel, recalled that "John Henry was there when I went to Big Bend. . . . Always singing when he worked. He was a sort of song-leader." D. R. Gilpin, who also worked at Big Bend, recalled that "John Henry was a good worker at driving steel," and that he "was a mighty powerful man" and was "the singingest man I ever saw." But he also added, "I don't know a thing about John Henry driving steel in a contest with a steam drill, and don't think I ever saw one at the tunnel." Yet John Hedrick, who was twenty-three years old when tunnel construction began, and who was manager of the woodwork (responsible for building shanties for the laborers), asserted "I knew John Henry . . . He drove steel with a steam drill at the east end, on the inside of the tunnel not far from the end." Hedrick admits that he "didn't see the contest," but recalled that John Henry won in the battle with the machine. His brother, George Hedrick, adds: "I often saw John Henry drive steel out there. I saw the steam drill too, when they brought it to the east end of the tunnel, but I didn't see John Henry when he drove in the contest with it. I heard about it right after." Neal Miller supplied the following: "I saw John Henry drive steel in Big Bend Tunnel. He was a great singer and always singing some old song when he was driving steel . . . The steam drill was brought to Big Bend Tunnel as an experiment, and failed because it stayed broke all the time." Miller also casts light on the final chapter of the story: "John Henry didn't die from getting too hot in the contest with the steam drill, like you say. He drove in the heading a long time after that. But he was later killed in the tunnel . . . The boys round the tunnel told me that he was killed from a blast of rock in the heading, and was put in a box with another Negro and buried at night under the big fill at the east end of the tunnel." However, Miller's credibility could be called into question because he told Johnson that he had actually seen part of the competition between John Henry and the steam drill but apparently refrained from making this same claim when interviewed by Chappell.

Did a worker named John Henry actually battle a steam drill in a contest such as the one described in the song? Not everyone has accepted the evidence gathered by Chappell, as I note below. And even some knowledgeable witnesses seemed dubious about the event; for example, Sam Wallace told Johnson that he doubted whether any such contest had ever taken place at Big Bend Tunnel: "In the first place, if it had happened I would have heard about it at the time because I was at the tunnel a great deal and I knew most of the steel drivers. In the second place, I'm sure there never was any steam drill at the tunnel. No, I think this John Henry stuff is just a tale somebody started."

Of course, the dispute over whether the steam drill was used at Big Bend might be explained by the fact that work on the tunnel took place simultaneously at five different sites, and thus most workers might never have seen the drill. An account from the time notes that the "breaking of machinery" delayed the construction of the tunnel. Further, Captain W. R. Johnson, who managed the project, was known to use steam machinery when it could be applied effectively and economically. Tunneling, especially the demanding type of work entailed at Big Bend Mountain, spurred innovation during the nineteenth century, such as improvements in drills and the use of explosives. Numerous patents and inventions in this area date back to the period. Above all, the advantages of the machine versus the laborer, a key theme in the ballad, were much analyzed in contemporary documents; for example, a report covering the period 1869 to 1874, the same time during which our hypothesized competition took place, notes that power drilling cost four cents per inch compared to nine and one-third cents for manual work. Finally, we are certain that contests and competitions between steel drivers were common, and were accompanied by wagers and drinking. The case of John Henry is circumstantial at best, but given the half century that had elapsed between the supposed event and the arrival of researchers on the scene, the body of facts gathered is impressive, as is their congruence with the ballad.

But other theories and additional evidence have come to light since the pioneering work of Johnson and Chappell. MacEdward Leach would later make a case for a Jamaican origin to the John Henry story. Leach was skeptical of the firsthand reports gathered by earlier researchers, noting that they tended to add few substantial details beyond what we already know from the song. During his fieldwork on the island in 1957, Leach had met with the principal emeritus of Jamaica College, Reginald Murry, who provided him with information on mountain folklore. Later, Murry sent him a map that he had made in 1894, on the back of which he had noted some proverbs and a song. It begins

Ten pound hammer it crush me pardner
Ten pound hammer it crush me pardner
Ten pound hammer it crush me pardner
Somebody dyin' every day.

John Henry is not mentioned at any point in the song, and the only link Leach offers is Murry's claim that it was called the "John Henry Song." But as we have seen, similar songs about nine-pound or ten-pound hammers in the United States sometimes mention John Henry. Leach also cites Walter Jekyll's research on Jamaican music and folklore, published in 1907, in which he discusses a song that mentions a "ten pound order" as well as the "number nine tunnel" and includes the phrase "Somebody dyin' here every day." Jekyll makes no reference to John Henry, but he does explain that the song relates to "an incident, or perhaps it were better to say an accident, in the making of the road to Newcastle. A man who undertook a piece of contract work for £10 was killed by a falling stone. The so-called tunnels are cuttings. Number nine had a very bad reputation." Leach conjectures that the worker killed was John Henry. On the basis of this tenuous body of evidence, he feels confident in concluding that the "oldest objective data concerning John Henry are the Jamaican songs," and he proposes that the protagonist of the ballad took on the identity of the Jamaican worker some time around 1900.

A more compelling case for an alternative to the Big Bend Tunnel was made in 2002 by John Garst, who gathered substantial evidence linking John Henry to the Oak Tunnel in Alabama. As noted above, in the 1920s Guy Johnson suggested that the Alabama claims provided the most reasonable alternative to the West Virginia hypothesis he eventually supported (although apparently influenced greatly by Chappell in this matter). Yet neither Johnson nor Chappell followed up on these leads with any rigor. In particular, Johnson had complained that his various informants had mentioned three locations in Alabama—Cruzee Mountain Tunnel, Cursey Mountain Tunnel, and Oak Mountain—and though he could locate Oak Mountain, situated southeast of Birmingham, the other names seemed to refer to no identifiable spot on the map. Garst has made a convincing case that "Cruzee" and "Cursey" are corruptions of the Coosa Mountain, and has shown that tunnels were made at both Coosa and Oak Mountains in 1887 and 1888. He has also taken names provided to Johnson and Chappell by their informants, and has linked them to individuals working for the railroad. In his research, Garst places considerable emphasis on validating the claims of C. C. Spencer, who sent letters to Johnson in the 1920s insisting that the John Henry story came from Alabama. Spencer offered many details of a competition between John Henry Dabner and a steam drill that took place, he asserted, on September 20, 1882. Spencer even claimed to have witnessed the event:

> The contractor told him that if he could beat this steam drill he would give him a new suit of clothes and fifty dollars, which was a large amount for that day and time. John Henry accepted the proposition providing they would buy him a fourteen-pound hammer. This the contractor did. . . . The agent had lots of trouble with his drill, but John Henry . . . kept pecking away with his fourteen-pound hammer. Of course, the writer was only about fourteen years old at that time, but I remember there were about three or four hundred people present. When the poor man with the hammer fell in the arms of his helper in a dead faint, they threw water on him and revived him . . . the last words he said were: 'Have I beat that old steam drill?' The record was twenty-seven and one half feet (27½'). The steam drill twenty-one (21'), and the agent lost his steam drill.

Spencer adds that he thought that John Henry was born a slave in the Dabner family, and was a native of Holly Springs, Mississippi. However, Johnson made inquiries at Holly Springs and found no information about John Henry, only a white family named Dabney. But Garst, using directories and newspaper articles, has identified a Frederick Yeamans Dabney, a civil engineer who worked for the Columbus and Western Railway at the time. In addition, Garst has undertaken research on Dabney's father and uncle, who according to the 1860 federal census collectively owned 162 slaves, including several males of an age that would make them possible candidates for the legendary John Henry. The first census after the abolition of slavery identifies a twenty-year-old black man, Henry Dabney, living with his wife Margaret in Copiah County, Mississippi. For Garst, Henry Dabney is a "specific candidate" for the historical John Henry.

Might this Henry Dabney really be the figure celebrated in the famous ballad? Garst offers additional circumstantial evidence, including a photo taken in 1930 of a steel drill stuck in the side of Oak Mountain near the east end of the tunnel—where it apparently stood for forty years as a tribute to Henry's prowess. The accumulated material Garst presents is impressive but far from conclusive—for example, the date and some other facts provided by the chief witness, C. C. Spencer, do not match completely with the results of Garst's research. Yet the overall picture is mostly consistent and coherent, and it has a ring of authenticity about it. It is unfortunate that, relative to the work done by Johnson and Chappell in West Virginia, no researcher in the 1920s devoted effort to following up on the Alabama claims. Had such fieldwork been undertaken, we might well have proof positive in hand.

Unless additional evidence comes to light, no clear resolution of this matter is likely. Yet the intensity with which claims have been staked and their merits debated attests both to the surprisingly complex diffusion of such songs, and even more to the universal appeal of the John Henry story. As Guy Johnson found out over seventy-five years ago, everyone wants to claim John Henry as a native son. In fact, it is perhaps worth noting that the latest proponent of a possible solution to the mystery, John Garst, was born and raised in Mississippi in the same part of the state where he locates the historical John Henry—just as Louis Chappell, who has best articulated the claims for the Big Bend Tunnel in West Virginia, was a longtime professor at West Virginia University and a noted advocate for the local music of that state. We can easily understand the attractions of the story and song for these zealous advocates and for others. Better than any other tale in American history, the John Henry ballad makes a compelling case that physical labor possesses its own poetry and grandeur; and that the worker can partake of those heroic qualities that, in other times and places, were attributed only to kings and warriors. Such values are clearly worthy of being commemorated in quasi-mythic form, especially in a democratic land where egalitarian views are espoused and sometimes even practiced. As such, this cherished ballad is much like the work songs that it inspired, and those that may in turn have contributed to its genesis. If workaday America has any right to claim such heroic virtues for its own, they would most certainly be found here, in this song and its antecedents and progeny.

CHAPTER NINE

The Cowboy

I've heard a thousand, but Lord, I kain't sing.

—Old-time cowboy, to a song collector

Our knowledge of the true songs of the cowboys would be all too meager were it not for a fortuitous event circa 1906 in the unlikely setting of a Harvard University classroom. Professor Barrett Wendell, then teaching a course on American literature, announced to his students that he had grown weary of reading essays on Hawthorne and Poe, Longfellow and Thoreau. This term he would require his students to look closer to home for inspiration: each would be responsible for preparing a thesis on the literary productions of the student's native region within the United States.

Inspired by this challenge, one of Wendell's older students, a middle-aged man of unprepossessing appearance but zealous disposition, who was taking courses at Harvard while on leave from a teaching job in Texas, feverishly composed a letter he sent to a thousand newspapers scattered across the West:

To the Editor: I am a member of the English faculty of the Texas Agricultural and Mechanical College on leave of absence for a year, which I am spending in the Graduate School of Harvard University. As a part of my work I am endeavoring to make a complete collection of the native ballads and songs of the West. It will hardly be possible to secure such a collection without the aid of the Press; for many of these songs have never been in print, but, like the Masonic ritual, are handed down from one generation to another by "word of mouth." . . . Eventually it is expected that the ballads will be published in book form. An editorial request from you to your readers for copies of frontier songs will doubtless result in valuable material. . . . Yours very respectfully, [signed] John A. Lomax

In response, correspondence from throughout the West began trickling into Lomax's Cambridge abode, and letters continued to find him after he returned to Texas armed with a Harvard master's degree and fellowship money to track down more American ballads. In fact, for the next twenty years, Lomax continued to receive letters in response to his initial solicitation for help. Four years after completing this class project, Lomax published the first edition of his seminal *Cowboy Songs* collection under the imprint of Sturgis and Walton, two intrepid New Yorkers who agreed to back the project after other publishers had rejected the manuscript. The book was a commercial success, but even more it was a landmark event in validating the nation's indigenous music as worthy of study and preservation. Lomax proudly claimed that it was the first published collection entirely comprised of vernacular American folk songs with accompanying music.

Many of the most cherished songs of the American West were first published in book form, with both words and music, as part of Lomax's collection. A fortune teller near the Fort Worth Stockyards provided Lomax with "Whoopee Ti Yi Yo"; a cowboy in a saloon reeled off innumerable verses of "The Chisholm Trail"—many of them unprintable at the time; an old hunter in Abilene contributed "The Buffalo Skinners." But perhaps Lomax's most fortuitous discovery came from Bill Jack Curry, a black saloonkeeper in San Antonio, who provided the researcher with the now-famous lyrics:

> Oh give me a home where the buffalo roam,
> Where the deer and the antelope play.
> Where seldom is heard a discouraging word,
> And the skies are not cloudy all day.

No music existed other than the saloonkeeper's sung melody, but a few weeks later Henry Leberman, a blind music teacher, sketched out an arrangement, and Lomax included the piece in his collection. Some years later, Franklin Roosevelt noted that "Home on the Range" was his favorite song, and propelled by this endorsement, as well as by the appealing sentimentality of the words and music, a legendary bit of Americana was lodged forever in the public consciousness. But another time-honored American tradition—litigation—would then rear its ugly head when an Arizona couple claimed ownership of the song and launched a copyright battle. Research spurred by this battle led to the discovery that the words to the song had been published in a newspaper as early as 1873.

Like many other cherished cowboy songs, "Home on the Range" is in three-quarters time. Curley Fletcher, composer of "The Strawberry Roan," thought that a three-quarter meter was the most suitable for a cowboy song. This rhythm matches neither the clip-clop-clip-clop of the horse, nor the up-and-down movements of the rider, yet this did not prevent "The Strawberry Roan" from joining "Home on the Range" as one of the most beloved cowboy songs.

> I was loafin' around just spendin' muh time,
> Out of a job and I hadn't a dime,
> When a feller steps up and sez he, "I suppose,
> That yore uh bronc fighter by the looks o' yer clothes."

Another classic, "The Streets of Laredo"—which with these two others surely ranks among the half dozen most famous cowboy songs—is also in three-quarters time.

> As I walked out in the streets of Laredo,
> As I walked out in Laredo one day,
> I spied a dear cowboy wrapped up in white linen,
> Wrapped up in white linen as cold as the clay.
> "I see by your outfit that you are a cowboy—"
> These words he did say as I boldly stepped by.
> "Come sit down beside me and hear my sad story;
> I am shot in the breast and I know I must die."

Although such ballads related the stories of cowboys, they did little to capture the true rhythms and sounds of their daily activities. Sentimental tales, humorous stories, and the adventures of lawmen and desperadoes were especially popular with the cowboys and figured prominently in songs such as "Jesse James," "The Old Chisholm Trail," "The Dying Cowboy," and "Red River Valley." Much of this music, however, was only loosely connected with the realities of life on the range. "The Streets of Laredo," for instance, with its odd imagery of fife and drum, actually draws from an old Irish song. "Red River Valley" originated among British troops in Manitoba, the Red River Valley of the north. Yet the cowboys adopted these songs as their own, whatever their origins. In a process familiar to ethnomusicologists, these foreign elements were assimilated and became adapted to their new native soil, just as traditional ballads, shanties, and other folk idioms traveled and developed new roots in locales far distant from their places of origin. And especially when compared with the later cowboy music of Hollywood invention, these songs stand out as paragons of authenticity, despite their foreign roots.

But in this regard the songs of the West were just like the people who sang them, most of whom were recent arrivals from distant lands. The cowboy vocation—which looms so large in the native consciousness of America—had the shortest life of any of the professions discussed in this book. True, there were precedents and rough equivalents elsewhere—the Argentinean *gauchos*, the *llaneros* of Colombia and Venezuela, and most notably the *vaqueros* of Mexico (their name inspired the Americanism "buckaroo"). And the term "cowboy" itself boasted a venerable history dating back before the settlement of the West (it was adopted during the Revolutionary War to refer to marauders who stole cattle, and even earlier usages can be found in the Old World). But none of these predecessors prepare us for the new character who emerged West of the Mississippi during the middle decades of the nineteenth century. He took on the dress and accouterments of a Mexican *vaquero*, the homespun practicality of a Yank, the firearms of a soldier, the outdoor savvy of a traditional herder, and the manners and personal hygiene of a prospector, but added to all of these a spirit of independence and devil-may-care brashness that was uniquely his own. This is *our* cowboy, the one studied and celebrated later by Lomax and so many others.

The authentic music of the American cowboy reflects strong affinities to the songs of the herders discussed in chapter 3; indeed, the profession of the "cow-boy" represents, in many ways, the final, most romanticized evolution of the cattle-herding lifestyle. Although few commentators have detailed the linkages between the pastoral music of shepherds and the open-range songs of cowboys, even a casual listener can hear the similarities—sometimes on a musical level but more often on an emotional one. A plaintive, nostalgic quality is often evident in the music of both professions. A pronounced lyricism, missing in many work song traditions, is equally prominent. The stronger rhythms of digging and hammering songs are rarely heard in these songs, replaced instead by a more stately sense of internal momentum. Perhaps the most striking and surprising connection between pastoral music and that of the open range is the prominence of yodeling in both groups of songs. The sound of the yodeling cowboy was even carried over into early commercial country music, as witnessed by the recordings of Jimmie Rodgers, the Carter Family, Hank Williams, and many others. Yes, these are generalizations, and exceptions can be found with little effort, but the overall convergence of cowboy and older herding song styles demonstrates likely historical connections, ones that we can only dimly trace at the present date.

But other traditions also fed into the music of the modern American cowboy, and these too have frequently been overlooked. For example, how much of the cowboy song tradition can be traced back to the Mexican vaquero? "I find it strange," writes Katie Lee, that "there isn't any Spanish, or Mexican, influence on the cowboy songs close to the border where I came from, or around Santa Fe, which was at one time the northern capital of New Spain." Yet most researchers of cowboy music may have simply neglected to document a tradition that was probably richer than our surviving sources can convey. Américo Paredes, who began collecting the songs of the Texas-Mexican border region in the 1920s, noted that men working on horseback frequently sang as part of their labors. Compared to field workers, the horsemen's "performance was usually higher pitched and at a slightly faster tempo. It was also much louder, with a few reflective *gritos* here and there. While the singer in the fields sang only loud enough to be heard by his fellow workers, the man on horseback seemed to take in the whole landscape as his potential audience." Texas folklorist J. Frank Dobie has published several vaquero songs, some of them learned from his brother Elrich H. Dobie, who had served as *caporal*, or boss, of a cow outfit on a south Texas ranch during 1916 and 1917. Even earlier, John Lomax had published two vaquero songs in Spanish in a 1915 issue of the *American Journal of Folk-Lore*. But these latter examples, it is worth adding, came not from his fieldwork but from a Harvard student who had done vacation work at a ranch in the southern Rio Grande country. In 1934, Lomax and his son Alan undertook field recordings of vaquero songs in this region. But by then the lifestyle that gave birth to this music had all but disappeared.

And, by this time, the American cowboy was also disappearing from the western plains—although his music would be more thoroughly documented by later researchers than that of his Mexican antecedents. His demise had little to do with the hostile forces found in western films and books—varmints and bad men, gunslingers and tribes on the warpath; instead, more subtle changes marked his departure. The first cars came West as novelties—driven by insurance salesmen, land agents, and other suspicious folks in soft occupations—but around the time Lomax's book was published, motor vehicles would start replacing horses in greater numbers as the preferred means of transportation. Shoes also supplanted boots. Denim jeans, impeccably made by Mr. Levi Strauss of San Francisco, were substituted for chaps. The cowboy hat would remain for longer, but even it would soon become more an affectation or a sign of deference to a tradition than a functional accessory. Moreover, as cultivation spread west, many ranch hands worked as farmers as well as among cattle. Gradual urbanization would introduce other ways of earning a livelihood, and spur additional changes in attitudes and lifestyles. In short, little would soon remain but an image—a powerful, haunting image nonetheless—supplemented by some history, much folklore, and a few songs.

In short, John Lomax was documenting a dying tradition even during these early years of the twentieth century, decades before the singing cowboys of Hollywood would sound the final death knell for authentic cowboy music. But this was only part of the challenge facing folklorists of the Wild West. Despite the well-meaning help of correspondents and academics, Lomax frequently encountered indifference or outright resistance from the cowboys themselves, who put little stock in Harvard degrees and fellowships. "To capture the cowboy music proved an almost impossible task," Lomax lamented. "The cowboys would simply wave away the large horn I carried and refused to sing into it! Not one song did I ever get from them except through the influence of generous amounts of whiskey, raw and straight from the bottle or jug."

But this indifference pales beside the outright hostility shown to Lomax by other song collectors and writers, who disparaged his methodology, questioned his honesty, and derided his results. Austin Fife, a meticulous gatherer of songs and folklore of the West, refers to the "pretentious Lomax books," which were "based on relatively small and fragmentary field resources," and he faults the author for his "subjectivity and limited historical perspective." D. L. Wilgus, in his study *Anglo-American Folksong*

Scholarship since 1898, also minimizes Lomax's achievement, categorizing his efforts as part of the pejoratively named "Local-Enthusiastic Tradition" in fieldwork, and lamenting the fact that the published versions of songs were often *composites* drawn from many different source documents, which Lomax combined based on (horrors!) his own judgments. Jack Thorp, another great collector of cowboy songs whose work predated that of Lomax, was peeved both at the latter's greater fame and by his belief that Lomax had borrowed from his collection without acknowledgment. Curley Fletcher, author of "The Strawberry Roan," sent a heated two-page letter to Lomax when he was not credited in the first edition of *American Ballads and Folk Songs*—although Fletcher was placated when he was later mentioned in the enlarged edition of *Cowboy Songs and Other Frontier Ballads*. True enough, Lomax was neither the first nor the most obsessive gatherer of cowboy material; and in his publications he could be silent about the specific sources of songs, which sometimes came to him in the mail rather than from the mouths of wranglers. And, contrary to today's practice, Lomax combined different texts of songs into finished versions, relying only on his own aesthetic tastes, cutting, juxtaposing, and fixing unmetrical lines in the process. In general, he often played fast and loose with copyright and intellectual property issues, so critically important today when millions of dollars would be at stake for songs as successful as "Home on the Range." Lomax stands guilty as charged on all these counts.

But let's also give the man his due. No one did more than Lomax to bring authentic cowboy music to the attention of the broader public, as well as spur others into efforts to preserve American vernacular music. In 1925, Moe Asch found a copy of Lomax's *Cowboy Songs* at a bookstall in Paris, and the excitement with which he read it contributed in no small degree to his later decision to found Folkways, a record label that did more to foster and preserve traditional music than any other of its time. Lomax's efforts also garnered the support of many other powerful forces—Harvard academics, publishing houses, concert promoters, the former president Teddy Roosevelt (who penned an endorsement for the *Cowboy Songs* volume), and later the Library of Congress, as well as a host of other individuals (the list should start with his son Alan) and organizations. The cumulative efforts of all the critics named above could not begin to match the impact of this one man—who was almost forty years old when he began his preservation efforts in earnest, literally only devoting half a career to it! As for his "borrowings" from Thorp, John West has gathered the facts and concluded that a "jury evaluating the evidence would have a difficult time agreeing beyond a reasonable doubt that John Lomax ever saw a copy of the little book Jack Thorp published in 1908. Almost no piece that Thorp published turned up in precisely the same form in Lomax's printing—words, phrases, punctuation, and even titles were different." It is not going too far to suggest that in his zeal to compete with Lomax, Thorp himself was inspired to expand his cowboy song collection in a follow-up edition of his book. So even when making enemies, Lomax contributed to progress in the field. And certainly Lomax's success contributed to many commercial publishers' willingness to issue and promote books of cowboy songs and folklore by other authors. In short, many of Lomax's harshest critics were undoubtedly beneficiaries of his unflagging efforts.

Jack Thorp's *Songs of the Cowboys* predates Lomax's publication by two years. Yet Thorp, despite claims sometimes made on his behalf, was neither the first to research nor the first to publish cowboy songs. Even if we exclude newspaper and broadside publications, precedence must go to Stanley Clark, whose forty-one-page pamphlet from 1897, *Life and Adventures of the American Cow-Boy*, included some cowboy songs. Mention should also be made of John A. Stone (known as "Old Put"), whose songsters published in California in the aftermath of the Gold Rush include songs of cattle drivers; as well as Joaquin Miller, the "poet of the Sierras," some of whose works were later set to music. But perhaps the most interesting document from the nineteenth century comes from Owen Wister, author of *The Virginian*, who noted in a diary entry from 1893 that he had "come upon a unique song." Wister then proceeded to transcribe the now famous words to "Git along Little Dogies":

> As I walked out one morning for pleasure,
> I met a cow-puncher a-jogging along.
> His hat was thrown back and his spurs was a-jinglin,'
> And as he advanced he was singing this song.
> Sing hooplio get along my little dogies,
> For Wyoming shall be your new home.

Andy Adams, in 1903, refers briefly to the same song, and only quotes two lines:

Ip-e-la-ago, go along little doggie,
You'll make beef steer by-and-by.

It was left for John Lomax to substitute "Whoopee ti yi yo, git along little
dogies," and provide the form in which the song would become widely
known. Whether drawing on better sources, or merely exercising (again!)
his audacious editorial skills, Lomax undoubtedly served as mid-wife at
the birth of another American classic.

No, Thorp was not the earliest researcher to document cowboy music,
but he was the first to collect these songs in a systematic manner, as well
as the first to devote an entire book-length manuscript to them. Even
more than the Harvard-educated Lomax, who at least was a Texan and
grew up (as he liked to point out) beside a branch of the Chisholm Trail,
Jack Thorp was an unlikely advocate for the music of the Wild West. A
native New Yorker born in 1867, he was the son of a prominent family and
received a polished education few cowboys could match at St. Paul's
School in Concord, New Hampshire, where John Jacob Astor, one of the
richest Americans of his day, was enrolled at the same time. But instead of
attending college, Thorp headed to New Mexico, where he traded in
horses and soon began hunting down cowboy songs. "Songs of the range
had a special appeal for me," he later wrote. "I was a singin' cowboy
myself, by adoption."

Like Lomax, Thorp also struggled to secure the cooperation of the
cowboys. In 1889 and 1890 Thorp traveled on horseback through New
Mexico and Texas, covering some fifteen hundred miles in his efforts to
collect the songs and ballads of the open range. In all that time, he claimed
never to have heard a cowboy with a good voice. And the ones who *could*
muster a melody, he complained, never managed to remember a whole
song. "It is generally thought that cowboys did a lot of singing around the
herd at night to quiet them on the bed ground. I have been asked about
this, and I'll say that I have stood my share of night watches in fifty years,
and I seldom heard any singing of that kind. What you would hear as you
passed your partner on the ground, would be a kind of low hum or
whistle, and you wouldn't know what it was. Just some old hymn tune,
like as not—something to kill time and not bad enough to make the herd
want to get up and run." Margaret Larkin reached a similar conclusion
while researching her 1931 book *Singing Cowboy.* "Very few melodies were
original; it may be that none of them were. Some were so wrenched out of

shape by the demands of their new words as to be nearly unrecognizable
. . . 'I've heard a thousand, but Lord, I kain't sing,' says the Old Timer
when you ask him for a song." Louise Pound offered an even harsher
critique in her 1959 study *Nebraska Folklore,* in which she attempted to
distinguish "genuine cowboy pieces"—namely those "related very closely
to the life of the communities which originated and preserved them"—
from songs that reflected outsider influence or were borrowed from
other occupations and settings. Alas, Pound came to conclude that the
"real" cowboy songs were more likely to be "crude and nearly formless,
without literary quality or individual touch." In other words, the closer
one got to the essence of cowboy music, the uglier it sounded. In our day,
when "authenticity" is held up as the ultimate compliment for traditional
music making, this is a bitter truth to embrace.

Perhaps these obstacles and embarrassments should not surprise us.
The nature of the cowboy's livelihood—unlike, say, agricultural labor—
made it all but impossible for them to sing together while at work.
"Working cowboys sang and still sing for recreation," writes Guy Logsdon. "Since their work is non-rhythmic, they did not and still don't sing
much while they work." The songs that Thorp encountered were always
sung by an individual, never a group. Even when the cowboy's life kept
him on the ground in one place, the vocation elicited little on-the-job
singing. Men standing at work will sing. Men sitting at work will sing.
Even a walking man is likely to carry a tune. But once a man is moving at
rapid pace on a horse or a steam engine, or at a machine, the work song
begins to lose its organic connection to physical labor, its ability to organize the behavior of limbs and torso, its linkages to productivity, and,
above all, its ability to impart vitality and energy to an undertaking. The
tasks now have a stronger and more insistent force of momentum behind
them.

Yet the image of the singing cowboy would become firmly lodged as a
powerful symbol in the American psyche. When Eck Robertson, the first
documented rural southern musician to be recorded, came to New York
for his 1922 audition, he dressed in cowboy attire for the event. Even city
slickers soon followed suit—for example, John White, who captivated
audiences as the "Lonesome Cowboy"—dressing the part if they hoped to
gain credibility in singing this music. In 1925, cowboy music achieved its
first genuine hit record with Carl T. Sprague's version of "When the
Work's All Done This Fall," which sold almost one million copies and was

covered by dozens of other artists in the following decades. But an even greater impetus to the music at this time came from a technological innovation—the advent of "talking" motion pictures. Although western plots had been a preoccupation of silent films, the advent of sound to the cinemas of America furthered the idealization of the semi-mythical "singing cowboy" figure. From the mid-1930s until the early 1950s, the character was a staple of Hollywood output. Gene Autry, who made his movie debut in 1934 with *In Old Santa Fe,* epitomized the role, parlaying it into a successful career in other areas. Autry's net worth eventually surpassed $300 million—making him the most successful singing cowboy in history—quite an achievement for someone who couldn't ride a horse, shoot a gun, or rope a calf when he first came to Hollywood. But he could sing passably well, and looked good in the saddle or with a guitar in his hand: these advantages, combined with the mystique of the Wild West, were enough to propel him to fame and fortune. His success as a performer proved so irresistible, that a host of other cowboy stars imitated it. Even John Wayne was prodded into singing on-screen (his voice, however, was dubbed by a professional).

This success ironically led to undeserved obscurity for the true music of the West. In the 1930s, publishers released countless collections of so-called cowboy songs, but they were mostly the work of Tin Pan Alley hacks who had never ventured anywhere near where deer and antelope play. Few of these songs had been sung—or would ever be taken up by—real cowboys. But this did not prevent them from finding a ready audience. The proliferation of cowboy music fed off the glamour of cinema westerns, and even film stars who could hardly hold a tune issued their own songbooks: the 1935 publication *Tom Mix Western Songs,* published by M. M. Cole of Chicago, gives composer credits to this silent movie cowboy; and Ken Maynard, who was a flop as a singer (after bringing him into the studio, Columbia smartly decided to keep locked up in the vaults most of the nasally, kazoo-like vocals they had recorded) could issue successful music books under his imprimatur. Long before the end of the Great Depression, cowboy music had stopped being a folk genre and instead had become just another commercial category for the entertainment industry.

The popular imagination, fed by these business interests, continues to fixate on a romanticized image of the "lonesome cowboy" who sings to counter the isolation and anomie of his solitary profession. How much historical truth is contained in this stereotyped character? As already noted, much of the singing took place in the evenings, around the campfire, as part of the socializing after the end of the day's labors. But in other instances, cowboys sang to encourage their four-legged companions. A persistent belief among muleskinners held that that mule would work harder and longer if entertained by a song. Some animals were even said to come to their master the moment they heard singing. As Teddy Blue Abbott, in his firsthand account of cowboy life, *We Pointed Them North: Recollections of a Cowpuncher,* explains: "One reason I believe there were so many songs about cowboys was the custom we had of singing to the cattle on night herd. The singing was supposed to soothe them and it did . . . I know that if you wasn't singing any little sound in the night—it might be just a horse shaking himself—could make them leave the country; but if you were singing they wouldn't notice it." Charles Siringo, in his classic nineteenth-century memoir, *A Texas Cowboy,* concurs, and he tells how it was necessary to sing "melodious songs" and lullabies to stop a herd from stampeding. Other old-timers dismissed such romantic recollections. "They whistled and yelped at their cattle to keep them on the move," writes Margaret Larkin, "or at most employed the eerie, wailing Texas yodel. If they sang, they declare prosaically, it was to keep themselves awake." One surmises that, although some cowhands sang on the job, it was not required for employment—only in Hollywood would a cowboy's vocal skills be tested during the audition. John Lomax managed to record some cattle calls, and also attempted to document how they were used, but the results were fairly unimpressive—a few pathetic whoops, not much different than one might hear wandering by the swinging doors to the saloon in any number of western towns even today. Other collectors hardly concerned themselves with such tepid material, which lacked the allure of the cowboy ballads; but even if they had it is unlikely that the cattle call would ever rival the field holler or shanty in the pantheon of American work songs.

In the final analysis, the music of the cowboy is important more for its symbolism, for its rich imagery, than for the insights it gives us into the existence of the working men and women of the West. Yet this symbolism should not be dismissed as useless fantasy. These melodic memorials to unfettered freedom and to the untarnished outdoors, these reminders of simple human relationships and conflicts between Good and Evil writ large with capital letters: these very emblems of what Americans wanted the West—and to some extent wanted their entire Nation—to represent, are the very ingredients that have made this music so timeless and moving. Even the cowboys themselves could not resist its appeal, often deriving their most resilient images of their work and their society from these simple lyrics. True, no occupational songs had less connection with real labor; yet, by the same token, no music told better the ideal of work to which we should all aspire. As such, for all its sentimentality and affectations, its rough edges and perhaps rougher interior, and despite all the later attempts to commercialize and commoditize its allure, this music has the greatest claim to being enshrined as the quintessential vernacular music of the New World.

 **CHAPTER TEN**

The Miner

Pick, pick, pick,

That's the music down the mine.

I learned to play the tune

When I was scarcely nine.

—Nineteenth-century English

coal miner song

Archie Green, a pre-eminent expert on the songs of miners, has lamented the tendency of folklorists to overlook these musical notes from the underground in favor of the cultural legacy of those who plied their trades in the great outdoors. Green attributes this practice to the in-grained bias against industrialization among folklorists, and he notes that "songs of cowboys as well as shantymen (maritime) and shantyboys (lumbering) were viewed more romantically than miners or steel mill men." Even within the comparatively egalitarian world of folklore, a pecking order exists—or so it seems—one in which these workers with dirty faces are, just as in their subterranean jobs, left forgotten far below, on a lower rung than everyone else. Green has suggested, further, that the trade union and communist influence in these industrial workplaces aggravated the situation, making folksong collectors even more reluctant to get involved in preserving and promoting the songs of miners and factory workers.

Green's complaint is legitimate. But he can take some consolation in knowing that mining songs, though they may have charmed few folklorists, exerted a tangible impact on the labor movement. Only the textile industry could approach mining in showing how music could mobilize workers and be brought to bear in the fight to improve wages and labor conditions. In all fairness, folklorists were not indifferent to these gains. Moreover, they may have preferred other types of occupational music, not from ideological considerations, or because they were sung out in the sunshine, or were more upbeat and picturesque, but more likely because the songs of the outdoor professions revealed more direct ties with the realties of work and the working life, in some instances forming a natural part of it—in contrast to the industrial songs, which often commented on labor conditions from a distance. And even when the outdoor songs were not sung during physical labor—as with the songs of the logging camp and the cowboys' campfire, or the forecastle ballads of the sailors—they were performed in the evening after work was done, and served as a culmination and celebration of the day's events. For folklorists, obsessed as they are with authenticity, this was a great merit. In contrast, the mining songs that Green cherishes are far more acculturated.

Certainly some miners sang while at work—as firsthand accounts testify —but only a few so-called songs of miners came into existence in such an overtly functional manner. One such example, from the turn-of-the-century phosphate mines of Florida, is recounted by Dorothy Scarborough in her 1925 study *On the Trail of Negro Folksongs*: "The song leader would be called a 'Phosphate Jesse,' and all he had to do was to inspire the singing. Under the thrill of music, the workers would compete madly with each other to see who could 'lay the rest out,' until all but one had dropped in exhaustion, almost denuded of clothes." Such references, however, are comparatively rare, especially when contrasted with the numerous citations of songs in other centers of work—plantations, sailing ships, levee camps, prison gangs—where music seemed to blossom spontaneously from the tasks at hand. To the extent that miners sang or performed music, it was typically not as laborers per se, but rather as members of their communities—at taverns, in town bands, with friends in small vocal groups—much like what one would find in any other working-class neighborhood.

Perhaps the most distinguishing feature of this music was less its ties to the mining life and more its sheer abundance. "Music was not discouraged by operators when it helped to keep their employees contented," writes George Korson. "Some even subsidized local bands and provided mining sinecures for bandsmen whom fellow workers nicknamed 'gob roosters.' There were bands everywhere; the little town of Dugger, Indiana, with a population of only 1,500 supported a sixty-piece band until it was wiped out by a mine disaster. There were also quartets, sextets, and choruses of male and female voices who sang for the sheer love of singing. In some camps, singing schools were conducted. Appalachian mountaineer coal miners joined in all-day 'sing-in's' with their neighbors on June Sundays." Korson calls particular attention to the traditions of the Welsh miners, whose "musical life centered around two institutions, the *Gymanfa Ganu* and the *Eisteddfod*." The Gymanfa Ganu (which means "congregational singing") provided an opportunity for communal music making, primarily the performance of traditional church hymns. The Eisteddfod, important both in Wales and among Welsh immigrant communities in the United States, involved competitions in vocal and instrumental music, among other areas, and culminated in the "chairing of the bard," an honor awarded for skill in composing poetry that relied on traditional meters and alliteration.

As such examples suggest, the vast majority of songs performed in mining communities had only loose ties with excavation. Especially in the early days of the mining industry—which did not become a major source of employment in America until around 1840—the music reflected the traditions that the miners brought from their native lands. "The music in early coal camps was a transplanted one," adds Korson. "The Welsh sang Welsh songs, the Scotch their songs, and other nationalities the songs of their home countries." In time, new music was created, drawn from the current experiences of the workers, often serving to provide a commentary on the trials and tribulations of the mining life. Yet in many other instances, as we shall see, the most famous "mining songs" were composed by outsiders with few or no ties to these communities. Within the often politically charged world of folk song collectors and preservationists, such a situation raises obvious questions of authenticity and value. But Archie Green reverses the typical argument, challenging Korson's preference for ballads composed by miners themselves —an attitude that Green describes as an obsession with preserving "purity against contamination."

Yet, more than any other individual, Korson deserves our praise not only for preserving the music but for legitimizing it as a valuable part of American culture. True, as early as 1908 the Edison Concert Band recorded "Down in a Coal Mine"—but a "Concert Band" is far removed from real mining life. Some thirty-seven years would elapse before any substantial recordings of actual working coal miners were made on location. Finally, in 1935, Korson and Melvin LeMon documented dozens of songs of anthracite miners in Pennsylvania. Before Korson's pioneering efforts, even when a coal miner was given a chance to record—as Moran Lee (Dock) Boggs did in 1927 for Brunswick and in 1930 for Lonesome Ace—he did not address the miner's occupation in his songs. For example, a number of performances of Slovak-American *csardas*, made by musicians drawn from the Pennsylvania coal mining communities, were recorded by the Victor and Columbia labels in the late 1920s and early 1930s, and these have been reissued with the evocative subtitle *Dance Tunes from the Pennsylvania Coal Mines*. But the name is misleading: the music contains no references to mining, and it was not recorded in Pennsylvania but rather at the Victor studio in Camden, New Jersey, and at a Columbia location in New York. Preserving the local musical culture of American miners was almost exclusively left up to researchers such as Korson—those literally willing to go to the coal face to find, preserve, and promote these otherwise neglected songs.

Born in the Ukraine, and moving to Wilkes-Barre, Pennsylvania, when he was thirteen years old, George Korson first supported himself as a journalist while devoting his spare time to documenting the cultural milieu of mining communities. Like many pioneering American ethnomusicologists and folklorists, Korson lacked academic training for this pursuit, but rather was led by happenstance as well as by an unfailing personal interest to undertake the preservation of the music and folklore of the miners. When Korson graduated from high school in 1917, the coal mining industry dominated the local economy by employing some 150,000 workers and extracting over one hundred million tons of coal per year. By the time of his death in 1967, however, the mining industry was in decline: its production down 90 percent from a half century before and only a few workers left toiling in an occupation that had increasingly become the domain of machines, not men. Korson's *Songs and Ballads of the Anthracite Miner*, published in 1927, captured the ethos and spirit of these laborers during the booming pre-Depression years and, along with Korson's later books, made a convincing case that American folklore was not limited to farming communities and the great outdoors. In time, Korson's work gained the support of influential parties: he won a Guggenheim fellowship, was supported by the Ford Foundation, and was lauded by John L. Lewis of the United Mine Workers of America.

Few later researchers followed in the path that Korson had blazed. Although in 1933 John Lomax recorded Blind James Howard's "The Hard-Working Miner" in Harlan County, Kentucky, which may have been the first attempt to record a coal-mining related song in the bituminous region—he did little to follow up on this effort. Jean Thomas, in her 1939 study *Ballad Makin' in the Mountains of Kentucky,* devoted a few pages to coal mining songs, but perhaps did more harm than good with her romanticized approach to folklore research, which (as I describe below) led her to stretch truth to the breaking point. No worthy successor to Korson would appear in the United States for almost half a century after the publication of his first book. Not until the release of Archie Green's meticulously researched survey *Only a Miner,* in 1972, would the study of the songs and folklore of American miners again take center stage in a book that did justice to the subject.

But researchers in other countries were paying attention to Korson's work and pursuing comparable projects to preserve and publish the songs of the mining industry. During the years following World War II, research into this area gained momentum in Britain, largely due to the efforts of A. L. Lloyd. In 1951 Lloyd arranged a competition, with the aid of the recently nationalized industry, in which "miners were invited to submit any songs they knew, of the life, work, pastimes, disasters and union struggles in the coalfields." More than one hundred entries were submitted, and prizes were awarded to those deemed to be the best "finds." Lloyd's research culminated in *Come All Ye Bold Miners,* published in 1952. "It is doubtful whether any other industry in Britain has such a body of balladry related to the job itself, or to the life, diversions and struggles of the men engaged in that job," he wrote in his introduction. Although most of the songs collected in the book originated during the late nineteenth century or early twentieth, some material was far older, such as "The Colliers' Rant," which was first published in 1793 yet probably was sung for decades or generations before seeing print. "The Recruited Collier" had appeared as early as 1808 in a collection of ballads in the Cumberland dialect, and "Walker Pits" had been published in John Bell's *Rhymes of the Northern Bards* from 1812. The majority of the songs, however, made their first appearance in book form as a result of Lloyd's pioneering efforts.

The coal mining industry in Canada also boasted a rich song tradition, but early researchers took only the most passing interest in it. Helen Creighton uncovered a few songs, but her main interests lay in other areas. Starting in the 1960s, John C. O'Donnell began collecting coal mining songs in Canada, and published an extensive collection in 1992. Much as Lloyd had done in England, O'Donnell drew on the results of a contest, organized by Creighton and the Miners' Folk Society of Cape Breton. O'Donnell gathered songs from individuals throughout Canada, although his research efforts focused on eastern Canada, especially Cape Breton Island. Here O'Donnell, like his counterparts in the United States and England, was faced with a declining industry. The downturn had begun in the 1950s, driven by a shift in demand to cleaner-burning fuels such as natural gas and oil. At the time of its closure on January 8, 1976, Cape Breton's Princess mine ranked as the oldest-producing coal site in North America, yielding more than thirty million tons during its century of operation. Yet even in their final hours these epicenters of toil and the precarious livelihoods they supported could inspire music, such as the following tribute to Caledonia—the most commonly mentioned mine in the Cape Breton songs—which O'Donnell learned from its composer Hattie Batemen:

> Farewell to Caledonia, the sea laden mine;
> All your tunnels dark with memories.
> Now you're all closed up and you never more shall be.
> There were many a shift you provided for me.

The mining industry is marked by many such booms and busts in production and employment. The location of mining jobs—and their associated songs—is determined not solely by the situation of the natural resources to be tapped, but perhaps even more, by the costs of extraction and the diffusion of demand. As such, communities prosper or decline on the basis of global trends and circumstances beyond the control of workers or, ultimately, even bosses and owners. The development of the British coal mining industry, for example, had little to do with the discovery of good excavating sites or the cost effectiveness of labor, but rather gained momentum from industrialization and the concomitant demand for energy to fuel the mills. These same factors have led to an inexorable shift of mining jobs to the developing world. This process, underway for many decades, has eradicated the occupational songs from communities in advanced economies while spurring their emergence in other locations half a world distant. For instance, "Joban Tanko Bushi," which originated as a Japanese work song of the miners of Ibaragi prefecture, is often sung today, although primarily by school choirs rather than by actual miners. Central Europe was once rich in mining songs—some appeared in print in German as early as 1531—and the old Silesian miners' refrain "Glück-auf, der Steiger kommt" is still performed today, but no longer by the pitmen themselves. Dr. Gerhard Heilfurth, born in 1909 in Neustaedtel, the son of a silver miner, collected mining songs as part of his researches into the coal industry of his native region. But his work—like the labors of Korson, Lloyd, and O'Donnell—serves as testimony to the past rather than as an indication of the present and future of mining.

To some extent, mining songs have been preserved in virtually all regions of the world, and almost everywhere their lyrics convey, to some degree, a pronounced spirit of melancholy or malaise, sometimes border-ing on despair. Vladimir Propp, in his collection of Russian folk lyrics, includes several songs drawn from mine workers, such as the following lament about conditions at the Zmeinogorsk mine, referred to here as the Golden Snake:

> To the ore they have sent us
> They keep flogging and abusing us . . .
> Over a dam, over the water
> Stands the mine Golden Snake,
> But we hate it. Our mining work
> Gives us troubles.

Propp also includes the following example, with its doleful admonitions about the travails of the miner's life.

> Peasants, you peasants,
> In a word—fools!
> You haven't been in the mines—
> You haven't seen need and sorrow.
> You haven't been in the mines
> You haven't seen need and sorrow,
> Come to the mines with us
> You'll find out all about it. . . .

Doesn't take a scythe in hand,
Doesn't put money in the coffer.
The miner knows cold, the miner knows hunger,
But neither bread nor water.

Few occupational songs from other trades or industries can match the dolorous and desperate tone of these lyrics, a legacy of the Tsarist days.

Similar examples could be cited from many locales; the details may vary but the underlying sense of mournfulness remains. Sulfur mining no longer takes place in Sicily, but Alan Lomax was able to record its poignant music while the industry still played a significant role in the local economy surrounding Sommatino. "Nor had I arrived on the scene a moment too soon," he later recounted. Here, in the summer of 1954, he recorded one of the most moving performances of his long career. Accompanied only by a Jew's harp, Rocco Meli intones: "Mi scuordo, mi scurdà, scurdattu sugnu" ("I forget, I have forgotten, I am forgotten"). Then the singer continues, in words of extraordinary sadness:

I have forgotten my own life.
I have forgotten the goodness of my mother,
She was sweeter, even better than you.
I have forgotten the goodness of my father,
Who crossed the ocean three times for me.
I have forgotten my friends and my brothers,
I forget the saints, but not you.

The song is haunting in its intensity. The culture that gave it birth is now gone, replaced by a society that learns its songs almost entirely from radios and home entertainment centers. Its preservation may be but a small victory, yet it serves as an important reminder that the spontaneous songs of day-to-day life can match the poetic inspiration of the most acculturated art music.

Projects such as those undertaken by Lomax, Korson, Lloyd, O'Donnell, and others were a great boon in advancing our knowledge of work songs, but still only partly filled the gap in this area. In particular, admirers of this music must regret the few chances that real miners had to record their songs in the environment that gave them birth. But this paucity of on-site documentation is only one aspect of the challenges facing researchers attempting to trace the history of this body of occupational music. As noted above, the music of the mines, more than almost any other type of labor song, was often composed and disseminated by outsiders—by musicians who had never been down a shaft. Indeed, blind singers seemed to have particular fondness for these songs, such as Andrew Jenkins, composer of "The Dream of the Miner's Child," who sought inspiration for song-writing from radio broadcasts, Braille books and stories read to him by others, rather than from first-hand experience; or James William Day, a blind fiddler who later regained his eyesight through an operation, and came to adopt the more colorful (and successful) identity Jilson Setters, under which name he composed and recorded the protest song "Coal Creek Troubles." It was difficult, and sometimes impossible, to trace the lineage of any number of songs of this sort back to the coal face. Even when a miner was involved in composing or performing a song, the role might be a surprising one. Ted Chestnut who recorded "Only a Miner" in the 1920s, had actually worked in a mine for the Harding-Burlington Company, but he later told researcher Archie Green that he learned the song not at the mine but from his father, who was a preacher, and sang the song while accompanying himself on the home parlor organ as though it were a hymn. At his mining job, Chestnut had to teach the song to another worker, who not only was unfamiliar with it but also preferred to make a parody of the lyrics.

In other ways, however, the mining industry was a rich source of authentic folk songs, although often for the most tragic reasons. No work environment inspired more "disaster songs." Songs such as "Only a Miner," "Avondale Mine Disaster," and "New Made Graves in Centralia" commemorated the workers killed in these all-too-frequent events. When the Bureau of Mines published its *Historical Summary of Coal-Mine Explosions in the United States, 1810–1958*, it found no shortage of calamities to mention, including almost two hundred diagrams or photographs of various disasters and their horrible consequences. In the days before the Civil War, slave owners often considered mining jobs as a punishment for their more intractable workers, so awful were the conditions and so high the rate of casualties. Some profit-motivated owners hired out their slaves for such work, at the same time purchasing insurance to compensate for their potential losses—yet, by 1850, most insurance companies refused to cover such risky undertakings.

The occupational hazards of the miner's life were not only limited to accidents but also sometimes resulted from the frequent conflicts caused by labor unrest. For example, during the 1913 strike in the copper mines of Calumet, Michigan, company agitators created a panic at a Christmas party for the workers' children, allegedly shouting "Fire!" but locking the doors to the outside. Seventy-three youngsters were either smothered or trampled to death in the ensuing confusion. Music often served to document and protest the casualties of these labor conflicts, sometimes bringing them to the attention of the whole nation. For example, Woody Guthrie's song "1913 Massacre" has served as a lasting reminder of the Calumet incident. As performed by Bob Dylan (at Carnegie Hall in 1961), or by Ramblin' Jack Elliot or Woody Guthrie or his son Arlo Guthrie, "1913 Massacre" testifies to the power of song to preserve and convey not only the facts but, even more, the emotional impact of historical events. The following year, a strike in Colorado led to open conflict between miners and an armed militia, marked by gunfire and a deadly blaze set among the workers' tents by the drunken soldiers. The song "Ludlow Massacre," also by Guthrie, describes the scene in vivid detail.

> That very night your soldiers waited,
> Until all us miners were asleep,
> You snuck around our little tent town,
> Soaked our tents with your kerosene.
> You struck a match and in the blaze that started,
> You pulled the triggers of your gatling guns,
> I made a run for the children but the fire wall stopped me.
> Thirteen children died from your guns.

Are tragedy and turmoil the inescapable subjects of mining songs? No, not always. Although most investigation into mining songs has focused on the coal industry, gold prospectors also possessed a rich musical culture worthy of documentation. And in gold mining we encounter music of a far different tone and spirit—more akin to the boisterous songs of the lumberjacks and sailors described in previous chapters. Jean Murray, who began researching the songs of the Alaska-Klondike Gold Rush in 1989, found that no book had been written on the subject, although almost a century had transpired since prospectors had descended on the Yukon in search of their fortune. In many such cases, the music of these people would be all but lost after so many years had passed. Yet by the time Murray published her work on the subject a decade later, she had collected over one hundred songs. Some came from dance halls, others were sung by the miners in their tents; many prospectors brought instruments, such as harmonicas or banjos, with them on their travels. One intrepid music lover even had a piano dismantled, wrapped in yarn, and hauled over the steep and hazardous Chilkoot Pass.

The song "Yukona," from Murray's collection, makes clear the much cheerier demeanor of the music of those miners who spent their days in pursuit of gold, not coal. The piece won a 1901 competition conducted by the *Daily Klondike Nugget* for the best song about the gold rush and the Klondike: " 'Yukona' has been received with great favor by all who have heard the song," proclaimed the paper when announcing the winner of the contest.

> All hail, all hail the Yukon,
> Mighty, rich and glorious!
> We seeking came, content remain
> O'er fiercest gale victorious.

"The Carmack Song," also included in Murray's collection, describes the discovery of gold in 1896. The song was mentioned in several diaries of the era. The following version was transcribed by Anchorage musician Paul Roseland from an old resident in the 1960s. Here we see the same zeal for storytelling and light humor characteristic of the ballads of the lumber camp.

> George Carmack in Bonanza Creek went out to look for gold.
> Old-timers said it was no use, the water was too cold.
> I wonder why, I wonder why, I wonder why.
> They said that he might search the creek until the world would end.
> They said the willows on the creek, the other way would bend,
> And not enough gold he would find, a postage stamp to send.

In his autobiography John Lomax briefly notes having discovered, while going through boxes of uncataloged material at the University of California's Bancroft Library, information on the songs of the miners who had come to California during the Gold Rush. From the facts Lomax provides, we can tell that his reference is to the work of John A. Stone, who called himself "Old Put." Stone, who made it rich in California during the Gold Rush (in 1853 he apparently found a single nugget worth $15,000), published numerous songs before his death in the 1860s. Few researchers have seen fit to look into Stone's life and times, but in his day his music must have been widely sung. My copy of *Put's Original California Songster*, published in 1868 as the fifth edition, notes that some twenty-five thousand copies had been sold—a stunning figure given that the entire population of San Francisco, according to the 1860 census, was fewer than 57,000 souls, and Los Angeles was still a modest pueblo of 2,300 people. Dedicating the book to the "Miners of California," Stone aimed to provide "in a few words what would occupy volumes, detailing the hopes, trials and joys of a miner's life."

> When gold was found in '48, the people said 'twas gas,
> And some were fools enough to think the lumps were only brass;
> But soon they all were satisfied, and started off to mine,
> They bought their ships, came round the Horn, in the fall of '49.

Stone's songsters deserve to be better known. He had a good ear for colloquial language and local color, as well as a knack for storytelling. As with the material collected by Murray, Stone's works remind us of the sentimental and humorous ballads composed by Larry Gorman, Joe Scott, and the other minstrels of the lumber camps discussed in chapter 7.

The California Gold Rush probably produced more boisterous and entertaining music than any other gathering of miners known to us. The cultural diversity of this group, and their music, was far wider than one might suspect. One collection of Gold Rush songs includes material from over a dozen different countries, including China, France, and Chile. Even Australians found it easier to reach the West Coast of the United States than did most Americans—the trip took them a scant six weeks compared to half a year for those who wanted to come 'round the Horn from New York or Boston. It is even possible that Australian miners played an important role in disseminating the most famous mining song —"My Darling Clementine"—which usually, but incorrectly, is dated thirty years after the Gold Rush and attributed to Percy Montrose.

> In a cavern, in a canyon,
> Excavating for a mine,
> Dwelt a miner forty-niner,
> And his daughter Clementine.

In researching folk songs, the early collectors often documented the words, sometimes the music, but only rarely provided detailed information about performance styles. Yet in the years before World War II, Eleanora Black and Sidney Robertson were able to piece together from various sources a vivid account of how the prospectors performed their music:

> Some evidence of the manner in which these songs were sung has survived in written descriptions and in songs learned from Forty-Niners . . . A five-stringed banjo (picked, not strummed), is the natural accompaniment for them; a guitar will do. During the Gold Rush, as today, the singing of a folk song was an exceedingly serious business, no matter how humorous the words. Enunciation had to be distinct, so that the story would be clear to every hearer; but an emphatic rhythm, usually audibly tapped out by one toe, was an integral part of the folk singer's performance, even when the idea expressed in the text would not seem to require this monotonous accent. The style was never emotionally interpretative, for convention required understatement. Delivery was dead-pan rather than dramatic. Moreover, when a folk-singer came to the end of his song he stopped without warning; there was no 'letting the old cat die' by broadening the rhythm to bring his tale to a gradual close.

This passage is noteworthy not only for its acuteness of observation—which is exemplary and rarely matched in other early literature on occupational songs—but also for the clear indications it gives that the "cool" or "laid-back" style of musical performance, associated with West Coast music in the 1950s and 1960s, was in fact part of California performance styles as early as the Gold Rush.

Edward Hammond Hargraves, an Australian who had traveled to the California Gold Rush, felt that comparable geological conditions in his own country clearly indicated the presence of the precious metal. His success spurred another Gold Rush, followed by similar finds in New Zealand. As in California, these activities left behind a body of music commemorating the events and describing the miners' lives and times. Like John Stone, Charles Thatcher made the transition from miner to entertainer. His trip to Wakamarina in 1864 inspired the following:

> On the banks of the Wakamarina,
> A walk out from Nelson about thirty miles
> A splendid gold yield's been discovered, a field

Where dozens are making their piles.
Well they work with a pan in the river-bank sand
And in many a crevice, I'm told,
With knives they can dig out the nuggets so big,
A nice easy way to get gold.

Another of Thatcher's songs—"Gold's a Wonderful Thing"—marks the changes to the landscape caused by the onslaught of prospectors.

This place at one time was a Maori peach grove,
Now thousands of diggers all over it rove.
They mark out their claims on this marvelous rush,
And put up machinery, quartz here to crush.

As suggested above, the richest sources of mining music in recent decades are found, like the mineral deposits themselves, in the developing world. The African tradition is especially impressive, and has even exerted an influence on global pop music. The rich Zulu style of a cappella music known as *mbube* was developed primarily by men working in mines and factories. The name comes from the word for "lion," and its musical associations are derived from the 1939 hit song "Mbube (the Lion)," by Solomon Linda's Original Evening Birds, which later became well known as the pop hit "The Lion Sleeps Tonight." The vocal group Ladysmith Black Mambazo, launched to international fame after being featured on Paul Simon's highly successful *Graceland* recording from 1986, further developed the popularity of this style of music. However, only a few researchers have sought out the authentic music of the African miners themselves. Hugh Tracey made a significant contribution in this area with his writings and recordings, still insufficiently well known except among specialists. Tracey's 1952 book *African Dances of the Witwatersrand Gold Mines* is lavishly documented with dozens of photos and a discography; but the fact that the latter only cites recordings made by the author himself is all too revealing—no, not of Tracey's vainglory, but of the paucity of other researchers willing to tap into this rich source of traditional music. Tracey, who founded the International Library of African Music in 1954, received funding from the mining industry to support his efforts. He had been studying African music since the 1920s, when he arrived in Southern Rhodesia (now Zimbabwe) from England to farm tobacco with his older brother, who had received a land grant as a recompense for being wounded as a soldier in World War I. Tracey learned the Shona/Karanga language and soon was singing with his Karanga workers while out in the fields. During this period he developed a deep conviction that the indigenous cultures of Africa possessed little-known artistic riches, which needed to be preserved for future generations. His recordings of the music of African miners represent but a small part of the more than two hundred recordings made by this pioneering researcher before his death in 1977.

Half a world away, Luiz Heitor Corrêa de Azevedo worked to preserve the songs of the black miners of Brazil, performances that were, in the words of Morton Marks, "some of the most African-sounding music in all of Brazil." Corrêa de Azevedo had already developed a reputation as a leading expert on folk culture when he traveled to the United States in the early 1940s to serve as a consultant to the Music Division of the Pan American Union. Here he received encouragement and support from Charles Seeger and Alan Lomax and, perhaps even more important, the loan of portable recording equipment from the Library of Congress. Returning to Brazil, he initiated an ambitious plan of field recordings, involving arduous travels to Goiás (1942), Ceará (1943), Minas Gerais (1944), and Rio Grande do Sul (1945). In Minas Gerais, he found that most of the laborers' music had been forgotten, but old-timers remembered a few *vicungos,* or work songs, of the diamond miners. In discussing the music of these laborers, John Storm Roberts has explained: "In the Brazilian mining district of Minas Gerais, black diamond-miners sang songs with the Bantu-sounding name *vissungo.* . . . The texts of the vissungo mixed Portuguese words with others apparently from some corrupted African dialect. Like many African or African-derived songs they were accompanied by sounds made with the working tools." These plaintive recordings not only capture a bygone era of Brazilian culture but also expand our understanding of the linkages between African music and the songs of the New World. Listening to them, one may well agree with Roberts's conclusion that "on the whole the work songs of any country are among the more African styles of that country."

As the examples from Africa make clear, the music of miners occasionally influences the commercial world of pop songs. A large body of successful American and British popular music also found inspiration, or originated, in various coal mining communities. A number of miners' children have become well-known popular singers—Loretta Lynn, Merle

Travis, Tom Jones, Bryan Ferry, and the Everly Brothers come to mind. The mining life sometimes becomes part of the public image of these performers—for example, Lynn, whose life story was titled "Coal Miner's Daughter," or Travis, who composed the song "Sixteen Tons." Travis came up with the idea for the latter song the night before a recording session for the Capitol label. Looking for inspiration, he recalled two comments from family members. The opening of the song's chorus came from a letter his brother had written him during World War II, lamenting the death of journalist Ernie Pyle while covering the war in the Pacific. This missive from John Travis had complained: "It's like working in the coal mines. You load sixteen tons and what do you get? Another day older and deeper in debt." The closing line came from a comment his father had often made: "I can't afford to die. I owe my soul to the company store." From its first release in 1947, the song generated interest and controversy—a deejay in Chicago was reportedly advised by the FBI not to play it because of crypto-communist significations in the lyrics—but its moment of fame would not arrive for some eight years, when Tennessee Ernie Ford revived it, first on his daily NBC show in 1955. The network received over one thousand letters asking about the song, and in July of that year Ford performed it in front of thirty thousand people at a state fair in Indiana, where he received a tumultuous ovation. Based on this response, Ford decided to record the song for Capitol in September, but the song was put on the B side of the single, giving the more prominent position to "You Don't Have to Be a Baby to Cry," which the record company executives thought had more hit potential (not surprisingly, since pop tunes about romance outsell those about hard labor by a ratio of about ten thousand to one). But this was one of the few times when the worker's complaint outdistanced the lover's lament. Within eleven days of release, some four hundred thousand copies were sold. By November "Sixteen Tons" ranked number one on every chart in the industry, and before the close of the year, two million copies had been sold. For Ford, who had been a music conservatory student before springing to fame as a hillbilly disk jockey and performer of stylized songs such as "Mule Train" and "The Shot Gun Boogie," this would be the biggest hit of his career, forever linking him in the public's mind with the travails of the miner's life.

More rare than successful children of miners, but still significant, are the miners who made the transition themselves from backbreaking labor in the shafts to noteworthy performing careers. One such case was Ike

Everly, father of the Everly Brothers. Less famous yet very influential within the musical community is Roscoe Holcomb, whose forceful and heartrending singing style has been praised by Bob Dylan and admired by numerous folk singers and blues performers. Holcomb might never have recorded had it not been for the fieldwork of John Cohen, who was researching the music of Kentucky at the close of the 1950s. Cohen embarked on this project with hopes of finding the authentic music of people who "plowed with mules, canned beans and tomatoes from their gardens, and reclined on front porches with slatted wooden swings attached to rafters by metal chains. . . . Their music reflects a whole way of life, a total experience of hard work and hard living." Asking local dwellers to point him in the direction of old music and traditional songs, Cohen tracked down hosts of banjo players, fiddlers, and singers, but it was a random decision that led to his most spectacular find.

Having checked out all of the local players to whom he had been referred, Cohen decided to take his chances by leaving the blacktop and traveling up the first dirt road he found that would bring him into the hills. This route led over a small bridge and across railroad tracks to a row of wooden houses. Here he asked a loitering child whether any banjo players were thereabouts. The youngster pointed to a house in the distance, from which the sound of string music could be heard. Here Cohen met Holcomb, the former miner who in time would be justifiably lauded as one of the finest traditional American musicians of the recorded era.

A quarter of a century earlier, Jean Thomas had attempted to create a colorful figure of the mountains of Kentucky, named Jilson Setters, a homespun fiddler who could sing of the plight of miners and deal with various other traditional themes, all with unblemished authenticity. She convinced J. W. Day to take on this new name and began promoting him as the "Singin' Fiddler of Lost Hope Hollow." This may have been a good commercial move, but did little to legitimize research into the authentic music of miners. It crossed the line, even by the standards of folklorists, who by definition dwell at that liminal place where Truth and Legend meet, and sometimes forget their respective roles. Yet everything that Thomas had hoped to create with the semifictitious Jilson Setters, Cohen had found live and in the flesh with Roscoe Holcomb. "It was as if I'd felt this music already even though I had never heard it before," Cohen would recall almost forty years later. "At the first song he sang for me, with his guitar tuned like a banjo and his intense, fine voice, I was deeply moved, for I knew this was what I was searching for—something that went right to my inner being, speaking directly to me."

A short time later, Holcomb would be celebrated as "a true genius of the white blues and the Anglo-American ballad," with one writer praising Cohen for creating "one of the greatest records in the entire literature of American folk song." Holcomb would tour overseas, record commercial projects, and serve as the subject of a documentary, but at the time of his first encounters with Cohen he was a man marked by hard labors, his life, his music, his very features shaped by constant toil. His hands were cracked and worn by work (as was, in fearful symmetry, his banjo itself), his back stooped as a result of extreme physical labor, and his speech interrupted by an asthmatic cough aggravated by black lung disease and smoking. He had broken his back in a work mishap. His wife was the widow of a man who had died in a mining accident, and Holcomb was raising their children. At times he apologized for being too tired from his day's labors to perform with vitality for the Swiss-made Magnamite recorder that Cohen had brought to the Kentucky mountains for the project.

But when he sang, Holcomb revealed a vitality and energy that belied his broken-down body and excuses. His voice offered the timeless testimony of a working man, in which the strength of endurance and the cry for relief were woven together with mesmerizing force. Much of Holcomb's appeal no doubt related to this very fact. In an age in which performers of music had been set apart from men of work, he stood as a rare and vibrant representative of a different state of affairs. Although Holcomb would build a quasi career from the notoriety gained through the Cohen recordings—making several more records and performing at various concert halls around the United States and Europe—he never fully developed the mind-set of a professional musician. On stage and off, his attitude toward music remained one of intense personal commitment. He was "simply content," in the words of one observer, "with singing his lonesome songs to himself." For some listeners, this preoccupied attitude may have lessened their enjoyment of the music. But at least a few among them must have found it refreshing to encounter, at such a late date, this uncompromising aesthetic—so typical of the oldest blues and traditional music, and always at the root of the work song— that derives its strength from the inner resources of the singer and worries not a whit about the fickle applause of an audience.

CHAPTER ELEVEN

The Prisoner

What can be done in hell? They sang.

For where there is no more hope, song remains.

—*Victor Hugo*

Here flows the American Nile. The vast alluvial plain of the Yazoo Delta stretches from the eastern bank of the Mississippi River some seventy-five miles to Chickasaw Ridge, and runs from Vicksburg for two hundred miles to Memphis. This is a troublesome land of floods and humid subtropical weather, of hungry Delta mosquitoes who refuse to accept that humans should reside unchallenged at the top of the food chain, and of even more voracious bosses and overseers. But the fame of this region has little to do with these trifling inconveniences. It derives instead from the two major products of this parcel of earth: cotton and song. The fertility of the soil here is a matter of record. The fecundity of the music is the stuff of legend.

Despite its importance, the Yazoo River remains little known, its fame overshadowed by the grandeur of its neighbor, the "Ol' Man River" Mississippi. Alas, it narrowly missed its chance for popular renown. One day in 1851, composer Stephen Foster strolled into the office of his brother Morrison, and asked "What is a good name of two syllables for a Southern river? I want to use it in this new song 'Old Folks at Home.'" After pondering a while, Morrison suggested "Yazoo." But his brother was unimpressed. "Way down upon the *Yazoo* river?" Hardly! Eventually the two consulted a map, and found an obscure stream in Florida that emptied into the Gulf of Mexico. Its name: Swanee River.

Sprung to fame in Foster's song, the soon-to-be-mythic river later inspired Gershwin's song "Swanee" and was emblazoned in the public's memory by Al Jolson's performance (as well as by many parodies of the same) on bended knee. The same river was mentioned in Irving Berlin's "Alexander's Ragtime Band" and commemorated in his "Swanee Shuffle"; it was celebrated in Ellington's "Swanee River Rhapsody" and served as the title of the 1939 film *Swanee River*. Over the period of a century, the unimpressive Swanee flowed straight out of obscurity and into the realm of myth, where it came to symbolize an entire region, and call to mind its music.

The Yazoo—its unmelodic name comes from a Choctaw word of disputed meaning—would have been a far better choice. But what the Yazoo lacks in Tin Pan Alley glitter it makes up for in the gritty authenticity of its musical roots, a lineage that the poor Swanee will never be able to match. Was this the land that gave birth to the blues? Robert Johnson, Son House, Charley Patton, Bukka White, Muddy Waters, Big Bill Broonzy, Howlin' Wolf, B. B. King—the names linked with the region literally define the essence of this African American art form. Travel outside the range of this river and its environs, and all the blues you find will be a mere footnote to what happened here, sprouting from the brown, moist topsoil of the Delta region.

Perhaps the largest and most depressing landmark in this entire hothouse landscape, the former site of the legendary Parchman Farm, spreads over fifteen thousand acres watered by a disproportionate share of human blood, sweat, and tears. Social historians might quibble at the name: Parchman was no farm, they will insist. It was a prison, or even worse than a prison, if such is possible. In 1972, Judge William C. Keady stepped in to set matters aright, deeming that Parchman's operations were in violation of the First Amendment, the Eighth Amendment, the Fourteenth Amendment, and probably a book full of other ordinances, laws, and statutes—not to mention those basic laws of human decency that judges sometimes take into account, and sometimes don't. As a result, the federal government put an end to Parchman Farm, the institution that Keady described as a "backward, shabby, trusty-run plantation." Today a modern penitentiary stands in its place, with a grim façade, imposing double gates, and a large contingent of armed guards securing its perimeter. This represents progress, or at least as close as one gets among those unfortunate enough to be incarcerated in the State of Mississippi.

In its prime the old Parchman Farm hardly looked the part of a repressive penal institution. No walls or barriers kept its inmates in check. Yes, there was a front gate, but it was free-standing, not linked to fences or any other structure. People came and went freely, including the "lewd women" who worked with little interference among the inmates. There were no cells, either. The convicts lived in large dormitories that to a casual glance might be mistaken for army barracks. The facility, in fact, represented nothing less than a miniature economic community, the cultivated farmland supplemented by a dairy, a brickyard, a canning facility, a sawmill, a slaughterhouse, and other operations that contributed to Parchman's self-sufficiency.

Yet Parchman's innocent appearance was very much the cause of its disgrace. No, it didn't look like a prison. It looked like nothing less than an old-style plantation from the antebellum era. Parchman was a throwback to a different world, almost a vestigial reminder of the days when African Americans were forced to pick cotton for idle slaveowners. Over a century after the Emancipation Proclamation, Parchman continued this disreputable tradition. The inmates, who were almost exclusively black, toiled in the sun under the supervision of an administrative organization that was primarily white.

Parchman was caught in a time warp. But the very conditions that constituted Parchman's shame were a boon to the researchers attempting to trace the forgotten history of African American song. John Lomax and his son Alan first traveled to the prison farm in the 1930s, at a time when few historians felt inclined to tap into the rich vein of traditional material trapped within the nation's various places of incarceration. In fact, songs by prisoners were held in such low esteem at the time, that when John Lomax wrote to prisons about his project he had to stress that he wanted to "secure copies of the songs, *no matter how crude or vulgar they may be.*" When he arrived at one prison, the warden angrily thrust a copy of the letter under Lomax's nose and yelled "What in hell do you want with dirty songs? And did you think we would violate postal laws to send indecent stuff through the mails?"

Even after the pioneering efforts of John and Alan Lomax and their followers, our knowledge of the long history of prison music is all too incomplete. The vast masses of convicts through the ages, along with their stories and songs, are mostly lost to us. True, kings and other high-born individuals held in captivity sometimes managed to have their firsthand accounts—and even their songs—preserved. For example, a song supposedly composed by Richard the Lionhearted while held prisoner by Leopold of Austria laments that "no man in prison can speak his thoughts aptly without doing so as a griever; and yet for comfort's sake he can make a song." It is unlikely, though, that such songs originated as part of prison labor. In fact, a song from the imprisoned Franciscan poet Jacopone da Todi, held captive by Pope Boniface VIII in 1298, explains how he gained weight while in custody despite his scanty diet (mostly of bread) because he had no chance to exercise. A number of experts on the history of prisons—such as Dario Melossi, Massimo Pavarini, Michael Ignatieff, Orlando Lewis, and, even earlier, John Howard—have shown how the link between imprisonment and daily labor emerged only gradually in the modern era. Howard, who traveled over forty thousand miles visiting European prisons in the late eighteenth century, noted the objection that permitting prisoners to work was tantamount to "furnishing felons with tools for mischief or escape." But over time a host of motives—some driven by the desire to rehabilitate, others by economic factors or punitive schemes—gradually transformed prisons into places of daily labor. For example, the influential theorist Jeremy Bentham envisioned that inmates at his model prison, which he called the "panopticon," would "exercise to martial tunes and sing at their work." For the most part, historians of incarceration have paid scant attention to such songs, although occasional references from various sources provide us with odd glimpses into the musical life of those held in captivity.

In some instances, entire songs have come down to us. The folk song "Die Moorsoldaten" ("The peat bog soldiers") originated among prisoners digging ditches at the Börgemoor concentration camp at Papenburg, near the Dutch border, in 1933. The Soviet Union also produced its own body of prison camp songs, but even earlier such songs and verses were known in nineteenth-century Russia, both authentic laments composed by the prisoners themselves, as well as more literary equivalents by Pushkin and Lermontov, among others. Some of these were adapted for use as revolutionary songs. The following, drawn from the play *Na Dne* ("Lower depths") by Gorky, was apparently sung frequently in the early years of the twentieth century.

> I cannot stroll, as I used to,
> During the dark night along the forests,

My youth has faded
In jails and prisons.
Black raven, black raven,
Why are you soaring above me?
Or do you scent booty?
Black raven, I am not yours.

The limited documentation of this music is somewhat surprising. The general public has long had a fascination with the music of criminals and prisoners—even today, I am told, so-called Mafia songs are exceptionally popular in Italy, and the Greek tradition of songs about the underworld is even richer; while the history of outlaw ballads in English is long and extensive although, like the other regional styles of criminal tales set to music, beyond the scope of this book to address. Despite this widespread popular interest, the stories and songs of the criminal have typically been created by law-abiding citizens, who perhaps garner, along with their audience, vicarious satisfaction from the fast-and-loose exploits of the protagonists of these works. Yet only rarely have outlaws or prisoners been given the opportunity to present the songs of their own invention in their own voices.

John Lomax is often credited as the pioneer of this field of study, and though he and his son remain the most influential advocates of this music, they were not the first to go inside American prisons in search of songs. A few years earlier, the researchers Howard Odum and Guy Johnson had taken the bold move of including a chapter on "Songs of Jail, Chain Gang and Policemen" in their 1926 study *Negro Workaday Songs*. For readers of the 1920s, the very idea of devoting a book to the work songs of America's black population must have itself seemed like a trivial or misguided exercise. To the extent that African American music was valued at all by mainstream white America, it was primarily for spirituals or, in a few instances, for popular music (much of which was written by whites who mimicked the sound of authentic black music). But work songs? Sure, everyone knew they existed, and most Americans had probably heard them in the flesh at one time or another, but few would deign them worthy of the attention of two university scholars. Yet Odum and Johnson went even farther. Their opinion that convicted criminals might be especially gifted performers of this "art" was, circa 1926, certain to be repellent to a large cross-section of the American population. Where others saw only social outcasts, Odum and Johnson granted special status: "If one wishes to obtain anything like an accurate picture of the workaday Negro he will surely find much of his best setting in the chain gang, prison, or in the situations of the ever-fleeing fugitive from 'chain-gang houn', high sheriff or policeman." Here, among the convicts, "one may listen to high-pitched voices, plaintive and wailing, until the haunting melody will abide for days." Odum and Johnson provide few details of the fieldwork they undertook in documenting the prison songs in their collection, but they did pause to comment on the extraordinary abundance of the material found in these desolate settings. "One youngster about twenty-one years of age, periodic offender with experience on the chain gang and in jail, sang more than one hundred songs or fragments and the end was not yet. They cannot be described; selections are not adequate."

Around this same time, Robert Winslow Gordon published a summary of his researches into "jailhouse songs" in an article in the *New York Times Magazine*. "Nearly every type of song is to be found in our prisons and penitentiaries," Gordon explained. He documented numerous examples, including the following forerunner of "The Midnight Special," usually attributed to Leadbelly, who would record it seven years later, but clearly drawing on material that may have been fairly widely known among prisoners of the era.

> Every Monday mornin'
> When the ding-dong rings.
> You go to the table,
> See the same damn thing.
> Oh let the Midnight Special
> Shine a light on me.
> Let the Midnight Special
> Shine an ever-lovin' light on me.

Almost fifty years later, the band Creedence Clearwater Revival would transform "The Midnight Special" into a hit FM rock song, marking the final rehabilitation of this anguished and rough-hewn refrain born amid convicts and outcasts.

Only recordings could do justice to this large and imperfectly documented body of prison songs. Few, it is true, would make their way onto the Billboard charts, despite the example of "The Midnight Special," but if the emotional intensity of music counts for anything, these recordings deserve our attention. Gordon and others would contribute to this preservation effort, but it would be left primarily for John and Alan Lomax to emerge as the "recording angels" in this harrowing chapter of American folklore, as the main protagonists in preserving and promoting the riches only hinted at by earlier researchers. In addition to the cultural obstacles facing such a project—which were many given the barriers between white and black, prisoner and freeman—John Lomax also encountered equally daunting personal challenges at the time. His prison fieldwork developed in earnest at the bleakest moment in the Great Depression. In 1932 Lomax was in debt and unemployed, and had just suffered the death of his first wife, Bess Brown Lomax. His own health was poor but he needed to generate income—two of his four children depended on him for support, including Alan, who was still a teenager. In this precarious condition, "worth less than nothing" as he later wrote, Lomax secured a contract and payment from the Macmillan Company to compile the collection of songs eventually published as *American Ballads and Folk Songs*. The following June, father and son set out in a Ford automobile packed to the brim with cots, bedding, cooking equipment, clothes, and a 350-pound "pile of iron and wire and steel" that served as a primitive yet effective recording device. They were embarking on a song-collecting expedition that would take them through Texas, Louisiana, Mississippi, Tennessee, and Kentucky on their first four-month trip, and on later journeys, bring them to Florida, George, North Carolina, South Carolina, Alabama and Virginia. The Lomaxes sought out remote communities, lumber camps, plantations—anywhere, in short, where groups outside the mainstream of American society had been able to preserve their musical culture with minimal interference from external forces. "Our best field was the southern penitentiaries," Lomax later surmised. The prisoners provided a wealth of musical material, as well as encouragement for an endeavor that from others elicited mostly indifference or hostility: "Except for Negro convicts, we found little interest or sympathy manifest for our project."

Although the documentation of prison work songs in the United States began with these pioneering efforts, researchers such as Gordon, Odum, Johnson, and Lomax actually arrived fairly late on the scene. Beginning in the 1870s, many southern prisons had initiated a profitable practice of leasing convicts out to private businesses for work in farming, mining,

railroad construction, and other demanding occupations, with little regard paid to their health and safety or even to their basic needs for shelter,
food, and clothing. Although by the late 1920s this practice had fallen out
of favor, its termination had little to do with humanitarian concerns—
rather, state officials simply realized that they didn't need to share the
profits of the convicts' labor with private businesses. Large farms, such as
Parchman, could be economic enterprises unto themselves. With thousands of acres of cultivated land and with virtually enslaved labor at its
disposal, Parchman was merely an old-style plantation transferred into
the twentieth century. True, the "master" was now called warden, but
little else had changed. The shift from leased-labor to self-sustained
prison businesses must have also served, in some degree, to reduce the
free flow of work songs in and out of the prison grounds. Had some
daring researcher attempted to document convict songs circa 1900, they
may well have found an even wider range of material than the gold vein of
traditional music discovered by Lomax in 1933. Yet even as enclosed
systems of labor, the southern prisons still stood out as the richest source
of work songs and related music that any ethnomusicologist has yet
encountered.

This was true even when prison officials took steps to staunch the flow.
At Angola State Farm in Louisiana, the Lomaxes were dismayed to learn
that the prisoners were not allowed to sing while they worked. Yet one
convict, born as Huddie Ledbetter but more often referred to by the
stalwart (and soon famous) name of "Leadbelly," made the visit to Angola a major milestone in the career of the Lomaxes, and, for that matter,
in the history of American vernacular music. Leadbelly knew so many
songs, despite the senseless injunction against their use, that John Lomax
"quite resolved," as he later wrote, "to get him out of prison and take him
along as a third member of our party." Although some have accused
Lomax of being patronizing and paternalistic in his attitudes to his "discovery," few would dare deny the instrumental role he played in the
transformation of the one-time convict into a commercially successful
performer of traditional African American music. The turnabout in the
convict's life was rapid and profound: Leadbelly was released from prison
on August 1, 1934; his schedule for the last week in December of that year
included performances for the MLA gathering in Philadelphia, for an
afternoon "tea" at Bryn Mawr, and for an informal gathering of professors from Columbia and NYU. Even by the standards of the entertain-

ment industry, known for the unpredictability of its careers and the fickleness of its audiences, this was a remarkable transformation.

Each day was bringing new surprises for the Lomaxes. At Central State Farm in Sugarland, Texas, they encountered a sixty-three-year-old convict named Iron Head who knew so many songs that John Lomax dubbed him "a black Homer" and noted in a letter that it would take "a volume of 500 pages" to encompass his repertoire. In Louisiana, they met Henry Truvillion, a preacher and leader of a railroad track crew who was familiar with a wealth of musical material. The first recording session was hampered, however, by Mrs. Truvillion's insistence that her husband sing only spirituals and "sanctified" songs. As the session continued, the couple was prevailed upon and secular music was performed—but only after all the doors and windows were closed, despite the sultry weather, for fear that congregation members would hear their preacher singing "low-down blues."

But an even more fertile source of traditional songs lay ahead for the two intrepid collectors. On August 10, 1933, John and Alan Lomax arrived at Parchman Farm. Here they would hear, for the first time, "Big Leg Rosie," "Stewball," "Po Lazarus," "Diamond Joe," and many other songs now considered as constitutive parts of America's musical heritage. At Parchman, the sheer abundance of African American music was overwhelming, but aspects of European musical culture also could be detected in this unlikely setting. Take, for example, the frequently encountered prison work song "Stewball": its origins can be traced at least as far back as a London ballad published in 1822, celebrating a race that occurred in Kildare, Ireland. The ballad's history takes many twists and turns, but eventually it is linked to another horse race ballad about a noteworthy July 4, 1878, encounter between the Kentucky thoroughbred Ten Broeck and the mare Miss Molly McCarthy at Churchill Downs (then known as the Louisville Race Track). "Stewball" probably entered the African American song repertoire at southern racetracks, where many blacks served as jockeys and stable workers and often worked side by side with poor Irish immigrants. By the time Lomax recorded "Stewball" at Parchman, the various details of the story had coalesced into a strange concoction: the horse is described as white and red in the opening phrases of the song, but midway through it becomes black; the setting of the song moves from California to Chicago to Texas; and at its close the song switches gears, leaving the racetrack behind and moving to a description of horses pulling a wagon—perhaps a more expected subject for a work song than a century-old race in Ireland. But the strange juxtapositions do not detract from the Parchman version of "Stewball." Instead, the shifting particulars of the story remind us of the essence of myth—a genre with which the work song shares more than a few similarities. Myths almost always survive in numerous and often contradictory forms, finding strength in this mutability. The flexibility that allows each user to recast some details of the story helps it achieve what all great art aspires to: a universality that rises above the particulars of place and date, evoking timeless elements of the human condition.

Song served many important functions for the prisoners of this era. As with workers on the outside, convicts relied on the music to alleviate the drudgery of their labor and coordinate the effort of the individual with the rest of the group. The words of the songs also no doubt played a symbolic role, and must often have served as a type of code language within the inner circle of participants. John Storm Roberts has noted that the "use of oblique or cryptic references" is a striking characteristic of African music, one that clearly became highly useful in the New World among slaves or in prison settings where the rights of protest, or even of communication, were frequently curtailed. These songs must also have helped to protect the individuals who sang them. As Bruce Jackson has explained: "They kept a man from being singled out for whipping because he worked too slowly. The songs kept all together, so no one could be beaten to death for mere weakness." Violence of this sort was a real risk in southern prisons, where the threat of the leather strap was ever present. At Parchman "the bat," as it was called, was four feet long and a quarter of an inch thick, with holes in the last foot of leather to increase its biting force. Four men would hold the offender flat on the ground, face down, while a fifth applied the strap to the convict's bare backside.

Yet prisoners also derived more positive, if somewhat intangible, benefits from this body of music. By offering a rare opportunity for self-expression—or rather group expression—in the midst of suffering, the songs provided, as Jackson points out, an "outlet for the inmates' tensions and frustrations and angers." Singing and ire rarely coexist comfortably: the music must have imperceptibly mitigated the harshness of the surroundings, so as to soften tempers and make it marginally easier to cope. It has sometimes been suggested that the songs also had another role: to entertain others, such as guards or overseers. And though this may have been the case in certain rare instances, I doubt that it ever stood out as an important factor. In general, we should be wary of imposing our modern views of music, derived from experiences with professional performers and entertainers, on the much different world of the work song. But even more to the point, we cannot hear this music or listen to the stories of those who created it without sensing that it was motivated by intrinsic needs rather than by the expectations of others. Above all, it served as a tool for the prison workers, one that was perhaps even more important than the axes and hammers they held in their hands.

I am reminded here of a central passage in Alexander Solzhenitsyn's novel *One Day in the Life of Ivan Denisovich*—an odd scene that takes up almost a tenth of the novel's length. In this passage the author depicts the construction of a wall by the protagonist and his fellow prisoners, who work feverishly at their task and continue even after the signal is given to stop. This section of the book no doubt perplexes many readers, who must wonder why such attention is lavished on an interlude that does little to advance the plot or develop the characters involved. Yet as a depiction of the psychological and emotional reality of work in the "flow state" of consciousness, to borrow Csikszentmihalyi's term, the passage is unparalleled. Of course, the great irony here is that Ivan Denisovich is little more than a slave laborer who has no real reason to give himself up so completely to the task at hand. I suspect that the intensity of this part of the book was one of the reasons why Soviet officials allowed its publication, despite its sharp criticism of the prison system it described: it fit well with the Marxist psychological view that individuals work from their inherent desire to accomplish things, and not because of external rewards from the capitalist economy. But, more than this, Denisovich and his wall demonstrate the puzzling, contradictory human capability to find commitment and meaning in workaday contexts that seem totally devoid of such values, to discover beauty in the midst of the most demeaning labor. What we are dealing with here is an odd juxtaposition of a survival mechanism with an aesthetic predilection.

In another work of fiction, but in a section that seems to draw on real life events, Victor Hugo noted the same contradiction among nineteenth-century prisoners. When Hugo asks, "What can be done in hell?" he quickly answers his own question: "They sang. For where there is no more hope, song remains . . . The poor poacher Survincent, who had passed through the cellar prison of the Châtelet, said, 'It was the rhymes that sustained me.'" Hugo continues: "All the songs, some melodies of which have been preserved, were humble and sad to the point of tears." But even here, he detected powerful positive emotions, sometimes even tenderness, and in his final verdict on the music of the incarcerated, he states: "Try as you will, you cannot annihilate that eternal relic of the human heart, love."

This same strange beauty comes back to me when I listen to the Parchman recordings. The work conditions were, if anything, even more dehumanizing at Parchman than for the fictional Denisovich or the prisoners described by Hugo. At Parchman black convicts started their workday long before dawn, at 4 AM. Their first actions were to run at gunpoint to the fields where they worked, sometimes a mile or more distant, with prison guards pursuing them on horseback. Their labors continued until nightfall. "Everywhere we heard of men working till they dropped dead or burnt out with sunstroke," Alan Lomax later wrote. One convict Lomax met, known as the River-Ruler, had been the lead worker on the top gang at Parchman for many years, but his "feet had turned into masses of pulpy bones from the long years of pounding the earth of the penitentiary fields. In the words of the song, he had run and walked 'till his feet got to rollin', just like a wheel.'" Beyond this physical abuse, the black prisoners carried a heavy psychic load as well, knowing that even on the outside, if and when they left Parchman, they would still remain outcasts as members of an exploited underclass; that even being freed from this hellish prison did not really give them true freedom, just a slightly lesser degree of servitude.

Given the long and exhausting workday, and the warden's unwillingness to compromise its demands for the eccentric purposes of his visitors, only a small part of each day could be used for recording. The Lomaxes were granted a brief spell at noon to record, along with a somewhat longer period starting at 9 PM, when the prisoners returned to their barracks to sleep. Given these restrictions, John Lomax determined that "it would require many months to secure all the song material available among these two thousand black men." In point of fact, he was far too optimistic. It took decades to complete the project of documenting the musical riches of Parchman. Both father and son would return on many occasions, and each time found the prison farm to be an almost inexhaustible source of songs.

On John Lomax's follow-up visit in 1936, four full days were required to record the music, and his assistant at the time, former prisoner James

"Iron Head" Baker—the aforementioned "black Homer" of Sugarland—attested that he had never seen "such a mess" of singing convicts. The piece "I'm Going to Leland," sung by Frank Jordan and a group of other prisoners during this visit, is an especially noteworthy performance. Describing its power, Alan Lomax has noted that it is "scarcely music in the ordinary sense of the word," but rather represents "direct expressions in sound of the driving thrust of group labor, of the pain in the hearts of men who are cut off from ordinary human contact, of the desperation of men who have no tenderness or warmth in their lives." Lomax's effusiveness and sentimentality—trademarks of his prose that have troubled those who associate scholarly value with academic coldness—hit the mark here. This is a hard song of hardened men put to the test too often.

> I went to Leland, Lord, I thought I was lost.
> I went to Leland, Lord, I thought I was lost.
> When I went to Leland, Lord, I thought I was lost.
> Lord, I walked around the corner, spied my walking boss.
> Walking boss, Lord my walking boss.
> Walked around the corner, spied my walking boss.

In 1939, John Lomax embarked on another major song-collecting odyssey, this time accompanied by his second wife, Ruby Terrill Lomax. "Miss Terrill" as he continued to call her during their fourteen years of marriage, proved to be a capable assistant in the arduous work of finding and recording the hitherto unknown custodians of the country's vernacular music tradition. A trained classicist—she counted Alan Lomax among her Latin students—Terrill had met the elder Lomax during a college visit to lecture on cowboy music. She handled most of the documentation of the 1939 fieldtrip, transcribed lyrics, organized and arranged singers and musicians, and helped to resolve many of the day-to-day challenges of operating a movable recording studio and archive. From February 8 through June 14, the couple traveled over 6,500 miles in their 1939 Plymouth, traversing eight southern states before concluding their journey in Washington, D.C. John Lomax was seventy-one years old at the time, yet he had lost none of his zeal for ferreting out new, undiscovered sources of American music. Some six hundred songs were recorded during this period, featuring more than three hundred performers. The archive of material from this trip, now housed in the Library of Congress, amounts to 267 acetate recording discs and one linear foot of printed materials.

The 1939 trip included visits to chain gangs and penitentiaries in Texas, Mississippi, Florida, and South Carolina. At Clemens State Farm in Brazoria, Texas, they recorded a group of African American convicts whose songs were not without a dose of sarcastic humor:

> Oh, I b'lieve I git religion an' jine de church;
> I'll be a black-jack preacher, an' not have to work.

That same day, Tommy Woods led a group of convicts in a far more bitter song, one that addressed that inevitably recurring theme in this type of music: going home.

> Cap'n, I got a home in Oklahoma, Cap'n, I got a home in Oklahoma,
> Well, well, well.
> Cap'n, I sho' wanta see my Mamma, Cap'n, jes' one more time.
> Cap'n, I sho' wanta see Black Alma, (Well, well), Cap'n, I can't go home.
> Cap'n, I sho' wanta see Black Alma, (Oh, Lawdy), Cap'n, I can't go home.
> Cap'n, I b'lieve I'll write my Mama one more letter, (Well, well, well)
> Tell her to pray for me. (Lawd, have mercy)
> Cap'n, I b'lieve I'll write my Mama one more letter, (Well, well, well)
> Will you please pray for me?
> Cap'n, it's all black an' cloudy—
> But it ain't goin' rain.

Although Lomax had heard many of the prisoners' songs before, he still found it worthwhile doing fieldwork among convicts because, as he notes in his report on the trip, "the constantly shifting penitentiary population makes new folk song material available among such groups. In the solitude and loneliness of confinement the Negro recalls the songs that he learned as a child, and readily learns others from his prison associates as they work together."

By this time, however, the work songs at southern prisons were already becoming an artifact of the past. Younger prisoners often disdained the practice of singing at work, which they associated with the days of slavery. The Hawes-Cooper Act of 1929 and the Ashurst-Sumners Act of 1935 had essentially prohibited interstate distribution of prison-made goods, and signaled that the use of convicts as de facto slave laborers would soon become a marginal activity limited to a handful of trades. Above all, the decline of work songs outside the prison walls was inevitably leading to their demise inside them as well. John Lomax's death in January 1948 might well have led a disinterested observer to conclude that this important chapter in the history of American ethnomusicology had come to an end.

Yet by the time of the elder Lomax's death, his son Alan had already shown that he had inherited his father's determination to seek out the vernacular music of his native country—and, increasingly, of other countries—wherever it might be found. As such, he decided in 1947 and 1948 to embark on additional fieldwork at Parchman Farm in an attempt to find new singers and songs to supplement the extensive body of work documented on earlier visits. He also hoped to benefit from important advances in recording technology made since the end of World War II. With his new equipment, which used tape instead of disks, he believed he could capture nuances of sound that had been lost during early fieldtrips to Parchman.

A few years earlier, Alan Lomax's major claim to fame had been derived from his family connection to his father, the pioneering ballad-hunter who had almost single-handedly legitimized the study of traditional music in America. But Alan's individual achievements during the 1930s and 1940s were also noteworthy and served as tokens of a promising future career pursuing projects of his own choosing. By the time of the 1947–1948 Parchman recordings, one might even have debated whether the father or son was the greater contributor to the preservation of traditional music, and with each passing year the balance of evidence was tilting increasingly toward the younger member of the family. Born in 1915 in Austin, Texas, Alan's training and education had taken place partly in academic institutions but mostly on the road with his father; he eventually took time away from his studies at Harvard and the University of Texas in order to assist on recording trips and in the preparation of the volume *American Ballads and Folk Songs*—Lomax father and son even traveled together to New York to deliver the manuscript, housed in a laundry-shirt box, to the publisher in October 1933.

During these early years of his career, Alan participated in the fieldwork undertaken by his father that resulted in the debut recordings of an impressive roster of American music legends in the making, including Muddy Waters, Woody Guthrie, and Leadbelly. But even before Pearl

Harbor, Lomax had begun building a resume of his own: working for the Archive of American Folksong at the Library of Congress, first as assistant curator then replacing his father as curator in 1940; embarking on music-collecting expeditions to Haiti and the Bahamas; recording more than eight hours of Jelly Roll Morton's piano playing, singing, and story-telling—which formed important documents in the history of early jazz as well as the source material for a later biography (*Mr. Jelly Roll*); and writing and producing *American Folk Songs,* a radio survey that ran on CBS. His broadcasting continued as part of the war effort, and afterward he broadened the scope of his work by recording *Blues in the Mississippi Night* in 1946, a pathbreaking and controversial discussion of the origin and meaning of the blues, featuring Memphis Slim, Sonny Boy Williamson, and Big Bill Broonzy. Here Lomax showed that, even more than his father, his interests went beyond documenting African American music and extended to critiquing the harsh social conditions and racial divisions of midcentury American life. The following year, around the time he embarked on his new Parchman field recording project, Lomax was selected as one of 135 individuals in the Americas to be awarded a Guggenheim fellowship, honored that year alongside Ansel Adams, Gwendolyn Brooks, and Arthur Schlesinger Jr. In short, the Alan Lomax who arrived at Parchman Farm in 1947 was a major scholar and researcher, a leader in his field, transformed markedly from the teenage apprentice who had first visited its grounds fourteen years earlier.

Throughout his career, Lomax tended to depict his fieldwork and recording efforts in quasi-mythic language. Even more than his father, he invariably sought the symbolic element in what he documented. And what he documented he saw less as music making and more as legend making—although like all good legends it needed to be grounded in historical reality. On the Parchman recordings from 1947 and 1948, these tendencies came to the fore. The many singers recorded take on—like Leadbelly and Muddy Waters before them—evocative nicknames. Indeed, even decades after the event Lomax is so caught up with these alternative identities that he disdains providing the singer's given names. The accompanying notes to the commercial recordings featuring these postwar Parchman singers merely refer to 'Bama, Tangle Eye, C. B., Fuzzy Red, Hard Hair, Little Red, and—most enigmatically of all—to two convicts simply called "22" and "88." The mythic ethos of the project also comes across in the recorded interviews and monologues—which take on greater prominence in the work of the younger Lomax. During these sessions at Parchman, convicts were encouraged to tell tall tales for the recording device, or speculate about the folklore hero John Henry, or recount the parable of the prodigal son in their own words. Occasionally, the realities of prison life intruded, as in a song that dealt directly with the subject of incarceration:

> Ain't but one thing I done wrong,
> Ain't but one thing I done wrong,
> Ain't but one thing I done wrong,
> Stayed in Mississippi just a day too long.
> A day too long, Lordy, day too long,
> In Mississippi, a day too long.

Or in a song about the much-awaited time when they would be paroled:

> I'm goin' to Memphis when I get my 'role.
> I'm goin' to Memphis when I get my 'role.
> I'm goin' to Memphis when I get my 'role.
> Stand on the levee, hear the big boat blow.
> Big boat blow, baby, big boat blow,
> Stand on the levee, hear the big boat blow.

Lomax clearly understood that he wanted to move beyond what his father had done. Instead of merely recording traditional songs, he aimed to translate them into something grander, accentuating their folkloric elements and presenting them as part of the rich cultural tapestry in which they were embedded. Some researchers in his situation might have dreamed of discovering the next Charley Patton or Robert Johnson. But Alan Lomax, though he may not have admitted it to himself in such blunt terms, aspired to create another Paul Bunyan or John Henry, a Johnny Appleseed or Pecos Bill. We can see this process at work as early as his efforts with Jelly Roll Morton; here Lomax reaches for the most colorful elements—the bawdy houses of Storyville, the brashness and exaggerations of his protagonist—in crafting a tale in which music provides a mere soundtrack and is never the central focus of the endeavor. For better or worse, views of New Orleans jazz are still colored by this tawdry romanticism, thanks in no small part to Lomax. Now at Parchman, he was again looking beyond the songs, searching both for the larger cultural context as well as for any elements that could contribute toward the mythologizing of the men who made the music and their surroundings. He came close to succeeding, as evidenced by Parchman's now-prominent place in the imaginative landscape of southern folklore. And whether one likes or dislikes the transformation of this unseemly prison into a legendary bit of Americana suitable for tour guides and nostalgic reminiscences, one must marvel at the sheer audacity of the move. In the midst of unvarnished human misery, Alan Lomax was determined to find heroes and legends.

Yet the linkages with his father's pioneering fieldwork at the prison farm were also evident. Often this sense of continuity was provided by the prisoners themselves, perhaps most notably by Dobie Red, who had been pointed out to John Lomax during his initial visit as the best song leader at Parchman. With a thick bristle of red hair that contrasted sharply with his dark-brown complexion, Dobie Red would have stood out from his fellow convicts even if it had not been for his greatly admired vocal skills. But when he began singing his distinction was even more apparent: his voice, Lomax later recalled, "carried the shock of a bugle call." Muscular and assertive, it conveyed an unusual degree of energy for a work song. Remember this music was meant to keep a steady, manageable pace to the work, not push it as hard as possible. More often than not, the song leaders had higher-pitched voices (the opposite of what one expects based on movies and stereotypes of prison work gangs) probably for the good reason that they could be heard more clearly above the din of work. Yet Dobie Red seemed oblivious to the need to pace himself. True, the actual tempo of his singing was unrushed, but the vitality he exuded was all the more remarkable for this fact. And the other prisoners responded with a rare degree of enthusiasm, given their circumstances. An uninitiated listener, on first hearing Dobie Red leading his fellow prisoners in a rendition of "Stewball," might be mistaken into thinking that this music was recorded in an especially fervent southern church, given the ecstatic emotions of the call-and-response.

The prison officials must have been equally impressed by the prisoners' response to Dobie Red. When John Lomax returned to Parchman, he found that the authorities had made him into a guard, since Red's ability to lead the prisoners apparently was thought to extended to matters other than music. Taking advantage of this new role, Dobie Red disappeared one day—leaving for the North, according to friends left behind. But his freedom was short-lived. Alan Lomax now found him back at Parchman in the late 1940s, broken down in spirit and voice. He told Lomax at that time that he had spent twenty-seven years of his life in incarceration. But he still managed to demonstrate an evocative field holler for the recording equipment, later issued as part of the commercial releases documenting the 1947 and 1948 fieldwork at Parchman.

In the late 1950s and early 1960s—at a time when group singing at work began to disappear from penitentiaries—few researchers showed an interest in following up on the early initiatives by John and Alan Lomax. As a result, only a small number of recording projects were undertaken during these final years in which songs were regularly sung as part of prison labor. Harry Oster, who pursued important fieldwork at Angola Prison at the end of the 1950s, was a most unlikely champion of this music. This son of Jewish immigrants from Russia had served in the U.S. Air Force during World War II, then completed a degree in English at Harvard. (It is interesting to note that all of the major protagonists in recording American prison music, including Oster, Robert Winslow Gordon, and both of the Lomaxes, could boast of Harvard ties.) After leaving Harvard, Oster began preparing for a commercial career at Columbia's School of Business, spending his spare time performing as a singer and guitarist, mostly in a group specializing in Yiddish folk music. After a brief, unhappy period in the business world, however, Oster returned to Cornell to complete a doctorate in English, then embarked on a fruitful career tracking down living artistic traditions in places where few academics dared to go. Lugging his secondhand Ampex 600 tape recorder along on his travels, Oster documented Cajun performers, bluegrass, old-time country music, and blues—mostly in Louisiana—and also went into Mexico to conduct field recordings of Hispanic musical traditions. In 1957, Oster made his first visit to Angola Prison, where he initiated one of the last major work song recording projects in the United States. "I actually operated rather differently than some of the people who've found old time blues singers," Oster later explained to interviewer Ranko Vujosevic. "Usually they track down someone who recorded in the '20s or 30s and disappeared from sight for a while. I sort of went about it in a quite different way, which in fact produced some interestingly different results, more offbeat performances and more unusual repertoire." In essence, Oster was looking to document the still-vibrant musical traditions of the South rather than re-create the styles of the past. In the area of work songs, this presented an acute challenge. "I've always been fascinated with black worksongs," Oster noted in the same interview. "I had heard that they were essentially extinct in the regular world because of mechanization of farming, and the only place to find them would be in southern prison farms."

By 1957, the public's perception of music behind bars had been permanently altered by alien cultural influences—some nuanced and others merely nonsensical. After all, this was the year that Elvis Presley graced the silver screen in *Jailhouse Rock*—stamping on the collective consciousness the lasting image of dancing, gyrating, *hard-rockin'* convicts—while, half a world away, Shostakovich debuted his Eleventh Symphony, drawing on Russian prison songs for some of his thematic material. Who would believe that, at the dawn of the space age, real inmates still made music of extraordinary pathos and intensity? Yet Oster's end-of-an-era efforts at Angola were amply rewarded. Here he recorded a rich variety of music, not just work songs but also exceptional performances of blues and spirituals, much of which has been released commercially. One prisoner, Odea Matthews, provided a rare glimpse of the songs of female prisoners. While scrubbing clothes on a washboard, Matthews sang of the man who "put her out" after five years of bringing him her paycheck from her job at a sawmill. "Next man I marry he got to work, and bring me some gold." In another recording James Russell, one of the few younger prisoners who sang work songs, also lamented "I had five long years" in a slow-drag work song often used for hoeing or cutting cane. Rodney Mason, known at Angola as "Big Louisiana," led a group in a poignant version of "Berta"—a recurring female figure in prison work songs. In this instance, Roosevelt Charles served as a foil, interjecting cynical comments on the fidelity of the woman outside the prison walls. These hard-hitting performances rank among the finest recorded examples of work music, and would compare favorably with many commercial blues and pop recordings of the day.

Indeed, Oster's legacy of recordings from Angola reveal how much prison music, by this late date, had learned from commercial music styles. The figure of 'Berta shows up in Russell's song, which literally repeats the lyric of a different work song tradition ("Alberta, Let Your Bangs Go Long"). But Russell's song also is a variant of "Makes a Long Time Man Feel Bad," which was recorded by John Lomax in 1934 in the woodyard of an Arkansas prison and which surprisingly later entered the repertoires of unlikely singers such as Bobby Darrin and Harry Belafonte.

Odea Matthews, in contrast, borrowed from a popular singer in her lament, which echoes a jukebox hit from 1952, "Five Long Years" by Eddie Boyd. In this regard, it is perhaps worth noting that only five years after Oster made his last prison recordings, Charles Neville—best known as the second-oldest member of the Neville Brothers—was incarcerated in Angola for possession of marijuana. By then the call-and-response singing tradition of prison workers was mostly a dim memory at the prison; however, Neville learned one song, "Angola Bound," which he made into a pop recording after his release. Here, in its final phase, the work song tradition was still evolving—drawing on soul, R&B, and blues elements and creating extraordinary hybrids. This borrowing and cross-fertilization may upset purists (who are unhappy to see songs from the Hit Parade enter the repertoires of traditional singers, and are only slightly less peeved when traditional singers themselves make the Hit Parade) or confuse discographers trying to assign a song title to a performance that is "half a' this" and "half a' that." But it also reflects an often-forgotten aspect of this music: work songs were not intended to be presented in three or four minute installments on commercial recordings; they need to keep going, just like the laborer, until the work finishes. Given this requirement, work song leaders would invariably draw on whatever snippets of lyrics came into their heads, no matter what the source. In the hot sun with a heavy hammer or axe in hand, a manual laborer had no leisure to worry about the "integrity" of the song or, needless to say, issues of copyright infringement.

Around this same time, Alan Lomax made a return visit to the Mississippi penitentiaries. As Oster had found at Angola, Lomax discovered that some work songs were still sung by prisoners at the end of the 1950s, although this would be the last time he would record them in this setting. Many of the songs were familiar ones, although Lomax also documented new music and, like Oster, he was struck by the high caliber of the performances he heard. Leading a group of prisoners whose voices blend in supple harmony behind him, Ervin Webb intones his poignant lament "I'm Goin' Home," which in my opinion is the single most heart-wringing performance from Lomax's long career of preserving prison work songs.

I'm goin' home, oh yes,
I'm goin' home, oh yes,

I'm goin' home,
Lord, Lord,
I'm going home.
My baby sister's cryin,'
My baby sister's cryin,'
Brother come home,
Lord, Lord,
Brother come home.
My old mother's cryin,'
My old mother's cryin,'
Come on home,
Lord, Lord,
Come on home.

But even if Lomax had not uncovered new material of such quality, the fieldtrip might have been justified for the memorable version of the old song "Po' Lazarus," which he recorded at Lambert. This performance, oddly destined to be featured on a Grammy-winning album, finds James Carter re-telling the story of the title protagonist, who represents neither of the two differently afflicted Lazaruses of the New Testament, but rather an outlaw determined never to suffer the indignity of arrest and incarceration. Lazarus eludes the authorities, until his final confrontation with the sheriff:

O then Laz'rus, he tol' the High Sheriff,
Says, "I've never been arrested,
By no one man, Lord, Lord,
By no one man."
Oh well, the Sheriff, he shot Laz'rus,
Yes, he shot him with a great big number.
With a forty-five, Lord, Lord,
With a forty-five.
O then they taken po Laz'rus,
An' they laid him on the commissary galley.
He said, "My wounded side, Lord, Lord,"
He said, "My wounded side."

The vitality of this music could not hide the anachronisms of the settings that produced it. Within the next decade the tradition of prison singing would be extinguished from penitentiaries in the South.

Yet, around this same time—when one might have thought no more fieldwork and recordings would be made in this area—researcher Bruce Jackson embarked on a final, successful attempt to preserve the dying tradition of work songs at various Texas prisons. Beginning in 1964, Jackson visited more than a dozen facilities, documenting the greatest amount of material at three of them—Ramsey, Ellis, and Wynne—where older convicts predominated. Again, the quality of the music and the intensity of the performances are worthy of note. Memorable recordings of "Down the Line," "Captain Don't Feel Sorry for a Longtime Man," and "Long Hot Summer Days" can be found on the commercial release *Wake Up Dead Man*, drawn from Jackson's tapes. "Grizzly Bear," which Jackson recorded twelve separate times with five different leaders (a dramatic version is also included on *Wake Up Dead Man*) is a mini-epic, which traces the bear as he eludes captors and wreaks havoc in several states before being killed. Different informants provided Jackson with conflicting details about which person inspired the protagonist of the song. Yet the prison-oriented symbolism of the story—at one point the bear is locked in a zoo but manages to escape—imparts a poignancy to the piece that transcends whatever facts surrounded its creation. Jackson notes with surprise that this popular prison song was not documented before 1951 and hence never surfaced in the earlier fieldtrips by John and Alan Lomax. Then again, the story conveys an antihero ethos that is very much in line with the characters popularized by Hollywood movies in the 1950s and 1960s. The grizzly bear of this tale would have been out of place in a Parchman convict song of the Great Depression, but in the cold war era the hard-edged call-and-response might well have served as part of the soundtrack for a Marlon Brando or James Dean film. "The songs, sometimes, are compellingly beautiful," Jackson would write of this music; "the subject, always, has to do with making it in Hell." He continues: "The songs are sung outdoors. They are sung in daylight only. They do not exist in the dark. But it is darkness or absence or lostness or vacancy or deprivation that they are about. This is not an easy thing (or group of things, if you think those words are different) to sing about. But neither is it an easy thing to experience and perceive, and the singing somehow makes it a little more bearable."

Michel Foucault has taught us that the essence of the modern penal system is the subjugation of the psyche, just as half a millennium ago punishment aimed to lacerate the body. The lash has been relegated to the dustbin—even at Parchman—and replaced by the counselor and thera-pist. Perhaps this move represents a greater clemency, or perhaps merely the quest for a deeper and even more dominating subjugation of the convict. In either case, the prisoner's work song has played an equivocal role in the new order of things. Truly the inmate's very soul was held captive, as witnessed by these heartfelt songs through which the prisoner embraced his laborious punishment. Or are we perhaps misreading the situation? Was the work song a subversive attempt by the convict to hold onto his individuality and maintain his spirit in the face of his degraded state?

Both interpretations are true. And this duality of the work song is one of its most mysterious and alluring features. It can denounce work or celebrate it, or—most extraordinary of all—do both at the same time. Bruce Jackson reached essentially this same conclusion at the close of his fieldwork collecting these songs in Texas prisons:

> I confess a certain ambivalence toward the songs and their contexts . . . I experience an unmediated loathing for the context that made and makes these songs possible and necessary. . . . But at the same time I am (obviously) drawn to the songs and the people who make them. On a cognitive level there is something in them significant of a world I hope will never be mine or be that of anyone I ever know (but there is that academic catholicism that tells me that anything affecting so many people must be a part of my world in some way), and that something is there in strikingly human terms. . . . Our world is so dissonant, so incongruous, it is hard to make sense of things sometimes yet it is so tempting to try: Beauty must be kept, wherever it is found, however foul its genesis. Les Fleurs du Mal are still flowers.

Perhaps this complexity in the work song helps us understand how a performance such as "Po Lazarus," recorded at the Mississippi State Peni-tentiary in 1959, could become the lead track on a Grammy-winning recording in the year 2002—beating out Michael Jackson and Mariah Carey for the unlikely honor. The tremendous popular response to the soundtrack to the film *O Brother, Where Art Thou?*—the recording of which sold a staggering seven million copies—must have seemed a puz-zling phenomenon to entertainment industry executives gathered at the Grammy ceremonies. Indeed, much of the music could hardly be de-scribed as "commercial"—whether the term is defined narrowly as "likely to succeed in the marketplace" or even defined loosely as "intended for commerce." This prison work song was so integrated into its day-to-day setting that James Carter, who was the lead performer, even forgot his role in making the recording. His surprise bordered on stupefaction when he was presented with a platinum record and a royalty check for $20,000 almost forty-two years after his performance for the visiting Alan Lomax. Interviewed by the *New York Times,* Carter admitted that he had no memory whatsoever of Lomax's visit. But when told that his recording was outselling Michael Jackson, Carter took a puff on his cigarette, mused for a moment, then replied: "You tell Michael that I'll slow down so that he can catch up with me."

CHAPTER TWELVE

The Labor Movement and Songs of Work

Then come comrades rally

And the last fight let us face.

The Internationale Unites the human race.

—*The Internationale*

In 1821 various supporters of the utopian visionary Henri de Saint-Simon gathered together at the estate of a wealthy businessman with progressive leanings to enjoy the premier of a new type of work song, described as a "Chant des industriels." Saint-Simon had enlisted the assistance of Claude-Joseph Rouget de Lisle, composer of "La Marseillaise," in his attempt to create this new work song celebrating the "children of industry"—as well as praising Saint-Simon's generous supporter, Guillaume Ternaux, the owner of the estate and a prominent woolens manufacturer.

The song was written in the first-person plural, which encouraged the workers attending the premier to join in the singing—as many in fact did. Their voices blended together, the workers proclaimed:

Honor to us, children of industry.
Honor, honor to our fortunate labors!

Vanquishing our rivals, in all the arts,
Let us be the hope and pride of the fatherland!

This industrial song would prove to be Saint-Simon's first as well as last foray into the world of ideological music—although many of his followers would strive to fill the void. But the ambiguity of the relationship of music to the working movement would remain unresolved. "Au peuple," a Saint-Simonian song written by the most fervent of the Saint-Simonian composers, Félicien David, needed to have its text changed when it was discovered that it was better to have the song sung by the workers rather than at the workers out of the mouths of the intellectuals.

Later, Jules Vinçard, artisan and leader of the Parisian "family" of Saint-Simonians, played a prominent role in composing songs for the group. These were styled "songs for workers"—but it is doubtful whether many laborers were able to master the strange metrics and two-range octave demanded by the music. One colleague complained to Vinçard that "your devilish songs have an irregularity of rhythm which forces you to make lines of very differing meters. This is an obstacle which prevents anyone other than you to sing them, to set them to different music, or to put yours into score for an accompanist."

Yet for all the limitations of this music, the approach adopted by Vinçard and the other Saint-Simonians would serve as harbinger of a new and significant tendency in worker's music—namely the growing use of song to create class consciousness among laborers and to serve as a rallying point for political and industrial movements; in short, to become an instrument of advocacy and social change. Exactly fifty years after the debut of the "Premier chant des industriels," another, more memorable, song, also of French origin—"The Internationale"—would reveal the hitherto untapped potential of this new tool. "The Internationale," composed in 1871 by Eugene Pottier, a woodworker from Lille, with music supplied by factory worker Pierre Degeyter, achieved the ends to which the Saint-Simonians had merely aspired. "The Internationale" was originally an anthem for workers at the fall of the Paris Commune—which forced member Pottier to flee to England—but then came to be adopted by a wide range of groups and individuals, from Marxist revolutionaries to more peaceful socialist organizations. The song proved to have enormous staying power and adaptability. During the Paris unrest of 1968, tens of thousands of protesters marched through the streets, many singing the venerable melody, still relevant despite the very changed circumstances of the times. In 1989 it was repeatedly sung by the protesting students in Tiananmen Square, just as it had been used by the early supporters of the very regime they were attacking. During the course of its long history, "The Internationale" has been translated into several dozen different languages, including Japanese, Farsi, Maori, Zulu, and Esperanto. In English, the chorus proclaims:

> Then come comrades rally
> And the last fight let us face.
> The Internationale
> Unites the human race.

Of course, laborers had long used songs to complain about their work conditions. A surviving song from ancient Egypt offers the worker's lament: "Must we spend all day carrying barley and white emmer?" Sometimes the singer protested openly, as in this instance; perhaps more often the rebuke was couched in metaphorical terms that might escape the notice of an overseer, or hidden behind the appearance of servility. One must be deaf to nuances to miss the disingenuousness of many of the surviving memorials to long dead tyrants. We hear it, for example, in this fragment quoting the Old Kingdom Egyptian servant who carries the master in his chair: "Happy are they that bear the chair. Better it is for us when full than when it is empty."

We are tempted to view the birth of the workers' protest song as intimately linked to the Industrial Revolution in Britain. But even earlier British workers expressed their dissatisfactions in the form of songs. "The Cutty Wren," composed at the time of the 1381 peasants' revolt, stirred the emotions of the rebels with its description of the capture of a wren, symbolizing the king, and its division among the poor. "The Diggers' Song" commemorated the exploits of a group of radical squatters from the mid-seventeenth century. Their experimental community on St. George's Hill, near Weybridge, survived little more than a year, but would later be viewed as a forerunner of the collectivist models of the nineteenth and twentieth centuries. And only a decade before Saint-Simon's experiments with music, the Luddites had created songs to celebrate their attack on the machines that were making many jobs obsolete.

This latter rebellion against the inexorable forces of industrialization began in Nottingham, with members of the local working class forming together into a secret army, showing up at factories in disguise to demand concessions and, if necessary, to wreak damage on the offending machinery. The members of this guerrilla movement sang about their agenda, personified for them in the figure of General Ludd. The singers accorded him the honors once associated with an earlier hero of Nottingham, who had also fought for the rights of the poor:

> Chant no more your old rhymes about bold Robin Hood,
> His feats I but little admire.
> I will sing the Achievements of General Ludd
> Now the Hero of Nottinghamshire.

Another Luddite song commemorates the destruction of a mill located between Horbury and Ossett:

> Come all ye croppers stout and bold,
> Let your faith grow stronger still,
> Oh, the cropper lads in the county of York
> Broke the shears at Forster's Mill.
> The wind it blew,
> The sparks they flew,
> Which alarmed the town full soon.
> And out of bed poor people did creep
> And ran by the light of the moon;
> Around and around they all did stand,
> And solemnly did swear,
> Neither bucket nor kit nor any such thing
> Should be of assistance there.

The movement eventually spread to Yorkshire, Lancashire, and other industrial regions. A conflict at a Lancashire power loom mill in April 1812 may have involved more than a thousand members of the working class, armed mostly with sticks and rocks. When the well-armed guards rebuffed the attack, the Luddites burned down the house of the mill owner. The deployment of troops, along with the trial of sixty-four followers of "General Ludd" and the subsequent hanging of three, deflated the movement, but its memory continued to inspire later critics of industrialization. Collective movements aiming to destroy machinery would still flare up on occasion—in England the tradition dated back to 1663 and would continue at least until 1831—but most workers shifted their attention to other means of confrontation and negotiation.

The labor protest song of the modern era was different from any of these earlier melodic testimonials to worker unrest. It stood out as a more ambitious and purposive enterprise, less a spontaneous outpouring of the worker's feelings and more often a deliberate effort to spur change and rally support. In many instances, the desired change was a local matter of wages and conditions, but sometimes a more revolutionary transformation was envisioned, in which economic structures would be reconfigured and the owners of the means of production stripped of their powers. And, as we have already seen with Saint-Simon and his colleagues, the creators and propagators of this new labor music did not necessarily need to be members of the working class. Progressive and revolutionary thinkers of various affiliations would take on this responsibility, if class consciousness did not arise spontaneously among the laborers. In 1885, for example, the Socialist League in London issued a one-penny pamphlet, *Chants for Socialists*, containing songs by William Morris, the Oxford-educated heir of an affluent family. A half-century later, the Harvard-educated Charles Seeger, whose ancestors had sailed to America on the Mayflower, adopted the nom de plume "Carl Sands" for his work as a composer of consciousness-raising songs for laborers. Yet this affinity of establishment scions for radical music merely reflected the larger intellectual climate, where the ideological support for revolutionary politics found sustenance in the writings of Karl Marx (son of a lawyer), Friedrich Engels (son of a wealthy industrialist), Vladimir Lenin (son of a Russian nobleman), Georg Lukács (son of a banker), and others with similarly entitled backgrounds. Like the intellectual climate that surrounded it, the modern labor song could frequently boast of an upper-crust pedigree, even if its allegiances were squarely with the working class.

The simpler purposes that work songs had embraced in the past—to make the hours of toil more tolerable; to express the deeply felt emotions of a worker; to amuse or inspire; to coordinate movements and activities; or to assert the inherent dignity of all labor, even the most grueling—were seen as no longer adequate, or perhaps even proper, roles for music. Under the old scheme of things, singing workers seemed to acquiesce in their own oppression. They presented an image of contentment that served to obscure the exploitative relationships of the work environment, and as such might even be harmful to the true interests of labor. The protest song—conceived as a critique of work rather than an accompaniment to it—would now emerge as the quintessential music of organized labor.

Yet, from another perspective, this new music of labor shared striking similarities with the call-and-response songs of old. Like the work song, this music was noted for its ability to organize individuals into groups. Both types of song were about survival in the face of adversity and about helping to improve the quality of a worker's life. In essence, both embraced the tools of art to meet functional ends. The utility of the traditional work song was obvious: it made the hours of labor pass more quickly and alleviated in some small degree the drudgery and drain of physical exertion. The functional role of the new labor song was not dissimilar—it too aimed to reduce the negative aspects of work—but how music achieved this end was now far more complex and multifaceted. Certainly the songs of the labor movement served to protest work conditions, but they did much more than just articulate grievances. They rallied individuals around a common cause and won adherents among the undecided through the infectious quality of music. They blurred the line between politics and art, and as such reached people and places when more conventional methods of advocacy might have failed. When used effectively, they succeeded in spurring genuine reform. But even when they failed in this larger goal, the songs still served a purpose. In an age in which many newspapers and official channels of communication tended to exclude the views of the working class, such songs played a vital role in describing and interpreting events. They offered, in essence, an alternative source of information, a different type of historical record. And, in an age in which many workers were illiterate, they might very well be more than an alternative medium, but rather serve as the preferred method of disseminating ideas.

In some countries, a snapshot history of the modern workers' movement could almost be constructed from the songs alone. The memorable events of the German labor movement and revolutionary politics, for example, can be traced over the course of a turbulent century by studying the musical statements they left behind. "Achtzehnter März" captures the bitter sentiments of radical groups following the failure of the uprisings of 1848. "Bundeslied" was penned by poet Georg Herwegh in response to the founding of the General German Workers' Union in 1863 (although it borrowed heavily from an English poem by Shelley). "Ich bin Soldat" conveyed the sentiments of revolutionary groups at the time of the 1870–1871 Franco-Prussian War. "Sozialistenmarsch" was first sung at the second convention of the Sozialdemokratische Partei Deutschlands (SPD) in October 1891, when Marxist doctrine was formally embraced as the official philosophy of the party. "Auf, Auf, Zum Kampf" was reworked in response to the suppression of the Spartacus Revolt and the murder of Rosa Luxemburg and Karl Liebknecht in 1919. Hans Eisler and Erich Weinert composed their well-known song "Der Rote Wedding" to protest police attacks on demonstrators on May 1, 1929—which was viewed as a betrayal by the social democratic police chief of Berlin Karl Zörgiebel.

Left, left, left, left,
In spite of Fascists and police!
Remember May 1st!
Remember the bloodied face of the ruling class
and the disgrace of the Socialist Party!

Weinert later adapted the lyrics in response to other topical issues. Whenever important events transpired, it seems that they were invariably preceded, followed, or accompanied by songs tailored for the exigencies of the moment.

Often, songs were the only lasting result of labor unrest. We see this, for instance, in the history of the last major worker revolt in England. This 1830 uprising, which began in Kent, soon moved west into Sussex, Hampshire, and Dorset, and north into Wiltshire and Berkshire, eventually reaching into the Midlands. Reprisals were severe. Over six hundred men were executed, but not before they had burned down workhouses, destroyed machines, and called attention to the need for higher wages. A song recounting the struggles, "The Owslebury Lads," circulated for over seventy-five years as popular oral history before being transcribed in a collector's notebook. Its survival is a telling reminder of the power of music to preserve the memory of events, as well as to offer interpretations of them contrary to those found in "official" channels. Here song is more than protest; it is also *samizdat*:

The thirtieth of November, eighteen hundred and thirty,
The Owslebury lads they did prepare all for the machinery,

And when they did get there, my eye! how they let fly.
The machinery flew to pieces in the twinkling of an eye.
The mob, such a mob, you never did see before.
And if you live one hundred years you never will no more.

The prediction offered in these lyrics proved to be all too true. Future rumblings of unrest in Britain failed to erupt into major uprisings. When Dorset farm workers attempted to organize four years later, authorities acted quickly to deport the ringleaders, and matters soon calmed down. From then on, workers and their leaders might dream of an armed uprising, but their actions increasingly focused on unionization rather than revolution, a shift that was also reflected in the songs of the movement.

Song also figured prominently in the workers' movement in the United States. In fact, it perhaps filled an even more vital role on American soil, given the typically less-confrontational nature of class conflicts in the United States during the first century of the nation's history. A great burst of unionization and labor organization marked the years following the Civil War. The Knights of Labor were formed in Philadelphia in 1869— originally as a secret society with esoteric rituals but eventually as a public institution fighting for an eight-hour workday, the end of child labor, and other progressive causes. The so-called Molly Maguires, another secret organization with roots in Ireland, became prominent in the United States around this same time, serving as an assertive and sometimes violent force in advocating the rights of Pennsylvania miners in the 1870s. The Federation of Trades and Labor Unions was established in 1881—five years later it changed its name to the American Federation of Labor (AFL); the United Mine Workers was started in 1890, and the Teamsters in 1903. In little more than a generation, the labor movement had emerged as a significant force in American public life.

This was also a great era for labor songs and poems. As the labor press expanded, growing from a few scattered publications in the 1860s to hundreds of influential newspapers and periodicals in the 1880s, these songs did not decline in status but instead became an important part of the new media. "Almost without exception," writes Clark Halker, "only marginal, irregular publications, or those first published in the 1890s, excluded original song-poetry. Otherwise, song-poetry appeared in publications representing an array of occupations—typographers, coal miners, iron molders, machinists, coopers, seamen, granite cutters, railway carmen, saddle makers, cigar makers, printers, window glass workers, brakemen, locomotive engineers, and bakers." However, as Philip Foner, in his work *American Labor Songs of the Nineteenth Century*, points out: "The chances are that many never got off the printed page." It would be left for the next generation to take the potential of songs such as these and make them a vital part of the workers' movement in the United States.

No group would do more in this regard than the Industrial Workers of the World (IWW), or the "Wobblies" as they were often called. The IWW was formed in Chicago in June 1905, at a meeting attended by many key figures in radical labor and political movements: Mother Jones, the organizer for the United Mine Workers, may have looked the part of a demure grand-mother, but her fiery rhetoric and indefatigable efforts in labor conflicts were reminiscent of nothing less than the tactics of a battlefield general; Eugene V. Debs, who had run for president the previous year as candidate for the Socialist Party, would continue to be the party's standard-bearer for many years, garnering close to one million votes in 1912; Lucy Parsons, a labor activist and champion of the rights of African Americans, had risen to notoriety after her husband Albert Parsons was convicted of murder and hanged in the aftermath of the Haymarket bombing; and Big Bill Haywood, the confrontational former cowboy, was the current leader of the Western Federation of Miners, known for his prominent role in championing an eight-hour work day: his celebrated refrain was "Eight hours of work, eight hours of play, eight hours of sleep—eight hours a day!" The organization that resulted from this gathering of labor luminaries embraced more am-bitious goals than any previous American union. The Wobblies criticized other worker organizations, especially the AFL, for being too narrowly focused and far too willing to collaborate with ownership. In contrast, the preamble to the constitution of the IWW proclaimed: "The working class and the employing class have nothing in common." Confrontation was not only to be accepted as an occasional tactic, but encouraged as an on-going strategy; even sabotage, in the name of workers' rights, was seen as an acceptable tool of social and economic change. Such systemic friction and envisioned transformation of society was beyond the scope of existing labor organizations, whose energies were consumed by their specific and local concerns. The Wobblies aspired, instead, to creating "One Big Union" that could mobilize all members of the working class in forging a new basis for economic life.

Among the IWW's many other criticisms of the American Federation of

Labor loomed the noteworthy charge, according to the *Industrial Worker* of May 27, 1916, that the AFL "had no songs." The Wobblies took steps to rectify this oversight. A songbook was issued along with every union card, announcing on its cover that the music's purpose was "to fan the flames of discontent." Some Wobblies went so far as to suggest that the union might be better served by ceasing the distribution of pamphlets, instead focusing on the circulation of these songs. One IWW organizer enthused, shortly after the publication of the *Little Red Song Book:* "There are 38 songs in the I.W.W. song book, and out of that number 24 are educational, and I can truthfully say that every one of them is almost a lecture in itself." During the Lawrence, Massachusetts, textile industry strike of 1912, the value of this approach could be seen in the efficacy of song in organizing workers of forty different nationalities, a situation in which linguistic barriers might have hindered other methods of communication. Writing in the *American Magazine* of May 1912, Ray Stannard Baker noted: "It is the first strike I ever saw which sang. I shall not soon forget the curious lift, the strange sudden fire of the mingled nationalities at the strike meetings when they broke out into the universal language of song. And not only at the meetings did they sing, but in the soup houses and in the streets. I saw one group of women strikers who were peeling potatoes at a relief station suddenly break into the swing of the 'Internationale.' They have a whole book of songs fitted to familiar tunes."

No one contributed more to the success of *The Little Red Song Book* than labor songwriter and activist Joe Hill. Hill would in time become famous for much more than his songs—he was convicted of murder and executed in Salt Lake City in 1915 in a case that served as a rallying point for members of the IWW. In time, his life story would meld with the renown of his music in creating one of the quasi-mythic figures of the early-twentieth-century labor movement. By both birth and education, Hill possessed an unlikely background for an American folk musician. Born in Sweden on October 7, 1879, as Joel Emmanuel Haggland, one of nine children of railroad worker Olof Haggland and his wife Margareta, Hill had no musical training as a youngster and remained in his native country until early adulthood. Here he worked at a rope factory and shoveled coal until the age of twenty-three, when he moved to the United States. In this new setting, he traveled and worked at a wide range of jobs, laying pipe, working on docks, cleaning bars, serving onboard merchant ships, and laboring underground in mines. At some point during this period he also changed his name, first to Joseph Hillstrom and finally to Joe Hill.

While working on the docks in San Pedro, California, in 1910, Hill was exposed to the radical aims of the IWW and became an active member and organizer in its ranks. His work in the trenches for the IWW brought him to the scene of many labor conflicts, but it soon became clear that his greatest contribution to the movement would be through his music. For many years he had sketched out songs and poems—he called them "scribbles"—which drew on his experiences as a working man. Now as a union organizer he put this talent to use, creating a body of protest songs that aimed at mobilizing workers. In many ways, his limited musical background may have been an advantage for Hill. He did not hesitate to borrow well-known melodies for his words, often reconfiguring old material to meet his current needs. In one of his most famous songs, Hill reworked the classic "Casey Jones"—turning Casey into a strikebreaker who kept the Southern Pacific in business during a labor conflict. This practice of adapting familiar tunes would prove to be a great asset in teaching and propagating the songs, and would give Hill the type of influence that more highly trained composers would hardly have been able to achieve.

Perhaps the greatest—and most effective—source of inspiration for these new protest songs would be religious hymns. Far more than traditional work songs, these sacred compositions set the proper tone for the new music of labor. With their fervor and their promise for a better world in the future, the sacred songs offered both powerful imagery as well as familiar melodies, easy for workers to sing and share. For instance, Joe Hill's song "There Is Power in a Union" drew on the melody of the well-known Christian hymn, "There Is Power in the Blood of the Lamb." Brenda McCallum, in her research into the rise of jubilee gospel quartet music in the Birmingham area from the 1910s to the 1930s, found hundreds of singing groups, many of them with ties to companies and industries. McCallum notes the often memorable mixture of religious and labor movement themes in these songs, as in the musical reenactment of the Last Supper, at which Jesus tells his apostles "Stay in Union!" First-hand accounts of singing at factories in American history often stress the religious tenor of the songs; hence it comes as no surprise that these same melodies were among the very first ones drawn on when uprisings against working conditions inspired a spontaneous protest song.

In 1913 Hill traveled to Utah, where the following year he was charged in the shooting death of Arling Morrison, a youngster who worked with his father in a small grocery store. On the night of January 10, 1914, two gunmen had entered the store around closing time, their features obscured by hats and handkerchiefs. In the confrontation that ensued, the boy was shot, and the intruders fled without taking any money, at least one of them wounded in the encounter. Hill, who went to a local doctor that same night to be treated for a gunshot wound, which he claimed he received in an argument over a woman, became the prime suspect in the murder. Hill refused to testify on his own behalf in the resulting trial, and many motives have been offered for this silence: guilt, orders from the IWW, his code of honor, and the like. The jury had no doubts, however, as to how the events should be interpreted, and they returned a guilty verdict after deliberating only a few hours. When given the option of execution by hanging or firing squad, Hill told the judge: "I'll take the shooting. I've been shot a couple times before, and I think I can take it." The verdict caused an outcry in many circles: not only Wobblies but the AFL and individuals ranging from Helen Keller to W. A. F. Ekengren, the Swedish minister to the United States, lobbied President Wilson to intervene. And though Wilson refrained from issuing a presidential pardon, he attempted to convince Governor Spry of Utah to delay the execution while the matter was reviewed. Spry refused to bow to these pressures, however, and on November 19, 1915, Hill was executed by a firing squad. In one of the last messages from his cell, Hill advised Big Bill Haywood "Don't waste time mourning. Organize!" The phrase became a frequently repeated motto in the labor movement, becoming almost as well known as Hill's songs.

Joe Hill's influence continued to be felt long after his death, and songs about him soon came to join his own compositions as part of this musical legacy. Alfred Hayes's poem "I Dreamed I Saw Joe Hill," was set to music by Earl Robinson. This tribute has been translated into a dozen languages, popularized by Paul Robeson, sung by the Loyalists during the Spanish Civil War, and performed by Joan Baez at Woodstock in front of four hundred thousand people.

I dreamed I saw Joe Hill last night,
Alive as you or me.
Says I, 'But Joe, you're ten years dead.'

'I never died,' said he.
'I never died,' said he.

In the following decades, many labor supporters took Hill's admonition to heart by organizing rather than mourning, and frequently using the same musical tools that Hill had employed in their causes. These efforts involved not only workers but also some of the most illustrious composers and music scholars in America, most notably in the formation of the Composers Collective and its publication, in 1934, of its first *Workers Songbook*. The Composers Collective boasted around two dozen members along with various sympathizers who supported their efforts—those connected to the group include Aaron Copland, Henry Cowell, Elie Siegmeister, and Charles Seeger. The foreword to the *Workers Songbook* left little doubt about the ideology behind the work:

> Music Penetrates Everywhere
> It Carries Words With It
> It Fixes Them in the Mind
> It Graves Them in the Heart
> Music is a Weapon in the Class Struggle

At times, the tension between artistic and political goals led to differences among the members. For example, the Composers Collective initiated a competition in 1934 to create an appropriate May Day song, with the members preferring Aaron Copland's contribution, a setting to music of Alfred Hayes's "Into the Streets May 1." But Charles Seeger snickered that Copland's piece required a very rhythmic piano accompaniment to give it its intended march beat—and what worker would be able bring a piano on a march? In contrast, Seeger and Elie Siegmeister attempted to provide critiques of the capitalist system that could easily be learned by anyone who heard them a few times. Siegmeister contributed:

> There were three brothers named Dupont. Patriots are they.
> They make their money from munitions, in an honest way.
> They love their country right or wrong.
> But when yen or lira come along
> They always very cheerfully to anyone will sell
> Shells that will armor pierce, and armor that will stop each shell.

Here is Seeger's attack on Henry Ford:

> Henry Ford and a hundred thousand men
> bargained up a hill and down again.
> Henry got the money and the men did the work.

And Siegmeister's lament for John Pierpont Morgan:

> Poor Mr. Morgan cannot pay his income tax.
> Pity poor Morgan, he cannot pay.
> He's dead broke, he hasn't got a cent.

But more often, the songs of the Composers Collective were far too complex for genuine popularity. Henry Cowell, a leading experimentalist who was also a member of the group, believed that proletarian music would be enhanced by mixing dissonant tone clusters with work songs. The idea that serious composers could provide musical material to inspire the masses of workers was not without precedent. In Germany Hanns Eisler had been able to combine progressive politics and equally progressive compositional techniques in his songs, which were sung by musically untrained workers on mass marches. Even Seeger pushed the envelope with a song, attacking Chiang Kai-shek in five-four meter with five measure phrases.

Before long, however, signals from the Soviet Union made it clear that the revolution might topple regimes and businesses, churches and universities, but the basic bourgeois tastes in harmony and melody were not to be touched. Dmitri Shostakovich, the greatest composer in the Soviet world, was taken to task by the Communist Party for the supposed cacophonies and musical chaos of his opera *Lady Macbeth of Mzensk*. Indeed, the opera had been drawing enthusiastic capacity audiences for some two years, but the authorities felt compelled to denounce its dangerous "formalism"—an especially egregious sin under Soviet rule, and a worrisome one for artists, since "formalism" could be construed to mean almost anything depending on the situation. In this instance, however, the formalism to be avoided was soon evident to aspiring revolutionary composers. As Arthur Berger explains: "For worker songs, the model was to be simple traditional folk-like accompaniments, and for orchestral music, though this was not officially spelled out, composers were to keep someone like Tchaikovsky in mind despite his personal bourgeois leanings."

The Composers Collective, for all the extraordinary talent it channeled into the effort, was unable to match the success of far less sophisticated worker-songwriters, such as Joe Hill or Pierre Degeyter. Much of the most lasting workers' music from this era came from the efforts of other working-class musician-activists. Mary Magdalene Garland, better known as Aunt Molly Jackson, may have released only one commercial recording during her lifetime—"Kentucky Miner's Wife," made for Columbia 1931—but she was embraced by left-wing progressives as the musical voice of the Kentucky miners. When a fact-finding group of writers, led by Theodore Dreiser and John Dos Passos, investigated the unrest in Harlan County, they were impressed by Jackson's spirited performance of her song "*Hungry Ragged Blues.*" Before long she came to New York to sing in fundraising efforts for the miners, where she became well known as an activist and performer. Although her Columbia recording career was brief, over 150 of Jackson's performances were documented by the Library of Congress, some of which have been commercially released.

Woody Guthrie was neither a singing worker nor a union organizer, yet he deserves mention here if only for his symbolic role as the musical spokesman for a large portion of the American working class during the middle decades of the twentieth century. Guthrie, born in Okemah, Oklahoma on July 14, 1912, came to California as part of the great migration of the mid-1930s. There his 1937 radio broadcasts on KFVD in Los Angeles and on XELO across the border in Mexico brought him to the public's attention. In 1939, he moved to New York where his plain-spoken views and traditional music established him as one of the most well-loved musicians associated with progressive politics. He distinguished himself as a composer, a preserver of traditional music, and a prose stylist—his semiautobiographical *Bound for Glory* is a classic of American literature.

The meeting between Guthrie and Pete Seeger at a benefit concert on March 3, 1940, has sometimes been described as the "birth of folk music." Later that year, the two activist musicians helped form the Almanac Singers, a collective group that also counted Lee Hays, Millard Lampell, Sis Cunningham, Sonny Terry, and Brownie McGhee among its members. On the last day of 1945, around thirty people gathered in Pete Seeger's basement in Greenwich Village to establish a new organization designed to create politically progressive music. From 1946 to 1949, People's Songs, Inc. fostered music about workers, labor conditions, civil liberties and peace. Its recruiting document stated the organization's focus as follows: "People all over the world and all over this country have always been making up songs about the things that were on their minds. Work songs, play songs, nonsense songs, religious songs and fighting songs. Put them all together—that's what we call 'People's Songs.'" As part of its efforts People's Songs, Inc. began publishing a monthly bulletin, established a booking agency, organized events, created a library and issued books, filmstrips and records. The organization may have failed in its goal to politicize the masses through music, but it served as a contributor to the growing folk music movement in the United States, and set the foundation for the rebirth of the protest song, albeit in a different form, in the late 1960s.

It is perhaps ironic that this body of music would have its greatest impact far away from workers and places of employment. During the Vietnam era, student-led movements, not organized workers, proved to be the main inheritors of the protest song tradition. Instead of local labor conditions, the far different circumstances of combat in Southeast Asia served as the spur to action. Yet given the declining power of labor unions in America during the last half of the twentieth century, this passing of the baton to teenagers and young adults focused on national and international issues may well have been the only way of keeping this song tradition vital and of exerting an influence on public discourse. No, the *Little Red Song Book* did not spur a revolution—nor could it, according to classic Marxist theory, in which songs are part of the mere "superstructure" of culture, while only changes in the "economic base" could trigger a final upheaval. Yet the efforts of Joe Hill, Aunt Molly Jackson and Woody Guthrie were not without lasting influence on the social landscape of American life. They made possible the work of Bob Dylan, Joan Baez, and other protest singers, as well as the emergence of what might be called "popular music with a conscience," a category that encompasses everything from John Lennon to Bruce Springsteen. Much of this earlier tradition of labor music could be assimilated into these new movements led by students and entertainment-industry celebrities. When Fowke and Glazer's anthology of labor songs, *Songs of Work and Freedom,* was reissued in 1973, the title was changed to *Songs of Work and Protest* and a picture of an unshaven hippie with a guitar was put on the cover, but little else required updating to make the songs relevant to the new generation of folk singers addressing social themes. We can predict with a fair degree of confidence that future social movements, caused by events and circumstances that we can now only dimly perceive, will also reach back to this legacy, finding inspiration in these efforts to give musical voice to the plight of industrial workers.

CHAPTER THIRTEEN

Music and the Modern Worker

Heigh-ho, heigh-ho

To make your troubles go

Just keep on singing

All day long, heigh-ho,

Heigh-ho, heigh-ho.

— *Snow White and the Seven Dwarfs*

The noise of the manufacturing equipment is almost deafening. Many workers are wearing earplugs or cumbersome mufflers to block out the din. But even louder, the sound of rock star Rod Stewart booms out, resounding above the whirring and pounding of equipment. The sound of the radio blaring on the factory floor can even be heard half a building away in the office of the plant manager.

Wake up Maggie I think I have somethin' to say ta yooooou! "Try turning off the radio," the plant manager explains to me, "and it is the closest you will get to an organized labor strike." After a moment he adds, "I don't even notice it any more. I guess I just block it out." *All you did was wreck my bed. . . . and in the mornin' kick me in the head . . . .*

This scene—so striking to see; so excruciating to hear—is repeated daily across the industrialized world. Recorded music is so pervasive in modern manufacturing sites that it remains even when all other amenities of the workplace are removed. Writer William Branigin, exploring the hidden sweatshops that support the New York garment industry, found illegal immigrants working for less than minimum wage in rooms with poor ventilation and no fire exits, and where bosses would scream, throw objects, or even pull hair to get their attention. Toiling at machines for up to sixty hours per week, these long-suffering laborers enjoyed none of the prerogatives of the modern manufacturing worker. But even here the employer continued to provide music, with songs in Spanish resounding over the din of the machinery. As with the work song of old, this modern-day music of labor means the most to those who have the least. It is the last inviolable "perk."

And it is a perk that is defended with zeal. When employers are unwilling to provide music in the modern workplace, the employees take matters into their own hands. The efforts they expend in this cause are often remarkable, and counter the claims of commentators who depict today's worker as passive and indifferent. In his classic memoir of assembly line life, *Rivethead,* Ben Hamper tells of his co-worker Hogjaw's single-minded goal: namely, to ensure that the factory floor was enveloped with the high-volume reverberations of rock-and-roll oldies. General Motors prohibits the use of factory electricity for this purpose, allowing only battery-operated radios for employee use. But Hogjaw and his colleagues wanted their music very loud—at a level far beyond the capability of EverReady and DuraCell to deliver. As a result, Hogjaw lugged to work each day a huge car battery to run his stereo system. "You would see him strainin' his way through the parking lot every afternoon, a lunch bucket curled under one arm and his trusty Delco Weatherbeater on top of his other shoulder. Trailing behind him would be a couple of riveters with their arms locked around the speakerboxes—pallbearers bringing around the tombs of the Dead Rock Stars." The factory security guards eventually put a halt to this daily ritual, and barred all employees from bringing car batteries inside the factory. Rather than face defeat the men on the line began plotting to restore the music, using the same degree of focus and determination that Ronnie Biggs and his cohorts brought to pulling off the 1963 Great Train Robbery. With a little invention, some behind-the-scenes construction, and a large dose of audacity, they contrived to steal electricity from the company power source, threading hidden wires through a hollowed-out leg of a workbench and bringing them out behind a water fountain where they could be plugged in without being noticed by the bosses. To a casual observer, the stereo seemed to be powered by ordinary batteries—no other electricity source could be seen. Only the ear-piercing volume hinted that something odd was afoot.

Hamper understood the value of this music. True, it provided diversion and entertainment. Yes, it gave the employees some small sense of power over their otherwise tyrannical work environment. But the music achieved more than this. It had become part of the work itself, inseparable from the labor of making the car. "As for the popularity of the Dead Rock Stars on the Rivet Line, I've settled upon this private theory," Hamper writes. "The music of the Dead Rock Stars is redundant and completely predictable. We've heard their songs a million times over. In this way, the music of the Dead Rock Stars infinitely mirrors the drudgery of our assembly jobs."

Conventional wisdom tells us that the work song is dead. And it is true that the shanties and field hollers, the hammering and digging songs, and the rich abundance of vocal music that accompanied labor a century ago have all passed away, apparently never to return. Yet, from another perspective, music and labor are on more intimate terms today than ever before. Visit factories and construction sites, stroll around malls and inside shops, sit alongside the trucker on the road or the taxi driver in the cab, watch the mechanic at the tune-up bay or the dentist drilling teeth, and you will quickly reach the conclusion that the work song has not disappeared, it has merely been transformed. Can music and commercial interests co-exist? Not only can they, they must. They need each other.

The very acts of buying and selling have embraced music with a persistence and vigor that no force—technological, cultural, or political—has been able to eradicate or even diminish. Few psychologists have bothered to study the (fascinating) subject of how songs make us fall in love or go to war, but intense interest has been expended in learning how music encourages us to shop. Here is musicology that pays dividends. Researchers have camped out in supermarkets, restaurants, and malls, seeking their own equivalent of the lost chord, the magical sounds that inspire us to open our wallets, write our checks, hand over our credit cards.

Ah, this is not new, nor is the backlash—which time has shown is as inevitable as it is futile. A hundred years ago, street vendors sang melodic snippets to attract customers to their wares.

'Tatoes! Peaches! 'n cents a basket!

or

> I got shad. Ain't you glad?
> I got shad. So don't get mad.

or

> Blackberries fresh an' fine,
> I got blackberries, lady, fresh from de' vine.

A 1908 ban in New York on musical street cries failed to halt this singing commerce. Prohibitions on these songs are, of course, almost as old as capitalism itself. During the reign of Queen Elizabeth I, Parliament passed two acts suppressing street music, but with little effect, setting a precedent of futility in this area of legislation that would be repeated over and over again. In the mid-1860s, another failed campaign to stamp out street music earned the support of Dickens, Tennyson, and others. To no one's surprise, New York vendors evinced no more respect for government interference in their livelihood than had their Elizabethan or Victorian counterparts. A researcher for the Federal Writers' Project, investigating the practice as late as 1938, documented numerous examples of the still-vibrant tradition.

Yet the following year a more powerful counterforce than either Parliament or the New York Police Department was unleashed on the peddlers' music: Pepsi Cola unveiled its first radio jingle, revolutionizing the nascent field of mass media advertising, and creating a song that was so insistent it became a hit record.

> Pepsi-Cola hits the spot.
> Two full glasses, that's a lot.
> Twice as much for a nickel too.
> Pepsi-Cola is the drink for you!

The makers of Coca-Cola did not respond until 1941, but by then the rules of the game had changed. From now on the so-called Cola Wars—along with every other battle for share of the consumer's wallet—would be fought with songs. How could " 'Tatoes! Peaches!" compete with the memorable song, introduced in 1944,

I'm Chiquita banana and I've come to say
Bananas have to ripen in a certain way.
When they are fleck'd with brown and have a golden hue
Bananas taste the best and are best for you.

Or match the haiku-like intensity of this hypnotic innovation from 1952:

N-e-s-t-l-e-s
Nestle's makes the very best:
Chocolate!

The modern corporation needs a good theme song much as it requires property, plant, and equipment. If the jingle is strong enough, even the least-glamorous products and services, from Roto-Rooter to Oscar Meyer Wieners, can capture our fickle fancy. Where would Campbell's Soup be without "M'm m'm good!"? How would State Farm sell insurance without "Like a good neighbor." Even the most stodgy and hidebound institutions have learned this lesson. With the zeal of a Tin Pan Alley song plugger, the U.S. Army entered the 1980s by pumping millions into promoting its theme of "Be all you can be."

In Japan, corporate songs are more than just a tool in selling products. Even senior executives and white-collar workers see some benefit from periodically joining together in a rousing rendition of the company anthem. And Western businesses have tentatively embraced the practice as well. Here, for example, are some of the inspiring words to "Our Vision Is One Honeywell":

Showing pride and confidence
With customers every day
A partnership in business
Builds trust along the way. . . .
Our vision is one Honeywell
The future we can see.
We band together, spirits high.
At Honeywell, our quest is qualiteeeee!

Songs such as this one—or KPMG's "Our Vision of Global Strategy" or IBM's "Ever Onward"—are unlikely to hit the charts any time soon. Yet they reflect a growing awareness in the citadels of capitalism of a truth that workers and their organizers learned long ago: namely, that participative singing can create solidarity and enthusiasm to a degree that mere words, no matter how eloquent, can never match. At the same time, a song that seems awkward, manipulative, or forced will only engender cynicism and contempt. In 2001, London-based computer programmer Chris Raettig established a web site devoted to corporate songs. Within one week he had attracted 200,000 visitors to the site—yet most of the audience, one suspects, came to mock, not admire, these outpourings of capitalistic fellow-feeling. But in an age in which the medium is the message, virtually all e-visibility is valued by the purveyors of products—even just being the butt of an e-joke, provided it generates enough "clicks." Although some company representatives objected that the anthems featured on the web site were not "official," not one of the corporations asked that their song be removed from the site.

Despite many protests to the contrary, music and the day-to-day demands of the capitalist economy seem to coexist on friendly terms most of the time. Songs get us to work in the morning, sustain us on the job, and even encourage us to buy the products that keep others employed. But unlike the work songs of days gone by, this music is mostly consumed passively. Corny corporate anthems notwithstanding, six-pack Jack, toiling at the assembly line, is hardly encouraged to break out into song during his nine-to-five stint. And certainly no one expects him to compose his own songs, to express himself in musical form as did so many lumberjacks, sailors and crew leaders of yore. At the most, he is allowed to "identify" with the words blasting out of the radio or loudspeaker. And this almost instinctive tendency to identify—to feel that the song on the radio expresses, in some small way, his own sentiments at second hand—explains why six-pack Jack usually wants to hear rock-and-roll at work, rather than Mozart or Mantovani. Rock is the custom-made sound of rebellion, of individualism, of freedom and defiance; and just as our worker threw this music into the teeth of his parents while growing up, he now blasts it out at bosses and cohorts. The more dehumanizing the work, the more in-your-face the music must be. As the GM assembly-line worker Hogjaw intuitively understood, the "Dead Rock Stars" are the best candidates to assert the individualism of the modern worker on the job. No, these may not be protest songs playing on the radio, but they are close surrogates.

Hence, it should come as little surprise that popular songs about work, at least these days, should inevitably be sarcastic and biting. For the last half century, composers of popular music have been increasingly unable to deal with the dignity of work as a theme for their songs. In contrast, the indignity of work is the subject that comes easy—as witnessed by "Nine to Five" or "Sixteen Tons" or the classic of the genre, "Take This Job and Shove It" by Johnny Paycheck. Only in the rarest instances—Jimmy Webb's "Witchita Lineman," Billy Joel's "Allentown," and Sting's "Work the Black Seam" come to mind—can a modern pop music icon manage to find real poetry and pathos, rather than just a nasty mood, in a workaday job. This poetry is there, sure enough, but few know where to look, and even fewer can translate it into the medium of song. In this regard, pop songs about work reflect the larger macrocosm of contemporary music (not to mention cinema, talk radio, and magazines), where irony, distance, and posturing, and sometimes arrogance and contempt, reign supreme. Obviously, the rise of rock and roll has contributed to this overriding tone in the music world, but even earlier Frank Sinatra pointed the way, showing he could add to the allure of a song by deflecting its emotional directness, by establishing a contrast between vulnerability and toughness—a contrast that captivated audiences with its piquant, modernistic twist. With Sinatra one always got a sense that he was offering us a critique of the lyrics while he was singing them, stepping into and stepping away from the words at the same time—a stance that in a later age would be called "deconstruction." Hence the oddity of Sinatra singing the quasi-work song "Ol' Man River" in the film 'Till the Clouds Roll By (1947)—a majestic musical declamation that needs to be sung without any touches of irony. Sinatra's performance in the film was further subverted by his lean, neatly groomed look, which was anything but the appearance of a rugged workman familiar with "Ol' Man River." Although Sinatra was perhaps the most charismatic performer of the century, he seems distinctly ill at ease here, and provides a telling contrast with Paul Robeson's extraordinarily poised, and much praised treatment of this song. The difference between the two versions encapsulates the sea change that was taking place in the public's tastes in the thirty years between Robeson and Sinatra: "Ol' Man River" is a song that even the slightest modernist twist will make sound ridiculous—with its "tote dat barge, lif' dat bale" lyrics.

Sinatra's awkward moment was simply a harbinger of things to come. Mick Jagger would have no more success than Sinatra in singing "Ol' Man River"; nor would Elton John, or Michael Jackson, or Madonna, and the list goes on and on. Of the many celebrity singers of recent decades, only a handful—maybe a Johnny Cash or a Willie Nelson, or possibly a Bob Dylan or Bruce Springsteen—might be able to interpret this piece, or an equivalent one addressing the dignity of work, with sufficient authenticity to convince a blue-collar audience that they should listen. Until this state of affairs changes, popular music about work is likely to continue to be permeated by dark humor and ambivalence, if not outright hostility.

This was not always the case. The songs of working people were once intimately bound up with the concerns of workaday life. Gerald Porter estimates that around half of the traditional songs in English composed from the seventeenth century to the nineteenth mention an occupation or type of work. These linkages to the world of work were not there to provide a jest or a target for ridicule but to add depth and substance to the story told in the song. In American popular songs of the nineteenth century, work and working conditions also figure prominently, either as a direct subject matter or as a setting. Stephen Foster, the most important American songwriter of the nineteenth century, stands out as an exemplar in this regard; in his songs, as his biographer reminds us, "Men and women work . . . cooking or sweeping up a storm, hoeing the cornfield, toting the cottonwood. They toil not just because they're slaves or poor, but also because it's the human condition." We have come a long way from such times. Not only have we lost singing at work, but simply listening to songs *about* work is difficult for most people unless the tone is sufficiently infused with bitterness, irony, or ridicule. As I shall discuss in my concluding pages, such a state of affairs can only add to the alienation of the worker, the desolation of the work environment, and the poverty of our culture.

The growth of passively consumed music in places of employment occurred almost simultaneously with the decline in the older, more active style of singing at manual labor. It was almost as if the street peddler *needed to sing*, despite prohibitions and threats, until a technological alternative was in place. Workers at the most arduous manual jobs, like these vendors, also *required* their music, and would only stop making it themselves when a machine could do it for them. The years between the two World Wars saw the creation and dissemination of many such machines, and this same period witnessed the eradication of singing at work in the West. No, it wasn't the noise of the factory or the demands of the boss that put a halt to these traditional songs of labor: workers only stopped singing when others with better voices and full instrumental accompaniment took their place.

In the mid-1920s, while the first serious research into African American work songs was underway, inventor George Owen Squier was taking a decisive step in replacing this traditional style of work singing with a superior technology, one that would bring affordable, professionally performed music into the workplaces and stores of America. Yet, as is often the case, the inventor himself did not initially envision the result of his efforts. Squier, who had served as a chief signal officer with the army, was instead focused on the role that such a technology could play in battlefield communications. Radio signals could only be sent twenty miles before being lost in an ocean of static, and even within that range it was possible for enemy forces to listen to the broadcast. Squier dreamed of combining the two great inventions of his day—telephone and radio—into a new hybrid that would "pipe" sounds over longer distances, thus offering superior privacy and clarity. Over time, the inventor began to realize that civilians, too, might find benefit in this technology, which eventually became known as "Muzak." Squier's role models in this endeavor were the utility and phone companies, who were then establishing networks in the municipalities of America, bringing power, water, and communications to entire neighborhoods. Why, Squier wondered, couldn't the same thing be done for music?

At almost the same time, others were looking at the potential impact of music on worker productivity. The National Phonograph Company, founded by Thomas Edison, had already enlisted the services of psychologist Walter Bingham, a pioneering advocate of assessment testing, in exploring the use of recordings in commercial settings. On October 13, 1920, Bingham announced the establishment of the Thomas A. Edison Prize for "meritorious research" on the various effects of music, which included "modification of moods by music" and "effects of contrasting types of music on muscular activity." These studies had little practical impact at the time. A surviving note from Edison to William Maxwell, a vice president in his company, reads: "You will end in throwing all these things in the wastebasket after infinite trouble and irritation." But the desire to channel the power of music to serve practical ends was very much part of the spirit of the age, and Bingham's concerns were echoed in the work of other researchers, for example Charles M. Diserens, who waxed enthusiastically about the importance of this field of inquiry in his 1926 book *The Influence of Music on Behavior*. In this volume, Diserens collected the available research on music's effect on workers, and shared the results of his own experiments on its efficacy in reducing fatigue and enhancing endurance. His findings were encouraging, and inevitably suggested a business opportunity for the visionary entrepreneur who could combine the promised efficiencies of Taylorism with the new technologies of the entertainment industry.

Squier only gradually perceived the scope and nature of this opportunity. His early efforts led to the establishment of a new enterprise to tap the demand for a "music utility," a business that was initially called Wired Radio. At first the company focused on households as the obvious market for its services—after all, if the modern home came equipped with running water, why shouldn't it have a "tap" for songs as well? But it soon became clear that it was not households but rather businesses that were most receptive to Squier's new wired sounds. Even in the midst of the Great Depression, many were willing to pay for canned music. In the mid- 1930s, Wired Radio was rechristened Muzak (Squier created the name by combining the word "music" with a futuristic-sounding brand name of his day, "Kodak") and the company moved from Cleveland to New York where its managers set about establishing an ideology and body of research to support further expansion. In lieu of its previous goal of providing household entertainment, Muzak instead aimed to serve as nothing less than the universal soundtrack for the capitalist economy. Here was an inspiring vision of the future: just as sound movies had made silent ones obsolete, businesses wired for music would gain ascendancy in the modern marketplace, replacing those enterprises unable or unwilling to march to the beat of their own drummer.

The late 1930s stand out as an especially fascinating time in the history of workers and their music. Researchers were documenting the old work songs at the same time that Muzak managers were aiming to create new ones. Hollywood churned out picture after picture featuring singing cowboys—celebrating an image of the working westerner that bore little resemblance to historical reality. In 1936, the newly formed RCA Victor signed Hank Snow and began promoting him as the "Singing Ranger," much as its predecessor company, Victor Talking Machine, had done with the "Singing Brakeman" Jimmie Rodgers. The following year saw the theatrical release of *The Singing Marine* and *The Singing Buckaroo.* Every occupation, it seems, would be given a chance to belt out a few tunes on screen or on disk. But these offerings were paragons of authenticity in comparison to the saccharine image of singing laborers presented to movie goers at the end of that year. In the days leading up to Christmas, Walt Disney released his feature-length cartoon *Snow White and the Seven Dwarfs*, which promoted not one but two upbeat pop work songs—"Heigh-Ho" and "Whistle While You Work." This strange idealization of work came at a time when there was all-too-little work to go around: unemployment, which had dipped below 20 percent in the previous year, started rising again, and even those fortunate enough to have a job feared losing it as the Great Depression approached its eighth anniversary. Right around the time that *Snow White* was released, the economy seemed to be entering into another tailspin. In this environment, in which nothing was more precious than a chance to work, who can wonder at the fetishization of labor in these cheery movie songs—whether sung by cowboys, marines, or dwarfs? Needless to say, the impact on the public's psyche was enormous. Even today, long after the other cultural offerings of 1937 are all but forgotten, the Disney songs are still recalled, sung, whistled, and—even more often—parodied or used in a sarcastic light. Only the previous year, Charlie Chaplin had released his film *Modern Times*, which also obsessively focused on the rhythms and processes of the workaday life, idealizing them as some quasi-mystical ritualistic activity. But with very little sound (it might very well be called, with only a bit of exaggeration, the last great silent film) and its stark black-and-white format, Chaplin's effort could not match Disney in his ability to mythologize labor and its music. And, in the midst of the greatest shortage of jobs in American history, the public was far more willing to fantasize about fairy-tale working conditions in vivid, cartoonish color than to critique their alienating modernistic aspects in harsh black and white. During this same period, John and Alan Lomax were making tremendous strides in their efforts to document work songs and traditional music. In so doing they were engaging in more than a little myth making of their own—as evidenced by, among other signs, their successful advocacy of prisoner-turned-entertainer Leadbelly, who had moved to New York to capitalize on the public's interest in exploring a somewhat more authentic slice of the working-man's musical life. Whether real or a product of Disney, or behind bars or merely on barstools, the music of work seemed to be on the brink of a resurgence, captivating the hearts and minds of the general public.

But just as (in Gresham's law) bad money drives out good, phoney culture squeezes out the real thing. It was Muzak, not the African American work song, that represented the music of these Modern Times. Indeed, the Muzak company completed its move to New York at virtually the same time Chaplin was releasing his film. The company's president, Waddill Catchings, had caught a glimmer of a truth forgotten by most of the music industry, namely that song could be a productivity tool as well as a form of entertainment, and he sought to use his piped-in link to businesses and stores as a gentle persuader and prodder. Muzak as wired music was not enough—it now needed to be an instrument of social engineering for the modern age. Muzak had already taken the lead in producing its own music rather than relying solely on the output of record companies; now the company's "programmers" went further. Under Catchings's guidance, all elements of the presentation—the sequencing of songs, tempos, use of vocals, and timing—were subject to scrutiny and manipulated to create the ideal sonic background to work.

But even more, Muzak required an ideology and supporting scientific research to further its ambitions. The publication, also in 1937, of *Fatigue and Boredom in Repetitive Work* by S. Wyatt and J. N. Langdon represented a major step forward in this regard. This study, funded by the Industrial Health Research Board of Great Britain, showed that a group of women exposed to a regular dose of morning music worked better and with less resentment than their musically deprived peers. A similar study, conducted by the Stevens Institute of Technology, found that "functional music" on the job served to reduce absenteeism. Another researcher, H. C. Smith, chimed in with a study showing that the vast majority of workers preferred to have music at their place of employment. John Lomax no doubt could have saved all these researchers the trouble and expense of conducting these studies, the results of which he could easily have predicted in advance. But Lomax had not understood the full commercial implications of these conclusions, at least not to the degree that Waddill Catchings and his colleagues at Muzak had done. Others both inside and outside the entertainment industry were also paying attention, as subsequent events made clear. In 1938 Warner Bros. acquired Muzak, which it combined with some of its own assets and resold to Catchings, Allen Miller, and William Benton the following year. Between 1939 and

1944, Muzak would open around a thousand new accounts, as more and more businesses responded to the pitch that music on the job would increase productivity and save them money.

In the 1950s, Muzak's researchers continued to push ahead with their positivistic efforts. Research now focused on the new concept of "Stimulus Progression," where music's intensity and pacing would match and adapt to the daily circadian rhythms of the body, providing the right amount of musical energy at precisely the proper time. Here was suitable musical accompaniment for the Cold War work week, fitting nicely with news articles about brainwashing, truth serums, electroshock therapy, propaganda, and other innovative techniques of getting inside the mind space of the modern worker. Gramsci might have called it "musical hegemony" had he deigned to treat the subject. But few thinkers thought much about Muzak—it was so unobtrusive and so well hidden in the background. Like a double agent, its success was driven very much by its ability not to call too much attention to what it was doing. And then in the 1980s, almost coinciding with the fall of the Berlin Wall, Muzak came out into the open with its new concept of "Foreground Music," which provided original-artist hits of well-known songs, designed to be an active (and louder) part of the commercial soundscape. Muzak had finally co-opted even the Dead Rock Stars.

The Muzak company has changed ownership several times in recent decades, with Teleprompter and Westinghouse included among its corporate owners. Today, the company boasts a quarter of a million accounts and some eighty million listeners. The company disdains the term "background music," preferring to call their service "audio architecture." This term focuses on the functionality of its offerings, supposedly as vital to workers as the walls, floors, and ceilings that surround them. In the 1990s Muzak even began offering "video architecture," in which images enhanced the impact of the music. Since its inception Squier's technology has improved many times over: cumbersome wires are no longer necessary and Muzak can be beamed to the workplace straight from a satellite in outer space. But the philosophy of musical manipulation continues.

Some might conclude that this process of corporate control and cultural hegemony is inevitable and irresistible. Workers can no more regain control of their music than they can seize the means of production or fire the board of directors at the next stockholders' meeting. Perhaps. But music has a funny way of resisting control from above. Since the emergence of the mass entertainment industry, every major revolution in music—bop, rock, new age, grunge, hip hop—has sprung up "on its own" outside of the purview of the major corporations, who later scramble to get a piece of the action. Authorities have a hard enough time controlling people and things, but fighting against sounds and rhythms is almost impossible; it's a guerrilla warfare in which the enemy eludes every battle, slipping back into the vapors and mists. In this light it is interesting to note that the most controversial business issue raised by the introduction of the Internet was the "illegal" downloading of music. Here again consumers took matters into their own hands, just like Hogjaw and his coworkers hauling their surreptitious sound equipment into the factory. The role of music in people's lives is too much a part of their identity for them ever to relinquish their control of it. The same phenomenon occurs everywhere: scratching, sampling, remixing, downloading, swapping, sharing, MP3ing, iPodding, just as an earlier generation of garage bands and basement ensembles were concocting their private brew of intoxicating sounds outside of the view of grownups and authority figures.

No, the work song of yore will never return. But workers can and will reclaim their music. It is, as noted above, the last inviolable perk, the part of the workers' inner lives that they are least willing to give up to the boss. The same inexorable "advance" in technologies that created the possibility for central control of the soundscape will, in their next iteration, provide the tools for subverting these imposed hierarchies. How this will play out is anybody's guess. Yet even the most cursory examination of the cultural scene makes it clear that one-way media are already being squeezed out or marginalized; the flourishing spheres of cultural life are interactive, viral, communal, flexible, maintaining a grassroots authenticity even when navigating through the global village—supported by technology but not driven by it. Even more than our political or economic life, our musical selves are morphing rapidly in the face of these new-found possibilities. Yes, I have seen the future of song—or at least caught a glimpse of it—and it is not MTV! And although the replacement of the sea shanty or field holler will sound nothing like the original, something of the spirit that gave rise to those fervent songs may still be rumbling below, waiting for the right moment to reemerge.

The Calling

Art is man's expression of his joy in labor.

—*William Morris*

My fascination with the songs of work was inspired, from the start, by several complementary motives. First and foremost, I aimed to make a compelling case that these songs deserve a more central place in the history of human music making. The sweep and power of this music has been scarcely appreciated for its inherent beauty, just as its role in the evolution of our capacity for organizing and imparting meaning to sound has been sorely neglected. But more than a curious preoccupation with antiquarian matters has motivated my efforts. As I outlined in the opening pages of this book, I hold firm to an ardent hope that the study of these songs can help us understand how music, even in today's post-industrial world, can enter more intimately into the fabric of our day-to-day lives. If music once exerted its powers of enchantment in the midst of the exigencies and hardships of labor, it must likewise have the potential to enrich and transform other spheres of our quotidian existence to a greater extent than we currently realize. As such, the study of work songs can serve as a touchstone, heightening our sensitivity to possible dimensions of our musical lives that we will never appreciate if our experience of song is limited to the aural effluvium of FM radio, music videos, and the Billboard charts.

These are important considerations, and they serve as the guiding principles in my efforts. But they are not the only ones. This book is about work just as much as it is about songs. And, from the start, this aspect of my subject has been as much on my mind as the melodies and rhythms, the sharps and flats, the recordings and transcriptions, and the singers and instrumentalists that make up the musical substance to the story I have told. By cherishing the musician, I have not forgotten the pressing needs of the laborer.

Put simply, I am convinced that this music opens for us a window onto our working selves, and it offers a much-needed opportunity to reexperience the dignity of human labor, and comprehend the potential elements of play and self-expression that are latent in all directed activities and enterprises. Some readers might be surprised by this perspective. For them, the work song tells us about the indignity of work and the abuse of human labor. And, true, the conditions that surrounded this labor were often degrading and corrupt. But the work itself—whether sowing or reaping, building or lifting, herding or weaving—could not be demeaned. The work of the poorest laborer is still a process of creating and of making something where before there was nothing. And such activities always carry something magical and awe-inspiring about them. The worker's song has always been part of this magic, and it serves as an important reminder that music and labor share an affinity—both are creative efforts with an aesthetic component that even the most crass commercial motives cannot totally negate.

For the most part, the dignity of this music has been obscured by the tainted conditions in which it came to life. As a result, some have been convinced that the songs themselves must be disgraceful, and thus would be best forgotten. Still others have valued only a small subset of work songs, primarily those that might serve some ideological or political end. And although the motives behind these views were often good and fair, the result was to miss what was most essential in the music, depriving the songs of their psychic and emotional depth, of their rough but rich beauty. Caught up in the particulars, the specific issues of time and place, we let go of what was most universal.

It is an easy mistake to make. After ordering from a catalogue a recording called *Georgia Work Songs and Religious Songs,* I was surprised to receive a compact disc containing purely Caucasian music: recorded in Caucasia, to be precise, these songs came from the Georgia located on the Black Sea, north of Turkey and Armenia. Yet the spirit of the recordings— strange to say—was not all that different from works songs made in the American state of Georgia. Both groups of workers managed to capture the strange, paradoxical combination of a wail of misery and an uplifting statement of human dignity as expressed in labor. Such music simultaneously complains and exults, denies and accepts, pushes forward and holds back. It is contradictory in the same way that people are contradictory, and that too is part of its complex beauty.

But it is perhaps wise to reflect for a moment on the Georgia of the American South, the land of plantations and slavery, for it may help us understand the multifaceted emotions that surround work music and the activities that gave it birth. It is worth recalling that the institution of slavery left both former slaves and masters with a sense that labor was inherently demeaning; that to work with one's hands was undignified and to be avoided at all costs. The reasons for this attitude were all too understandable. For the former slaves, manual labor was associated with their previous state of servitude. The former slaveowners, for their part, had felt that their social status was based on deigning not to work with their hands. As a result, the insidious view took root that only leisure and giving orders to others were compatible with a healthy sense of self-esteem and personal worth. These pernicious, ingrained attitudes left the South ill prepared for the modern era. While the North became a center of industrial activity and commercial success, the South remained comparatively impoverished, beset by racism and class envy and incapable of recognizing that the only path to success was by embracing the very work activities that all parties shunned. In essence, the dignity that comes only with perspiration and dirty hands needed to be reasserted, cherished, and celebrated.

In this regard, all of us can benefit from the lessons of this music: almost all of us, by now, have come to share in the ambivalent attitudes to labor described above. To the extent that we seek a deeper meaning in our life—a meaning that once came to us through the work of our hands—we are told to "self-actualize." Abraham Maslow, in his highly influential 1954 book *Motivation and Personality,* postulated that "self-actualization" was the deepest and most authentic source of human motivation. In his famous hierarchy of human needs, he postulated five levels:

1. *Physiological* (freedom from hunger, thirst, etc.)
2. *Safety* (the need for protection from physical and emotional harm)
3. *Social* (the need for affection, belonging, acceptance, friendship)
4. *Esteem* (such as the desire for self respect, autonomy, status, recognition)
5. *Self-actualization*

To clarify his fifth level, Maslow wrote: "A musician must make music, an artist must paint, a poet must write, if he is to be ultimately at peace with himself. What a man can be, he must be." And who dares to disagree? Should we not all aspire to the highest tier and be self-actualizers? The phrase, in making its way into the popular imagination, has come to mean different to things to different people, but the underlying message remains clear. We were told—and we are still told, in a myriad of ways—that happiness comes from obeying our own inner muse, our own inclinations. Laboring for others, especially when measured by the ticking of the time clock, can play no role in this scheme of things.

The myth of growth through self-actualization—for however beguiling, it is truly, I believe, a myth—is based on a view of individuals as atomized, as cut off from others, as dealing only with a reality within. The work song, with its emphasis on community, its integration of individual efforts into a more powerful whole, and its focus on mastery over the immediate demands of the here and now, reminds us of a different set of attitudes to life and labor. Although unfamiliar, these perspectives may be all the more valuable given the fragmented nature of our modern work world. From such a viewpoint, the call-and-response of the classic work song can serve as a useful metaphor for us even today, distant as we are from the world in which this music was made.

The concept of the "call" reminds me of the way people once spoke about their work and livelihood. It was a calling, a vocation—from the Latin *vocare*, to call. Recall, too, that this same Latin word serves as the source of many words associated with singing and chanting—from "invocation" to "vocalist." In our work is our song. Yet without the response, the call is meaningless; the calling makes sense only within a context in which there are others who are helped, even if only in some small way; others who respond with their own energy to our invitation. And in the modern world what we need most is a model of our interacting lives as a type of call-and-response, rather than as a collection of isolated individuals pursuing separate paths to self-actualization.

Today, we seldom hear the words "vocation" or "calling." They strike the ear as quaint and old-fashioned. More often we speak either of "careers" or "jobs." But these various terms are not interchangeable: a career is pursued for our own ends; a job is done for somebody else. But the terms calling or vocation convey the clear sense of usefulness to both others *and* ourselves: our calling finds its meaning only when we do something for others, and its benefit to us exists only to the extent that our labor reaches out into the surrounding community—perhaps only the community of our fellow-workers, although at times to larger social units. The calling involves, almost by definition, a responding.

The call-and-response is thus a rich metaphor to consider. But in the world of the work song—and here is the crux of the matter—this was more than a metaphor, but an actual way of navigating through the often brutal realities of a hostile environment. For this reason, the work song is especially deserving of our attention. It is a musical "genre" that is much more than a genre because it emerges as a transformational tool. Even more striking, this source of transcendence was reserved as a special support for those on the lowest rungs of the socioeconomic ladder—the most oppressed laborer and even the slave or prisoner. When all else was taken away, it remained inalienable. Members of the leisure class, representatives of the ruling powers, were all but excluded from tapping into its power. The nature of this social role—so strange and amorphous, yet so tightly defined—adds to the rich complexity of this body of music.

In closing, I am reminded of Rousseau, who dreamed of a community where men no longer spoke but sang, inspiring a reenchantment of the commonplace by means of music. No form of music making has come closer to realizing this unobtainable philosopher's dream than the work song. Here, more than anywhere else in human society, the most dreary realities of the day-to-day life, from the banal to the brutal, were transformed by song, were given a small touch of magic that made them into something better and more decent than they deserved to be. We may never be able to bring back such songs, but our ability to do so is not as important as re-creating an atmosphere in which such an integration of aesthetic creativity and the sheer perspiration of everyday work are possible. In such a world, the call would always be met by the response. We would find the two meanings of calling again reunited. Above all, people's work would also always be their song, even when no music could be heard.

 **NOTES**

Preface

ix **"I think these songs"**: See *Prison Songs: Historical Recordings from Parchman Farm 1947–48,* vol. 1, *Murderous Home* (Rounder CD 1714).

Introduction: Why Work Songs?

1 **"what an audience wants"**: Jeffrey Thomas quoted in Bernard D. Sherman, *Inside Early Music* (New York: Oxford University Press, 1997), p. 277.

1 **"separability principle"**: Lydia Goehr, *The Imaginary Museum of Musical Works: An Essay in the Philosophy of Music* (New York: Oxford University Press, 1994), p. 157.

1 **Ralph Vaughan Williams**: Ralph Vaughan Williams, *National Music and Other Essays* (Oxford: Clarendon Press, 1996), p. 205.

2 **"auditory cheesecake"**: The comparison of music to cheesecake and recreational drugs comes from Steven Pinker, *How the Mind Works* (New York: Norton, 1997), pp. 528, 534. See also Joseph Carroll, "Steven Pinker's Cheesecake for the Mind," *Philosophy and Literature* 22 (1998): 478–85.

2 **"There were very few songs"**: John Bierhorst, *A Cry from the Earth: Music of the North American Indians* (Santa Fe, N.M.: Ancient City Press, 1979), p. 3.

3 **"No drums are beaten uselessly"**: James Chalmers, *Adventures In New Guinea* (London: Religious Tract Society, 1886), p. 181. The passage here is cited in Ernest Crawley, *Dress, Drinks and Drums: Further Studies of Savages and Sex,* edited by Theodore Besterman (London: Methuen, 1931), p. 251, where Crawley adds: "The Papuans' remark applies universally."

3 **"The time for next things"**: Arthur C. Danto, *The State of the Art* (New York: Prentice Hall, 1987), p. 217.

4 **Christopher Small**: Christopher Small, *Music, Society, Education,* 2nd ed. (London: John Calder, 1980), *Music of the Common Tongue* (London: John Calder, 1987), and *Musicking: The Meanings of Performing and Listening* (Han-

over, N.H.: Wesleyan University Press, 1998). For works by all other authors cited in this paragraph, see the bibliography.

6 **The Imperfect Art**: Ted Gioia, *The Imperfect Art: Reflections on Jazz and Modern Culture* (New York: Oxford University Press, 1988).

6 **"The Dehumanization of Art"**: See José Ortega y Gasset, *The Dehumanization of Art and Other Writings on Art and Culture* (New York: Anchor, 1956). This now unjustifiably neglected essay, first published in 1925, was extraordinarily prescient in anticipating current theories of artistic production and consumption. It aptly states that the prevailing trend would be "to consider art as play and nothing else," "to be essentially ironical," "to regard art as a thing of no transcending consequence," etc. Mark Helprin recalls being so impressed by this essay, which enjoyed a brief flurry of notoriety during the cold war era, that he announced to his Harvard tutor a plan to write a lengthy novel, set in the Galápagos, in which no person or even animal figured, just lava, rocks, tides, and the like. Only his tutor's horror put a halt to the project.

8 **"A person may create"**: John Blacking, *How Musical Is Man?* (Seattle: University of Washington Press, 1973), p. 108.

8 **Austin and "performatives"**: See J. L. Austin, *How to Do Things with Words* (Cambridge: Harvard University Press, 1962). Victor Turner's influential writings on ritual and symbolism convey a similar point, namely that modern scholars are more comfortable analyzing social and artistic phenomena as types of "discourse" or as ways of communicating, whereas it is often more insightful to see them as ways of doing. In writing about symbols in Ndembu ritual, Turner notes: "I would like to raise the problem of what is involved in the 'meaning' of a ritual symbol. After attending a number of performances of different kinds of ritual and asking many informants, both during and after the performance, to interpret their symbolism, I began to realize that a symbol's meaning must include not only what was said about it but also how it was used: it had an *operational* meaning as well as an *interpretation*" (Victor Turner, *The Drums of Affliction: A Study of Religious Processes among the Ndembu of Zambia* [Ithaca: Cornell University Press, 1981], p. 14). In the present study I take a similar approach by seeking out the operational meaning of work songs over and beyond any merely musicological treatment. Such an approach to music is, I believe, a fruitful exercise and one that is likely to bring us close to the original meaning of musical "performance," a concept that includes in its essence both ritual (as defined by Turner) and Austin's "performatives" as sounds that do things.

8 **"For the Flathead"**: Alan B. Merriam, *Ethnomusicology of the Flathead*

Indian (New York: Wenner-Gren Foundation for Anthropological Research, 1967), p. 3.

9 **Charles Keil**: Charles Keil, *Tiv Song: The Sociology of Art in a Classless Society* (Chicago: University of Chicago Press, 1979), p. 27.

9 **Mungo Park**: Mungo Park, *Travels in the Interior Districts of Africa,* edited by Kate Ferguson Masters (Durham: Duke University Press, 2000), pp. 124, 129, 156, 169, 196, 242, 251, 277, 282, 295.

10 **survey of sixty-seven**: See John Sloboda, "Empirical Studies of Emotional Response to Music," in *Cognitive Bases of Musical Communication,* edited by Mari Riess Jones and Susan Holleran (Washington, D.C.: American Psychological Association, 1992), pp. 33–46.

11 **"We found, on average"**: For this study and the information below, see John A. Sloboda and Susan A. O'Neill, "Emotions in Everyday Listening to Music," in *Music and Emotion: Theory and Research,* edited by Patrik N. Juslin and John A. Sloboda (New York: Oxford University Press, 2001), pp. 415–29 (the passage quoted is on p. 418). In general, Sloboda's approach here and elsewhere can be seen as providing the psychological underpinnings for the historical and aesthetic concerns that are my main areas of focus.

11 **M. I. Finley**: M. I. Finley, *Early Greece: The Bronze and Archaic Ages* (New York: Norton, 1981), p. 139.

11 **"national disgrace"**: Tacitus, *The Annals of Imperial Rome,* translated by Michael Grant (New York: Penguin, 1978), p. 383.

11 **Aristotle's view**: Aristotle, *Aristotle's Politics,* translated by Benjamin Jowett (New York: Modern Library, 1943), pp. 326–27.

Chapter 1: The Hunter

13 **Reznikoff and Dauvois**: Iegor Reznikoff and Michel Dauvois, "La dimension sonore des grottes ornées," *Bulletin de la Société Préhistorique Française* 85, no. 8 (1988): 238–46. See also the research of Steven J. Waller on the acoustics of caves, most notably his paper "Psychoacoustic Influences of the Echoing Environments of Prehistoric Art," presented at the First Pan-American/Iberian Meeting on Acoustics, December 4, 2002, Cancun.

15 **homo sapiens first appeared**: Estimates here and below are from Richard B. Lee and Irven Devore, eds., *Man the Hunter* (Hawthorne, N.Y.: Aldine de Gruyter, 1968), pp. 3–5.

15 **"if Homo erectus bands"**: William H. McNeill, *Keeping Together in*

Time: Dance and Drill in Human History (Cambridge, Mass.: Harvard University Press, 1995), p. 30

17 **While visiting the Mandan:** George Catlin, *Letters and Notes on the Manners, Customs, and Conditions of North American Indians* (New York: Dover, 1973), vol. 1, p. 127.

17 **Among the Wahehe:** Rose Brandel, *The Music of Central Africa: An Ethnomusicological Study* (The Hague: Martinus Nijhoff, 1961), p. 32.

17 **The turtle-hunting song:** A. R. Radcliffe-Brown, *The Andaman Islanders* (Glencoe, Ill.: Free Press, 1948), p. 100.

17 **in Yamoussoukro:** Geoffrey Gorer, *Africa Dances: A Book about West African Negroes* (New York: Norton, 1962), pp. 224–25.

17 **an "opossum dance":** A. W. Howitt, *The Native Tribes of South-East Australia* (Canberra: Aboriginal Studies Press, 1996), p. 423.

18 **"We stretch forth our hands":** Knud Rasmussen, *Across Arctic America: Narrative of the Fifth Thule Expedition* (New York: G. P. Putnam's Sons, 1927), p. 32.

18 **Frances Densmore:** Frances Densmore. *Seminole Music*, Smithsonian Institution, Bureau of American Ethnology, Bulletin 161 (Washington, D.C.: Government Printing Office, 1956), p. 176.

18 **"kangaroo increase":** T. G. H. Strehlow, *Songs of Central Australia* (Sydney: Angus and Robertson, 1971), pp. 305–27.

18 **Writing of the Laplanders:** From John Scheffer, *The History of Lapland, wherein are shewed the Original Manners, Habits, Marriages, Conjurations, &c. of that People* (Oxford, 1674). The text can be found in Frank Harrison, *Time, Place and Music: An Anthology of Ethnomusicological Observation, c. 1550 to c. 1800* (Amsterdam: Fritz Knuf, 1973), pp. 74–75. See also Hugh Beach, *A Year in Lapland: Guest of the Reindeer Herders* (Seattle: University of Washington Press, 2001), p. 19.

19 **Israeli ethnomusicologist Simha Arom:** All of the types of Aka hunting music described here and below can be heard on the 1987 recording *Centrafique: Anthologie de la musique des Pygmees Aka* (Ocora C559012 13).

19 **the first human languages:** See *The New Science of Giambattista Vico*, translated by Thomas Goddard Bergin and Max Harold Fisch (Ithaca: Cornell University Press, 1984), p. 77.

19 **the only time they are silent:** Colin Turnbull, *The Forest People* (New York: Simon and Schuster, 1962), p. 58.

21 **to classify local bird lore:** Steven Feld, *Sound and Sentiment: Birds, Weeping, Poetics, and Song in Kaluli Expression*, 2nd ed. (Philadelphia: University of Pennsylvania Press, 1990), p. 45.

21   **Elias Canetti:** Elias Canetti, *Crowds and Power* (New York: Continuum, 1978), p. 31.

21   **demonstrated in stunning fashion:** Bruce Chatwin, *The Songlines* (New York: Viking, 1987), p. 13.

22   **The Bariba of Benin:** The melodic hunting calls of the Bariba can be heard on *Benin: Bariba and Somba Music* (UNESCO D 8057), recorded by Simha Arom.

22   **Teton Sioux medicine men:** Frances Densmore, *Teton Sioux Music,* Smithsonian Institution, Bureau of American Ethnology, Bulletin 61 (Washington, D.C.: Government Printing Office, 1918), p. 445.

23   **"The buffalo was part of us":** John (Fire) Lame Deer and Richard Erdoes, *Lame Deer Seeker of Visions: The Life of a Sioux Medicine Man* (New York: Touchstone, 1972), p. 255.

23   **Writing of the Yaqui:** Larry Evers and Felipe S. Molina, *Yaqui Deer Songs, Maso Bwikam: A Native American Poetry,* Sun Tracks: An American Indian Literary Series, Vol. 14 (Tucson: Sun Tracks; University of Arizona Press, 1987), p. 47.

24   **the *Shijing* from China:** See songs 103, 112, 127, 179, and 180 in Joseph R. Allen, ed., *The Book of Songs: The Ancient Chinese Classic of Poetry,* translated by Arthur Waley and Joseph R. Allen (New York: Grove Press, 1996).

24   **the *Kinkafu* from Japan:** See Noah Brannen and William Elliott, eds. and trans., *Festive Wine: Ancient Japanese Poems from the Kinkafu* (Tokyo: John Weatherhill, 1969), pp. 52–54.

24   **"I have shot a bull elephant":** From Verrier Elwin, *Folk-Songs of Chhattisgarh* (Madras: Oxford University Press, 1946), p. 136.

24   **"When hunting we found":** Charles Hofmann, *Drum Dance: Legends, Ceremonies, Dances and Songs of the Eskimos* (Toronto: W. J. Gage, 1974), p. 21.

24   **For the Netsilik Inuit:** Beverly Cavanagh, *Music of the Netsilik Eskimo: A Study of Stability and Change* (Ottowa: National Museums of Canada, 1982), vol. 1, pp. 80–81.

24   **Among the Mande:** Eric Charry, *Mande Music* (Chicago: University of Chicago Press, 2000), p. 64. See also Charles Bird, "Heroic Songs of the Mande Hunters" in *African Folklore,* edited by Richard M. Dorson (Bloomington: Indiana University Press, 1972), pp. 275–93.

24   **Among the Akan:** J. H. Nketia, *Drumming in Akan Communities of Ghana* (London: Thomas Nelson and Sons, 1963), p. 80.

25   **funeral dirges:** See Bade Ajuwon, *Funeral Dirges of Yoruba Hunter* (New York: NOK Publishers, 1982). The passage quoted is on p. 17.

25 **"first affluent societies"**: See Marshall D. Sahlins, "Notes on the Original Affluent Society," in *Man the Hunter,* edited by Richard B. Lee and Irven Devore (Hawthorne, N.Y.: Aldine de Gruyter, 1968), pp. 85–86.

25 **Napoleon Chagnon**: Napoleon Chagnon, *Yanomamo: The Fierce People,* 3rd ed. (New York: Holt, Rinehart and Winston, 1983), p. 4.

25 **Ba-Benjellé Pygmies**: Louis Sarno, *Songs from the Forest: My Life Among the Ba-Benjellé Pygmies* (New York: Houghton Mifflin, 1993), p. 70. For an account that is critical of researchers, including Sarno and Turnbull, for their lack of academic distance and tendency to identify with the society they were studying, see Michelle Kisliuk, *Seize the Dance! BaAka Musical Life and the Ethnography of Performance* (New York: Oxford University Press, 2001), pp. 3–5, 169.

26 **Chagnon explains**: Napoleon Chagnon. *Yanomamo: The Fierce People,* 3rd ed. (New York: Holt, Rinehart and Winston, 1983), p. 157.

27 **"Each time a shaman"**: Mircea Eliade, *Shamanism: Archaic Techniques of Ecstasy,* translated by Willard R. Trask (Princeton: Princeton University Press, 1964), p. 94.

27 **Among the Tungus**: Sergei M. Shirokogoroff, *Psychomental Complex of the Tungus* (London: Kegan Paul, Trench, Trubner and Co., 1935), p. 322.

27 **The Ndembu of Zambia**: Victor Turner, *The Drums of Affliction: A Study of Religious Processes among the Ndembu of Zambia* (Ithaca: Cornell University Press, 1981), pp. 15–16.

27 **"hunter's musician"**: Eric Charry, *Mande Music* (Chicago: University of Chicago Press, 2000), p. 64.

27 **Rose Brandel**: Rose Brandel, *The Music of Central Africa: An Ethnomusicological Study* (The Hague: Martinus Nijhoff, 1961), pp. 31–32.

27 **Among the Crow**: Robert H. Lowie, *The Crow Indians* (Lincoln: University of Nebraska Press, 1983), pp. 73–74.

27 **Luther Standing Bear**: Luther Standing Bear, *My People the Sioux* (Lincoln: University of Nebraska Press, 1975), p. 113.

28 **The Scythians**: From Plutarch's "Demetrius," cited in Walter Wiora, *The Four Ages of Music,* translated by M. D. Herter Norton (New York: W. W. Norton, 1967), p. 25.

28 **When Sir Laurens van der Post**: Laurens van der Post, *The Lost World of the Kalahari* (New York: Morrow, 1958), p. 239.

29 **Michael Harner**: Michael Harner, *The Jivaro: People of the Sacred Waterfalls* (Berkeley: University of California Press, 1984), p. 107.

29 **efficacy of the bow**: Victor Turner, *The Drums of Affliction: A Study of*

Religious Processes among the Ndembu of Zambia (Ithaca: Cornell University Press, 1981), pp. 214–16, 240–43.

30 **"The fundamental unity"**: Eric Charry, *Mande Music* (Chicago: University of Chicago Press, 2000), p. 75.

31 **In discussing their discovery**: Drago Kunej and Ivan Turk, "New Perspectives on the Beginnings of Music: Archeological and Musicological Analysis of a Middle Paleolithic Bone 'Flute,'" in *The Origins of Music*, edited by Nils L. Wallin, Bjorn Merker, and Steven Brown (Cambridge, Mass: MIT Press, 2000), p. 248.

31 **"In the spiritual horizon"**: Mircea Eliade, *Shamanism: Archaic Techniques of Ecstasy*, translated by Willard R. Trask (Princeton: Princeton University Press, 1964), p. 63.

31 **the "singing bone"**: See, for a summary, Walter Wiora, *The Four Ages of Music*, translated by M. D. Herter Norton (New York: Norton, 1967), pp. 19–24.

33 **St. Peterburg could boast**: See Jaroslaw de Zielinski, "Russian Hunting Music," *Musical Quarterly* (January 1917): 53–59.

33 **Reg Hall**: See Reg Hall's liner notes in *To Catch a Fine Buck Was My Delight: Songs of Hunting and Poaching* (Topic TSCD 668).

33 **Alexander Mackay-Smith**: See Alexander Mackay-Smith, *The Songs of Fox-Hunting* (Milkwood, Va.: American Foxhound Club, 1974). Less definitive but also valuable is John Sherard Reeve, ed., *Lyra Venatica: A Collection of Hunting Songs* (London: Arthur L. Humphreys, 1906), most of which contains songs collected by Reeve's father, Colonel John Reeve, who died in 1897. His son completed the project, which includes songs, correspondence, and prose relating to hunting, along with accompanying notes (the latter of which are rather incomplete).

34 **deer song tradition**: Larry Evers and Felipe S. Molina, *Yaqui Deer Songs, Maso Bwikam: A Native American Poetry*, Sun Tracks: An American Indian Literary Series, vol. 14 (Tucson: Sun Tracks; University of Arizona Press, 1987), pp. 14, 18.

Chapter 2: The Cultivator

36 **"The simplest form"**: Irmgard Bartenieff, with Dori Lewis, *Body Movement: Coping with the Environment* (Amsterdam: Gordon and Breach, 1980), pp. 73–74.

37 **Rose Brandel notes**: Rose Brandel, *The Music of Central Africa: An Ethnomusicological Study* (The Hague: Martinus Nijhoff, 1961), p. 34.

37 **a millstone grinding song**: This performance recorded by Patrick Kersale, identified as "Millstone Song," can be found on *Burkina Faso: Anthology of the Music of the Gan* (Buda Records/Musique du Monde 92709-2).

37 **Hahn Man-young transcribed**: Hahn Man-young, "Folk Songs of Korean Rural Life and Their Characteristics Based on the Rice Farming Songs," *Asian Music* 9, no. 2 (1978): 21–28. The author adds: "Korean folk song is almost always in triple meter. Triplets rather than dotted rhythms are characteristic" (p. 27). See also Tae Hung Ha, *Korea Sings: Folk and Popular Music and Lyrics* (Seoul: Yonsei University Press, 1958), pp. 18–21.

37 **The corn-grinding songs**: Natalie Curtis, *The Indians' Book: Songs and Legends of the American Indians* (New York: Dover Publications, 1968), pp. 430–37.

37 **a *hie*-pounding song**: Ryutaro Hattori, ed., "Hie-Pounding Songs" ("Hie tsuki bushi"), in *Japanese Folk Songs*, 7th ed. (Tokyo: Japan Times, 1971), pp. 88–90.

37 **the Garifuna of Belize**: "Grating Song" is included in *The Spirit Cries: Music from the Rainforests of South America and the Caribbean* (Rykodisc RCD 10250), recorded by Carol and Travis Jenkins in 1981.

37 **acorn grinding song**: This transcription made by E. G. Locke from a recording in the Phoebe Hearst Museum in Berkeley can be found in Karen W. Arlen, Margaret Blatt, Mary Ann Benson, and Nancie N. Kester, eds., *Days of Gold: Songs of the California Gold Rush* (Oakland, Calif.: Calicanto Associates, 1999), p. 64.

37 **Among the Navajo**: The song discussed here, listed as "Corn Grinding Song," can be found on the commercial release *Navajo Songs* (Smithsonian Folkways CD 40403), recorded by Laura Bolton.

37 **Gerhard Kubik**: See Gerhard Kubik, *Africa and the Blues* (Jackson: University of Mississippi Press, 1999), p. 76.

39 **"Must we spend all day"**: From Lise Manniche, *Music and Musicians in Ancient Egypt* (London: British Museum Press, 1991), p. 19.

40 **Lewis Henry Morgan**: Lewis Henry Morgan, *The League of the Ho-De'-No-Sau-Nee, or Iroquois* (North Dighton, Mass.: J. G. Press, 1995), p. 193.

40 **Frances Densmore interviewed**: Frances Densmore, *Yuman and Yaqui Music*, Smithsonian Institution, Bureau of American Ethnology, Bulletin 110 (Washington, D.C.: Government Printing Office, 1932), pp. 66–67.

41 **Judith Brown**: Judith Brown, "A Note on the Division of Labor by Sex," *American Anthropologist* 72, no. 5 (1970): 1073–78.

42 **"In Europe well into this century"**: Elizabeth Wayland Barber, *Women's Work: The First 20,000 Years* (New York: Norton, 1994), p. 85.

42 **Hem Barua:** Hem Barua, *Folk Songs of India* (New Delhi: Indian Council for Cultural Relations, 1963), pp. 61–62.

42 **"The upper voice"**: Comments from Shehan and the text of the Macedonian song can be found in Patricia K. Shehan, "Balkan Women," in *Women and Music in Cross-Cultural Perspective,* edited by Ellen Koskoff, Contributions in Women's Studies, no. 79 (Westport, Conn.: Greenwood Press, 1987), pp. 45–53, esp. pp. 48–49.

42 **In traditional Japanese:** See Toshijiro Hirayama, "Seasonal Rituals Connected with Rice Culture," in *Studies in Japanese Folklore,* edited by R. M. Dorson, Toichi Mabuchi, and Tokihiko Oto (Bloomington: Indiana University Press, 1963), p. 65.

43 **among the Kammu people:** Kristina Lindell, Håkan Lundström, Jan-Olof Svantesson, and Damrong Tayanin, *The Kammu Year: Its Lore and Music* (London: Curzon Press, 1982), p. 71.

43 **In a striking passage:** Leo Tolstoy, *What Is Art?,* translated by Aylmer Maude (New York: Thomas Crowell and Co., 1899), pp. 127–28.

43 **Walter Jekyll:** Walter Jekyll, ed., *Jamaican Song and Story* (New York: Dover, 1966), p. 158. For recorded examples of Jamaican "digging sings," see *Caribbean Island Music: Songs and Dances of Haiti, the Dominican Republic, and Jamaica* (Nonesuch 72047-2), recorded by John Storm Roberts.

44 **"Upon a rough calculation"**: "Negro Minstrelsy—Ancient and Modern," in *Putnam's Monthly Magazine of American Literature, Science and Art* 5, no. 25 (January 1855): 72–79. The passage quoted is on p. 79.

44 **Scarborough consulted Dr. Boyd:** Dorothy Scarborough, *On the Trail of Negro Folksongs* (Hatboro, Pa.: Folklore Associates, 1963), p. 210.

45 **Delta bluesman Muddy Waters:** Robert Gordon, *Can't Be Satisfied: The Life and Times of Muddy Waters* (Boston: Little, Brown, 2002), pp. 26–27.

45 **"With the exception"**: Eugene D. Genovese, *Roll, Jordan, Roll: The World the Slaves Made* (New York: Vintage, 1976), p. 315.

45 **In an interview with Bernice Lewis:** From Charles L. Perdue Jr., Thomas E. Barden, and Robert K. Phillips, eds., *Weevils in the Wheat: Interviews with Virginia Ex-Slaves* (Charlottesville: University Press of Virginia, 1976), p. 279.

46 **"Even after allowing"**: Roger D. Abrahams, *Singing the Master: The Emergence of African-American Culture in the Plantation South* (New York: Penguin, 1993), p. 5.

46 **"Dis cotton want a-pickin' "**: Song text and music can be found in Natalie Curtis-Burlin, *Negro Folk-Songs: The Hampton Series Books I–IV, Complete* (Mineola, N.Y.: Dover, 2001), pp. 89–97.

47 **"Way down in the bottom"**: "Five Fingers in the Boll," in Lydia Parrish, *Slave Songs of the Georgia Sea Islands* (Athens, Georgia: University of Georgia Press, 1992), pp. 247–48. For another example, for which no date or place is given, see *The Frank C. Brown Collection of North Carolina Folklore*, vol. 5, *The Music of the Folk Songs,* edited by Jan Philip Schinhan (Durham: Duke University Press, 1962), p. 137.

47 **only one firsthand account**: "Life and Travel in the Southern States," *Great Republic Monthly* 1 (1859): 80–84, reprinted in *Travels in the Old South: Selected from Periodicals of the Times,* edited by Eugene L. Schwaab (Lexington: University of Kentucky Press, 1974), vol. 2, pp. 487–93. The passage quoted is on p. 491.

48 **Olive Dame Campbell**: See Mike Yates, "Cecil Sharp in America: Collecting in the Appalachians," updated version published on the *Musical Traditions* Web site (www.mustrad.org.uk) on June 30, 2000.

49 **John Lomax boasted**: John Lomax's account of this visit can be found in John A. Lomax, *Adventures of a Ballad Hunter* (New York: Macmillan, 1947), p. 248.

50 **T. C. Singh**: On the influence of music on vegetation, notably in the work described here of Singh, Smith, Milstein, and Retallack, see Peter Tompkins and Christopher Bird, *The Secret Life of Plants* (New York: Harper and Row, 1973), pp. 145–213.

51 **A. W. Howitt**: A. W. Howitt, *The Native Tribes of South-East Australia* (Canberra: Aboriginal Studies Press, 1996), p. 397.

52 **Natalie Curtis; Béla Bartok; Verrier Elwin**: For the rainmaking songs mentioned here, see Natalie Curtis, *Songs and Tales from the Dark Continent* (Mineola, N.Y.: Dover Publications, 2002), pp. 20–23; Béla Bartok, *Turkish Folk Music from Asia Minor,* edited by Benjamin Suchoff (Princeton: Princeton University Press, 1976), pp. 82–85, 189; and Verrier Elwin, *Folk-Songs of Chhattisgarh* (Madras: Oxford University Press, 1946), p. 229.

52 **Curtis tells of a group**: Natalie Curtis, *The Indians' Book: Songs and Legends of the American Indians* (New York: Dover Publications, 1968), p. 364.

52 **ritual of southeastern Europe**: James G. Frazer, *The Golden Bough: A Study In Comparative Religion* (New York: Gramercy, 1981 [1890]), vol. 1, p. 16.

53 **"Frazer cites numerous other instances"**: See James G. Frazer, *The Golden Bough: A Study In Comparative Religion* (New York: Gramercy, 1981 [1890]), vol. 1, esp. pp. 71–98.

53 **Rainmaking is only one example**: These examples of songs to discourage animals come from Roy Palmer, *The Painful Plough: A Portrait of the Agricultural Labourer in the Nineteenth Century from Folk Songs and Ballads and Contemporary Accounts* (Cambridge: Cambridge University Press, 1972, pp. 8–9). See also G. F. Northall, *English Folk Rhymes* (Detroit: Singing Tree Press, 1968), pp. 319–21. For the musical scarecrows of Laos, see Kristina Lindell, Håkan Lundström, Jan-Olof Svantesson, and Damrong Tayanin, *The Kammu Year: Its Lore and Music* (London: Curzon Press, 1982), pp. 93–99.

54 **"Field calls grew up alongside work songs"**: Frederic Ramsey Jr. *Been Here and Gone* (New Brunswick: Rutgers University Press, 1960), p. 36.

55 **Frederick Law Olmsted**: This description by Olmsted of a field holler comes from his *A Journey in the Seaboard Slave States in the Years 1853–1854* (New York: G. P. Putnam, 1904), vol. 2, pp. 19–20. It is included, with commentary, in Dena J. Epstein, *Sinful Tunes and Spirituals: Black Folk Music to the Civil War* (Urbana: University of Illinois Press, 1977), p. 182.

55 **The Harvard archeologist**: Charles Peabody, "Notes on Negro Music," *Journal of American Folk-Lore* 16, no. 62 (July–September 1903): 148–52. The passage cited is on p. 151.

56 **"I have often been utterly astonished"**: Frederick Douglass, *Narrative of the Life of Frederick Douglass, An American Slave, Written by Himself* (New York: Signet, 1997), p. 30.

56 **ethnomusicologist Rose Brandel**: Rose Brandel, *The Music of Central Africa: An Ethnomusicological Study* (The Hague: Martinus Nijhoff, 1961), pp. 32–33.

56 **Robert Nathaniel Dett**: R. Nathaniel Dett, "Review of *Negro Workaday Songs*," in "The R. Nathaniel Dett Reader," special issue, *Black Sacred Music* (fall 1991): 52–53.

57 **In his book *Tiv Song***: Charles Keil, *Tiv Song: The Sociology of Art in a Classless Society* (Chicago: University of Chicago Press, 1979), p. 199.

57 **Matthew Lewis**: Passages here and below are from Matthew Lewis, *Journal of a West India Proprietor* (New York: Oxford University Press, 1999), pp. 203–4.

59 **"We have all experienced times"**: Mihaly Csikszentmihalyi, *Flow: The Psychology of Optimal Experience* (New York: Harper and Row, 1990), p. 3.

59 **"They do also by singing alleviate"**: Extract from Charles de Rochefort comes from the John Davies translation of *Histoire naturelle et morale des Iles Antilles* (Rotterdam, 1658), published as *The History of the Caribby-Islands* in London in 1666. The text can be found in Frank Harrison, *Time, Place and*

Music: An Anthology of Ethnomusicological Observation, c. 1550 to c. 1800 (Amsterdam: Fritz Knuf, 1973), pp. 54–55.

59 **"It go so better when you singing"**: Alan Lomax, *The Land Where the Blues Began* (New York: Pantheon, 1993), p. 263.

59 **Csikszentmihalyi has stated**: Mihaly Csikszentmihalyi, *Flow: The Psychology of Optimal Experience* (New York: Harper and Row, 1990) p. 7.

60 **Thomas F. Johnston speculated**: Thomas F. Johnston, "The Function of Tsonga Work-Songs," *Journal of Music Therapy* 10, no. 3 (fall 1973): 156–64. The passage quoted is on pp. 156–57.

60 **A few researchers have explored**: See, for example, V. J. Walter and W. Grey Walter, "The Central Effects of Rhythmic Sensory Stimulation," *Electroencephalography and Clinical Neurophysiology* 1 (1949): 57–86: Andrew Neher, "Auditory Driving Observed with Scalp Electrodes in Normal Subjects," *Electroencephalography and Clinical Neurophysiology* 13 (1961): 449–51; Melinda C. Maxfield, "The Journey of the Drum," in *Music and Miracles,* edited by Don Campbell (Wheaton, Ill: Quest Books, 1992), pp. 137–55; and Gilbert Rouget, *Music and Trance: A Theory of the Relations between Music and Possession,* translated by Brunhilde Biebuyck (Chicago: University of Chicago Press, 1985).

61 **A. L. Lloyd has suggested**: A. L. Lloyd, *Folk Song in England* (St. Albans: Paladin, 1975), p. 83.

62 **Victor Hanson**: Victor Hanson, *The Other Greeks* (New York: Free Press 1995), p. 3.

Chapter 3: The Herder

64 **The Roman author Columella**: Translation from Kathryn J. Gutzwiller, *Theocritus Pastoral Analogies: The Formation of a Genre* (Madison: University of Wisconsin Press, 1991), p. 31.

64 **Macrobius notes**: Macrobius, *Commentary on the Dream of Scipio,* translated by William Harris Stahl (New York: Columbia University Press, 1952), p. 195.

64 **"It is generally assumed"**: Raymond Williams, *The Country and the City* (New York: Oxford University Press, 1973), p. 14.

64 **As one expert on pastoral literature remarks**: J. E. Congleton, in the entry "Pastoral" in *Princeton Encylopedia of Poetry and Poetics*, edited by Alex Preminger (Princeton: Princeton University Press, 1974), p. 603.

65 *yoik* or *joik*: See Heikki Laitinen, "The Many Faces of the Yoik," update in October 2000 and posted on the Web site of the Finnish Music Information

Centre (http://www.fimic.fi/fimic/fimic.nsf). For a good contemporary account of life among the Sami, see Hugh Beach, *A Year in Lapland: Guest of the Reindeer Herders* (Seattle: University of Washington Press, 2001).

65   **The following yoik**: From Johan Turi, "Songs of the Sami," in *In the Shadow of the Midnight Sun: Contemporary Sami Prose and Poetry*, edited by Harald Gaski (Karasjok, Norway: Davvi Girji, 1997), p. 46.

66   **A. Hyatt King**: A. Hyatt King, "Mountains, Music and Musicians," *Musical Quarterly* 31, no. 4 (October 1945): 395–419.

66   **"I am the Good Shepherd"**: John 10:11. The translation here is from the King James Version of the Bible.

67   **"The Lord is my Shepherd"**: Psalms 23:1–4. The translation here is from the King James Version of the Bible.

68   **When Alan Lomax**: From "Saga of a Folksong Hunter," originally written for *HiFi/Stereo Review* (May 1960) and reprinted in the booklet accompanying *The Alan Lomax Collection Sampler* (pp. 42–57). For Lomax's account of the Spanish shepherd described here, see p. 52.

68   **"She had no education"**: See Francesca Alexander's preface to John Ruskin, ed., *Roadside Songs of Tuscany*, 2nd ed., translated and illustrated by Francesca Alexander (New York: John Wiley and Sons, 1887), p. 2.

69   **"When I was a shepherd boy"**: From Albert B. Lord, *The Singer of Tales*, 2nd ed., edited by Stephen Mitchell and Gregory Nagy (Cambridge, Mass.: Harvard University Press, 2000), p. 21.

69   **"As the Corsicans are"**: from Wolfgang Laade, "The Corsican Tribbiera: A Type of Work Song," *Ethnomusicology* 6, no. 3 (September 1962): 181–85. The passage cited is on p. 181.

69   **With the emigration of many Basque**: For information on the Basque role in American shepherding, see Catherine A. Kilker and Charles R. Koch, *Sheep and Man: An American Saga* (Denver: American Sheep Producers Council, 1978), pp. 9, 92–99. For the Basque *bertsolari* singing tradition in America, see Louis Irigaray and Theodore Taylor, *A Shepherd Watches, A Shepherd Sings* (New York: Doubleday, 1977), pp. 86–87. For more on this style of song, see Gorka Aulestia, *Improvisational Poetry from the Basque Country*, translated by Linda White (Reno: University of Nevada Press, 1995).

69   **In Albania, A. L. Lloyd**: This music can be found in *Folk Music of Albania* (Topic TSCD904), recorded by A. L. Lloyd.

69   **The Kuria of East Africa**: John P. Varnum, "The Ibirongwe of the Kuria: A Cattle Herding Flute in East Africa," *Ethnomusicology* 14, no. 3 (September 1970): 462–67. The passages quoted are on p. 463.

70   **the cracking of whips**: For a fascinating discussion of the rhythmic sound of whips as a signaling device among European herders, see Jan Ling, *A History of European Folk Music,* translated by Linda Schenck and Robert Schenck (Rochester, N.Y.: University of Rochester Press, 1997), pp. 22–23.

70   **"The music both comforts and directs"**: From the essay accompanying the Smithsonian Folkways recording *Mountain Music of Peru*, vol. 1 (Smithsonian Folkways SFCD 40020).

70   **In the nearby Mantaro Valley**: See the recording *Traditional Music of Peru,* vol. 2, *The Mantaro Valley* (Smithsonian Folkways SFCD 40467), compiled and edited by Raúl R. Romero.

70   **In *Somali Pastoral Work Songs***: Axmed Cali Abokor, *Somali Pastoral Work Songs: The Poetic Voice of the Politically Powerless* (Uppsala, Sweden: Department of Social and Economic Geography, Uppsala University, 1993), p. 38.

70   **A. L. Lloyd describes Bulgarian herders**: Described in A. L. Lloyd's accompanying notes to his collection *Folk Music of Bulgaria* (Topic TSCD905), p. 4.

71   **Milking songs are found**: The milking songs of Mongolia can be found on *Vocal and Instrumental Music of Mongolia* (Topic TSCD 909), recorded by Jean Jenkins. Jenkins's comments in the text come from the accompanying notes to this release. Milking songs from the Hebrides can be found in Margaret Fay Shaw, *Folksongs and Folklore of South Uist* (Edinburgh: Birlinn, 1999), pp. 157–63. The example cited is on p. 161. Sula Benet's description of a milking incantation from Poland can be found in Sula Benet, *Song, Dance, and Customs of Peasant Poland* (Cornwall Bridge, Conn.: Polish Heritage Publications, 1996), p. 69. For Rivers and Emeneau, see M. B. Emeneau, *Toda Songs* (Oxford: Clarendon Press, 1971), pp. xli–xlv, 30–108. Those still anxious to learn more are referred to an intriguing report that "The Blue Danube Waltz" increases milking output—see Joseph Lanza, *Elevator Music: A Surreal History of Muzak, Easy Listening and Other Moodsong* (New York: St. Martin's Press, 1994), p. 43. For a more recent study that also confirms the positive influence of music in milking, see K. Uetake, J. F. Hurnik, and L. Johnson, "Effect of Music on Voluntary Approach of Dairy Cows to an Automatic Milking System," *Applied Animal Behaviour Science* 53, no. 3 (June 1997): 175–82.

71   **"Makes no difference"**: "Shear Um," in Alton C. Morris, *Folksongs of Florida* (Gainesville: University of Florida Press, 1990), p. 184.

72   **"Come all my jolly boys"**: Bob Copper, *A Song for Every Season: A Hundred Years of a Sussex Farming Family* (Devon, England: Country Book Club, 1972), pp. 236–37.

72 **"Along came a jumbuck"**: A "jumbuck" is a sheep. The "matilda" is the name of the bedroll or pack carried by the shearer on his travels. The "tucker bag" holds food. And the "billabong" is a water hole. Finally, "waltzing" does not refer to dance, but rather derives from the German *auf der walz*, which indicates the period of traveling that an apprentice undertakes while learning a trade. In the Australian context it refers to a type of walkabout while looking for work. Australia boasts a rich tradition of shearing songs: for examples see Thérèse Radic, ed., *Songs of Australian Working Life* (Elwood, Victoria: Greenhouse Publications, 1989), pp. 8–19.

72 **Butter churning songs**: Chuck Perdue, "Come Butter Come: A Collection of Churning Chants from Georgia," *Foxfire* 3, no. 1 (spring 1969): 20–24, 65–72. Frank C. Brown, *The Frank C. Brown Collection of North Carolina Folklore*, vol. 7, *Popular Beliefs and Superstitions from North Carolina* (Durham: Duke University Press, 1964), pp. 439–46.

73 **Among the Nuer**: E. E. Evans-Pritchard, *The Nuer* (Oxford: Oxford University Press, 1940). The passage quoted is on pp. 18–19.

74 **Although the Nuer are not unaware of drumming**: For the use of drums in the religious life of the Nuer, see E. E. Evans-Pritchard, *Nuer Religion* (New York: Oxford University Press, 1974), p. 51.

74 **"The tonal patterns"**: Nils L. Wallin, *Biomusicology: Neurophysiological, Neuropsychological, and Evolutionary Perspectives on the Origins and Purposes of Music* (Stuyvesant, N.Y.: Pendragon, 1991), p. 377.

74 **only one surviving member**: See *Burkina Faso: Anthologies de la Musique Gan* (Musique du Monde label 902709-2), as well as the notes that accompany the recording.

74 **herding songs of China**: See Antoinet Schimmelpenninck, *Chinese Folk Songs and Folk Singers: Shan'ge Traditions in Southern Jiangsu* (Leiden: CHIME Foundation, 1997), pp. 79–81, 138.

75 **Balint Sarosi**: Balint Sarosi, *Folk Music: Hungarian Musical Idiom*, translated by Maria Steiner (Budapest: Corvina, 1986), pp. 22–23. For a comparison with the abundance of music from herding communities found by earlier researchers, see "Appendix 1: Lists of Places of Origin of the Tunes Contained in the Recent Collections," in Béla Bartok, *Hungarian Folk Music*, translated by Michael D. Calvocoressi (London: Oxford University Press, 1931), pp. 81–96.

75 **Violet Alford**: From Violet Alford, "Music and Dance of the Swiss Folk," in *Musical Quarterly* 27, no. 4 (October 1941): 500–15. The passage quoted is on p. 506.

75 **Frederick Law Olmstead**: From Frederick Law Olmstead, *A Journey in the*

Seaboard Slave States, With Remarks on their Economy (New York: Dix and Edwards, 1856), cited by Lydia Parrish in *Slave Songs of the Georgia Sea Islands* (Athens: University of Georgia Press, 1992), p. 216.

75 **Emperor Julian**: This early description of yodeling is summarized in Manfred Bukofzer, "Popular Polyphony in the Middle Ages," *Musical Quarterly* 26, no. 1 (January 1940): 31–49, especially p. 47.

76 **Hugo Zemp**: Zemp's comment comes from his notes accompanying *"Jüüzli": Jodel du Muotatal Suisse* (Le Chant du Monde LDX 274 716).

76 **James Leary**: James P. Leary, *Yodeling in Dairyland: A History of Swiss Music in Wisconsin* (Mount Horeb, Wisc.: Wisconsin Folk Museum, 1991). For a general overview of the topic, see Bart Plantenga, *Yodel-Ay-Ee-Oooo: The Secret History of Yodeling Around the World* (New York: Routledge, 2004).

77 **Nils Wallin**: Nils L. Wallin, *Biomusicology: Neurophysiological, Neuropsychological, and Evolutionary Perspectives on the Origins and Purposes of Music* (Stuyvesant, N.Y.: Pendragon, 1991), p. 509. The quote about song as a tool is from p. 390.

Chapter 4: Thread and Cloth

79 **Clay shards dating from this period**: See James M. Adovasio, Olga Soffer, and Bohuslav Klima, "27,000 Years Old Textile Fragments," *Textile Forum* (June 1996): 10–11.

79 **the "String Revolution"**: See Elizabeth Wayland Barber, *Women's Work: The First 20,000 Years* (New York: Norton, 1994), pp. 42–70.

80 **Judith Brown**: Judith Brown, "A Note on the Division of Labor by Sex," *American Anthropologist* 72, no. 5 (1970): 1073–78.

80 **beneficiaries of this work**: Elizabeth Wayland Barber, *Women's Work: The First 20,000 Years* (New York: Norton, 1994), pp. 59–60.

80 **Remy de Gourmont**: Remy de Gourmont, *The Natural Philosophy of Love*, translated by Ezra Pound (New York: Liveright, 1942), p. 252.

81 **"Sweet mother"**: This translation of Sappho comes from Diane J. Rayor, ed. and trans., *Sappho's Lyre: Archaic Lyric and Women Poets of Ancient Greece* (Berkeley: University of California Press, 1991), p. 63. Readers are also encouraged to enjoy the powerfully evocative, if loosely translated, enactment of this song in Walter Savage Landor's poem "Mother, I Cannot Mind My Wheel."

81 **"Ladies suffer"**: Quoted in Elizabeth Wayland Barber, *Women's Work: The First 20,000 Years* (New York: Norton, 1994), p. 190.

81 **St. John Chrysostom**: The quote from Chrysostom, drawn from his *Patrologia Graeca,* comes from a longer passage with many interesting comments on work songs, and can be found in Peter Dronke, *The Medieval Lyric* (Suffolk, U.K.: D. S. Brewer, 1996), p. 15.

81 **the *chansons de toile* of France**: A comprehensive overview, with close to one hundred pages of examples, is given in Michel Zink, *Les Chanson de Toile* (Paris: Champion 1978). See also E. Jane Burns, "Sewing Like a Girl: Working Women in the Chansons de Toile," in *Medieval Woman's Song: Cross-Cultural Approaches,* edited by Anne L. Klinck and Ann Marie Rasmussen (Philadelphia: University of Pennsylvania Press, 2002), pp. 99–126.

81 **"ladies and queens of days"**: From *Guillaume de Dole* (lines 1148–151), composed in the Liege area circa 1210. Translation from Christopher Page's liner notes to *The Spirits of England and France,* vol. 2, *Gothic Voices* (Hyperion CDA66773).

81 **Charles Bertram Lewis**: Charles Bertram Lewis, "The Origin of the Weaving Songs and the Theme of the Girl at the Fountain," *Publications of the Modern Language Association of America* 37, no. 2 (June 1922): 141–81.

82 **work songs of the Assam region**: Hem Barua, *Folk Songs of India* (New Delhi: Indian Council for Cultural Relations, 1963), p. 70.

82 **Ruth Rubin**: Ruth Rubin, *Voices of a People: The Story of Yiddish Folksong* (Urbana: University of Illinois Press, 2000), p. 290.

83 **In Galicia in 1952**: "Canto de espadela," from *World Library of Folk and Primitive Music,* vol. 4, *Spain* (Rounder 11661 1744-2), recorded by Alan Lomax and Jeannette Bell. The translation from Spanish used here is from the liner notes to this release.

83 **In Balkan culture**: Patricia K. Shehan, "Balkan Women," in *Women and Music in Cross-Cultural Perspective,* Contributions in Women's Studies, no. 79, edited by Ellen Koskoff (Westport, Conn.: Greenwood Press, 1987), pp. 45–53, especially p. 48.

84 **"The ends of a length"**: Margaret Fay Shaw, *Folksongs and Folklore of South Uist* (Edinburgh: Birlinn, 1999), p. 72.

84 **Each line of the verse**: Examples of waulking songs are from Margaret Fay Shaw, *Folksongs and Folklore of South Uist* (Edinburgh: Birlinn, 1999), pp. 207, 209, 219. See also Donald MacCormick, *Hebridean Folksong: A Collection of Waulking Songs,* edited by J. L. Campbell (Oxford: Clarendon Press, 1969). The MacCormick songs, which remained unpublished for seventy-six years, were probably taken down from the singing of his sister and mother in 1893. Waulking songs can be heard on the commercial recording *Scottish Tradition 3: Waulking Songs from Barra* (Greentrax CDTRAX 9003), edited by Peter Cooke.

85 **a "charm that I cannot express"**: For Rousseau's remarks, see *The Confessions*, translated by J. M. Cohen (London: Penguin, 1953), pp. 22–23.

85 **the unlikely source of Mungo Park**: Mungo Park, *Travels in the Interior Districts of Africa*, edited by Kate Ferguson Masters (Durham: Duke University Press, 2000), pp. 196–98.

86 **"Spin, ladies, spin all day"**: Dorothy Scarborough, *On the Trail of Negro Folksongs* (Hatboro, Pa.: Folklore Associates, 1963), p. 215.

86 **Mildred Carter**: Cited in Charles L. Perdue Jr., Thomas E. Barden, and Robert K. Phillips, eds., *Weevils in the Wheat: Interviews with Virginia Ex-Slaves* (Charlottesville: University Press of Virginia, 1976), p. 70.

86 **Michael Harner**: Michael Harner, *The Jívaro: People of the Sacred Waterfalls* (Berkeley: University of California Press, 1984), p. 69.

89 **"I am a hand-weaver"**: A. L. Lloyd, *Folk Song in England* (St. Albans: Paladin, 1975), p. 303–4.

90 **"The Poor Cotton Weaver"**: A. L. Lloyd, *Folk Song in England* (St. Albans: Paladin, 1975), p. 305.

90 **"The Hand-Loom Weaver's Lament"**: The version here is from *The Iron Muse: A Panorama of Industrial Folk Music* (Topic TSCD465). See also Karl Dallas, ed., *One Hundred Songs of Toil* (London: Wolfe Publishing, 1974), pp. 131–32.

90 **"Poverty, poverty knock!"**: A. L. Lloyd, *Folk Song in England* (St. Albans: Paladin, 1975), p. 309.

91 **"Pukala Sam Lenek"**: For a recording of this song and many others associated with spinning and weaving, see Carla Sciaky, *Spin the Weaver's Song* (Green Linnet GLCD 2106).

92 **"You stood all day"**: Unnamed interviewee, described as a female Catholic mill worker who was born in 1898 and began working in 1910. From Betty Messenger, *Picking Up the Linen Threads: A Study in Industrial Folklore* (Austin: University of Texas Press, 1980), p. 27.

92 **"Tilly is our doffing mistress"**: Unamed interviewee, described as a male Catholic spinning master who was born in 1904 and began working in 1916. From Betty Messenger, *Picking Up the Linen Threads: A Study in Industrial Folklore* (Austin: University of Texas Press, 1980), p. 55.

93 **"Oh! Isn't it a pity"**: Quoted in Evelyn Alloy, *Working Women's Music: The Songs and Struggles of Women in the Cotton Mills, Textile Plants and Needle Trade* (Somerville, Mass.: New England Free Press, 1976), p. 7.

93 **"Come all ye weary"**: "The Lowell Factory Girl," in John Greenway,

American Folksongs of Protest (Philadelphia: University of Pennsylvania Press, 1953), pp. 125–26.

93 **By 1890, garment manufacturing**: Catherine Reef, *Working in America: An Eyewitness History* (New York: Facts on File, 2000), p. 293.

94 **"We run by water then"**: Jacquelyn D. Hall, James Leloudis, Robert Korstad, Mary Murphy, Lu Ann Jones, and Christopher B. Daley, *Like a Family: The Making of a Southern Cotton Mill World* (Chapel Hill: University of North Carolina Press, 1987), p. 88.

94 **"Mill Mother's Lament"**: John Greenway, *American Folksongs of Protest* (Philadelphia: University of Pennsylvania Press, 1953), pp. 251–52.

95 **"Cotton Mill Colic"**: For more information on "Cotton Mill Colic," see Doug DeNatale and Glenn Hinson, "The Southern Textile Song Tradition Reconsidered," in *Songs About Work: Essays in Occupational Culture*, edited by Archie Green (Bloomington: Indiana University, 1993), pp. 77–107.

96 **Like McCarn, a number of mill workers**: For information on radio and recordings in the life of southern mill workers, see Jacquelyn D. Hall, James Leloudis, Robert Korstad, Mary Murphy, Lu Ann Jones, and Christopher B. Daley, *Like a Family: The Making of a Southern Cotton Mill World* (Chapel Hill: University of North Carolina Press, 1987), pp. 258–61.

97 **"Xe chi luon kim"**: "Xe chi luon kim," Included in *Music from Vietnam*, Caprice Records (CAP 21406).

Chapter 5: The New Rhythms of Work

99 **"Each city has four gates"**: Quoted in David S. Landes, *Revolution in Time* (Cambridge, Mass.: Harvard University Press, 1983), p. 26.

100 **"The Alba hymn was the song of dawn"**: From Tey Diana Rebolledo and María Teresa Márquez, eds., *Women's Tales from the New Mexico WPA: La Diabla a Pie* (Houston: Arte Público Press, 2000), p. 24. For an apparent parallel from *The Book of Songs*, see Joseph R. Allen, ed., *The Book of Songs: The Ancient Chinese Classic of Poetry*, translated by Arthur Waley and Joseph R. Allen (New York: Grove Press, 1996), pp. 69, 77.

100 **"Time and the calendar"**: David S. Landes, *Revolution in Time* (Cambridge, Mass.: Harvard University Press, 1983), p. 63. The passage quoted below is on p. 61.

101 **For St. Basil**: Quotations from St. Basil and Pope Gregory, in the context of a discussion of these ideas, can be found in Thomas Merton, *Contemplative Prayer* (New York: Image Books, 1992), pp. 49–51.

101   **In Artois in 1355**: Jacques Le Goff, *Time, Work and Culture in the Middle Ages,* translated by Arthur Goldhammer (Chicago: University of Chicago Press, 1980), p. 36.

102   **"Big Jacqueline"**: These names, as well as the quote from the chronicler Chastellain, are from Johan Huizinga, *The Waning of the Middle Ages,* translated by Herfsttijd der Middeleeuwen (New York: St. Martin's Press, 1984), pp. 2–3.

102   **"Whoever cares to peer"**: John Frederick Rowbotham, *The History of Music* (London: Richard Bentley and Son, 1893), pp. 15–16.

102   **Writing in 1772, Charles Burney**: Charles Burney, *Dr. Burney's Musical Tours in Europe,* vol. 2, *An Eighteenth Century Musical Tour in Central Europe and the Netherlands,* edited by Percy A. Scholes (London: Oxford University Press, 1959), p. 64.

102   **"Wherever the missionaries"**: R. Murray Schafer, *The Tuning of the World* (New York: Knopf, 1977),

102   **Alain Corbin**: Alain Corbin, *Village Bells: Sound and Meaning in the Nineteenth-Century French Countryside,* translated by Martin Thom (London: Papermac, 1999), p. 207.

103   **"God confound the man"**: These lines come from *Boeotia,* a play attributed to Plautus, and are included in Aulus Gellius, *Noctes Atticae,* translated by J. C. Rolfe (New York: Putnam, 1927), p. 247. They are also cited in David S. Landes, *Revolution in Time* (Cambridge, Mass.: Harvard University Press, 1983), pp. 15–16.

104   **Peter Drucker writes**: Peter Drucker, "Beyond the Information Revolution," *Atlantic Monthly* 284, no. 4 (October, 1999): 47–57.

104   **"Singing and steam"**: William L. Alden, "Sailor Songs," *Harper's New Monthly Magazine* 65, no. 386 (July 1882): 281.

105   **A source in Arabic**: See the passage from Yâqût, a Greek residing in Baghdad in the twelfth century, in N. Levtzion and J. F. P. Hopkins, eds., *Corpus of Early Arabic Sources for West African History,* translated by J. F. P. Hopkins (Princeton: Markus Wiener Publishers, 2000), p. 169. For the example from the *Book of Songs* of Abu al-Faraj al-Isfahani, see Julian Ribera, *Music in Ancient Arabia and Spain,* translated by Eleanor Hague and Marion Leffingwell (Stanford: Stanford University Press, 1929), p. 39.

105   **Antoinet Schimmelpenninck**: See Antoinet Schimmelpenninck, *Chinese Folk Songs and Folk Singers: Shan'ge Traditions in Southern Jiangsu* (Leiden: CHIME Foundation, 1997), pp. 85–86.

106   **"Then you will notice"**: Alexander Tcherepnin, "Music in Modern

China," *Musical Quarterly* 21, no. 4 (October 1935): 391–400. The passage cited is on p. 392.

106 **In 1687, Marcellus Laroon:** Sean Shesgreen, ed., *The Criers and Hawkers of London: Engravings and Drawings by Marcellus Laroon* (Stanford: Stanford University Press, 1990). See also Charles Hindley, *A History of the Cries of London: Ancient and Modern* (Detroit: Singing Tree Press, 1969). For early French street cries, see also Nicole Crossley-Holland, *Living and Dining in Medieval Paris: The Household of a Fourteenth-Century Knight* (Cardiff: University of Wales Press, 1996), especially "Appendix 5: Early Street Cries of Paris," pp. 220–26.

107 **In 1908, Commissioner Theodore Bingham:** See B. A. Botkin, *Sidewalks of America: Folklore, Legends, Sagas, Traditions, Customs, Songs, Stories and Sayings of City Folk* (Indianapolis: Bobbs-Merrill, 1954), pp. 567–68.

107 **Thirty years later:** Terry Roth, "Street Cries and Criers of New York," Federal Writers' Project report, dated November 3, 1938, eight pages. For additional information on the cries and songs of street peddlers, see Elizabeth Hurley, "Come Buy, Come Buy," in *Folk Travelers: Ballads, Tales, and Talk,* edited by Mody C. Boatright, Wilson M. Hudson, and Allen Maxwell (Dallas: Southern Methodist University Press, 1953), pp. 115–38. This essay focuses primarily on examples from Texas, but also gives a brief historical overview that covers other locations. For more examples, see B. A. Botkin, *Sidewalks of America: Folklore, Legends, Sagas, Traditions, Customs, Songs, Stories and Sayings of City Folk* (Indianapolis: Bobbs-Merrill, 1954), pp. 567–77; and Maud Karpeles, *An Introduction to English Folk Song* (London: Oxford University Press, 1973), pp. 64–66. An account of street cries can also be found in R. Murray Schafer's fascinating book *The Tuning of the World* (New York: Knopf, 1977), pp. 64–67. See also chapter 13 of the present volume for more examples and a further discussion.

108 **As Luigi Russolo pointed out:** Luigi Russolo, *The Art of Noises,* translated by Barclay Brown (Hillsdale, N.Y.: Pendragon Press, 1986), p. 23.

109 **Frederika Bremer:** Frederika Bremer, *The Homes of the New World: Impressions of America,* translated by Mary Howitt (New York: Harpers and Brothers, Publishers, 1854), vol. 2, pp. 509–10.

109 **By the time Dorothy Scarborough:** Dorothy Scarborough, *On the Trail of Negro Folksongs* (Hatboro, Pa.: Folklore Associates, 1963), p. 206–7.

109 **The tobacco industry of Cuba:** For this and the following information on music at Cuban and Dominican Republic cigar factories, see Harold G. Hagopian's liner notes to *Cigar Music: Tobacco Songs from Old Havanna* (Traditional Crossroads CD 4282).

110 **Creola Johnson**: Glenn Hinson, *Virginia Traditions: Virginia Work Songs* (Ferrum, Va.: Blue Ridge Institute, Ferrum College, 1983), pp. 14, 33–34.

110 **In the fifteenth century, Venetian war galleys**: An account of early uses of automated production techniques can be found in Melvin Kranzberg and Joseph Gies, *By the Sweat of Thy Brow* (New York: Putnam, 1975), pp. 116–25.

111 **Karl Bucher's 1896 book**: Karl Bucher, *Arbeit und Rhythmus* (Leipzig: B. G. Teubner, 1909 [1896]). For Nettl's critique, see Bruno Nettl, *Music in Primitive Culture* (Cambridge, Mass.: Harvard University Press, 1956), p. 63. See also Michael Golston, " 'Im Anfang war der Rhythmus': Rhythmic Incubations in Discourses of Mind, Body, and Race from 1850–1944," *Stanford Humanities Review* 5, supplement (1996): 1–24.

111 **Certainly there are instances**: For a good account of the use of music in organizing military operations, see William H. McNeill, *Keeping Together in Time: Dance and Drill in Human History* (Cambridge, Mass.: Harvard University Press, 1995). The writings of Henry George Farmer, although out of date, also provide valuable information in this area. The topic of "war songs" deserves a separate study in its own right, which I hope to write at a later date.

112 **We know, for instance**: For various references from ancient literature on the use of music to accompany athletes, see M. L. West, *Ancient Greek Music* (Oxford: Clarendon Press, 1994), p. 30.

112 **Hans Jenny devoted years**: See Hans Jenny, *Cymatics: A Study of Wave Phenomena and Vibration,* translated by D. Q. Stephenson (Newmarket, N.H.: Macromedia, 2001).

112 **Thaddeus Bolton published**: Thaddeus L. Bolton, "Rhythm," *American Journal of Psychology* 6, no. 2 (January 1894): 145–238. The passages quoted are on pp. 235–36.

112 **Yet less than twenty years later**: Christian A. Ruckmich, "The Role of Kinaesthesis in the Perception of Rhythm," *American Journal of Psychology* 24, no. 3 (July 1913): 305–59. The passages quoted are on pp. 305–6.

112 **Describing the "general steps"**: Frederick Winslow Taylor, *The Principles of Scientific Management* (Mineola, N.Y.: Dover, 1998), p. 61.

Chapter 6: Sea and Shore

115 **"Nothing is more common"**: Richard Henry Dana, *Two Years before the Mast: A Personal Narrative of Life at Sea* (New York: Penguin, 1986), pp. 53–54. The quote in the lines following is from p. 342.

116 **Egyptian fishermen**: Lise Manniche, *Music and Musicians in Ancient Egypt* (London: British Museum Press, 1991), p. 21.

116 **Greek legend tells of Jason**: W. K. C. Guthrie, *Orpheus and Greek Religion* (Princeton: Princeton University Press, 1993), p. 28.

116 **The first recorded observation**: See Reginald Laubin and Gladys Laubin, *Indian Dances of North America: Their Importance to Indian Life* (Norman: University of Oklahoma Press, 1977), p. 3.

117 **Henry Farmer has speculated**: Henry Farmer, *The Rise and Development of Military Music* (London: Wm. Reeves, 1912), pp. 12–15.

118 **the "solace of our people"**: Quoted in David Proctor, *Music of the Sea* (London: Her Majesty's Stationary Office, 1992), p. 22.

118 **"Vayra, veyra, vayra, veyra"**: Stan Hugill, *Shanties from the Seven Seas* (Mystic, Conn.: Mystic Seaport Museum, 1994), p. 3.

119 **William Doerflinger believes**: William Main Doerflinger, *Songs of the Sailor and Lumberman* (Glenwood, Ill.: Meyerbooks, 1990), pp. xiv, 93.

119 **In 1780, a group of black Americans**: W. Jeffrey Bolster, *Black Jacks: African American Seamen in the Age of Sail* (Cambridge, Mass.: Harvard University Press, 1997), p. 5.

120 **The autobiography of the African**: Olaudah Equiano, *The Life of Olaudah Equiano, or Gustavus Vassa, the African* (Mineola, N.Y.: Dover, 1999), p. 169.

120 ***Providence City Directory***: See W. Jeffrey Bolster, *Black Jacks: African American Seamen in the Age of Sail* (Cambridge, Mass.: Harvard University Press, 1997), pp. 159–60.

120 **"Reuben Ranzo"**: Stan Hugill, *Shanties from the Seven Seas* (Mystic, Conn.: Mystic Seaport Museum, 1994), p. 175.

121 **Dana tells of the difficulty**: Richard Henry Dana, *Two Years before the Mast: A Personal Narrative of Life at Sea* (New York: Penguin, 1986), p. 343.

122 **W. F. Arnold**: F. T. Bullen and W. F. Arnold, *Songs of Sea Labor (Chanties)* (London: Orpheus Music Publishing Company, 1914), p. viii.

122 **Joanna Colcord**: Joanna C. Colcord, *Songs of American Sailormen* (New York: Oak Publications, 1964), p. 28.

122 **Hugill speculates**: Stan Hugill, *Shanties from the Seven Seas* (Mystic, Conn.: Mystic Seaport Museum, 1994), pp. 8, 22–23.

122 **Roger Abrahams**: Roger D. Abrahams, *Deep the Water, Shallow the Shore: Three Essays on Shantying in the West Indies* (Mystic, Conn.: Mystic Seaport Museum, 2002), pp. 7–14. A number of interesting firsthand accounts

from early sources have been collected in Roger D. Abrahams and John F. Szwed, eds., *After Africa: Extracts from British Travel Accounts and Journals of the Seventeenth, Eighteenth, and Nineteenth Centuries Concerning the Slaves, Their Manners, and Customs in the British West Indies* (New Haven: Yale University Press, 1983), see pp. 282, 308–9, 327–28.

122 **Despite these differences**: W. Jeffrey Bolster, *Black Jacks: African American Seamen in the Age of Sail* (Cambridge, Mass.: Harvard University Press, 1997), p. 217.

123 **"Many a Chantyman"**: F. T. Bullen and W. F. Arnold, *Songs of Sea Labor (Chanties)*, (London: Orpheus Music Publishing Company, 1914), p. vi.

123 **"white sailors spent"**: W. Jeffrey Bolster, *Black Jacks: African American Seamen in the Age of Sail* (Cambridge, Mass.: Harvard University Press, 1997), p. 217.

124 **Hugill surmises that**: Stan Hugill, *Shanties from the Seven Seas* (Mystic, Conn.: Mystic Seaport Museum, 1994), p. 19.

124 **Konrad Tegtmeier, for example**: The information from Tegtmeier and the German shanty quoted in the text are from Joanna C. Colcord, *Songs of American Sailormen* (New York: Oak Publications, 1964), p. 26.

124 **"Ah, hoo-e la-e"**: Frederick Pease Harlow, *The Making of a Sailor, or Sea Life aboard a Yankee Square-Rigger* (New York: Dover, 1988), p. 339. "Sum go cool-ie" and the comment below are from pp. 333–34.

125 **The various cultures**: For the examples cited here, see Murasaki Shikibu, *The Tale of Genji*, translated by Edward G. Seidensticker (New York: Knopf, 1994), pp. 237, 388, 393–94; Matsuo Bashô, "The Narrow Road of Oku," translated by Donald Keene, in *Anthology of Japanese Literature, from the Earliest Era to the Mid-Nineteenth Century*, edited by Donald Keene (New York: Grove Press, 1960), p. 366; Sir James George Scott, *The Burman: His Life and Notions* (New York: Norton, 1963), p. 359; Abbasuddin Ahmad, "Music and Folklore of East Pakistan," in *Music in Southeast Asia*, edited by Petronilo A. Buan and Lourdes A. Zaldarriaga (Manila: UNESCO National Commission of the Philippines, 1956), p. 95; R. H. Barnes, *Sea Hunters of Indonesia: Fishers and Weavers of Lamaler* (Oxford: Oxford University Press, 1996), p. 285; and Mervyn McLean, *Weavers of Song: Polynesian Music and Dance* (Honolulu: University of Hawaii Press, 1999), p. 373 (see also p. 182); and Richard Moyle, *Tongan Music* (Auckland: Auckland University Press, 1987), pp. 184–94.

125 **"John Kanaka"**: Stan Hugill, *Shanties from the Seven Seas* (Mystic, Conn.: Mystic Seaport Museum, 1994), pp. 212–13.

126 **Tracing the history of the classic**: See Stan Hugill, *Shanties from the*

Seven Seas (Mystic, Conn.: Mystic Seaport Museum, 1994), pp. 74–80, and *Shanties and Sailors' Songs* (New York: Frederick A. Praeger, 1969), p. 127; and Lydia Parrish, *Slave Songs of the Georgia Sea Islands* (Athens: University of Georgia Press, 1992), pp. 197, 206–8. For the version from the Bahamas recorded in 1935, refer to *Deep River of Song: Bahamas 1935: Chanteys and Anthems from Andros and Cat Island* (Rounder 11661-1822-2), recorded by Alan Lomax and Mary Elizabeth Barnicle.

128 **"The most beautiful chanty"**: John Masefield, "Sea Songs," *Temple Bar*, London, January 1906, p. 56.

128 **Herman Melville's 1849 novel**: Quoted and discussed in Roy Palmer, ed., *The Oxford Book of Sea Songs* (Oxford: Oxford University Press, 1986), p. xviii. Melville's novels are often a surprisingly rich source of musical observation; see, for example, Jan LaRue, "Melville and Musicology," *Ethnomusicology* 4, no. 2 (May 1960): 64–66; Agnes Dicken Cannon, "Melville's Use of Sea Ballads and Songs," *Western Folklore* 23 (1964): 1–16; and the chapter "Fiction and Folksong" in Kevin J. Hayes, *Melville's Folk Roots* (Kent, Ohio: Kent State University Press, 1999), pp. 13–24.

129 **"Black watermen"**: Eileen Southern, *The Music of Black Americans: A History* (New York: Norton, 1971), p. 148.

129 **The diverse workforce**: Stan Hugill, *Shanties from the Seven Seas* (Mystic, Conn.: Mystic Seaport Museum, 1994), p. 17.

129 **Frederika Bremer**: Frederika Bremer, *The Homes of the New World: Impressions of America,* translated by Mary Howitt (New York: Harper and Brothers, 1854), vol. 2, p. 174.

130 **William Alden**: William L. Alden, "Sailor Songs," *Harper's New Monthly Magazine* 65, no. 386 (July 1882): 281–86.

130 **Mary Wheeler**: Mary Wheeler, *Steamboatin' Days: Folk Songs of the River Packet Era* (Baton Rouge: Louisiana State University Press, 1944).

130 **Samuel Clemens**: Mark Twain, *Life on the Mississippi* (New York: Signet, 2001), pp. 43, 95.

130 **"In order to make"**: Mary Wheeler, *Steamboatin' Days: Folk Songs of the River Packet Era* (Baton Rouge: Louisiana State University Press, 1944), p. 60.

130 **In 1939, Herbert Halpert**: Sam Hazel performing "Heaving the Lead Line," recorded by Herbert Halpert in Greenville, Mississippi. In 1939, reissued on *Negro Work Songs and Calls* (Rounder CD 1517).

131 **As a New England engineer**: Quoted in Alan Lomax, *The Land Where the Blues Began* (New York: Pantheon, 1993), p. 217.

313 **The levee camp "hollers"**: For recorded examples, see *Negro Blues and*

Hollers (Library of Congress, Archive of Folk Culture, Rounder CD 1501), recorded by Alan Lomax, John W. Work, and Lewis Jones. Note that the term "levee camp" came to be used in describing many construction sites unrelated to the building of levees; hence these songs also played a role in work life far from the banks of the Mississippi.

131 **R. Emmet Kennedy**: R. Emmet Kennedy, *Mellows: A Chronicle of Unknown Singers* (New York: Albert and Charles Boni, 1925), pp. 164–65.

131 **"Michael, Row the Boat"**: William Francis Allen, Charles Pickard Ware and Lucy McKim Garrison, *Slave Songs of the United States* (Bedford, Mass.: Applewood Books, 1996), p. xvi.

133 **Captain Hudnall Haynie**: Quoted in Glenn Hinson, *Virginia Traditions: Virginia Work Song* (Ferrum, Va.: Blue Ridge Institute, Ferrum College, 1983), p. 13.

133 **Johann Hüttner**: Johann Christian Hüttner, "Ein Ruderliedchen aus China mit Melodie," *Journal des Luxus und der Moden* 11 (1796): 37–40; reprinted and translated in Frank Harrison, *Time, Place and Music: An Anthology of Ethnomusicological Observation, c. 1550 to c. 1800* (Amsterdam: Fritz Knuf, 1973), pp. 190–91.

134 **The collection *Min River Boat Songs***: Stella Marie Graves, *Min River Boat Songs*, collected by Malcolm Farley (New York: John Day Company, 1946).

134 **Huang Bai**: Huang Bai, "Haozi-Working Cries Turned into Art," in *Chime: Journal of the European Foundation for Chinese Music Research* 5 (spring 1992): 42–49.

134 **Antoinet Schimmelpenninck**: Antoinet Schimmelpenninck, *Chinese Folk Songs and Folk Singers: Shan'ge Traditions in Southern Jiangsu* (Leiden: CHIME Foundation, 1997), pp. 82–83.

135 **In the mid-1950s, Alan Lomax**: Lomax's description comes from "Saga of a Folksong Hunter," originally written for *HiFi/Stereo Review* in May 1960, and reprinted in the booklet accompanying *The Alan Lomax Collection Sampler*, pp. 53–54.

135 **When seeking out these songs**: Guggino's interviews quoted in Burton Bollag, "Notes from Academie: Italy," *Chronicle of Higher Education* (November 21, 1997): B2.

135 **When composer David Fanshawe**: David Fanshawe, *African Sanctus: A Story of Travel and Music* (New York: New York Times Book Company, 1975), pp. 101–2.

135 **when the pearl diving songs returned**: These songs can be heard on *Bahrain: Fidjeri: Songs of the Pearl Divers* (UNESCO D 8046), recorded by Habib Hassan Touma.

136   **In an important essay, "Sailor Songs"**: William L. Alden, "Sailor Songs," *Harper's New Monthly Magazine* 65, no. 386 (July 1882): 281–86. The passage quoted is on p. 281.

136   **As poet John Masefield wrote**: John Masefield, "Sea Songs," *Temple Bar*, London, January 1906, p. 80.

136   **Richard Henry Dana reminds**: Richard Henry Dana, *Two Years before the Mast: A Personal Narrative of Life at Sea* (New York: Penguin, 1986), pp. 161–62, 194.

136   **Frederick Pease Harlow**: Frederick Pease Harlow, *The Making of a Sailor, or Sea Life aboard a Yankee Square-Rigger* (New York: Dover, 1988), p. 273.

Chapter 7: The Lumberjack

137   **An ancient record**: See Sir Alan Gardiner, *The Egyptians* (London: Folio Society, 2000), p. 39. I have retained the conventional terminology of "cedars," although some scholars have preferred to substitute the word "pine" in this context.

137   **An ancient relief from Karnak**: See Russell Meiggs, *Trees and Timber in the Ancient Mediterranean World* (Oxford: Clarendon Press, 1982), plates 2 and 16A.

138   **"Chop, chop they cut"**: Joseph R. Allen, ed., *The Book of Songs: The Ancient Chinese Classic of Poetry*, translated by Arthur Waley and Joseph R. Allen (New York: Grove Press, 1996), p. 87. For the indication of the deforestation caused by harvesting timber, see p. 233. See also pp. 110, 137–38.

138   **"Now the men carry big wood"**: From *Huai nan zi*, written by Liu An, cited in Yang Yinliu, *Zhongguo gudai yinyue shigao* [Draft history of ancient Chinese music] (Beijing: People's Music Publishing House, 1981), vol. 1, p. 3. I am indebted to Antoinet Schimmelpenninck for calling my attention to this passage.

138   **An old travel journal**: Fynes B. Moryson, *An Itinerary Containing His Ten Yeeres Travell through the Twelve Dominions of Germany, Bohmerland Sweitzerland, Netherland Denmarke, Poland Italy, Turky France, England Scotland and Ireland* (Glasgow: J. MacLehose and Sons, 1907), vol. 1, p. 391.

139   **The initial logging camps**: For a good account of the gradual development and expansion of logging activities, see Horace P. Beck, *The Folklore of Maine* (Philadelphia: J. P. Lippincott, 1957), esp. pp. 220–26.

139   **Ethnomusicologists have provided us**: For the Warao, see Dale A. Olsen,

Music of the Warao of Venezuela (Gainesville: University Press of Florida, 1996), pp. 347–62. Feld's recording can be found on *Bosavi: Rain Forest Music from Papua New Guinea* (Smithsonian Folkways SFW CD 40487).

140   **As the late Canadian folklorist**: Edith Fowke, *Lumbering Songs from the Northern Woods* (Austin: University of Texas Press, 1970), p. 11–12.

140   **Stan Hugill has also called attention**: Stan Hugill, *Shanties from the Seven Seas* (Mystic, Conn.: Mystic Seaport Museum, 1994), p. 27.

141   **Doerflinger assigned its origins**: William Main Doerflinger, *Songs of the Sailor and Lumberman* (Glenwood, Ill.: Meyerbooks, 1990), p. 210.

141   **Fowke writes that**: The comment from Edith Fowke and the version presented here of the "Lumbercamp Song" are from Edith Fowke, *Lumbering Songs from the Northern Woods* (Austin: University of Texas Press, 1970), pp. 34–36. For a recording of one of these lumber camp songs, listed as "Colley's Run-i-o," see *Cowboy Songs, Ballads, and Cattle Calls from Texas* (Library of Congress, Archive of Folk Culture, Rounder CD 1512), recorded by John A. Lomax and Rae Korson.

141   **Edward Ives recalls**: Edward D. Ives, *Folksongs of New Brunswick* (Fredericton, New Brunswick, Canada: Goose Lane Editions, 1989), p. 58.

142   **"I am a jolly shanty boy"**: "The Jolly Shanty Boy," from E. C. Beck, *Songs of the Michigan Lumberjacks* (Ann Arbor: University of Michigan Press, 1941), p. 62. John Stone, the song writer who commemorated the miners of the California Gold Rush, takes credit for a similar composition in his collection *Put's Golden Songster* (San Francisco: D. E. Appleton and Co., 1858), p. 43: "I am a happy miner; I love to sing and dance. I wonder what my love would say, if she could see my pants."

142   **"When you pass through the dense city"**: "The Logger's Boast" from Roland P. Gray, ed., *Songs and Ballads of the Maine Lumberjack With Other Songs from Maine* (Cambridge, Mass.: Harvard University Press, 1924), p. 19.

143   **cited by Jeff Ferrell**: Jeff Ferrell, "The Brotherhood of Timber Workers and the Culture of Conflict," in *Songs About Work: Essays in Occupational Culture, for Richard A. Reuss,* edited by Archie Green (Bloomington: Folklore Institute, Indiana University, 1993), pp. 287–302.

143   **"Jimmy Judge"**: From Edith Fowke, *Lumbering Songs from the Northern Woods* (Austin: University of Texas Press, 1970), pp. 104–5.

144   **Edward Ives recounts**: Edward D. Ives, *Folksongs of New Brunswick* (Fredericton, New Brunswick, Canada: Goose Lane Editions, 1989), p. 34.

144   **"I cut down trees"**: From "The Lumberjack Song," composed by Terry Jones, Michael Palin, and Fred Tomlinson. This song figures prominently in a

comedy sketch by the Monty Python troupe, which they performed, with slight variations, on television, stage, and film. The routine typically began with a man (initially Michael Palin, later Eric Idle) who complains about his current job, finally exclaiming, "I didn't want to do this job. I wanted to be a lumberjack!" See, for example, the recording *Monty Python Sings* (Virgin 86253).

145 **"Lumberjack songs are not"**: Paul Glass and Louis C. Singer, *Songs of Forest and River Folk* (New York: Grosset and Dunlap, 1967), p. 5.

145 **"Story-tellers were almost as welcome as a good cook,"**: Donald MacKay, *The Lumberjacks* (Toronto: McGraw Hill Ryerson, 1978), p. 243; the quote following is on p. 240.

145 **After publicizing his project**: Edward D. Ives, *Larry Gorman: The Man Who Made the Songs* (Bloomington: Indiana University Press, 1964), pp. 3–4.

145 **William Doerflinger writes**: William Main Doerflinger, *Songs of the Sailor and Lumberman* (Glenwood, Ill.: Meyerbooks, 1990), pp. 213–14.

146 **Gorman even commemorated**: Quoted in Donald MacKay, *The Lumberjacks* (Toronto: McGraw Hill Ryerson, 1978), p. 246.

146 **"My name is Nellie Harrison"**: The sections from "Young Billy Crane" included here come from William Main Doerflinger, *Songs of the Sailor and Lumberman* (Glenwood, Ill.: Meyerbooks, 1990), p. 259–60.

147 **Edward Ives, who wrote**: Edward D. Ives, *Joe Scott: The Woodsman-Songmaker* (Urbana: University of Illinois Press, 1978), p. 42.

147 **"Uncle Joe" Patterson**: William Main Doerflinger, *Songs of the Sailor and Lumberman* (Glenwood, Ill.: Meyerbooks, 1990), p. 247; the full text and music of "The Plain Golden Band" appear on pp. 247–49.

148 **"Now I am only Sacker Shean's"**: "Sacker Shean's Little Girl," included in Edward D. Ives, *Joe Scott: The Woodsman-Songmaker* (Urbana: University of Illinois Press, 1978), p. 325.

148 **"He used to get twenty-five cents"**: Thomas Hoy, quoted in Edward D. Ives, *Joe Scott: The Woodsman-Songmaker* (Urbana: University of Illinois Press, 1978), p. 55.

149 **Spurgeon Allaby told**: Edward D. Ives, *Folksongs of New Brunswick* (Fredericton, New Brunswick, Canada: Goose Lane Editions, 1989), pp. 16–17.

Chapter 8: Take This Hammer!

151 **"Take my hammer"**: Newman I. White, *American Negro Folksongs* (Hatboro, Pa.: Folklore Associates, 1965), p. 259.

151 **"I say that's all about the hammer"**: Harold Courlander, *Negro Folk Music, U.S.A.* (Mineola, N.Y.: Dover, 1992), p. 101.

151 **"Today, since I'm the anvil"**: From Irving Brown, *Deep Song* (New York: Harper and Brothers, 1929), p. 153.

152 **"Dubinuška, uxnem"**: Vladimir Propp, *Down along the Mother Volga,* edited and translated by Roberta Reeder (Philadelphia: University of Pennsylvania Press, 1975), p. 33.

152 **A. L. Lloyd**: A. L. Lloyd, *Folk Song in England* (St. Albans: Paladin, 1975), p. 300. Gershon Legman quoted in "Unprintable Folklore? The Vance Randolph Collection," *Journal of American Folk-Lore* 103, no. 409 (1990): 261.

153 **Writing of the Bambara**: See Harold Courlander, with Ousmane Sako, *The Heart of the Ngoni: Heroes of the African Kingdom of Segu* (New York: Crown Publishers, 1982), p. 7. For references to other examples of magical powers attributed to African blacksmiths, see Hutton Webster, *Magic: A Sociological Study* (New York: Octagon, 1973), pp. 166–67.

154 **B. A. Botkin and Alan Lomax**: See the notes by B. A. Botkin and Alan Lomax to the collection *Negro Work Songs and Calls* (Library of Congress, Archive of Folk Culture, Rounder CD 1517), p. 10.

154 **Frederick Burton**: Frederick R. Burton, *American Primitive Music, with Especial Attention to the Songs of the Ojibways* (Port Washington, N.Y.: Kennikat Press, 1969), p. 126.

154 **But in the 1934 recording**: This performance can be found in *Negro Work Songs and Calls* (Library of Congress, Archive of Folk Culture, Rounder CD 1517).

155 **"O brother"**: Verrier Elwin, *The Agaria* (Oxford: Oxford University Press, 1991), p. 171.

155 **"Here's a health"**: See "Twankydillo" in Peter Kennedy, ed., *Folksongs of Britain and Ireland* (New York: Oak Publications, 1984), p. 619.

155 **Pip responds**: Charles Dickens, *Great Expectations* (Oxford: Oxford University Press, 1987), p. 89.

155 **Barton could not help**: William Eleazar Barton, "Recent Negro Melodies," *New England Magazine,* February 1899, reprinted in Bernard Katz, ed., *The Social History of Early Negro Music in the United States* (North Stratford, N.H.: Ayer Company Publishers, 2000), pp. 106–18 (the passages cited appear on pp. 107, 112). A commentary on Barton's research, in the context of a useful discussion of hammering songs, can be found in Archie Green, *Only a Miner: Studies in Recorded Coal-Mining Songs* (Urbana: University of Illinois Press, 1972), pp. 329–67.

156 **"Boss is call-in—huh!"**: "Hammer Song," in Natalie Curtis-Burlin, *Negro Folk-Songs: The Hampton Series Books I–IV, Complete* (Mineola, N.Y.: Dover, 2001), pp. 140–48.

157 **Dorothy Scarborough was the first**: Texts from Dorothy Scarborough, *On the Trail of Negro Folksongs* (Hatboro, Pa.: Folklore Associates, 1963), pp. 220–21.

157 **"This yere hammer"**: Joanna Colcord, *Songs of American Sailormen* (New York: Oak Publications, 1964), p. 181.

158 **"I've been a-hammering"**: "Swannanoa Town," in Cecil Sharp, *English Folk Songs from the Southern Appalachians*, edited by Maud Karpeles (London: Oxford University Press, 1960), vol. 2, pp. 42–43. Colcord, however, disputes the British origin of this material; see Joanna Colcord, *Songs of American Sailormen* (New York: Oak Publications, 1964), p. 181.

158 **Robert Winslow Gordon**: Robert Winslow Gordon, *Folk Songs of America* (New York: National Service Bureau, WPA Federal Theatre Project, 1938), p. 16.

158 **The year after Scarborough's book**: The passage from Odum and Johnson can be found in Howard W. Odum and Guy B. Johnson, *Negro Workaday Songs* (New York: Negro Universities Press, 1969), p. 106. Song texts from this volume included here are "This Ol' Hammer" (p. 111) and "If I Could Hammer Like John Henry" (p. 236).

160 **The work songs may have come first**: Johnson's comments here are from Guy B. Johnson, *John Henry: Tracking Down a Negro Legend* (New York: AMS Press, 1969), p. 85. Archie Green's response is from Archie Green, *Only a Miner: Studies in Recorded Coal-Mining Songs* (Urbana: University of Illinois Press, 1972), p. 337. The best book-length summary of the John Henry legend and research into its origins remains Brett Williams, *John Henry, A Bio-Biography* (Westport, Conn.: Greenwood Press, 1983). Two excellent articles are Paul Garon, "John Henry: The Ballad and the Legend," *AB Bookman's Weekly*, February 17, 1997, pp. 509–16; and John Garst, "Chasing John Henry in Alabama and Mississippi," *Tributaries: Journal of the Alabama Folklife Association*, no. 5 (2002): 92–129.

161 **"John Henry said to his Captain"**: The version of "John Henry" quoted here, one of innumerable published versions, comes from Brett Williams, *John Henry, A Bio-Biography* (Westport, Conn.: Greenwood Press, 1983), p iv.

161 **Here are some extracts**: For additional portions of these, and other letters, received by Johnson while searching for the identity of the real John Henry, see Guy B. Johnson, *John Henry: Tracking Down a Negro Legend* (New York: AMS Press, 1969), pp. 8–32.

162 **"What a pity"**: Guy B. Johnson, *John Henry: Tracking Down a Negro Legend* (New York: AMS Press, 1969), p. 33.

162 **Beginning in 1922, Louis Chappell**: Louis Chappell, *John Henry: A Folk-Lore Study* (Jena, Germany: Frommannsche Verlag Walter Biedermann, 1933).

163 **George Jenkins, who worked**: Quotes here are from Louis Chappell, *John Henry: A Folk-Lore Study* (Jena, Germany: Frommannsche Verlag Walter Biedermann, 1933), pp. 44–53.

164 **"In the first place"**: Quoted in Guy B. Johnson, *John Henry: Tracking Down a Negro Legend* (New York: AMS Press, 1969), p. 34–35.

165 **"Ten pound hammer"**: From MacEdward Leach, "John Henry," in *Folklore and Society: Essays in Honor of Benj. A. Botkin,* edited by Bruce Jackson (Hatboro, Pa.: Folklore Associates, 1966), pp. 93–106. For the passages cited here and below, see pp. 98–99, 104.

165 **Leach also cites**: Song text and comments from *Jamaican Song and Story,* edited by Walter Jekyll (New York: Dover, 1966), pp. 268–69.

166 **Garst has made a convincing case**: John Garst, "Chasing John Henry in Alabama and Mississippi," *Tributaries: Journal of the Alabama Folklife Association,* no. 5 (2002): 92–129.

166 **"The contractor told him"**: C. C. Spencer quoted in Guy B. Johnson, *John Henry: Tracking Down a Negro Legend* (New York: AMS Press, 1969), pp. 19–20.

Chapter 9: The Cowboy

169 **"To the Editor"**: The full text of this letter can be found in John A. Lomax, *Adventures of a Ballad Hunter* (New York: Macmillan, 1947), pp. 34–35.

170 **"Oh give me a home"**: John A. Lomax and Alan Lomax, eds., *Cowboy Songs and Other Frontier Ballads* (New York: Macmillan, 1986), pp. 424–28.

171 **"I was loafin' around"**: The version of "The Strawberry Roan" quoted here comes from its first publication in 1915 in the *Arizona Record*. The song was then called "The Outlaw Bronco," and only became known as "The Strawberry Roan" two years later when included in a collection of poems by Fletcher. The entire original version, along with the history of the song, can be found in John I. White, "The Strange Career of 'The Strawberry Roan,'" in his *Git along Little Dogies: Songs and Songmakers of the American West* (Urbana: University of Illinois Press, 1989), pp. 137–47.

173 **But other traditions**: Katie Lee, *Ten Thousand Goddam Cattle: A History*

of the American Cowboy in Song, Story and Verse (Flagstaff Ariz.: Northland Press, 1976), p. 26; J. Frank Dobie, "Versos of the Texas Vaqueros (with Music)," in *Happy Hunting Ground,* Publications of the Texas Folklore Society, number 4, edited by J. Frank Dobie (Hatboro, Pa.: Folklore Associates, 1964), pp. 30–43; John A. Lomax, "Two Songs of Mexican Cowboys from the Rio Grande Border," *Journal of American Folk-Lore* 28, no. 110 (October–December 1915): 376–78; Américo Paredes, *A Texas-Mexican Cancionero* (Austin: University of Texas Press, 1976), pp. xx–xxi.

174 **"To capture the cowboy"**: John A. Lomax, *Adventures of a Ballad Hunter* (New York: Macmillan, 1947), p. 41.

174 **the "pretentious Lomax books"**: Austin E. Fife and Alta S. Fife, eds., *Cowboy and Western Songs: A Comprehensive Anthology* (New York: Clarkson N. Potter, 1969), p. x.

174 **D. L. Wilgus, in his study**: D. L. Wilgus, *Anglo-American Folksong Scholarship since 1898* (Westport, Conn.: Greenwood Press, 1982), pp. 156–65.

175 **Jack Thorp, another great**: For more information on the relationship between Lomax and Thorp, see Guy Logsdon's foreword to *Songs of the Cowboys,* compiled and edited by N. Howard (Jack) Thorp (Lincoln: University of Nebraska Press, 1984), pp. xii–xxi; and John O. West, "Jack Thorp and John Lomax: Oral or Written Transmission?" *Western Folklore* 26 (April 1967): 113–18. I find it hard to accept Logsdon's claim that "Lomax created the impression that all of the songs were collected in the field." As we have seen, Lomax was quite open about using newspaper editors as intermediaries in gathering songs, which were sent to him by mail. He not only discusses this technique in detail in his biography, but the very process of sending his solicitation letter to a thousand newspapers in the West, each of which he asked to publish his request, would seem to refute Logsdon's assertion that he was hiding this methodology. In point of fact, Lomax never claimed that he collected all the songs himself in the field, only that the material originated as part of a tradition of oral recitation before being transcribed in print. As Lomax's whole later career demonstrated, his preference was always to do this recording himself, but like any good scholar he relied on every possible means of gathering relevant material.

175 **In 1925, Moe Asch**: For a description of this event and the impact on Asch, see Peter D. Goldsmith, *Making People's Music: Moe Asch and Folkways Records* (Washington, D.C.: Smithsonian Institution Press, 1998), pp. 56–57.

176 **John West has gathered**: John O. West, "Jack Thorp and John Lomax: Oral or Written Transmission?" *Western Folklore* 26 (April 1967): 117.

176 **precedence must go to Stanley Clark**: Stanley Clark, *The Life and Adven-*

tures of the American Cow-Boy (Providence, R.I.: published by the author, 1897).

176 **John A. Stone (known as "Old Put")**: See "Crossing the Plains" (pp. 13–15) and "Sweet Betsey from Pike" (pp. 50–52), in John A. Stone, *Put's Original California Songster,* 5th ed. (San Francisco: D. E. Appleton and Co., 1868).

176 **as well as Joaquin Miller**: For Miller's poetry of the West, see Joaquin Miller, *Songs of the Sierras* (Boston: Roberts Brothers, 1877).

176 **But perhaps the most interesting**: For the passages from Wister and Adams in the context of a discussion of different versions of this song, see John I. White, *Git along Little Dogies: Songs and Songmakers of the American West* (Urbana: University of Illinois Press, 1989), pp. 17–19.

177 **"Songs of the range"**: N. Howard (Jack) Thorp, *Pardner of the Wind* (Lincoln: University of Nebraska Press, 1977), p. 22.

177 **"It is generally thought"**: N. Howard (Jack) Thorp, *Pardner of the Wind* (Lincoln: University of Nebraska Press, 1977), pp. 29–30. See also Guy Logsdon's foreword to *Songs of the Cowboys,* compiled and edited by N. Howard (Jack) Thorp (Lincoln: University of Nebraska Press, 1984), p. xv.

177 **Margaret Larkin reached**: Margaret Larkin, ed., *Singing Cowboy: A Book of Western Songs* (New York: Oak Publications, 1963), pp. 11–12.

178 **Louise Pound offered**: Louise Pound, *Nebraska Folklore* (Lincoln: University of Nebraska Press, 1989), pp. 159–60.

178 **"Working cowboys sang"**: From the accompanying notes to *Cowboy Songs on Folkways* (Smithsonian Folkways CD SF 40043), compiled and annotated by Guy Logsdon.

180 **"One reason I believe"**: E. C. (Teddy Blue) Abbott and Helena Huntington Smith, *We Pointed Them North: Recollections of a Cowpuncher* (New York: Farrar and Rinehart, 1939), pp. 261–62.

180 **Charles Siringo, in his classic**: Charles Siringo, *A Texas Cowboy; or, Fifteen Years on the Hurricane Deck of a Spanish Pony* (New York: Penguin, 2000), pp. 32–33.

180 **"They whistled and yelped"**: Margaret Larkin, ed., *Singing Cowboy: A Book of Western Songs* (New York: Oak Publications, 1963), p. 12.

180 **John Lomax managed**: Lomax's amusing attempts to coax cattle calls from Texan Sloan Matthews can be heard on *Cowboy Songs, Ballads, and Cattle Calls from Texas* (Library of Congress, Archive of Folk Culture, Rounder CD 1512), recorded by John A. Lomax and Rae Korson.

182 **Green attributes this practice**: Archie Green, *Only a Miner: Studies in Recorded Coal-Mining Songs* (Urbana: University of Illinois Press, 1972), p. 8.

183 **"The song leader"**: Dorothy Scarborough, *On the Trail of Negro Folksongs* (Hatboro, Pa.: Folklore Associates, 1963), p. 206.

183 **"Some even subsidized"**: This and the quote below are from George Korson, *Coal Dust on the Fiddle* (Philadelphia: University of Pennsylvania Press, 1943), pp. 17–19.

184 **But Archie Green reverses**: Archie Green, *Only a Miner: Studies in Recorded Coal-Mining Songs* (Urbana: University of Illinois Press, 1972), p. 150.

185 ***Dance Tunes***: These performances can be found on *Slovak Csardas: Dance Tunes from the Pennsylvania Coal Mines* (Interstate Music, East Sussex, England, HT CD 37).

185 **Korson's *Songs and Ballads***: George Korson, *Songs and Ballads of the Anthracite Miner* (New York: Frederick H. Hitchcock, 1927).

186 **Jean Thomas, in her 1939 study**: Jean Thomas, *Ballad Makin' in the Mountains of Kentucky* (New York: Oak Publications, 1964), see especially, pp. 195–97, 246–48.

186 **Not until the release**: Archie Green, *Only a Miner: Studies in Recorded Coal-Mining Songs* (Urbana: University of Illinois Press, 1972).

186 **In 1951 Lloyd arranged**: A. L. Lloyd, *Come All Ye Bold Miners: Ballads and Songs of the Coalfields* (London: Lawrence and Wishart, 1952), p. 9.

186 **"It is doubtful whether"**: A. L. Lloyd, *Come All Ye Bold Miners: Ballads and Songs of the Coalfields* (London: Lawrence and Wishart, 1952), p. 11.

187 **"Farewell to Caledonia"**: "Farewell to Caledonia," from John C. O'Donnell, *"And Now the Fields Are Green": A Collection of Coal Mining Songs in Canada* (Sydney, Nova Scotia: University College of Cape Breton Press, 1992), pp. 41–42.

188 **Central Europe was once**: See Gerhard Heilfurth, *Das Bergmannslied: Wesen, Leben, Function* (Kassel, Germany: Bärenreiter, 1954).

188 **Vladimir Propp, in his collection**: The lyrics included here are from an interesting section titled "Worker Songs" in Vladimir Propp, *Down along the Mother Volga*, edited and translated by Roberta Reeder (Philadelphia: University of Pennsylvania Press, 1975), pp. 222–27.

189 **Sulfur mining no longer**: The quote from Alan Lomax, and the original text and translation of the song "Surfarara" sung by Rocco Meli, can be found

in the notes accompanying *Italian Treasury: Sicily* (Rounder 11661-1808-2), recorded by Alan Lomax and Diego Carpitella.

190   **Ted Chestnut who recorded**: Archie Green, *Only a Miner* (Urbana: University of Illinois Press, 1972), p. 74.

191   **"1913 Massacre" and "Ludlow Massacre"**: Performances of both of these songs can be heard on volume 3 of Woody Guthrie's *The Asch Recordings* (Smithsonian Folkways Recordings SFW CD 40112).

191   **Jean Murray, who began**: Jean A. Murray, *Music of the Alaska-Klondike Gold Rush: Songs and History* (Fairbanks: University of Alaska Press, 1999).

192   **" 'Yukona' has been received"**: Quoted in Jean A. Murray, *Music of the Alaska-Klondike Gold Rush: Songs and History* (Fairbanks: University of Alaska Press, 1999), p. 21; for the music and lyrics of "Yukona," see p. 23.

192   **"George Carmack in Bonanza Creek"**: "The Carmack Song," in Jean A. Murray, *Music of the Alaska-Klondike Gold Rush: Songs and History* (Fairbanks: University of Alaska Press, 1999), pp. 16–17.

192   **In his autobiography**: John A. Lomax, *Adventures of a Ballad Hunter* (New York: Macmillan, 1947), p. 46.

193   **"When gold was found in '48"**: John A. Stone, *Put's Original California Songster*, 5th ed. (San Francisco: D. E. Appleton and Co., 1868), p. 7.

193   **One collection of Gold Rush songs**: Karen W. Arlen, Margaret Blatt, Mary Ann Benson, and Nancie N. Kester, eds., *Days of Gold: Songs of the California Gold Rush* (Oakland, Calif.: Calicanto Associates, 1999).

193   **It is even possible that Australian**: Few American popular songs present us with a more complicated lineage than "Oh My Darling Clementine." Many scholars assert that the song has no authentic connection to the California Gold Rush, since it was apparently published in 1884; see, for example, in Richard Dwyer and Richard Lingenfelter's *The Songs of the Gold Rush* (Berkeley: University of California Press, 1964). These authors credit the composition to Percy Montrose, who reportedly wrote it as a college song. In contrast, Jon W. Finson, in *The Voices That Are Gone: Themes in 19th-Century American Popular Song* (New York: Oxford University Press, 1994), pp. 90–92, correctly links "Clementine" to H. S. Thompson, who published it in Boston in 1863, when it was known as "Down by the River Lived a Maiden." However, the song may have an even more distant origin. Fern Zalin Jones has provided me with a transcript of a radio broadcast from May 25, 1958, in which research from Gold Rush historian Jay Monaghan was cited that indicates an Australian connection to the song. The transcript reads: "Incidentally, Monaghan says, Australians did much to popularize one of the best-known songs of the day, 'Clemen-

tine.' This song appears to have been popular in the London music halls, and it was printed at an early date in Australian newspapers. Undoubtedly it was sung by Aussies on their way to this country and may have been first brought into the gold fields by them. Certainly there is no record of American 49ers singing the song on their overland journey." It is unfortunate that Monaghan, who is now dead, did not provide any details of this research in his book *Australians and the Gold Rush: California and Down Under 1849–1854* (Berkeley: University of California Press, 1966)—a book that reveals his familiarity with Australian newspaper articles from the era but pays no attention to the songs of the miners. This may be a fruitful area of inquiry for a future researcher.

194 **Yet in the years before**: Eleanor Black and Sidney Robertson, *The Gold Rush Song Book* (San Francisco: Colt Press, 1940), pp. iv–v.

194 **His trip to Wakamarina**: Thatcher's songs "Wakamarina" and "Gold's a Wonderful Thing" are from Neil Colquhoun, ed., *Song of a Young Country: New Zealand Folksongs* (Folkestone, U.K.: Bailey Brothers and Swinfen, 1973), pp. 31, 34.

195 **Tracey's 1952 book**: Hugh Tracey, *African Dances of the Witwatersrand Gold Mines* (Johannesburg: African Music Society, 1952). Some of Tracey's recordings of the music of Zambian miners have been made commercially available in *From the Copperbelt: Zambian Miners' Songs* (Original Music OMCD 004).

196 **Half a world away**: Quote from Morton Marks comes from his essay accompanying the compact disk by L. H. Corrêa de Azevedo, *Music of Ceará and Minas Gerais* (Rykodisc; in conjunction with the American Folklife Center, Library of Congress, RCD 10404). See also Corrêa de Azevedo's essay "Vissungos: Negro Work Songs of the Diamond District in Minas Gerais, Brazil," in *Music in the Americas,* edited by George List and Juan Orrego-Salas (The Hague: Mouton and Co., 1967), pp. 64–67.

196 **In Minas Gerais he found**: John Storm Roberts, *Black Music of Two Worlds* (New York: Original Music, 1972), pp. 28–29.

198 **Cohen embarked on this project**: John Cohen's comments can be found in the essay accompanying *Mountain Music of Kentucky* (Smithsonian Folkways SF CD40077), pp. 3–4, and pp. 24, 29, 33.

199 **On stage and off**: From Tom Netherland's review of Roscoe Holcomb in *Musical Traditions,* online at http://web.ukonline.co.uk/mustrad/reviews/holcombe.htm.

201 **Perhaps the largest**: The best source of information on the history of Parchman Farm is William Banks Taylor, *Down on Parchman Farm: The Great Prison in the Mississippi Delta* (Columbus, Ohio: Ohio State University Press 1999).

202 **"What in hell do you want"**: The story of these early efforts to document prison songs is told in John A. Lomax, *Adventures of a Ballad Hunter* (New York: Macmillan, 1947), pp. 153–55. The italics in the quote are Lomax's.

203 **Richard the Lionhearted**: For medieval songs of imprisonment, including those cited here by Richard the Lionhearted and Jacopone da Todi, see Peter Dronke, *The Medieval Lyric* (Suffolk, U.K.: Boydell and Brewer, 1996), pp. 212–17.

203 **A number of experts**: For a description of the rise of labor as a constituent part of a convict's daily life, see especially Dario Melossi and Massimo Pavarini, *The Prison and the Factory: Origins of the Penitentiary System*, translated by Glynis Cousin (Totowa, N.J.: Barnes and Noble Books, 1981).

203 **"furnishing felons with tools"**: John Howard, *The State of the Prisons* (London: J. M. Dent and Sons, 1929), p. 24.

203 **"exercise to martial tunes"**: Quote from Janet Semple, *Bentham's Prison: A Study of the Panopticon Penitentiary* (New York: Oxford University Press, 1993), p. 128.

203 **"Die Moorsoldaten"**: For "Die Moorsoldaten," see Arthur Kevess, ed., *German Folk Songs* (New York: Oak Publications, 1968), pp. 88–90. See also Elinor Lipper, *Eleven Years in Soviet Prison Camps*, translated by Richard and Clara Winston (Chicago: Regnery Publishing, 1951), p. 304; and Paul F. Cummins, *Dachau Song* (New York: Peter Lang Publishing, 1992), pp. 89–91.

203 **"I cannot stroll"**: Vladimir Propp, *Down along the Mother Volga*, edited and translated by Roberta Reeder (Philadelphia: University of Pennsylvania Press, 1975), p. 216. See also pp. 42–45.

205 **"If one wishes to obtain"**: Quotes from Odum and Johnson can be found in Howard W. Odum and Guy B. Johnson, *Negro Workaday Songs* (New York: Negro Universities Press, 1969), pp. 71–73.

205 **Around this same time**: Robert Winslow Gordon, "Jailhouse Songs," in *Folk Songs of America* (New York: National Service Bureau, wpa Federal Theatre Project, 1938), pp. 48–54 (see esp. p. 51). This booklet, apparently printed in limited copies on mimeographed sheets, contains the original versions of the article written for the *New York Times* in 1927 and 1928. Gordon notes that the

Times frequently excised parts of his articles, but that in this collection they are "reprinted exactly as I wrote them" (p. iii). The article on "Jailhouse Songs" originally appeared in the *New York Times Magazine* on June 19, 1927, under the title "Folk-Songs of America: Jail Ballads." Gordon's contribution to the preservation of American folk music has often been unfairly obscured by the better-known efforts of his successor at the Library of Congress, John Lomax. However, Gordon's work did much to legitimize this music, and in the 1920s no one was doing more to preserve it on recordings. See Debora Kodish, *Good Friends and Bad Enemies: Robert Winslow Gordon and the Study of American Folksong* (Urbana: University of Illinois Press, 1986).

206 **In addition to the cultural obstacles**: Lomax's complaints about his personal situation in 1932 can be found in John A. Lomax, *Adventures of a Ballad Hunter* (New York: Macmillan, 1947), p. 106.

206 **"Our best field"**: John A. Lomax, *Adventures of a Ballad Hunter* (New York: Macmillan, 1947), pp. 106–12.

207 **John Lomax "quite resolved"**: John A. Lomax, *Adventures of a Ballad Hunter* (New York: Macmillan, 1947), p. 121. See also Charles Wolfe and Kip Lornell, *The Life and Legend of Leadbelly* (New York: Da Capo, 1999), esp. pp. 113–42.

208 **"Lomax dubbed him"**: See Nolan Porterfield, *Last Cavalier: The Life and Times of John A. Lomax, 1867–1948* (Urbana: University of Illinois Press, 1996), p. 299. For John Lomax and Henry Truvillion, readers may want to consult the May–December 2000 issue of *Journal of Folklore Research,* most of which is devoted to articles analyzing the relationship between Lomax and this friend and informant.

209 **John Storm Roberts has noted**: John Storm Roberts, *Black Music of Two Worlds* (New York: Original Music, 1972), p. 144.

209 **As Bruce Jackson has explained**: From the accompanying notes to *Wake Up Dead Man: Black Convict Worksongs from Texas Prisons,* recorded and edited by Bruce Jackson (Rounder CD 2013).

210 **Alexander Solzhenitsyn's novel**: Alexander Solzhenitsyn, *One Day in the life of Ivan Denisovich,* translated by Ralph Parker (New York: E. P. Dutton, 1963), pp. 90–106.

210 **"What can be done in hell?"**: Victor Hugo, *Les Miserables,* translated by Lee Fahnestock and Norman MacAfee, based on the version by C. E. Wilbour (New York: New American Library, 1987), pp. 992–93.

211 **"Everywhere we heard of men"**: Alan Lomax, *The Land Where the Blues Began* (New York: Pantheon, 1993), p. 258.

211 **"it would require many months"**: John A. Lomax, *Adventures of a Ballad Hunter* (New York: Macmillan, 1947), p. 126.

212 **Describing its power, Alan Lomax has noted**: Comments from Alan Lomax and the text of "I'm Going to Leland" are from the accompanying notes to *Afro-American Spirituals, Work Songs and Ballads* (Library of Congress, Archive of Folk Culture, Rounder CD 1510), p. 25.

213 **"Oh, I b'lieve I git religion"**: The words of this song, called "Driving Levee," as well as those below of "Cap'n, I Got a Home in Oklahoma," are from transcripts in the American Folklife Center, Library of Congress.

213 **Although Lomax had heard**: Quotes from John Lomax can be found in "Report of J. A. Lomax 1939 So. Rec. Trip Spring" in the American Folklife Center, Library of Congress.

214 **the 1947–1948 Parchman recordings**: Recordings of music and spoken words from the 1947 and 1948 visits to Parchman, including those referred to in the text, are available on two commercial releases. *Prison Songs: Historical Recordings from Parchman Farm 1947–48,* vol. 1, *Murderous Home* (Rounder CD 1714), and vol. 2, *Don'tcha Hear Poor Mother Calling?* (Rounder CD 1715), both recorded by Alan Lomax.

218 **"I actually operated"**: From Ranko Vujosevic's interview, "Dr. Harry Oster: His Life, Career and Field Recordings," *Blues Notes: Monthly Publication of the Johnson County Blues Society*, no. 9 (August 1995): 6. I am indebted to Ranko Vujosevic for making this material available to me.

219 **One prisoner, Odea Matthews**: Work songs from Oster's fieldwork have been released on the commercial recording *Prison Worksongs* (Arhoolie CD 448). All of the songs discussed in the text can be found on this release. For other recordings of female prisoners, although with less obvious ties to physical work, see the 1939 performances documented by Herbert Halpert, included in the compilation *Field Recordings,* vol. 8, *Louisiana, Alabama, Mississippi* (Document DOCD-5598). Samuel Charters discusses "Women's Blues from Parchman Prison Farm" in his *Walking a Blues Road: A Blues Reader, 1956–2004* (London: Marion Boyans, 2004), pp. 192–98. For Oster's recordings of the blues at Angola, see *Angola Prisoners' Blues* (Arhoolie CD 419), and *20 to Life: Prison Blues* (Fuel 200 Records 302 061 161 2).

220 **"I'm goin' home, oh yes"**: "I'm Goin' Home," performed by Ervin Webb and his group, can be found on *Southern Journey,* vol. 3. *Delta Country Blues, Spirituals, Work Songs and Dance Music* (Rounder CD 1703), recorded by Alan Lomax.

221 **"O then Laz'rus"**: Recording of James Carter and group singing "Po Lazarus" can be found on *Southern Journey,* vol. 5, *Bad Man Ballads: Songs of Outlaws and Desperadoes* (Rounder CD 1705), recorded by Alan Lomax.

222 **Memorable recordings of**: The recordings referred to in the text can be found on the commercial release *Wake Up Dead Man: Black Convict Worksongs from Texas Prisons* (Rounder CD 2013), recorded by Bruce Jackson.

222 **"The songs, sometimes"**: From the introduction to Bruce Jackson, ed., *Wake Up Dead Man: Afro-American Worksongs from Texas Prisons* (Cambridge, Mass.: Harvard University Press, 1972), p. xvi.

222 **Michel Foucault has taught us**: See Michel Foucault, *Discipline and Punish: The Birth of the Prison*, translated by Alan Sheridan (New York: Pantheon, 1977), esp. pp. 231–71.

223 **"I confess a certain ambivalence"**: Bruce Jackson, ed., *Wake Up Dead Man: Afro-American Work Songs from Texas Prisons* (Cambridge: Harvard University Press, 1972), pp. xx–xxi.

224 **Interviewed by the *New York Times***: From Bernard Weinraub, "An Ex-Convict, a Hit Album, an Ending Fit for Hollywood," *New York Times*, March 3, 2002, p. A1.

Chapter 12: The Labor Movement and Songs of Work

225 **"Honor to us"**: The song is included in full in Ralph B. Locke, *Music, Musicians and the Saint-Simonians* (Chicago: University of Chicago Press, 1986), pp. 238–39 (see also p. 33 and pp. 122–53).

226 **"your devilish songs"**: Cited in Ralph B. Locke, *Music, Musicians, and the Saint-Simonians* (Chicago: University of Chicago Press, 1986), p. 165.

227 **A surviving song**: Lise Manniche, *Music and Musicians in Ancient Egypt* (London: British Museum Press, 1991), p. 19. The quote at the end of the paragraph is on p. 20.

227 **"The Cutty Wren"**: Edith Fowke and Joe Glazer, *Songs of Work and Protest* (New York: Dover, 1973), pp. 175–77.

227 **"The Diggers' Song"**: See Roy Palmer, *The Sound of History: Songs and Social Comment* (London: Pimlico, 1996), p. 245.

228 **"Chant no more"**: Quoted in E. P. Thompson, *The Making of the English Working Class* (New York: Pantheon, 1964), p. 547. For a good overview of the Luddite revolts, see Frank Peel, *The Risings of the Luddites* (New York: Augustus M. Kelley Publishers, 1968). See also George Rudé, *The Crowd in History, 1730–1848* (New York: John Wiley and Sons, 1964), esp. pp. 79–92.

228 **"Come all ye croppers"**: Frank Peel, *The Risings of the Luddites* (New York: Augustus M. Kelley Publishers, 1968), p. 120.

230 **The memorable events**: The songs of the German workers' movement cited here can be found in full in Inke Pinkert-Sältzer, ed., *German Songs: Popular, Political, Folk, and Religious* (New York: Continuum, 1997), pp. 51–84.

231 **"Left, left, left, left"**: "Der Rote Wedding," translated by Alexandra Chciuk-Celt, in *German Songs: Popular, Political, Folk, and Religious*, edited by Inke Pinkert-Sältzer (New York: Continuum, 1997), pp. 78–81.

231 **"The thirtieth of November"**: "The Owslebury Lads," from Roy Palmer, *The Painful Plough: A Portrait of the Agricultural Labourer in the Nineteenth Century from Folk Songs and Ballads and Contemporary Accounts* (Cambridge: Cambridge University Press, 1972), p. 25.

232 **"Almost without exception"**: Clark D. Halker, *For Democracy, Workers and God: Labor Song-Poems and Labor Protest, 1865–95* (Urbana: University of Illinois Press, 1991), p. 31.

233 **However, as Philip Foner**: Philip S. Foner, *American Labor Songs of the Nineteenth Century* (Urbana: University of Illinois Press, 1975), p. xiv.

234 **the AFL "had no songs."**: Philip S. Foner, *American Labor Songs of the Nineteenth Century* (Urbana: University of Illinois Press, 1975), p. 168.

234 **"There are 38 songs"**: Cited in Philip S. Foner, *The Case of Joe Hill* (New York: International Publishers, 1965), p. 11.

234 **"It is the first strike"**: Ray Stannard Baker, quoted in Evelyn Alloy, *Working Women's Music: The Songs and Struggles of Women in the Cotton Mills, Textile Plants and Needle Trade* (Somerville, Mass.: New England Free Press, 1976), p. 13.

235 **Brenda McCallum, in her research**: See Brenda McCallum, "The Gospel of Black Unionism," from *Songs about Work: Essays in Occupational Culture, for Richard A. Reuss*, edited by Archie Green (Bloomington, Indiana: Folklore Institute, Indiana University, 1993), pp. 108–33; for Jesus's admonition "Stay in Union," see p. 125.

236 **In 1913 Hill traveled**: For an overview of the trial and conviction of Joe Hill as well as its aftermath, see Philip S. Foner, *The Case of Joe Hill* (New York: International Publishers, 1965). Foner's account is sympathetic to Hill and attempts to exonerate him from the charges that led to his conviction.

236 **"I dreamed I saw Joe Hill"**: For this and other songs about and by Joe Hill, see the compilation recording *Don't Mourn—Organize! Songs of Labor Songwriter Joe Hill* (Smithsonian Folkways CD SF 40026), produced by Elaine Taylor.

237 **"Music Penetrates"**: Quoted in Robbie Lieberman, *"My Song Is My Weapon": People's Songs, American Communism, and the Politics of Culture, 1930–1950* (Urbana: University of Illinois Press, 1989), p. 28.

237 **"There were three brothers"**: Lyrics from the songs by Charles Seeger and Elie Siegmeister are included in David K. Dunaway, "Charles Seeger and Carl Sands: The Composers' Collective," *Ethnomusicology* 24, no. 2 (May 1980): 159–68. See also Ann M. Pescatello, *Charles Seeger: A Life in American Music* (Pittsburgh: University of Pittsburgh Press, 1992), pp. 109–19.

238 **"As Arthur Berger explains"**: Arthur Berger, "Copland and the Audience of the Thirties," *Partisan Review* (Fall 2001): 575.

239 **Aunt Molly Jackson**: For more information, see Shelly Romalis's biography of Jackson: *Pistol Packin' Mama: Aunt Molly Jackson and the Politics of Folksong* (Urbana: University of Illinois Press, 1999).

240 **"People all over the world"**: Quoted in Robbie Lieberman, *"My Song Is My Weapon": People's Songs, American Communism, and the Politics of Culture, 1930–1950* (Urbana: University of Illinois Press, 1989), p. 68.

240 **When Fowke and Glazer's anthology**: Edith Fowke and Joe Glazer, *Songs of Work and Protest* (New York: Dover, 1973).

Chapter 13: Music and the Modern Worker

243 **Writer William Branigin**: William Branigin, "Sweatshops Once Again Common," *Washington Post*, February 16, 1997, p. A1.

243 **In his classic memoir**: Ben Hamper, *Rivethead: Tales from the Assembly Line* (New York: Warner Books, 1991), p. xviii.

244 **Few psychologists have bothered**: For a few examples of this depressing and growing body of literature, see Charles Areni and David Kim, "The Influence of Background Music on Shopping Behavior, Classical Versus Top-Forty Music in a Wine Store," *Advances in Consumer Research* 20 (1993): 336–40; Judy Alpert and Mark Alpert, "Music Influences on Mood and Purchases Intentions," *Psychology and Marketing* 7, no. 2 (Summer 1990): 109–33; Ronald Milliman, "Using Background Music to Affect the Behavior of Supermarket Shoppers," *Journal of Marketing* 46 (1982): 86–91; Gerald Gorn, "The Effects of Music in Advertising on Choice Behavior: A Classical Conditioning Approach," *Journal of Marketing* 46 (Winter 1982): 94–101; James Kellaris, Anthony Cox, and Dena Cox, "The Effect of Background Music on Ad Processing: A Contingency Explanation," *Journal of Marketing* 57 (October 1993): 114–25; James Kellaris and Anthony Cox, "The Effects of Background Music in Advertising: A Reassessment," *Journal of Consumer Research* 16 (June 1989), pp. 113–18; Patricia Cain Smith and Ross Curnow, "'Arousal Hypothesis' and the Effects of Music on Purchasing Behaviour," *Journal of Applied Psychology* 50 (June 1966): 255–86.

244 " 'Tatoes! Peaches!'": Street cries here are from B. A. Botkin, *Sidewalks of America: Folklore, Legends, Sagas, Traditions, Customs, Songs, Stories and Sayings of City Folk* (Indianapolis: Bobbs-Merrill, 1954), pp. 573–76. See also other examples and references in chapter 5 of this volume.

245 **A researcher for the Federal Writers' Project**: Terry Roth, "Street Cries and Criers of New York," Federal Writers' Project report, dated November 3, 1938, eight pages. For prohibitions on street music, see R. Murray Schafer, *The Tuning of the World* (New York: Knopf, 1977), pp. 66–67.

245 **"Pepsi-Cola hits the spot"**: Alas, no Toynbee or Thucydides—or even a Nettl or Blacking—has come forward to write the authoritative history of the commercial jingle, perhaps the best-known music of the last century. But some amateur sleuths have documented this rich modern tradition on the Internet. See, for example, David Jackson Shields's research at www.classicthemes.com; Robin Johnson's work at http://www.geocities.com/foodedge/index.htm; and Pete Wilson's online archive at www.pete-wilson.net.

246 **"Our Vision Is One Honeywell"**: For the complete lyrics to this song, as well as information on many other corporate anthems, see Chris Raettig's web site devoted to the subject: *http://www.zdnet.co.uk/specials/2002/it-anthems/*.

249 **Gerald Porter estimates**: Porter, in *The English Occupational Song* (Umea: University of Umea, 1992), p. 11, judges from songs available in various collections.

249 **"Men and women work"**: Ken Emerson, *Doo-Dah: Stephen Foster and the Rise of American Popular Culture* (New York: Simon and Schuster, 1997), p. 166.

250 **At almost the same time**: See Eleanor Selfridge-Field, "Experiments with Melody and Meter, or the Effects of Music: The Edison-Bingham Music Research," *Musical Quarterly* 81, no. 2 (1997): 291–310 (the passages quoted are on pp. 295–96).

250 **Charles M. Diserens, who waxed**: Charles M. Diserens, *The Influence of Music on Behavior* (Princeton: Princeton University Press, 1926), pp. 96–97, 104–23, 155–205.

253 **Another researcher, H. C. Smith**: For an account of the scientific studies supporting the use of music at work, as part of a detailed history of Muzak, see Joseph Lanza, *Elevator Music: A Surreal History of Muzak, Easy Listening and Other Moodsong* (New York: St. Martin's Press, 1994), especially pp. 42–45.

Epilogue: The Calling

258 **Abraham Maslow, in his highly influential**: Abraham Maslow, *Motivation and Personality*, 2nd ed. (New York: Harper and Row, 1970), p. 48.

✳ RECOMMENDED LISTENING

The following list is not meant to be a complete discography of work songs, but instead offers a few suggestions for readers interested in listening to some recordings related to the subject matter of this book. As such, I have focused on music that has been made available in compact disc format and that can be found (for the most part) without resorting to archives and dealers in rare recordings.

Aboard the Cutty Sark (Greenwich Village GVRXCD 207), sung by Stan Hugill. This live recording, made in 1979, finds the great shanty scholar and singer in top form, as he discourses and performs aboard the *Cutty Sark*.

Afro-American Spirituals, Work Songs and Ballads (Rounder CD 1510), recorded by John Lomax. This collection includes some of the most important field recordings of traditional work songs made during the first half of the twentieth century.

American Industrial Ballads (Smithsonian Folkways CD SF 40058), sung by Pete Seeger. These two dozen ballads, from a range of sources and industries, were recorded by Pete Seeger in 1956.

Back in the Saddle Again (New World 80314-2), produced by Charles Seemann. This is the best available compilation of early cowboy music. The two discs include performances by real cowboys (Harry McClintock, Jules Verne Allen), record industry cowboys (Jimmie Rodgers, John I. White), and early movie cowboys (Ken Maynard, Gene Autry). But for cattle calls and field recordings, see John Lomax's *Cowboy Songs, Ballads, and Cattle Calls from Texas,* described below.

Bahrain: Fidjeri: Songs of the Pearl Divers (UNESCO D 8046), recorded by Habib Hassan Touma. These performances from 1976 document the revival of the pearl diving songs, which had fallen into disuse during the 1930s but are again sung widely, although now at weddings and other functions rather than in work situations.

Benin: Bariba and Somba Music (UNESCO D 8057), recorded by Simha Arom. This release includes good examples of hunting and grinding songs from West Africa.

Bosavi: Rain Forest Music from Papua New Guinea (Smithsonian Folkways SFW

CD 40487), recorded by Steven Feld. This set of three compact discs documents both traditional and contemporary music from the interior of Papua New Guinea, including a number of interesting work songs.

Burkina Faso: Anthology of the Music of the Gan (Buda Records/Musique du Monde 92709-2), recorded by Patrick Kersale. This release includes songs recorded between 1994 and 1997 that are used in threshing, grinding, the preparation of shea butter, and other daily tasks.

Caribbean Island Music: Songs and Dances of Haiti, the Dominican Republic, and Jamaica (Nonesuch 72047-2), recorded by John Storm Roberts. This collection includes excellent examples of Jamaican digging songs, as well as a recording of singing workers at a Dominican Republic tobacco-grinding factory.

Cattle Calls: Early Cowboy Music and Its Roots (Rounder CD 1101), compiled by Douglas B. Green. Although not as comprehensive as the New World collection described above, this is an excellent survey of early cowboy songs.

Coal Mining Women (Rounder CD 4025), produced by Guy and Candie Carawan. These twenty tracks combine the sensibilities of the protest song with the traditions of country and bluegrass music.

Cowboy Songs, Ballads, and Cattle Calls from Texas (Library of Congress, Archive of Folk Culture, Rounder CD 1512), recorded by John A. Lomax and Rae Korson. This collection includes cattle calls recorded in Texas in 1942, as well as an interesting comparison between a lumbercamp song, "Colley's Run-I-O," and its cowboy equivalent, "The Buffalo Skinners."

Cowboy Songs on Folkways (Smithsonian Folkways CD SF 40043), compiled and annotated by Guy Longsdon. There is no shortage of recorded cowboy music on the marketplace, but few recordings can match the authenticity of these performances drawn from the extensive catalogue of the Folkways label.

Deep River of Song, Bahamas 1935: Chanteys and Anthems from Andros and Cat Island (Rounder 11661-1822-2), recorded by Alan Lomax and Mary Elizabeth Barnicle. This collection includes fifteen shanties and launching songs, including an early version of the "Sloop John B," later popularized by the Weavers and the Beach Boys.

Deep River of Song: Big Brazos: Texas Prison Recordings, 1933 and 1934 (Rounder 11661-1826-2), recorded by John A. Lomax and Alan Lomax. These performances draw on the rich singing traditions from the large Texas prison farms along the Brazos and Trinity rivers.

Diamonds in the Rough: 25 Years with the Men of the Deeps (Men of the Deeps Music 02 50398), under the direction of John C. O'Donnell. This collection presents a variety of performances, recorded over the course of three decades by the Men of the Deeps, a Cape Breton coal miners' chorus.

Don't Mourn—Organize! Songs of Labor Songwriter Joe Hill (Smithsonian Folkways CD SF 40026), performed by various artists and produced by Lori Elaine Taylor. Fifteen songs by or about the noted labor songwriter, whose controversial conviction and execution on murder charges in 1915 served as a rallying point for the union movement.

Echoes of the Forest: Music of the Central African Pygmies (Ellipsis Arts 4020), recorded by Colin Turnbull, Jean-Pierre Hallet, and Louis Sarno. These recordings, accompanied by excellent notes and photographs, were made over several decades by different researchers and capture the hauntingly beautiful music of hunting communities from Central Africa.

Field Recordings, Vol. 1, *Virginia 1936–1941* (Document DOCD 5575), compiled and produced by Johnny Parth. This excellent release includes work songs recorded at the state penitentiary in Richmond, Virginia, in 1936.

Field Recordings, Vol. 2, *North and South Carolina, Georgia, Tennessee, Arkansas 1926–43* (Document DOCD 5576), compiled and produced by Johnny Parth. This compilation includes street cries for selling blackberries and flowers (from South Carolina), work songs (from Tennessee), and other interesting material.

Field Recordings, vol. 3, *Mississippi 1936–1942* (Document DOCD 5577), compiled and produced by Johnny Parth. This release brings together a number of fascinating field recordings, including Mississippi sounding calls, and an excellent example of a cornfield holler sung by Thomas Marshall.

Field Recordings, vol. 6, *Texas 1933–1958* (Document DOCD 5580), compiled and produced by Johnny Parth. This recording features many of John and Alan Lomax's most compelling recordings from the 1930s, including noteworthy performances by James "Iron Head" Baker, Jesse Bradley, Clyde Hill, and Henry Truvillion.

Folk Music of Albania (Topic TSCD904), recorded by A. L. Lloyd. This recording, made by A. L. Lloyd in 1965, features the music of the herders of the Albanian countryside.

Folk Music of Bulgaria (Topic TSCD905), recorded by A. L. Lloyd. This collection, including a number of work songs, draws on recordings made by A. L. Lloyd during two trips to Bulgaria in 1954 and 1963.

Harvest Song: Music from Around the World Inspired by Working the Land (Ellipsis Arts 4040), compiled by Jeffrey Charno. This accessible recording documents harvest and field music from a range of cultures and includes detailed notes and photographs.

The Iron Muse: A Panorama of Industrial Folk Music (Topic TSCD465), compiled and produced by Tony Engle. This release, addressing a number of occupations, features songs drawn from the rich archives of Topic Records.

Italian Treasury: Sicily (Rounder 11661-1808-2), recorded by Alan Lomax and

Diego Carpitella. This compilation, recorded in 1954, includes a variety of fascinating work songs, including threshing and reaping songs as well as performances by miners and carters.

Ivory Coast: Music of the Wè (Le Chant du Monde CNR 2741105), recorded by Hugo Zemp. This collection of music from West Africa, recorded in 1965 and 1967, includes songs involved in hunting, tree felling, and sowing rice.

"Jüüzli": Yodel of the Muotatal (Le Chant du Monde LDX 274 716), recorded by Hugo Zemp. This compilation includes close to one hour of yodeling from Switzerland, recorded in 1979.

Leadbelly: Take This Hammer (RCA Bluebird 82876-50957-2), recorded by R. P. Wetherald and Alan Lomax. These 1940 tracks feature the great blues and folk singer performing traditional work songs. These are somewhat more polished than the typical field recordings of these songs—especially when Leadbelly is accompanied by the Golden Gate Jubilee Quartet, who serve as the lead singer's "work gang" on most of the performances. The overall effect, however, is impressive and moving.

Mountain Music of Peru, vol. 1 (Smithsonian Folkways SF 40020), recorded by John Cohen. This release provides a glimpse of the music of isolated herding villages in Andean Peru.

Music from Vietnam (Caprice Records CAP 21406), recorded by Torbjorn Samuelsson. This project, from Hanoi in 1991, includes a traditional needle-threading song performed in a modernized arrangement.

Music of Ceará and Minas Gerais (Rykodisc: RCD 10404), recorded by Luiz Heitor Corrêa de Azevedo. These recordings, made between 1942 and 1945, document the folk music of Brazil, including the songs of the miners of Minas Gerais. The apparent linkages to traditional African music are striking.

Music of the Rainforest Pygmies (Lyrichord 7157), recorded by Colin M. Turnbull. This landmark release focuses on music from the Ituri rainforest, and includes hunting songs and a honey-gathering song.

Navajo Songs (Smithsonian Folkways SF 40403), recorded by Laura Bolton. These recordings from New Mexico and Arizona include representative examples of Navajo corn-grinding songs.

Negro Blues and Hollers (Library of Congress, Archive of Folk Culture, Rounder CD 1501), recorded by Alan Lomax, John W. Work, and Lewis Jones. These recordings, from 1941 and 1942, include examples of levee camp hollers and cornfield hollers.

Negro Work Songs and Calls (Library of Congress, Archive of Folk Culture, Rounder CD 1517), recorded by Herbert Halpert, John Lomax, Ruby T. Lomax, Alan Lomax, and Mary E. Barnicle. This release ranks among the best collections available of African American work songs.

Prison Songs: Historical Recordings from Parchman Farm, 1947–48, vol. 1, *Mur-*

derous Home (Rounder CD 1714), and vol. 2, *Don'tcha Hear Poor Mother Calling?* (Rounder CD 1715), recorded by Alan Lomax. These landmark recordings rank among the most important documents of prison work songs in America.

Prison Worksongs (Arhoolie CD 448), recorded by Harry Oster. This release contains nineteen performances, mostly recorded at Louisiana's Angola State Farm in the late 1950s.

Railroad Songs and Ballads (Library of Congress, Archive of Folk Culture, Rounder CD 1508), edited by Archie Green. This compilation includes train calling and track lining songs, as well as a number of ballads related to railroads.

A Salty Fore Topman (SHCD 002), recorded by Stan Hugill with Stormalong John. The singing by Hugill of these classic shanties is so energetic and prepossessing that is hard to believe that he was in his eighties when the music was recorded.

Scottish Tradition 3: Waulking Songs from Barra (Greentrax CDTRAX 9003), edited by Peter Cooke. This recording focuses on performances of the waulking songs used to accompany the preparation of tartan cloth.

Sea Songs and Shanties: Traditional English Sea Songs and Shanties from the Last Days of Sail (Saydisc CD-SDL 405), recorded by Peter Kennedy. These recordings, made between 1950 and 1960, provide a good introduction to the music of British sailors.

Songs and Ballads of the Anthracite Miners (Library of Congress, Archive of Folk Culture, Rounder CD 1502), recorded by George Korson. These recordings were made in Pennsylvania in 1946, and represent an important milestone in the documentation of occupational music in the United States.

Songs and Ballads of the Bituminous Miners (Library of Congress, Archive of Folk Culture, Rounder CD 1522), recorded by George Korson. Supported by a grant from the United Mine Workers, Korson made these recordings during his 1940 visits to mining communities in Pennsylvania, Ohio, Kentucky, West Virginia, and Alabama.

Southern Journey, vol. 1, *Voices from the American South* (Rounder CD 1701), recorded by Alan Lomax. This opening release in Rounder's noteworthy *The Alan Lomax Collection* includes original and re-created work songs, among them Bessie Jones singing a moving version of "Sink 'em Low" and Ed Lewis leading a group of prisoners in "Dollar Mamie."

Southern Journey, vol. 3, *Delta Country Blues, Spirituals, Work Songs and Dance Music* (Rounder CD 1703), recorded by Alan Lomax. This release includes several outstanding examples of prison work songs and field hollers, including "Stewball," led by Ed Lewis, and "I'm Goin' Home," led by Ervin Webb.

Spin the Weaver's Song (Green Linnet GLCD 2106), recorded by Carla Sciaky.

Compelling interpretations of traditional songs about spinning and weaving are offered here by Sciaky, who draws from more than a dozen different cultures.

To Catch a Fine Buck Was My Delight: Songs of Hunting and Poaching (Topic TSCD 668), produced by Tony Engle and Reg Hall. This collection, accompanied by extensive notes, presents a range of traditional songs about hunting drawn from the Topic Records catalogue.

Traditional Music of Peru, vol. 2, *The Mantaro Valley* (Smithsonian Folkways SFCD 40467), compiled and edited by Raúl R. Romero. This release includes a range of work-related songs, including those used in farming, building, and cattle raising.

A Treasury of Library of Congress Field Recordings (Rounder CD 1500), selected by Stephen Wade. This is perhaps the best single-disc compilation of traditional American music; it includes, among other gems, songs of workers recorded by John Lomax, Alan Lomax, and George Korson.

Virginia Traditions: Virginia Work Songs (Global Village Music CD1007), song selection and notes by Glenn Hinson. This excellent compilation features recordings from the 1930s through the 1980s. A forty-page accompanying book with in-depth commentary by Hinson is also available from the Blue Ridge Institute at Ferrum College, Virginia.

Vocal and Instrumental Music of Mongolia (Topic TSCD 909), recorded by Jean Jenkins. The compilation, recorded in 1974, includes milking songs of herding communities and other examples of traditional Mongolian music.

Wake Up Dead Man: Black Convict Worksongs from Texas Prisons (Rounder CD 2013), recorded and edited by Bruce Jackson. This recording documents the final days of prison work songs at a number of Texas penitentiaries in the 1960s.

We've Received Orders to Sail: Jackie Tar at Sea and on Shore (Topic TSCD 662), produced by Tony Engle and Reg Hall. These recordings, mostly unaccompanied vocals, capture the authentic music of sailors—sometimes rough, occasionally out of tune, but often deeply moving.

Women's Songs: A Musical Anthology of the Arabian Peninsula (VDE 783), recorded by Simon Jargy and others. This recording includes corn grinding and grain milling songs, as well as ceremonial songs associated with pearl diving.

Work and Pray: Historic Negro Spirituals and Work Songs from West Virginia (WVU Press Sound Archive 4), recorded by Cortez D. Reece. These recordings, made by Cortez Reece as part of his dissertation research from 1949 to 1953, include many excellent examples of songs performed by retired railroad workers.

World Library of Folk and Primitive Music, vol. 4, *Spain* (Rounder 11661 1744-2), recorded by Alan Lomax and Jeannette Bell. This fascinating release includes work songs for threshing, reaping, and making linen.

Yodeling Song of the Alps (Legacy International CD 310). This release includes yodels from Switzerland, Germany, and Austria.

BIBLIOGRAPHY

Abbott, E. C. (Teddy Blue), and Helena Huntington Smith. *We Pointed Them North: Recollections of a Cowpuncher.* New York: Farrar and Rinehart, 1939.

Abokor, Axmed Cali. *Somali Pastoral Work Songs: The Poetic Voice of the Politically Powerless.* Uppsala, Sweden: Department of Social and Economic Geography, Uppsala University, 1993.

Abrahams. Roger D. *Deep the Water, Shallow the Shore: Three Essays on Shantying in the West Indies.* Mystic, Conn.: Mystic Seaport Museum, 2002.

———. *Singing the Master: The Emergence of African-American Culture in the Plantation South.* New York: Penguin, 1993.

Abrahams, Roger D., and John F. Szwed, eds. *After Africa: Extracts from British Travel Accounts and Journals of the Seventeenth, Eighteenth, and Nineteenth Centuries concerning the Slaves, their Manners, and Customs in the British West Indies.* New Haven, Conn.: Yale University Press, 1983.

Adovasio, James M., Olga Soffer, and Bohuslav Klima. "27,000 Years Old Textile Fragments." *Textile Forum* (June 1996): 10–11.

Ajuwon, Bade. *Funeral Dirges of Yoruba Hunters.* New York: NOK Publishers, 1982.

Alden, William L. "Sailor Songs." *Harper's New Monthly Magazine* 65, no. 386 (July 1882): 281–86.

Alford, Violet. "Music and Dance of the Swiss Folk." *Musical Quarterly* 27, no. 4 (October 1941): 500–15.

Allen, Joseph R., ed. *The Book of Songs: The Ancient Chinese Classic of Poetry.* Translated by Arthur Waley and Joseph R. Allen. New York: Grove Press, 1996.

Allen, Jules Verne. *Cowboy Lore.* San Antonio, Tex.: Naylor Company, 1943.

Allen, William Francis, Charles Pickard Ware, and Lucy McKim Garrison. *Slave Songs of the United States.* Bedford, Mass.: Applewood Books, 1996.

Alloy, Evelyn. *Working Women's Music: The Songs and Struggles of Women in the Cotton Mills, Textile Plants and Needle Trade.* Somerville, Mass.: New England Free Press, 1976.

Alpert, Judy, and Mark Alpert. "Music Influences on Mood and Purchases Intentions." *Psychology and Marketing* 7, no. 2 (summer 1990): 109–33.

Areni, Charles, and David Kim. "The Influence of Background Music on Shopping Behavior: Classical versus Top-Forty Music in a Wine Store." *Advances in Consumer Research* 20 (1993): 336–40.

Aristotle. *Aristotle's Politics*. Translated by Benjamin Jowett. New York: Modern Library, 1943.

Arlen, Karen W., Margaret Blatt, Mary Ann Benson, and Nancie N. Kester, eds. *Days of Gold: Songs of the California Gold Rush*. Oakland, Calif.: Calicanto Associates, 1999.

Attali, Jacques. *Noise: The Political Economy of Music*. Translated by Brian Massumi. Minneapolis: University of Minnesota Press, 1985.

Aulestia, Gorka. *Improvisational Poetry from the Basque Country*. Translated by Linda White. Reno: University of Nevada Press, 1995.

Austin, J. L. *How to Do Things with Words*. Cambridge, Mass.: Harvard University Press, 1962.

Bahr, Donald M., Joseph Giff, and Manuel Havier. "Piman Songs on Hunting." *Ethnomusicology* 23, no. 2 (May 1979): 245–96.

Bai, Huang. "Haozi-Working Cries Turned into Art." *Chime: Journal of the European Foundation for Chinese Music Research* 5 (spring 1992): 42–49.

Barber, Elizabeth Wayland. *Women's Work: The First Twenty Thousand Years*. New York: Norton, 1994.

Barnes, R. H. *Sea Hunters of Indonesia: Fishers and Weavers of Lamalera*. New York: Oxford University Press, 1996.

Bartenieff, Irmgard, with Dori Lewis. *Body Movement: Coping with the Environment*. Amsterdam: Gordon and Breach, 1980.

Bartok, Béla. *Hungarian Folk Music*. Translated by Michael D. Calvocoressi. London: Oxford University Press, 1931.

——. *Turkish Folk Music from Asia Minor*. Edited by Benjamin Suchoff. Princeton, N.J.: Princeton University Press, 1976.

Barty-King, Hugh. *The Drum*. London: Royal Tournament, 1988.

Barua, Hem. *Folk Songs of India*. New Delhi: Indian Council for Cultural Relations, 1963.

Bass, Robert Duncan. "Negro Songs from the Pedee Country." *Journal of American Folklore* 44, no. 174 (October-December 1931), 418–36.

Beach, Hugh. *A Year in Lapland: Guest of the Reindeer Herders*. Seattle: University of Washington Press, 2001.

Beck, E. C. *Songs of the Michigan Lumberjacks*. Ann Arbor: University of Michigan Press, 1941.

Beck, Horace P. *The Folklore of Maine*. Philadelphia: J. P. Lippincott, 1957.

Benet, Sula. *Song, Dance, and Customs of Peasant Poland*. Cornwall Bridge, Conn.: Polish Heritage Publications, 1996.

Berger, Arthur. "Copland and the Audience of the Thirties." *Partisan Review* (fall 2001): 570–76.

Bierhorst, John. *A Cry from the Earth: Music of the North American Indians.* Santa Fe, N.M.: Ancient City Press, 1979.

Black, Eleanor, and Sidney Robertson. *The Gold Rush Song Book.* San Francisco: Colt Press, 1940.

Blacking, John. *How Musical Is Man?* Seattle: University of Washington Press, 1973.

Boatright, Mody C., Wilson M. Hudson, and Allen Maxwell. *Folk Travelers: Ballads, Tales, and Talk.* Dallas: Southern Methodist University Press, 1953.

Bollag, Burton. "Notes from Academie: Italy." *Chronicle of Higher Education,* November 21, 1997, p. B2.

Bolster, W. Jeffrey. *Black Jacks: African American Seamen in the Age of Sail.* Cambridge, Mass.: Harvard University Press, 1997.

Bolton, Laura. *The Music Hunter.* New York: Doubleday, 1969.

Bolton, Thaddeus L. "Rhythm." *American Journal of Psychology* 6, no. 2 (January 1894): 145–238.

Botkin, B. A. *Sidewalks of America: Folklore, Legends, Sagas, Traditions, Customs, Songs, Stories and Sayings of City Folk.* Indianapolis: Bobbs-Merrill, 1954.

——, ed. *A Treasury of Western Folklore.* New York: Bonanza Books, 1980.

Bowra, Cecil Maurice. *Primitive Song.* New York: Mentor Books, 1963.

Brandel, Rose. *The Music of Central Africa: An Ethnomusicological Study.* The Hague: Martinus Nijhoff, 1961.

Brandolini, Raffaele. *On Music and Poetry (De musica et poetica; 1513).* Translated by Ann E. Moyer. Tempe: Arizona Center for Medieval and Renaissance Studies, 2001.

Brannen, Noah, and William Elliott, eds. and trans. *Festive Wine: Ancient Japanese Poems from the Kinkafu.* Tokyo: John Weatherhill, 1969.

——. *Songs They Sang in Ancient Japan: Isles of the Dragonfly.* Tokyo: Heine, 1995.

Bremer, Frederika. *The Homes of the New World: Impressions of America.* Translated by Mary Howitt. 2 vols. New York: Harper and Brothers, 1854.

Brown, Frank C. *The Frank C. Brown Collection of North Carolina Folklore.* Vol. 5, *The Music of the Folk Songs.* Edited by Jan Philip Schinhan. Durham, N.C.: Duke University Press, 1962.

——. *The Frank C. Brown Collection of North Carolina Folklore.* Vol. 7, *Superstitions from North Carolina.* Edited by Wayland D. Hand. Durham: Duke University Press, 1964.

Brown, Irving. *Deep Song: Adventures with Gypsy Songs and Singers in Andalusia and Other Lands, with Original Translations.* New York: Harper and Brothers, 1929.

Brown, Judith. "A Note on the Division of Labor by Sex." *American Anthropologist* 72, no. 5 (1970): 1073–78.

Browne, Ray B. "Some Notes on the Southern 'Holler.'" *Journal of American Folklore* 67, no. 263 (January-March 1954): 73–77.

Buan, Petronilo A., and Lourdes A. Zaldarriaga, eds. *Music in Southeast Asia.* Manila: UNESCO National Commission of the Philippines, 1956.

Bucher, Karl. *Arbeit und Rhythmus.* Leipzig: B. G. Teubner, 1909.

Bukofzer, Manfred. "Popular Polyphony in the Middle Ages." *Musical Quarterly* 26, no. 1 (January 1940): 31–49.

Bullen, F. T., and W. F. Arnold. *Songs of Sea Labor (Chanties).* London: Orpheus Music Publishing Company, 1914.

Burney, Charles. *Dr. Burney's Musical Tours in Europe.* Edited by Percy A. Scholes. 2 vols. London: Oxford University Press, 1959.

Burt, Struthers. *The Diary of a Dude-Wrangler.* New York: Charles Scribner's Sons, 1925.

Burton, Frederick R. *American Primitive Music, with Especial Attention to the Songs of the Ojibways.* Port Washington, N.Y.: Kennikat Press, 1969.

Canetti, Elias. *Crowds and Power.* New York: Continuum, 1978.

Cannon, Agnes Dicken. "Melville's Use of Sea Ballads and Songs." *Western Folklore* 23 (1964): 1–16.

Carroll, Joseph. "Steven Pinker's Cheesecake for the Mind." *Philosophy and Literature* 22, no. 2 (1998): 478–85.

Catlin, George. *Letters and Notes on the Manners, Customs, and Conditions of North American Indians.* 2 vols. New York: Dover, 1973.

Cavanagh, Beverly. *Music of the Netsilik Eskimo: A Study of Stability and Change.* 2 vols. Ottawa: National Museums of Canada, 1982.

Chagnon, Napoleon. *Yanomamo: The Fierce People.* 3rd ed. New York: Holt, Rinehart and Winston, 1983.

Chalmers, James. *Adventures in New Guinea.* London: Religious Tract Society, 1886.

Chappell, Louis. *John Henry: A Folk-Lore Study.* Jena, Germany: Frommannsche Verlag Walter Biedermann, 1933.

Charry, Eric. *Mande Music.* Chicago: University of Chicago Press, 2000.

Charters, Samuel. *Walking a Blues Road: A Blues Reader, 1956–2004.* London: Marion Boyars, 2004.

Chatwin, Bruce. *The Songlines.* New York: Viking, 1987.

Christian, Charles M. *Black Saga: The African American Experience.* New York: Houghton Mifflin, 1995.

Clark, Stanley. *The Life and Adventures of the American Cow-Boy.* Providence, R.I.: published by the author, 1897.

Coffin, Tristram Potter, and Hennig Cohen, eds. *Folklore from the Working Folk of America.* New York: Anchor Press, 1973.

Cohen, Norm. *Long Steel Rail: The Railroad in American Folksong.* Urbana: University of Illinois Press, 1981.

Colleu, Michel. "The Songs of the French Sailors: The Rediscovery of the French Tradition." Translated by Janet Russell and Paul Wright. *Musical Traditions* 9 (autumn 1991): 18–30.

Colquhoun, Neil, ed. *Song of a Young Country: New Zealand Folksongs.* Folkestone, U.K.: Bailey Brothers and Swinfen, 1973.

Cooke, Brett, and Frederick Turner, eds. *Biopoetics: Evolutionary Explorations in the Arts.* Lexington, Ky.: International Conference on the Unity of the Sciences, 1999.

Copper, Bob. *A Song for Every Season: A Hundred Years of a Sussex Farming Family.* Devon, U.K.: Country Book Club, 1972.

Corbin, Alain. *Village Bells: Sound and Meaning in the Nineteenth-Century French Countryside.* Translated by Martin Thom. London: Papermac, 1999.

Courlander, Harold. *Negro Folk Music, U.S.A.* Mineola, N.Y.: Dover, 1992.

——, with Ousmane Sako. *The Heart of the Ngoni: Heroes of the African Kingdom of Segu.* New York: Crown Publishers, 1982.

Cox, John Harrington. "John Hardy." *Journal of American Folk-Lore* 32, no. 126 (October-December 1919): 505–20.

Crafts, Susan D., Daniel Cavicchi, and Charles Keil. *My Music.* Hanover, N.H.: Wesleyan University Press, 1993.

Crawley, Ernest. *Dress, Drinks, and Drums: Further Studies of Savages and Sex.* Edited by Theodore Besterman. London: Methuen, 1931.

Creighton, Helen. *A Life in Folklore.* Toronto: McGraw Hill, 1975.

——. *Songs and Ballads from Nova Scotia.* New York: Dover, 1966.

Cremonesi, Carla. *"Chansons de geste" e "Chanson de toile."* Rome: Tipografia Cuggiani, 1943.

Crossley-Holland, Nicole. *Living and Dining in Medieval Paris: The Household of a Fourteenth-Century Knight.* Cardiff: University of Wales Press, 1996.

Cummins, Paul F. *Dachau Song.* New York: Peter Lang Publishing, 1992.

Curtis, Natalie. *The Indians' Book: Songs and Legends of the American Indians.* New York: Dover Publications, 1968.

——. *Songs and Tales from the Dark Continent.* Mineola, N.Y.: Dover Publications, 2002.

Curtis-Burlin, Natalie. *Negro Folk Songs: The Hampton Series Books I–IV Complete.* Mineola, N.Y.: Dover Publications, 2001.

Csikszentmihalyi, Mihaly. *Flow: The Psychology of Optimal Experience.* New York: Harper and Row, 1990.

Dallas, Karl, ed. *One Hundred Songs of Toil.* London: Wolfe Publishing, 1974.

Dana, Richard Henry. *Two Years before the Mast: A Personal Narrative of Life at Sea.* New York: Penguin, 1986.

Danto, Arthur C. *The State of the Art.* New York: Prentice-Hall, 1987.

De Gourmont, Remy. *The Natural Philosophy of Love.* Translated by Ezra Pound. New York: Liveright, 1942.

DeNora, Tia. *Music in Everyday Life*. Cambridge: Cambridge University Press, 2000.

Densmore, Frances. *Chippewa Music*. Smithsonian Institution: Bureau of American Ethnology, Bulletin 45. Washington, D.C.: Government Printing Office, 1910.

——. *Chippewa Music—II*. Smithsonian Institution: Bureau of American Ethnology, Bulletin 53. Washington, D.C.: Government Printing Office, 1913.

——. *Menominee Music*. Smithsonian Institution: Bureau of American Ethnology, Bulletin 102. Washington, D.C.: Government Printing Office, 1932.

——. *Seminole Music*. Smithsonian Institution: Bureau of American Ethnology, Bulletin 161. Washington, D.C.: Government Printing Office, 1956.

——. *Teton Sioux Music*. Smithsonian Institution: Bureau of American Ethnology, Bulletin 61. Washington, D.C.: Government Printing Office, 1918.

——. *Yuman and Yaqui Music*. Smithsonian Institution: Bureau of American Ethnology, Bulletin 110. Washington, D.C.: Government Printing Office, 1932.

Dett, R. Nathaniel. "Review of *Negro Workaday Songs*." In "The R. Nathaniel Dett Reader," special issue, *Black Sacred Music* (fall 1991): 52–53.

Deva, Indra. *Folk Culture and Peasant Society in India*. Jaipur, India: Rawat, 1989.

Dickens, Charles. *Great Expectations*. Oxford: Oxford University Press, 1987.

Diserens, Charles M. *The Influence of Music on Behavior*. Princeton, N.J.: Princeton University Press, 1926.

Dissanayake, Ellen. *Homo Aestheticus: Where Art Comes from and Why*. Seattle: University of Washington Press, 1995.

Dobie, J. Frank, ed. *Happy Hunting Ground*. Publications of the Texas Folklore Society, number 4. Hatboro, Pa.: Folklore Associates, 1964.

——. *Rainbow in the Morning*. Publications of the Texas Folklore Society, number 5. Hatboro, Pa.: Folklore Associates, 1965.

Doerflinger, William Main. *Songs of the Sailor and Lumberman*. Glenwood, Ill.: Meyerbooks, 1990.

Dorson, Richard M., ed. *African Folklore*. Bloomington: Indiana University Press, 1972.

Dorson, R. M., Toichi Mabuchi, and Tokihiko Oto, eds. *Studies in Japanese Folklore*. Bloomington: Indiana University Press, 1963.

Douglass, Frederick. *Narrative of the Life of Frederick Douglass, an American Slave, Written by Himself*. New York: Signet, 1997.

Dronke, Peter. *The Medieval Lyric*. Suffolk, U.K.: D. S. Brewer, 1996.

Dunaway, David K. "Charles Seeger and Carl Sands: The Composers' Collective." *Ethnomusicology* 24, no. 2 (May 1980): 159–68.

Dwyer, Richard A., and Richard E. Lingenfelter, eds. *The Songs of the Gold Rush*. Berkeley: University of California Press, 1964.

Eckstorm, Fannie Hardy, and Mary Winslow Smyth. *Minstrelsy of Maine: Folk-Songs and Ballads of the Woods and Coast.* Boston: Houghton Mifflin, 1927.

Eliade, Mircea. *Shamanism: Archaic Techniques of Ecstasy.* Translated by Willard R. Trask. Princeton, N.J.: Princeton University Press, 1964.

Elkin, A. P., and Trevor A. Jones. *Arnhem Land Music.* Oceania Monographs, no. 9. Sydney: University of Sydney, 1958.

Elson, Louis C. *Curiosities of Music: A Collection of Facts Not Generally Known, Regarding the Music of Ancient and Savage Nations.* Boston: Oliver Ditson and Co., 1880.

Elwin, Verrier. *The Agaria.* Oxford: Oxford University Press, 1991.

——. *The Baiga.* London: John Murray, 1939.

——. *Folk-Songs of Chhattisgarh.* Madras: Oxford University Press, 1946.

Emeneau, M. B. *Toda Songs.* Oxford: Clarendon Press, 1971.

Emerson, Ken. *Doo-Dah: Stephen Foster and the Rise of American Popular Culture.* New York: Simon and Schuster, 1997.

Epstein, Dena J. *Sinful Tunes and Spirituals: Black Folk Music to the Civil War.* Urbana: University of Illinois Press, 1977.

Equiano, Olaudah. *The Life of Olaudah Equiano, or Gustavus Vassa, the African.* Mineola, N.Y.: Dover, 1999.

Evans-Pritchard, E. E. *The Nuer.* Oxford: Oxford University Press, 1940.

——. *Nuer Religion.* New York: Oxford University Press, 1974.

——. *Witchcraft, Oracles and Magic among the Azande.* Oxford: Clarendon Press, 1937.

Evers, Larry, and Felipe S. Molina. *Yaqui Deer Songs, Maso Bwikam: A Native American Poetry.* Sun Tracks: An American Indian Literary Series, vol. 14. Tucson: Sun Tracks; University of Arizona Press, 1987.

Falkenhausen, Lothar von. *Suspended Music: Chime-Bells in the Culture of Bronze Age China.* Berkeley: University of California Press, 1993.

Fanshawe, David. *African Sanctus: A Story of Travel and Music.* New York: New York Times Book Company, 1975.

Farmer, Henry. *The Rise and Development of Military Music.* London: Wm. Reeves, 1912.

Feld, Steven. *Sound and Sentiment: Birds, Weeping, Poetics, and Song in Kaluli Expression.* Philadelphia: University of Pennsylvania Press, 1990.

Fenster, Mark. "Preparing the Audience, Informing the Performers: John A. Lomax and *Cowboy Songs and Other Frontier Ballads.*" American Music (fall 1989): 260–77.

Fife, Austin E., and Alta S. Fife, eds. *Cowboy and Western Songs: A Comprehensive Anthology.* New York: Clarkson N. Potter, 1969.

——. *Heaven on Horseback: Revivalist Songs and Verse in the Cowboy Idiom.* Western Texts Society Series, vol. 1, no. 1. Logan: Utah State University Press, 1970.

Finger, Charles J. *Sailor Chanties and Cowboy Songs*. Girard, Kans.: Haldeman-Julius Company, 1923.

Finley, M. I. *Early Greece: The Bronze and Archaic Ages*. New York: Norton, 1981.

Finson, Jon W. *The Voices That Are Gone: Themes in Nineteenth Century American Popular Song*. New York: Oxford University Press, 1994.

Foner, Philip S. *American Labor Songs of the Nineteenth Century*. Urbana: University of Illinois Press, 1975.

———. *The Case of Joe Hill*. New York: International Publishers, 1965.

Foner, Philip S., and Ronald L. Lewis, eds. *Black Workers: A Documentary History from Colonial Times to the Present*. Philadelphia: Temple University Press, 1989.

Foucault, Michel. *Discipline and Punish: The Birth of the Prison*. Translated by Alan Sheridan. New York: Pantheon, 1977.

Fowke, Edith. *Lumbering Songs from the Northern Woods*. Austin: University of Texas Press, 1970.

———, and Joe Glazer. *Songs of Work and Protest*. New York: Dover, 1973.

Frazer, James G. *The Golden Bough: A Study In Comparative Religion*. New York: Gramercy, 1981.

Gardiner, Alan. *The Egyptians*. London: Folio Society, 2000.

Garon, Paul. "John Henry: The Ballad and the Legend." *AB Bookman's Weekly*, February 17, 1997, pp. 509–16.

Garst, John. "Chasing John Henry in Alabama and Mississippi." *Tributaries: Journal of the Alabama Folklife Association*, no. 5 (2002): 92–129.

Gaski, Harald, ed. *In the Shadow of the Midnight Sun: Contemporary Sami Prose and Poetry*. Karasjok, Norway: Davvi Girji, 1997.

Genovese, Eugene D. *Roll, Jordan, Roll: The World the Slaves Made*. New York: Vintage, 1976.

Gillespie, Angus K. *Folklorist of the Coal Fields: George Korson's Life and Work*. University Park: Pennsylvania State University Press, 1980.

Gioia, Ted. *The Imperfect Art: Reflections on Jazz and Modern Culture*. New York: Oxford University Press, 1988.

Glass, Paul, and Louis C. Singer. *Songs of Forest and River Folk*. New York: Grosset and Dunlap, 1967.

Glassie, Henry, Edward D. Ives, and John F. Szwed. *Folksongs and Their Makers*. Bowling Green, Ohio: Bowling Green University Popular Press, 1970.

Goehr, Lydia. *The Imaginary Museum of Musical Works: An Essay in the Philosophy of Music*. New York: Oxford University Press, 1994.

Goldsmith, Peter D. *Making People's Music: Moe Asch and Folkways Records*. Washington, D.C.: Smithsonian Institution Press, 1998.

Golston, Michael. " 'Im Anfang war der Rhythmus': Rhythmic Incubations in Discourses of Mind, Body, and Race from 1850–1944." *Stanford Humanities Review* 5, supplement (1996): 1–24.

Gordon, Robert. *Can't Be Satisfied: The Life and Times of Muddy Waters.* Boston: Little, Brown, 2002.

Gordon, Robert Winslow. *Folk Songs of America.* New York: National Service Bureau, WPA Federal Theatre Project, 1938.

Gorer, Geoffrey. *Africa Dances: A Book about West African Negroes.* New York: Norton, 1962.

Gorn, Gerald. "The Effects of Music in Advertising on Choice Behavior: A Classical Conditioning Approach." *Journal of Marketing* 46 (winter 1982): 94–101.

Gover, Charles E. *The Folk-Songs of Southern India.* New Delhi: Rupa, 2002.

Grant, James Augustus. *A Walk Across Africa, or Domestic Scenes from My Nile Journal.* Edinburgh: William Blackwood and Sons, 1864.

Graves, Stella Marie. *Min River Boat Songs.* Collected by Malcolm Farley. New York: John Day Company, 1946.

Gray, Roland P., ed. *Songs and Ballads of the Maine Lumberjack, with Other Songs from Maine.* Cambridge, Mass.: Harvard University Press, 1924.

Grayston, Dave. "Music While You Work." *Industrial Management* 4 (June 1974): 38–39.

Green, Archie. "Labor Songs: An Ambiguous Legacy." *Journal of Folklore Research* 28, nos. 2–3 (1991): 93–102.

——. *Only a Miner: Studies in Recorded Coal-Mining Songs.* Urbana: University of Illinois Press, 1972.

——, ed. *Songs about Work: Essays in Occupational Culture, for Richard A. Reuss.* Folklore Institute, Indiana University, Special Publications, no. 3. Bloomington: Indiana University, 1993.

Greenleaf, Elisabeth Bristol. *Ballads and Sea Songs of Newfoundland.* Cambridge, Mass.: Harvard University Press, 1933.

Greenway, John. *American Folksongs of Protest.* Philadelphia: University of Pennsylvania Press, 1953.

Guthrie, W. K. C. *Orpheus and Greek Religion.* Princeton, N.J.: Princeton University Press, 1993.

Guttsman, W. L. *Workers' Culture in Weimar Germany: Between Tradition and Commitment.* Oxford: Berg, 1990.

Gutzwiller, Kathryn J. *Theocritus Pastoral Analogies: The Formation of a Genre.* Madison: University of Wisconsin Press, 1991.

Hahn Man-young. "Folk Songs of Korean Rural Life and Their Characteristics Based on the Rice Farming Songs." *Asian Music* 9, no. 2 (1978): 21–28.

Halker, Clark D. *For Democracy, Workers, and God: Labor Song-Poems and Labor Protest, 1865–95.* Urbana: University of Illinois Press, 1991.

Hall, Jacquelyn D., James Leloudis, Robert Korstad, Mary Murphy, Lu Ann Jones, and Christopher B. Daley. *Like a Family: The Making of a Southern Cotton Mill World.* Chapel Hill: University of North Carolina Press, 1987.

Hamper, Ben. *Rivethead: Tales from the Assembly Line*. New York: Warner Books, 1991.

Hanson, Victor. *The Other Greeks*. New York: Free Press, 1995.

Harker, Dave. *Fakesong: The Manufacture of British "Folksong," 1700 to the Present Day*. Milton Keynes, U.K.: Open University Press, 1985.

Harlow, Frederick Pease. *The Making of a Sailor, or Sea Life about a Yankee Square-Rigger*. New York: Dover, 1988.

Harner, Michael. *The Jívaro: People of the Sacred Waterfalls*. Berkeley: University of California Press, 1984.

Harrison, Frank, ed. *Time, Place and Music: An Anthology of Ethnomusicological Observation, c. 1550 to c. 1800*. Amsterdam: Fritz Knuf, 1973.

Hart, Mickey, and Fredric Lieberman, with D. A. Sonneborn. *Planet Drum: A Celebration of Percussion and Rhythm*. San Francisco: HarperCollins, 1991.

Hart, Mickey, and Jay Stevens, with Fredric Lieberman. *Drumming at the Edge of Magic: A Journey into the Spirit of Percussion*. San Francisco: Harper-Collins, 1990.

Hattori, Ryutaro, ed. *Japanese Folk Songs*. Tokyo: Japan Times, Ltd., 1971.

Hayes, Kevin J. *Melville's Folk Roots*. Kent, Ohio: Kent State University Press, 1999.

Heilfurth, Gerhard. *Das Bergmannslied: Wesen, Leben, Function*. Kassel, Germany: Bärenreiter, 1954.

Herodotus. *The History*. Translated by David Green. Chicago: University of Chicago Press, 1987.

Heth, Charlotte, ed. *Native American Dance: Ceremonies and Social Traditions*. Washington, D.C.: National Museum of the American Indian, Smithsonian Institution, 1992.

Hindley, Charles. *A History of the Cries of London: Ancient and Modern*. Detroit: Singing Tree Press, 1969.

Hinson, Glenn. *Virginia Traditions: Virginia Work Songs*. Ferrum, Va.: Blue Ridge Institute, Ferrum College, 1983.

Hofmann, Charles. *Drum Dance: Legends, Ceremonies, Dances and Songs of the Eskimos*. Toronto: W. J. Gage, 1974.

Honigsheim, Paul. *Music and Society: The Later Writings of Paul Honigsheim*. New York: John Wiley and Sons, 1973.

Howard, John. *The State of the Prisons*. London: J. M. Dent and Sons, 1929.

Howitt, A. W. *The Native Tribes of South-East Australia*. Canberra: Aboriginal Studies Press, 1996.

Huc, Evariste-Regis, and Joseph Gabet. *Travels in Tartary, Thibet and China, 1844–46*. London: George Routledge and Sons, 1928.

Hughes, David W. "Japanese 'New Folk Songs,' Old and New." *Asian Music* 22, no. 1 (fall/winter 1990–91): 1–49.

Hugill, Stan. *Shanties and Sailors' Songs*. New York: Frederick A. Praeger, 1969.

——. *Shanties from the Seven Seas*. Mystic, Conn.: Mystic Seaport Museum, 1994.

Hugo, Victor. *Les Miserables*. Translated by Lee Fahnestock and Norman Mac-Afee, based on the version by C. E. Wilbour. New York: New American Library, 1987.

Huizinga, Johan. *The Waning of the Middle Ages*. Translated by Herfsttijd der Middeleeuwen. New York: St. Martin's Press, 1984.

Hulting, Jane. *Muzak: A Study in Sonic Ideology*. Master's thesis, Annenberg School of Communications, University of Southern California, 1988.

Huntington, Gale. *Songs the Whalemen Sang*. New York: Dover, 1970.

Ignatieff, Michael. *A Just Measure of Pain: The Penitentiary in the Industrial Revolution, 1750–1850*. London: Penguin, 1989.

Irigaray, Louis, and Theodore Taylor. *A Shepherd Watches, A Shepherd Sings*. New York: Doubleday, 1977.

Ives, Edward D. *Folksongs of New Brunswick*. Fredericton, New Brunswick, Canada: Goose Lane Editions, 1989.

——. *Joe Scott: The Woodsman-Songmaker*. Urbana: University of Illinois Press, 1978.

——. *Larry Gorman: The Man Who Made the Songs*. Bloomington: Indiana University Press, 1964.

Jackson, Bruce, ed. *Wake Up Dead Man: Afro-American Work Songs from Texas Prisons*. Cambridge, Mass.: Harvard University Press, 1972.

Jekyll, Walter, ed. *Jamaican Song and Story*. New York: Dover, 1966.

Johnson, Guy B. *John Henry: Tracking Down a Negro Legend*. New York: AMS Press, 1969.

Johnston, Thomas F. "The Function of Tsonga Work-Songs." *Journal of Music Therapy* 10, no. 3 (fall 1973): 156–64.

Jones, Mari Riess, and Susan Holleran, eds. *Cognitive Bases of Musical Communication*. Washington, D.C.: American Psychological Association, 1992.

Juslin, Patrik N., and John A. Sloboda, eds. *Music and Emotion: Theory and Research*. New York: Oxford University Press, 2001.

Karpeles, Maud, ed. *Folk Songs of Europe*. London: Novello and Co., 1963.

——. *An Introduction to English Folk Song*. London: Oxford University Press, 1973.

Katz, Bernard, ed. *The Social History of Early Negro Music in the United States*. North Stratford, N.H.: Ayer Company Publishers, 2000.

Keene, Donald, ed. *Anthology of Japanese Literature, from the Earliest Era to the Mid-Nineteenth Century*. New York: Grove Press, 1960.

Keeney, Bradford, ed. *Kalahari Bushmen Healers*. Philadelphia: Ringing Rocks Press, 1999.

Keil, Charles. *Tiv Song: The Sociology of Art in a Classless Society*. Chicago: University of Chicago Press, 1979.

Kellaris, James, and Anthony Cox. "The Effects of Background Music in Advertising: A Reassessment." *Journal of Consumer Research* 16 (June 1989): 113–18.

Kellaris, James, Anthony Cox, and Dena Cox. "The Effect of Background Music on Ad Processing: A Contingency Explanation." *Journal of Marketing* 57 (October 1993): 114–25.

Kennedy, Emmet R. *Mellows: A Chronicle of Unknown Singers*. New York: Albert and Charles Boni, 1925.

Kennedy, Peter, ed. *Folksongs of Britain and Ireland*. New York: Oak Publications, 1984.

Kevess, Arthur, ed. *German Folk Songs*. New York: Oak Publications, 1968.

Kilker, Catherine A., and Charles R. Koch. *Sheep and Man: An American Saga*. Denver: American Sheep Producers Council, 1978.

King, A. Hyatt. "Mountains, Music and Musicians." *Musical Quarterly* 31, no. 4 (October 1945): 395–419.

Kisliuk, Michelle. *Seize the Dance! BaAka Musical Life and the Ethnography of Performance*. New York: Oxford University Press, 2001.

Klinck, Anne L., and Ann Marie Rasmussen, eds. *Medieval Woman's Song: Cross-Cultural Approaches*. Philadelphia: University of Pennsylvania Press, 2002.

Kodish, Debora. *Good Friends and Bad Friends: Robert Winslow Gordon and the Study of American Folksong*. Urbana: University of Illinois Press, 1986.

Korson, George. *Coal Dust on the Fiddle*. Philadelphia: University of Pennsylvania Press, 1943.

——, ed. *Pennsylvania Songs and Legends*. Baltimore: Johns Hopkins Press, 1960.

——. *Songs and Ballads of the Anthracite Miner*. New York: Frederick H. Hitchcock, 1927.

Koskoff, Ellen, ed. *Women and Music in Cross-Cultural Perspective*. Contributions in Women's Studies, no. 79. Westport, Conn.: Greenwood Press, 1987.

Kranzberg, Melvin, and Joseph Gies. *By the Sweat of Thy Brow*. New York: Putnam, 1975.

Kubik, Gerhard. *Africa and the Blues*. Jackson: University of Mississippi Press, 1999.

Kyagambiddwa, Joseph. *African Music from the Source of the Nile*. New York: Frederick A. Praeger, 1955.

Laade, Wolfgang. "The Corsican Tribbiera: A Type of Work Song." *Ethnomusicology* 6, no. 3 (September 1962): 181–85.

Lai, T. C., and Robert Mok. *Jade Flute: The Story of Chinese Music*. New York: Schocken Books, 1985.

Lame Deer, John (Fire), and Richard Erdoes. *Lame Deer Seeker of Venus: The Life of a Sioux Medicine Man*. New York: Touchstone, 1972.

Landes, David S. *Revolution in Time*. Cambridge, Mass.: Belknap Press, 1983.

Lanza, Joseph. *Elevator Music: A Surreal History of Muzak, Easy Listening and Other Moodsong*. New York: St. Martin's Press, 1994.

Larkin, Margaret, ed. *Singing Cowboy: A Book of Western Songs*. New York: Oak Publications, 1963.

LaRue, Jan. "Melville and Musicology." *Ethnomusicology* 4, no. 2 (May 1960): 64–66.

Laubin, Reginald, and Gladys Laubin. *Indian Dances of North America: Their Importance to Indian Life*. Norman: University of Oklahoma Press, 1977.

Le Goff, Jacques. *Time, Work, and Culture in the Middle Ages*. Translated by Arthur Goldhammer. Chicago: University of Chicago Press, 1980.

Leary, James P. *Yodeling in Dairyland: A History of Swiss Music in Wisconsin*. Mount Horeb: Wisconsin Folk Museum, 1991.

Lee, Katie. *Ten Thousand Goddam Cattle: A History of the American Cowboy in Song, Story and Verse*. Flagstaff, Ariz.: L. Northland Press, 1976.

Lee, Richard B., and Irven Devore, eds. *Man the Hunter*. Hawthorne, N.Y.: Aldine de Gruyter, 1968.

Legman, Gershon. "Unprintable Folklore? The Vance Randolph Collection." *Journal of American Folklore* 103, no. 409 (1990): 259–300.

Levtzion, N., and J. F. P. Hopkins, eds. *Corpus of Early Arabic Sources for West African History*. Translated by J. F. P. Hopkins. Princeton, N.J.: Markus Wiener Publishers, 2000.

Lewin, Olive. *"Rock It Come Over": The Folk Music of Jamaica*. Kingston, Jamaica: University of the West Indies Press, 2000.

Lewis, Charles Bertram. "The Origin of the Weaving Songs and the Theme of the Girl at the Fountain." *Publications of the Modern Language Association of America* 37, no. 2 (June 1922): 141–81.

Lewis, Matthew. *Journal of a West India Proprietor*. New York: Oxford University Press, 1999.

Lewis, Orlando F. *The Development of American Prisons and Prison Customs, 1776–1845*. Montclair, N.J.: Patterson Smith, 1967.

Lieberman, Robbie. *"My Song Is My Weapon": People's Songs, American Communism, and the Politics of Culture, 1930–1950*. Urbana: University of Illinois Press, 1989.

Lindell, Kristina, Håkan Lundström, Jan-Olof Svantesson, and Damrong Tayanin. *The Kammu Year: Its Lore and Music*. London: Curzon Press, 1982.

Ling, Jan. *A History of European Folk Music*. Translated by Linda Schenk and Robert Schenk. Rochester, N.Y.: University of Rochester Press, 1997.

Lingenfelter, Richard E., and Richard A. Dwyer, eds. *Songs of the American West*. Berkeley: University of California Press, 1968.

Lipper, Elinor. *Eleven Years in Soviet Prison Camps.* Translated by Richard Winston and Clara Winston. Chicago: Regnery Publishing, 1951.

Lipsitz, George. *Rainbow at Midnight: Labor and Culture in the 1940s.* Urbana: University of Illinois Press, 1994.

List, George, and Juan Orrego-Salas. *Music in the Americas.* The Hague: Mouton and Co., 1967.

Lloyd, A. L. *Come All Ye Bold Miners: Ballads and Songs of the Coalfields.* London: Lawrence and Wishart, 1952.

——. *Folk Songs of the Americas.* New York: Oak Publications, 1966.

——. *Folk Song in England.* St. Albans: Paladin, 1975.

Locke, Ralph B. *Music, Musicians, and the Saint-Simonians.* Chicago: University of Chicago Press, 1986.

Logsdon, Guy, ed. *"The Whorehouse Bells Were Ringing" and Other Songs Cowboys Sing.* Urbana: University of Illinois Press, 1995.

Lomax, Alan. *The Land Where the Blues Began.* New York: Pantheon, 1993.

——. *Selected Writings, 1934–1997.* New York: Routledge, 2003.

Lomax, Alan, Woody Guthrie, and Pete Seeger. *Hard-Hitting Songs for Hard-Hit People.* New York: Oak Publications, 1967.

Lomax, John A. *Adventures of a Ballad Hunter.* New York: Macmillan, 1947.

——. "Two Songs of Mexican Cowboys from the Rio Grande Border." *Journal of American Folk-Lore* 28, no. 110 (October-December 1915): 376–78.

Lomax , John A., and Alan Lomax. *American Ballads and Folk Songs.* New York: Macmillan, 1934.

——, eds. *Cowboy Songs and Other Frontier Ballads.* New York: Macmillan, 1986.

Lonsdale, Steven. *Animals and the Origins of Dance.* New York: Thames and Hudson, 1981.

Lorant, Stefan, ed. *The New World: The First Pictures of America.* New York: Duell, Sloan and Pearce, 1946.

Lord, Albert B. *The Singer of Tales.* Edited by Stephen Mitchell and Gregory Nagy. Cambridge, Mass.: Harvard University Press, 2000.

Lowie, Robert H. *The Crow Indians.* Lincoln: University of Nebraska Press, 1983.

Luboff, Norman, and Win Stracke. *Songs of Man: The International Book of Folk Songs.* New York: Walton Music Corporation, 1969.

Luce, S. B. *Naval Songs: A Collection of Original, Selected, and Traditional Sea Songs.* Portland, Maine: Longwood Press, 1976.

MacCormick, Donald. *Hebridean Folksong: A Collection of Waulking Songs.* Edited by J. L. Campbell. Oxford: Clarendon Press, 1969.

MacGillivray, Allister. *The Men of the Deeps: The Continuing Saga.* New Waterford, Nova Scotia: Men of the Deeps Music, 2000.

MacKay, Donald. *The Lumberjacks.* Toronto: McGraw Hill Ryerson, 1978.

Mackay-Smith, Alexander. *The Songs of Fox-Hunting.* Milkwood, Va.: American Foxhound Club, 1974.

Macrobius. *Commentary on the Dream of Scipio.* Translated by William Harris Stahl. New York: Columbia University Press, 1952.

Mahar, William J. *Behind the Burnt Cork Mask: Early Blackface Minstrelsy and Antebellum American Popular Culture.* Urbana: University of Illinois Press, 1999.

Malone, Bill C. *Singing Cowboys and Musical Mountaineers: Southern Culture and the Roots of Country Music.* Athens: University of Georgia Press, 1993.

Manniche, Lise. *Music and Musicians in Ancient Egypt.* London: British Museum Press, 1991.

Masefield, John. "Sea Songs." *Temple Bar.* January 1906, pp. 56–80.

Maslow, Abraham. *Motivation and Personality.* New York: Harper and Row, 1970.

Matthews, Washington. *The Night Chant: A Navaho Ceremony.* Salt Lake City: University of Utah Press, 1995.

McAllester, David P., ed. *Readings in Ethnomusicology.* New York: Johnson Reprint Corporation, 1971.

McClary, Susan. *Conventional Wisdom: The Content of Musical Form.* Berkeley: University of California Press, 2000.

McLean, Mervyn. *Weavers of Song: Polynesian Music and Dance.* Honolulu: University of Hawaii Press, 1999.

McNeill, William H. *Keeping Together in Time: Dance and Drill in Human History.* Cambridge, Mass.: Harvard University Press, 1995.

McRandle, James H. *The Antique Drums of War.* College Station: Texas A&M Press, 1994.

Meiggs, Russell. *Trees and Timber in the Ancient Mediterranean World.* Oxford: Clarendon Press, 1982.

Melossi, Dario, and Massimo Pavarini. *The Prison and the Factory: Origins of the Penitentiary System.* Translated by Glynis Cousin. Totowa, N.J.: Barnes and Noble Books, 1981.

Merriam, Alan B. *Ethnomusicology of the Flathead Indian.* New York: Wenner-Gren Foundation for Anthropological Research, 1967.

Messenger, Betty. *Picking Up the Linen Threads: A Study in Industrial Folklore.* Austin: University of Texas Press, 1980.

Miller, Joaquin. *Songs of the Sierra.* Boston: Roberts Brothers, 1877.

Milliman, Ronald. "Using Background Music to Affect the Behavior of Supermarket Shoppers." *Journal of Marketing* 46 (1982): 86–91.

Moberg, Carl-Allan. *Studien zur Schwedischen Volksmusik.* Studia Musicologica Upsaliensia Nova Series 5. Uppsala, Sweden: Acta Universitatis Upsaliensis, 1971.

Monaghan, Jay. *Australians and the Gold Rush: California and Down 1849–54*. Berkeley: University of California Press, 1966.

Morgan, Lewis Henry. *The League of the Ho-De'-No-Sau-Nee, or Iroquois*. North Dighton, Mass.: J. G. Press, 1995.

Morris, Alton C. *Folksongs of Florida*. Gainesville: University of Florida Press, 1990.

Moryson, Fynes B. *An Itinerary Containing His Ten Yeeres Travell through the Twelve Dominions of Germany, Bohmerland Sweitzerland, Netherland Denmarke, Poland Italy, Turky France, England Scotland and Ireland*. Vol. 1. Glasgow: J. MacLehose and Sons, 1907.

Moyle, Richard. *Tongan Music*. Auckland: Auckland University Press, 1987.

Mullen, Patrick B. "The Dilemma of Representation in Folklore Studies: The Case of Henry Truvillion and John Lomax." *Journal of Folklore Research* 37, nos. 2–3 (May-December 2000): 155–74.

Murray, Jean A. *Music of the Alaska-Klondike Gold Rush: Songs and History*. Fairbanks: University of Alaska Press, 1999.

"Negro Minstrelsy—Ancient and Modern." *Putnam's Monthly Magazine of American Literature, Science and Art* 5, no. 25 (January 1855): 72–79.

Neher, Andrew. "Auditory Driving Observed with Scalp Electrodes in Normal Subjects." *Electroencephalography and Clinical Neurophysiology* 13 (1961): 449–51.

Nettl, Bruno. *Music in Primitive Culture*. Cambridge, Mass.: Harvard University Press, 1956.

Nettl, Bruno, and Philip V. Bohlman, eds. *Comparative Musicology and Anthropology of Music: Essays on the History of Ethnomusicology*. Chicago: University of Chicago Press, 1991.

Nketia, J. H. *Drumming in Akan Communities of Ghana*. London: Thomas Nelson and Sons, 1963.

Northall, G. F. *English Folk-Rhymes: A Collection of Traditional Verses Relating to Places and Persons, Customs, Superstitions, Etc.* Detroit: Singing Tree Press, 1968.

O'Donnell, John C. *"And Now the Fields Are Green": A Collection of Coal Mining Songs in Canada*. Sydney, Nova Scotia: University College of Cape Breton Press, 1992.

Odum, Howard W. "Folk-Song and Folk-Poetry as Found in the Secular Songs of the Southern Negroes." *Journal of American Folk-Lore* 24, no. 93 (July-September, 1911): 255–94.

Odum, Howard W., and Guy B. Johnson. *The Negro and His Songs: A Study of Typical Negro Songs in the South*. Hatboro, Pa: Folklore Associates, 1964.

——. *Negro Workaday Songs*. New York: Negro Universities Press, 1969.

Ohrlin, Glenn. *The Hell-Bound Train: A Cowboy Songbook*. Urbana: University of Illinois Press, 1973.

Olsen, Dale A. *Music of the Warao of Venezuela*. Gainesville: University Press of Florida, 1996.

Ortega y Gasset, José. *The Dehumanization of Art and Other Writings on Art and Culture*. New York: Anchor, 1956.

Palmer, Roy, ed. *The Oxford Book of Sea Songs*. Oxford: Oxford University Press, 1986.

——, ed. *The Painful Plough: A Portrait of the Agricultural Labourer in the Nineteenth Century from Folk Songs and Ballads and Contemporary Accounts*. Cambridge: Cambridge University Press, 1972.

——. *The Sound of History: Songs and Social Comment*. London: Pimlico, 1996.

Paredes, Américo. *A Texas-Mexican Cancionero*. Austin: University of Texas Press, 1976.

Park, Mungo. *Travels in the Interior Districts of Africa*. Edited by Kate Ferguson Masters. Durham: Duke University Press, 2000.

Parrish, Lydia. *Slave Songs of the Georgia Sea Islands*. Athens: University of Georgia Press, 1992.

Peabody, Charles. "Notes on Negro Music." *Journal of American Folk-Lore* 16, no. 62 (July–September 1903): 148–52.

Peel, Frank. *The Risings of the Luddites*. New York: Augustus M. Kelley Publishers, 1968.

Pendle, Karen, ed. *Woman and Music: A History*. Bloomington: Indiana University Press, 1991.

Perdue, Charles L. Jr., Thomas E. Barden, and Robert K. Phillips, eds. *Weevils in the Wheat: Interviews with Virginia Ex-Slaves*. Charlottesville: University Press of Virginia, 1976.

Perdue, Chuck. "Come, Butter, Come: A Collection of Churning Chants from Georgia." *Foxfire* 3, no. 1 (spring 1969).

Perrow, E. C. "Songs and Rhymes from the South." *Journal of American Folklore* 25 (1912): 137–55; 26 (1913): 126–73; 28 (1915): 129–90.

Pescatello, Ann M. *Charles Seeger: A Life in American Music*. Pittsburgh, Pa.: University of Pittsburgh Press, 1992.

Pinker, Steven. *How the Mind Works*. New York: Norton, 1997.

Pinkert-Sältzer, Inke, ed. *German Songs: Popular, Political, Folk, and Religious*. New York: Continuum, 1997.

Plantenga, Bart. *Yodel-Ay-Ee-Oooo: The Secret History of Yodeling around the World*. New York: Routledge, 2004.

Porter, Gerald. *The English Occupational Song*. Umea, Sweden: University of Umea, 1992.

——. "Women's Working Songs." *Lore and Language* 10, no. 2 (1991): 25–37.

——. "'Work the Old Lady Out of the Ditch': Singing at Work by English Lacemakers." *Journal of Folklore Research* 31, nos. 1–3 (1994): 35–55.

Porterfield, Nolan. *Last Cavalier: The Life and Times of John A. Lomax, 1867–1948.* Urbana: University of Illinois Press, 1996.

Pound, Louise. *Nebraska Folklore.* Lincoln: University of Nebraska Press, 1989.

Price, T. Dougals, and Anne Birgitte Gebauer. *Last Hunters—First Farmers.* Santa Fe, N.M.: School of American Research Press, 1995.

Proctor, David. *Music of the Sea.* London: Her Majesty's Stationary Office, 1992.

Prokhorov, Vadim. *Russian Folks Songs: Musical Genres and History.* Lanham, Md.: The Scarecrow Press, 2002.

Propp, Vladimir. *Down along the Mother Volga: An Anthology of Russian Folk Lyrics.* Edited and translated by Roberta Reeder. Philadelphia: University of Pennsylvania Press, 1975.

Quasten, Johannes. *Music and Worship in Pagan and Christian Antiquity.* Translated by Boniface Ramsey. Washington, D.C.: National Association of Pastoral Musicians, 1983.

Radcliffe-Brown, A. R. *The Andaman Islanders.* Glencoe, Ill.: Free Press, 1948.

Radic, Thérèse, ed. *Songs of Australian Working Life.* Elwood, Australia: Greenhouse Publications, 1989.

Ramsey, Frederic, Jr. *Been Here and Gone.* New Brunswick, N.J.: Rutgers University Press, 1960.

Rasmussen, Knud. *Across Arctic America: Narrative of the Fifth Thule Expedition.* New York: G. P. Putnam's Sons, 1927.

——. *Songs and Stories of the Netsilik Eskimos.* Translated by Edward Field. Cambridge, Mass.: Education Development Center, 1968.

Rayor, Diane J., ed. and trans. *Sappho's Lyre: Archaic Lyric and Women Poets of Ancient Greece.* Berkeley: University of California Press, 1991.

Rebolledo, Tey Diana, and María Teresa Márquez, eds. *Women's Tales from the New Mexico WPA: La Diabla a Pie.* Houston: Arte Público Press, 2000.

Reef, Catherine. *Working in America: An Eyewitness History.* New York: Facts on File, 2000.

Reeve, John Sherard. *Lyra Venatica: A Collection of Hunting Songs.* London: Arthur L. Humphreys, 1906.

Reuss, Richard A. *Songs of American Labor, Industrialization and the Urban Work Experience: A Discography.* Ann Arbor: Labor Studies Center, University of Michigan, 1983.

Reznikoff, Iegor, and Michel Dauvois. "La dimension sonore des grottes ornées." *Bulletin de la Société Préhistorique Française* 85, no. 8 (1988): 238–46.

Ribera, Julian. *Music in Ancient Arabia and Spain.* Translated by Eleanor Hague and Marion Leffingwell. Stanford: Stanford University Press, 1929.

Richmond, Michael L. "The Music of Labor: From Movement to Culture." *Legal Studies Forum* 23, no. 1 (1999): 211–34.

Roberts, Helen H. *Ancient Hawaiian Music.* New York: Klaus Reprint Company, 1971 [1926].

Roberts, John Storm. *Black Music of Two Worlds*. New York: Original Music, 1972.

Romalis, Shelly. *Pistol Packin' Mama: Aunt Molly Jackson and the Politics of Folksong*. Urbana: University of Illinois Press, 1999.

Roth, Terry. "Street Cries and Criers of New York." Federal Writers' Project report, dated November 3, 1938, eight pages.

Rouget, Gilbert. *Music and Trance: A Theory of the Relations between Music and Possession*. Translated by Brunhilde Biebuyck. Chicago: University of Chicago Press, 1985.

Rousseau, Jean-Jacques. *The Confessions*. Translated by J. M. Cohen. London: Penguin, 1953.

Rowbotham, John Frederick. *The History of Music*. London: Richard Bentley and Son, 1893.

Rubin, Ruth. *Voices of a People: The Story of Yiddish Folksong*. Urbana: University of Illinois Press, 2000.

Rudé, George. *The Crowd in History, 1730–1848*. New York: John Wiley and Sons, 1964.

Ruskin, John, ed. *Roadside Songs of Tuscany*. 2nd ed. Translated and illustrated by Francesca Alexander. New York: John Wiley and Sons, 1887.

Russolo, Luigi. *The Art of Noises*. Translated by Barclay Brown. Hillsdale, N.Y.: Pendragon Press, 1986.

Sachs, Curt. *The Rise of Music in the Ancient World: East and West*. New York: Norton, 1943

——. *The Wellsprings of Music*. Edited by Jaap Kunst. New York: Da Capo, 1977.

Sarno, Louis. *Songs from the Forest: My Life Among the Ba-Benjellé Pygmies*. New York: Houghton Mifflin, 1993.

Sarosi, Balint. *Folk Music: Hungarian Musical Idiom*. Translated by Maria Steiner. Budapest: Corvina, 1986.

Scarborough, Dorothy. *On the Trail of Negro Folksongs*. Hatboro, Pa.: Folklore Associates, 1963.

Schafer, R. Murray. *The Tuning of the World*. New York: Knopf, 1977.

Schimmelpenninck, Antoinet. *Chinese Folk Songs and Folk Singers: Shan'ge Traditions in Southern Jiangsu*. Leiden, Netherlands: CHIME Foundation, 1997.

Schwaab, Eugene L., ed. *Travels in the Old South: Selected from Periodicals of the Times*. 2 vols. Lexington: University of Kentucky Press, 1974.

Scott, James George. *The Burman: His Life and Notions*. New York: Norton, 1963.

Sedjo, Roger A. "The Forest Sector: Important Innovations." Discussion Paper 97–42. Washington, D.C.: Resources for the Future, August 1997.

Seeger, Pete, and Bob Reiser. *Carry It On! A History in Song and Picture of the Working Men and Women of America*. New York: Simon and Schuster, 1985.

Selfridge-Field, Eleanor. "Experiments with Melody and Meter, or the Effects of Music: The Edison-Bingham Music Research." *Musical Quarterly* 81, no. 2 (1997): 291–310.

Semple, Janet. *Bentham's Prison: A Study of the Panopticon Penitentiary.* New York: Oxford University Press, 1993.

Sharp, Cecil. *English Folk Songs from the Southern Appalachians.* Edited by Maud Karpeles. London: Oxford University Press, 1960.

Shaw, Margaret Fay. *Folksongs and Folklore of South Uist.* Edinburgh: Birlinn, 1999.

Shelemay, Kay Kaufman. *Soundscapes: Exploring Music in a Changing World.* New York: Norton, 2001.

Sherman, Bernard D. *Inside Early Music.* New York: Oxford University Press, 1997.

Shesgreen, Sean, ed. *The Criers and Hawkers of London: Engravings and Drawings by Marcellus Laroon.* Stanford: Stanford University Press, 1990.

Shikibu, Murasaki. *The Tale of Genji.* Translated by Edward G. Seidensticker. New York: Knopf, 1994.

Shirokogoroff, Sergei. M. *Psychomental Complex of the Tungus.* London: Kegan Paul, Trench, Trubner and Co., 1935.

Sires, Ina, ed. *Songs of the Open Range.* Boston: C. C. Birchard, 1928.

Siringo, Charles. *A Texas Cowboy; or, Fifteen Years on the Hurricane Deck of a Spanish Pony.* New York: Penguin, 2000.

Small, Christopher. *Music of the Common Tongue.* London: John Calder, 1987.

——. *Music, Society, Education.* 2nd ed. London: John Calder, 1980.

——. *Musicking: The Meanings of Performing and Listening.* Hanover, N.H.: Wesleyan University Press, 1998.

Smith, Laura Alexandrine. *The Music of the Waters: A Collection of the Sailors' Chanties, or Working Songs of the Sea, of All Maritime Nations.* Detroit: Singing Tree Press, 1969.

Smith, Patricia Cain, and Ross Curnow. "'Arousal Hypothesis' and the Effects of Music on Purchasing Behaviour." *Journal of Applied Psychology* 50 (June 1966): 255–86.

Solzhenitsyn, Alexander. *One Day in the Life of Ivan Denisovich.* Translated by Ralph Parker. New York: E. P. Dutton, 1963.

Southern, Eileen. *The Music of Black Americans: A History.* New York: Norton, 1971.

Standing Bear, Luther. *My People the Sioux.* Lincoln: University of Nebraska Press, 1975.

Stone, John A. *Put's Golden Songster.* San Francisco: D. E. Appleton and Co., 1858.

——. *Put's Original California Songster.* 5th ed. San Francisco: D. E. Appleton and Co., 1868.

Strehlow, T. G. H. *Songs of Central Australia*. Sydney: Angus and Robertson, 1971.

Supicic, Ivo. *Music in Society: A Guide to the Sociology of Music*. Stuyvesant, N.Y.: Pendragon Press, 1987.

Tae Hung Ha. *Korea Sings: Folk and Popular Music and Lyrics*. Seoul: Yonsei University Press, 1958.

Tanaka, Jiro. *The San: Hunter-Gatherers of the Kalahari*. Translated by David W. Hughes. Tokyo: University of Tokyo Press, 1980.

Taylor, Frederick Winslow. *The Principles of Scientific Management*. Mineola, N.Y.: Dover, 1998.

Taylor, William Banks. *Down on Parchman Farm: The Great Prison in the Mississippi Delta*. Columbus: Ohio State University Press, 1999.

Tcherepnin, Alexander. "Music in Modern China." *Musical Quarterly* 21, no. 4 (October 1935): 391–400.

Thomas, Jean. *Ballad Makin' in the Mountains of Kentucky*. New York: Oak Publications, 1964.

Thomas, Joseph B. *Hounds and Hunting through the Ages*. New York: Windward House, 1933.

Thompson, E. P. *The Making of the English Working Class*. New York: Pantheon, 1964.

Thorp, N. Howard (Jack), and Neil M. Clark. *Pardner of the Wind*. Lincoln: University of Nebraska Press, 1977.

——, ed. *Songs of the Cowboys*. Lincoln: University of Nebraska Press, 1984.

Tolstoy, Leo. *What Is Art?* Translated by Aylmer Maude. New York: Thomas Crowell and Co., 1899.

Tompkins, Peter, and Christopher Bird. *The Secret Life of Plants*. New York: Harper and Row, 1973.

Touma, Habib Hassan. *The Music of the Arabs*. Portland, Oreg.: Amadeus Press, 2003.

Tracey, Hugh. *African Dances of the Witwatersrand Gold Mines*. Johannesburg: African Music Society, 1952.

Turnbull, Colin. *The Forest People,* New York: Simon and Schuster, 1962.

Turner, Frederick. *Natural Classicism: Essays on Literature and Science*. New York: Paragon House, 1985.

Turner, Victor. *The Drums of Affliction: A Study of Religious Processes among the Ndembu of Zambia*. Ithaca: Cornell University Press, 1981.

Twain, Mark. *Life on the Mississippi*. New York: Signet, 2001.

Uetake, K., J. F. Hurnik, and L. Johnson. "Effect of Music on Voluntary Approach of Dairy Cows to an Automatic Milking System." *Applied Animal Behaviour Science* 53, no. 3 (June 1997): 175–82.

van der Post, Laurens. *The Lost World of the Kalahari*. New York: Morrow, 1958.

Varnum, John P. "The Ibirongwe of the Kuria: A Cattle Herding Flute in East Africa." *Ethnomusicology* 14, no. 3 (September 1970): 462–67.

Vatuk, Ved Prakash. "Malhor: A Type of Work Song in Western Uttar Pradesh, India." *Asian Folklore Studies* 29 (1970): 251–74.

Vaughan Williams, Ralph. *National Music and Other Essays.* Oxford: Clarendon Press, 1996.

Vico, Giambattista. *The New Science of Giambattista Vico.* Translated by Thomas Goddard Bergin and Max Harold Fisch. Ithaca: Cornell University Press, 1984.

Vujosevic, Ranko. "Dr. Harry Oster: His Life, Career and Field Recordings." *Blues Notes: Monthly Publication of the Johnson County Blues Society*, no. 9 (August 1995): 1–9.

Wallaschek, Richard. *Primitive Music: An Inquiry into the Origin and Development of Music, Songs, Instruments, Dances, and Pantomimes of Savage Races.* London: Longmans, Green and Co., 1893.

Wallin, Nils L. *Biomusicology: Neurophysiological, Neuropsychological, and Evolutionary Perspectives on the Origins and Purposes of Music.* Stuyvesant, N.Y.: Pendragon, 1991.

Wallin, Nils, Bjorn Merker, and Steven Brown, eds. *The Origins of Music.* Cambridge, Mass: MIT Press, 2000.

Walter, V. J., and W. Grey Walter. "The Central Effects of Rhythmic Sensory Stimulation." *Electroencephalography and Clinical Neurophysiology* 1 (1949): 57–86.

Webster, Hutton. *Magic: A Sociological Study.* New York: Octagon, 1973.

Weinraub, Bernard. "An Ex-Convict, a Hit Album, an Ending Fit for Hollywood." *New York Times,* March 3, 2002, p. A1.

Wells, Evelyn Kendrick. *The Ballad Tree: British and American Ballads; Their Folklore, Verse and Music.* New York: Ronald Press Company, 1950.

West, John O. "Jack Thorp and John Lomax: Oral or Written Transmission?" *Western Folklore* 26 (April 1967): 113–18.

West, M. L. *Ancient Greek Music.* Oxford: Clarendon Press, 1994.

Wheeler, Mary. *Steamboatin' Days: Folk Songs of the River Packet Era.* Baton Rouge: Louisiana State University Press, 1944.

White, John I. *Git along Little Dogies: Songs and Songmakers of the American West.* Urbana: University of Illinois Press, 1989.

White, Newman I. *American Negro Folksongs.* Hatboro, Pa.: Folklore Associates, 1965.

Wilgus, D. L. *Anglo-American Folksong Scholarship since 1898.* Westport, Conn.: Greenwood Press, 1982.

Williams, Brett. *John Henry, A Bio-Biography.* Westport, Conn.: Greenwood Press, 1983.

Williams, Leonard. *The Dancing Chimpanzee: A Study of the Origins of Primitive Music*. London: Alison and Busby, 1980.

Williams, Raymond. *The Country and the City*. New York: Oxford University Press, 1973.

Wiora, Walter. *The Four Ages of Music*. Translated by M. D. Herter Norton. New York: Norton, 1967.

Wolfe, Charles, and Kip Lornell. *The Life and Legend of Leadbelly*. New York: Da Capo Press, 1999.

Work, John D., Lewis Wade Jones, and Samuel C. Adams Jr. *Lost Delta Found: Rediscovering the Fisk University–Library of Congress Coahoma County Study, 1941–1942*. Edited by Robert Gordon and Bruce Nemerov. Nashville, Tenn.: Vanderbilt University Press, 2005.

Work, John W. *American Negro Songs*. Mineola, N.Y.: Dover, 1998.

Yang, Yinliu. *Zhongguo gudai yinyueshi gao* (Draft history of ancient Chinese music). 2 vols. Beijing: People's Music Publishing House, 1981.

Yates, Mike. "Cecil Sharp in America: Collecting in the Appalachians." Revised version published on the web site of *Musical Traditions* (www.mustrad.org .uk), June 30, 2000.

Yurchenco, Henrietta. "Trouble in the Mines: A History in Song and Story by Women of Appalachia." *American Music* (summer 1991): 209–24.

Zevik, Emma, and Zou Xianping. "Sichuan Street Songs. The Everyday Cries of Street Vendors in Chengdu." CHIME, nos. 12–13 (spring/autumn 1998): 87–97.

Zielinski, Jaroslaw de. "Russian Hunting Music." *Musical Quarterly* (January 1917): 53–59.

Zink, Michel. *Les chanson de toile*. Paris: Champion, 1978.

American Labor Songs of the Nineteenth Century (Foner), 233
American Negro Folk Songs (White), 151
American Songbag, The (Sandburg), 132, 159
American South, music in, 129. See also African American music; Slavery
American West, songs of. See Cowboy songs
Anglo-American Folksong Scholarship since 1898 (Wilgus), 174–175
Animals destroying crops, music to prevent, 53–54. See also Agricultural songs
Appalachian ballads, 48–49
Arbeit und Rhythmus (Bucher), 111, 112
Arkwright, Richard, 88
Armstrong, Louis, 126
Arnold, W. F., 122
Arom, Simha, 19
Art: in day-to-day lives, 4–5; lowbrow, 1–2; separability principle as dominant view in, 10; ways of relating to, 2–4
Artistic movements, positivistic model of, 5–6
Art of Noises, The (Russolo), 108
Asch, Moe, 175
Asia, fishing and rowing songs in, 125–126
Assembly line, and rhythm of work, 110–111. See also Work efficiency, and singing
Astor, John Jacob, 177
Austin, J. L., 8
Autry, Gene, 179

Baez, Joan, 236–237, 240
Bailey, DeFord, 33
Baker, James "Iron Head," 211–212
Baker, Ray Stannard, 234

Ballad Makin' in the Mountains of Kentucky (Thomas), 186
Barber, Elizabeth Wayland, 42
Barnes, R. H., 125
Barnicle, Mary Elizabeth, 132
Bartenieff, Irmgard, 36
Bartok, Bela, 52, 75
Barton, William Eleazar, 155
Barua, Hem, 42, 82
Battle music, 117
Beck, E. C., 141–142
Belafonte, Harry, 219–220
Bell, John, 186
Bells: marking time, 101; in modern times, 102; and protest, 102–103
Benet, Sula, 71
Bentham, Jeremy, 203
Benton, William, 253
Berger, Arthur, 238–239
Berlin, Irving, 201
Bernardi, Beatrice, 68–69
Berry, Charley, 55
Bessemer, Henry, 104
Bierhorst, John, 2–3
Big Bend. See Henry, John
Bingham, Theodore, 107
Bingham, Walter, 250
Biomusicology (Wallin), 74
Bivins, Lester Pete, 95
Black, Eleanora, 194
Blacking, John, 4, 8
Blake, William, 88
Blues in the Mississippi Night (A. Lomax), 215
Boggs, Moran Lee, 185
"Boilermakers' deafness," 108
Bolster, W. Jeffrey, 122, 123
Bolton, Laura, 37
Bolton, Thaddeus, 112–113
Bone, David, 127
Boniface VIII (pope), 203
Book of Songs (Abu al-Faraj al-Isfahani), 105

Printing, of songs, 128–129

Prison songs, 160, 200–224; documentation of, 206–207; function of, 209; loss of, 202–203; popular interest in, 204; professional recordings of, 205–206; recording projects of, 218–222; and slavery, 213–214; subject matter of, 222–223; in works of fiction, 210–211. *See also* Parchman Farm

Prison Worksongs (Oster), 160

Professional recordings: of cowboy songs, 178–179; of labor protest songs, 239–240; of prison songs, 205–206

Propp, Vladimir, 152, 188

Prospectors, songs by, 191–192, 194

Protest songs, 225–242; and bells, 102–103; composers creating, 238; function of, 230; labor songs as, 229–230; and laborers, 225–227; in logging camps, 143–144; and poems, 232–233; and religious hymns, 235–236; staying power of, 231–232; in textile industry, 94–95; work songs as, 39, 230

Pyle, Ernie, 197

Radio, replacing song, 49, 245–246, 250–251

Raettig, Chris, 247

Rainmaking songs, 51–53

Ramsey, Frederick, 54–55

Rassmussen, Knud, 18

Record companies, signing mill workers, 96. *See also* Professional recordings

Red, Dobie, 217

Redburn (Melville), 128

Reece, Cortez, 160

Reese, Doc, 61

Religious hymns, and protest songs, 235–236

Ren Mei, 134

Retallack, Dorothy, 50, 51

Revolution in Time (Landes), 100

Reznikoff, Iegor, 13, 27–28

Rhapsody in Blue (Gershwin), 50

Rhymes of the Northern Bards (Bell), 186

Rhythm: of farm songs, 37; of nature and pulse of labor, 99–114 (*see also* Work efficiency, and singing). *See also* Meter

Richard the Lionhearted, 203

Riley, James Whitcomb, 146

Rituals, rainmaking, 51–52

Rivers, W. H. R., 71

Rivethead (Hamper), 243

Roadside Songs of Tuscany (Ruskin), 68–69

Roberts, John Storm, 196, 209

Robertson, Eck, 178

Robertson, Sidney, 194

Robeson, Paul, 236, 248

Robinson, Earl, 236

Rochefort, Charles de, 59

Rock music, effect of, on plants, 50–51

Rodgers, Jimmy, 96–97, 173, 251

Romero, Raúl R., 70

Roosevelt, Franklin, 170

Roosevelt, Teddy, 175

Roseland, Paul, 192

Roth, Terry, 107

Rouget, Gilbert, 60

Rousseau, Jean-Jacques, 85, 260

Rowing songs, 116, 125. *See also* Sailing songs; Shanties

Rubin, Ruth, 82

Ruckmich, Christian, 113

Ruskin, John, 68–69

Russell, James, 219

Russolo, Luigi, 108

Sailing songs, 115–136; compared with lumberjack songs, 144–145;

Thorp, Jack, 175–178
Thucydides, 62, 116
'Till the Clouds Roll By (film), 248
Timber, historical value of, 138–139
Time: bells marking, 101; passage of, and organization of labor, 100
Tiv Song (Keil), 57
Tobacco industry songs, 109–110
Toda Songs (Emeneau), 71
Todi, Jacopone da, 203
Tolstoy. Leo, 43–44
Tom Mix Western Songs (M. M. Cole), 179
Tongan Music (Toyle), 125
Tools: and manual laborers, 150–168; mystical power of, 152; as part of work songs, 155. See also Hammers
Tracey, Hugh, 195, 196
Travels in the Interior Districts of Africa, 9–10
Travis, Merle, 197
Tree-cutting songs, 139–140. See also Logging camps; Lumberjacks
Troxler, Ignaz, 66
Trumpet, on ships, 116–117
Truvillion, Henry, 208
Turi, Johan, 65
Turk, Ivan, 31
Turnbull, Colin, 19–20
Turner, Frederick, 4
Turner, Joseph, 157
Turner, Victor, 29
Twain, Mark, 130
Two Years before the Mast (Dana), 115

Unity, music's influence on, 112–113

Van der Post, Laurens, 28–29
Van Swieten, Baron, 85
Vaquero songs, 173
Varnum, John, 69–70
Vaughan Williams, Ralph, 1, 3
Verdi, Giuseppe, 61
Vico, Giambattista, 19

Victor Records, 96
Vinçard, Jules, 226
Virgil, 64, 66, 67
Virginian, The (Wister), 176
Virility, hammers as symbols of, 152–153
Voices of a People (Rubin), 82

Wagner, Richard, 32, 85
Wake Up Dead Man (compilation), 222
Wallin, Nils L., 74, 77
Walter, V. J., 60
Walter, W. G., 60
"Waltzing Matilda," 72
Ware, Charles Pickard, 131
Water Music (Handel), 32
Waters, Muddy (McKinley Morganfield), 45, 201, 214
Waulking songs, 83–84
Wayland, Elizabeth, 80
Wayne, John, 179
Weaving, 132; loom for, 103–104; songs of, 80–81, 90–91; and women, 81–83. See also Cloth production; Garment manufacturing; Textile industry
Webb, Ervin, 220
Webb, Jimmy, 248
Wedgwood, Josiah, 104, 110–111
Weelkes, Thomas, 106
Weinert, Erich, 231
Wendell, Barrett, 169
We Pointed Them North: Recollections of a Cowpuncher (Abbott), 180
West, American, songs of. See Cowboy songs
West, John, 176
What is Art? (Tolstoy), 43–44
Wheeler, Mary, 130
"Whistle While You Work," 252
White, Bukka, 201
White, John, 178
White, Newman, 151

TED GIOIA IS AN INDEPENDENT SCHOLAR.

Library of Congress Cataloging-in-Publication Data
Gioia, Ted.
Work songs / Ted Gioia.
p. cm.
Includes bibliographical references and index.
ISBN 0-8223-3726-6 (cloth : alk. paper)
1. Working class—Songs and music—History and criticism.
2. Work songs—History and criticism. I. Title.
ML3780.G56 2006
782.42'1593—dc22
2005026241